HIG

MW00813640

Encyclopedia of Canadian Rock Pop & Folk Music

by
RICK JACKSON

Other Quarry Press Rock Books

BRYAN
ADAMS

JONI
MITCHELL

E.P.L. HIG

GORDON
LIGHTFOOT

K. D.
LANG

Encyclopedia
of Canadian
Rock
Pop
&
Folk
Music
by
RICK JACKSON

ANNE
MURRAY

ALANNAH
MYLES

JANE
SIBERRY

SNOW

NEIL
YOUNG

TOM
COCHRANE

This book is dedicated to everyone in it.

Copyright © Rick Jackson, 1994.
All rights reserved.

The publisher gratefully acknowledges the assistance of The Canada Council, the Ministry of Canadian Heritage, the Ontario Arts Council, and the Ontario Publishing Centre.

Canadian Cataloguing in Publishing Data

Jackson, Rick
    Encyclopedia of Canadian rock, pop and folk

ISBN 1-55082-107-5 (bound)
ISBN 1-55082-098-2 (pbk.)

    1. Popular music — Canada — Encyclopedias.
2. Rock music — Canada — Encyclopedias.   3. Folk music — Canada — Encyclopedias.   I. Title.

ML102.P66J34 1994   781.64'0971   C94–900285-2

Design by Susan Hannah.
Typeset by Chris McDonell.
Printed in Canada by Webcom, Limited, Toronto, Ontario.

Published by Quarry Press, Inc.,
P.O. Box 1061, Kingston, Ontario K7L 4Y5.

Contents

Preface

At the time I began to compile *The Encyclopedia of Canadian Rock, Pop & Folk Music* in the early 1970s, there was only one book written about Canadian pop music culture, Ritchie Yorke's *Axes, Chops and Hot Licks*. Over the past twenty years the Canadian pop music industry has grown enormously, especially under the influence of the Canadian content (CANCON) regulations stipulated by the Canadian Radio-Television and Telecommunications Commission, but we have not yet seen a comprehensive account of Canada's music history.

The Encyclopedia of Canadian Rock, Pop & Folk Music looks at the history of Canadian music from the 1950s to the 1990s, and although it does not list every artist who put out a record during this era, the book does list the key groups and solo artists, from A–Z, from Newfoundland to British Columbia and even the Northwest Territories. Each entry includes a short biography plus a list of singles and albums or compact discs.

While researching this book, I found very few sources of information. *RPM Weekly*, *The Music Scene*, *Canadian Composer*, and various newspaper and magazine articles were used for the older artists and groups. *The Encyclopaedia of Music in Canada* was also helpful but was limited in the folk, pop, and rock categories. Another important source was the four volume *Made in Canada* compact disc series compiled by Paul White and released by BMG Music Canada Inc. The series spans the years 1960-1974 and includes over fifty hard-to-find and out-of-print tracks from artists such as The Beau-Marks, Little Caesar & the Consuls, Kensington Market, and Chilliwack. I was also able to talk to some of the artists who appear in this book.

The hit songs by each artist and group came from various sources. *The* CHUM *Chart Book* was used for those who had hits before 1965, while *A Chartology of Canadian Popular Music — January 1965 to December 1976* served as a guide for those after 1965. I also used individual charts from CFNB, Fredericton, New Brunswick (1967-1982); CKWS, Kingston, Ontario (1970-1975); CKLC, Kingston (1970-1979,

1992); and CKOC, Hamilton, Ontario (1976). A listing of single releases in *The Music Scene* from 1977 to 1986 proved useful for the non-hits. *Canadian Composer* was a good cross-reference.

The artist and groups listed in Appendix A deserve full entries, but information on them was not available by press time. Appendix B lists Canadian artists who have made their mark on popular music outside of the borders of their native country.

Although I have made every effort to be accurate and complete, it is possible that I have overlooked information in some cases. I welcome fans to provide me with correct information by writing to me in care of the publisher.

During the past twenty years, a number of people have assisted me in compiling this encyclopedia. They include Angie Flint at A&M Records; Joanne Dine at Warner Music; Anne Forbes, Liz McElheran and Klaus Northmore at EMI; Sonya Sorensen and Pam Gillies at Sony Music; Gerry Vogel at Polygram; Allison Mercer, Janet Roder, Paul White, and Julie Snell at BMG Music; Brian Ferriman and Dawn Costigan at Savannah Music (Nashville); Mary Arsenault at Be-Bop Communications; Pierre St-Georges at Audiogram Records; Susan Martinez; Steve Jordan, and Lindsay Gillespie at Kinetic Records; Julie Brown at Absolute; and the publicity departments at I.R.S. and Eureka Records.

I wish to express my gratitude to Bryan Olney, who worked as a disc jockey at CKWS (now CFFX) in Kingston, Ontario from 1956 to 1971 and, since 1971 has taught radio and media studies at Loyalist College in Belleville, Ontario.

I also would like to thank Richard Patterson (The Esquires) for answering all my queries about Canadian music.

For taking the time to discuss their careers with me, thanks to Valdy, Murray McLauchlan, Kate Fenner and Dave Wall (The Bourbon Tabernacle Choir), Larry Mercey (The Mercey Brothers), Jim Bertucci (Abraham's Children), Joey Frechette (The Beau-Marks), Cliff Edwards (The Bells), Johnny Fay (The Tragically Hip), Paul Huot (The Townsmen), Roy Lesperance (The Chantones), Dick Wendling (Copperpenny), James Keelaghan, Andrew Cash, Catherine McKinnon, Val Haas (Aglukark Entertainment Inc.), John Bermingham and Roger Cooke (Bob McCord and The Vibrations), Jean-Marc Pisapia (The Box), Les Emmerson (The Staccatos), Richard Cooper (The Cooper Brothers), John Allan Cameron, and the members of The Waltons. Terry McRae of Shantero Productions who introduced me to Murray McLauchlan, Valdy, and James Keelaghan, and Bernie Dobbin of The Dobbin Agency.

A special thank you to Sandy Nicholas, record librarian at CKLC in Kingston. Others who helped me in gathering information were Rob Bolton and Peggy Shanks at CFRC (Queen's University); Guy Brooks at CFMK; Ray Bergstrom and Lorne Matthews at CFFX; Jack Thompson and Scott O'Brien at CKLC; Greg Hinton at CFJR; Sheila Roussel at the CRTC Library in Hull, Quebec; Florence Hays at the National Library's Music Division; the staff of both the Music Library and Douglas Library of Queen's University; and the staff of the Kingston Public Library.

I wrote this book because of the dearth of material available in the marketplace for libraries, record collectors, and broadcasters. It has been a labor of love.

— Rick Jackson

Introduction

Kurt Cobain died today. Mere hours ago his body was discovered just south of me in his Seattle home. It appears the lead singer of Nirvana had decided he'd had enough of rock and roll fame and all that it brings. What a sad end to such a promising singer and songwriter. What Kurt may or may not have known is that rock and roll refuses to let its heroes, big or small, ever die.

Jim Morrison and the Doors continue to sell at least half a million albums a year, two decades removed from their glory days. Led Zeppelin, some fourteen years after they lost their heart and soul with the death of John Bonham, have sold close to 15 million albums without a tour or appearance of any kind.

What does this tell us about ourselves? Perhaps that we live our lives, however vicariously, through our musical artists. If there is even a modicum of truth to this statement, if we measure ourselves at all by the accomplishments of this country's singers and songwriters, its bands and balladeers, then the book you now hold is *the* reference manual.

Believe me, I'm a research freak. I have books, magazines, and computer print-outs reaching to the ceiling. Bags of research surround me, and piles of books are everywhere — books about the rock world, rock 'n' roll guides to Britain, the U.S.A., even the Third World. There are even a few that purport to cover the entire geographical spectrum, with artists from all four points of the globe. Canada, though, is generally poorly represented. Unless your last name is Adams, Murray, Young, or lang, mentions in these guides — mentions *anywhere* — are few and far between.

Finally, someone has incorporated the whole history of Canadian rock, pop, and folk music into one book. I found that while reading the pages memories came back to me . . . As you read this encyclopedia you'll find yourself remembering events, people, love, break-ups, school, weddings, grads . . .

I've been lucky enough to meet most of the people Rick has written about. From Joni Mitchell to The Guess Who in their very early days, to

Barry Allen/Wes Dakus and the Rebels, who owned Alberta, Saskatchewan, and Manitoba during the 1960s. I remember The Stampeders heading for Toronto and the "big time" from their home in Calgary, and all of them piling out of what I think was a hearse to sleep in my one bedroom apartment in Regina . . . six guys, one bed.

Rick has tried to cover an artist's career just enough so that the book remains a reference guide without straying into the waters of the multi-volume historical epic. Granted, for every artist or group mentioned in the book, there will be an expert out there, waiting to check the every fact, every album, every birthday. If Rick has missed the mark in an entry or two, fear not. He'll continue to make changes to the encyclopedia edition after edition, striving always for complete accuracy.

The Guess Who are there, of course. Expect to see Rush, Glass Tiger, Loverboy, Corey Hart, Chilliwack . . . I was delighted to discover information, new and old, on bands such as Crowbar, Lighthouse, Dr. Music, Heart (seven years in Vancouver). It was wonderful to see the talented line-ups of groups like Mandela, McKenna Mendleson Mainline (although I'm sure Joe thinks he deserves his own solo mention). It was great to see Mother Tucker's Yellow Duck included (Vancouver loved that band), as well as the unique talent and attitude of Pear of Pied Pumpkin and their ace-in-the-hole, Shari Ulrich.

It's great to see Bobby Taylor of Bobby Taylor and the Vancouvers (with guitar player Tommy Chong) get proper credit for discovering the Jackson Five and even better to read about a favorite of mine from the 1960s, Three's a Crowd. Think about it, Colleen Peterson, Brent Titcomb, the amazing Donna Warner, the brilliant but doomed David Wiffen, Richard Patterson, and a very young Bruce Cockburn. Live, they were great.

Sure, Neil Young and Tom Cochrane were givens, but I'd have thrown the book back on the shelf if Bim hadn't been included.

Rock and roll is known for its leading edge, those artists making music that ignores boundaries or definitions — speaking in a voice that hasn't been heard before. It's a much tougher accomplishment than most can ever realize. There are only so many notes and for the pure rocker only three chords.

Bands at the front edge can and will succeed. However, after that initial success they must forever answer the question, "What have you done for us lately?" Well, this book answers that question and any others that might be asked. It will help preserve this country's musical legacy.

Rick Jackson is to be commended for his dedication to the industry and his love of the music and the people that make it.

— *Terry David Mulligan*

**Aarons
and Ackley**

CHUCK AARONS
JIM ACKLEY

Both Chuck Aarons and Jim Ackley were born in the United States. Chuck had worked on the road with The Beach Boys before arriving in Toronto in 1969 to avoid the draft. Jim frequently came up to Toronto to play. They met through a mutual friend, producer Dennis Murphy, and in the fall of 1970 they decided to become music partners.

Jim Ackley had been working as a clerk in the promotion department at Capitol Records when he met Chuck. As Aarons and Ackley, they sent a demo to A&R Director Paul White at Capitol Records who took it to New York. This demo led to the recording of their first, self-titled album, which contained their first major hit, *Devil Song*.

Backing up the duo were two experienced musicians: bass player Jim Rolleston, who had worked with Seals and Crofts and Gordon Lightfoot; and Terry Clarke, a drummer from Vancouver who previously had worked with John Handy Shelley's Manhole and the Fifth Dimension.

After the release of AARONS AND ACKLEY, they spent the next two years producing albums for such artists as Bob McBride and the Irish Rovers. They also produced a series of jingles.

In December, 1974 Aarons and Ackley signed a contract with GRT Records. Their only single for the label was *Where Did the Music Go*.

Singles		
Devil Song 1971		*Bonnie Blue* 1972
Let It Shine 1971		*Where Did the Music Go* 1974
Girl I've Been Waiting 1971		

Album   AARONS AND ACKLEY   1971

**Abraham's
Children**

RON BARTLEY *(guitar)*   SHAWN O'SHEA *(guitar)*
JIM BERTUCCI *(bass)*   BOB McPHERSON *(keyboards)*
BRIAN COTTERILL *(percussion)*

The beginnings of Abraham's Children go back to the late 1960s when they were known as Just Us and Captain Midnight's Dirty Feet, a name taken from an American comic strip. When the owners of the strip would not allow the use of the name in the United States, they changed their name to Abraham's Children. Their first single was *Hot Love*, which was released in 1968 and later became the flip side to their 1972 hit *Goodbye Farewell* on G.A.S. Records.

During the early 1970s, the group was led by Jim Bertucci, one of the principal songwriters, and Ron Bartley. The group consisted of four members until April 1973 when Shawn O'Shea joined the band in time for their first international hit, *Gypsy*. After the success of *Goddess of Nature* in 1974, the group went for a heavier sound. That same year they became known as The Children.

When their commercial appeal faded, the quintet continued to play various concert venues before they dropped out of sight. Shawn O'Shea formed a new group called Bang in 1976 with Ron Bartley, Dave Babyn, and Joe Dinardo, formerly of Cycle.

Singles

Hot Love 1968	*Thank You* 1973
The Lovin' Things 1968	*Gypsy* 1972-73
Goodbye Farewell 1972	*Goddess of Nature* 1973-74

Album TIME 1973

Ronney Abramson

Born in Paris, France, Ronney Abramson moved with her parents to Montreal when she was a child. Her early musical training was in classical music, and when she was fourteen she wrote her first song. While still in her teens she gave her first public performance, a solo classical guitar recital in Montreal.

She attended McGill University. While there, she became involved in Montreal's folk club scene. Her success as a folk singer led to dates in Eastern Canada and New York, and a recording contract with Capitol Records. She recorded only one album with the label, the self-titled RONNEY ABRAMSON.

In 1972 she moved from Montreal to Toronto and became part of a rock trio with John-Mills Cockell. She later formed her own band and signed to True North Records. Her first single, *Question for an Answer* came out early in 1976. An album of original songs was released at the end of the year.

Her next album on True North was STOWAWAY in 1977. It marked a departure in her music from folk to rock. Bruce Cockburn and Moe Koffman were among the guest artists featured. Backing up Ronney was the Stowaway Band, including Pat Ringley on bass, John Sheard on keyboards, and Bob DiSalle on drums.

Singles

Question for an Answer 1976	*Trouble* (duet with David
Your Love Gets Me Around	Clayton-Thomas) 1979
1977	*I'm a Big Girl* 1980

Albums RONNEY ABRAMSON 1972   JUKEBOX OF PARIS 1978
STOWAWAY 1977

Acosta JOHN ACOSTA
Russell JAMES RUSSELL

This Scarborough-based duo have known each other since 1983. Both began writing at the age of twelve.

John Acosta was born in Uruguay where he was influenced by the Latin rhythms and passion of his parent's music. He also listened to The Beatles and learned to play various musical instruments, such as the drums, guitar, and keyboards.

James Russell grew up listening to James Brown, Sly and the Family Stone, and Marvin Gaye. Among the instruments he learned to master were the clarinet, saxophone, guitar, and piano. He later played with the Toronto Symphony. Before his fourteenth birthday, he discovered Prince and was impressed by his blend of rock and funk.

Together as Acosta Russell they form a unique hybrid of pop, R&B, and funk. Their self-titled debut album on Eureka Records produced the hit singles *Never Change My Mind* and *Call Me* in 1991. In 1992 came their second album, A LITTLE DEEP DIRECTION. *Deep in My Soul* was the first of four singles to be released.

Singles *Never Change My Mind* 1991   *You're So Tempting* 1992
Call Me 1991   *Do It to Me* 1993
Deep in My Soul 1992   *Wherever You Are* 1993
Running Out of Love
  (with Lisa Lougheed) 1992

CDs ACOSTA RUSSELL 1990   A LITTLE DIRECTION 1992

Bryan Adams Bryan Adams is Canada's reigning pop superstar. With the release of his album WAKING UP THE NEIGHBORS in 1991, he became Canada's most successful recording artist to date. By January 1992, the album had sold seven million copies worldwide.

The eldest son of English-born Jane and Conrad Adams, Bryan was born in Kingston, Ontario, on November 5, 1959. When his parents separated in 1975, he moved to Vancouver with his mother. After graduating from high school, he bought an Estey baby grand piano with the money his parents set aside for university. In 1977 Adams met Jim Vallance of the group Prism, and together the pair began a long and fruitful songwriting partnership. They wrote songs for Prism, Loverboy, and many others.

By 1980 Adams had recorded his self-titled debut album. During the next five years he managed to carve a niche for himself in the pop music scene. In 1985 he received the Diamond Award for selling one million copies of his RECKLESS album in Canada, a first for a Canadian artist. Six Top Ten singles were released from it: *Run to You, Heaven, Summer of '69, One Night Love Affair,* and *It's Only Love* (a duet with Tina Turner). The album also sold four million copies in the U.S.A. *Heaven* became the first Canadian single to reach number one on Billboard's Hot 100 since Anne Murray's *You Needed Me* in 1978.

Adams also wrote with Vallance and David Foster the Ethiopian famine relief anthem, *Tears Are Not Enough*, which brought many Canadian musicians together under one roof.

He also headlined the Prince's Trust Fund charity pop concerts in 1987 at Wembley Arena in London, England. Former Beatles Ringo Starr, George Harrison, and Paul McCartney, along with Eric Clapton, Boy George, and Mark King of the British pop group Level 42, joined the Canadian singer on three Beatles classics: *While My Guitar Gently Weeps, With a Little Help from My Friends,* and *Here Comes the Sun*. Other performers at the weekend concerts were Phil Collins, Paul Young, Midge Ure, and Dave Edmunds, who also performed with Adams and his band.

In 1991 Bryan wrote *Everything I Do (I Do It for You)* for the Warner Brothers film, *Robin Hood: Prince of Thieves*. The following year Adams made headlines when the Canadian Radio-television and Telecommunications Commission (CRTC) ruled that his album, WAKING UP THE NEIGHBORS could not be considered Canadian content because many of the songs were co-written with his producer, Robert "Mutt" Lange. At the time the CRTC only recognized songs 100 percent of which were written and performed by Canadians. In the face of protests by Adams and his fans, the regulatory body changed the requirement to 50 percent and WAKING UP THE NEIGHBORS was declared CANCON on January 29, 1993.

Since his rise in popularity in 1985, Adams has recorded a successful string of hit singles and albums.

Singles

Hidin' from Love 1980	*Cuts Like a Knife* 1983
Give Me Your Love 1980	*Straight through the Heart* 1983
Lonely Nights 1981	*This Time* 1983
Coming Home 1982	*Best Was Yet to Come* 1984
Fits Ya Good 1982	*Run to You* 1984-85

Somebody 1985
Heaven 1985
Summer of '69 1985
Diana 1985
One Night Love Affair 1985
Christmas Time 1985
It's Only Love
   (with Tina Turner) 1986
Heat of the Night 1987
Victim of Love 1987
Hearts on Fire 1987
Only the Strong Survive 1988

Everything I Do (I Do It
   For You) 1991
Can't Stop this Thing We
   Started 1991
There Will Never Be Another
   Tonight 1991-92
Thought I'd Died and Gone to
   Heaven 1992
Do I Have to Say the
   Words? 1992
Please Forgive Me 1993

Albums/CDs

BRYAN ADAMS 1980
YOU WANT IT, YOU GOT IT 1981
CUTS LIKE A KNIFE 1983
RECKLESS 1984

INTO THE FIRE 1987
WAKING UP THE NEIGHBORS 1991
SO FAR SO GOOD 1993

Greg Adams

For this Toronto singer/songwriter, success has not been easy.

After majoring in communications at Loyola University in Montreal, Greg Adams played at local coffeehouses as a folksinger. He was later offered an acting part in director Paul Almond's film *Journey* but turned it down for an editor's job at *Sporting Good News* because it meant a regular salary.

In the early 1970s Adams began peddling his songs to various record companies. A&M Records was the first to show any interest in 1972 and agreed to record some of his songs. The label released only one single, *Take the Road.*

Adams spent the next few years writing songs and jingles and taking the occasional acting job. He also met Eric Robertson, and together they formed a songwriting partnership. International recording star Roger Whittaker was one of the first to record Adams' songs, notably *River Lady,* which was a number one hit in Germany.

In 1977 Adams clinched a deal with Attic Records. His first single, *Hold On,* came out in November. In January 1978 the label released his self-titled debut album.

Singles

Take the Road 1972
Hold On 1977-78
Serene Serene 1978

Come Running 1978
Leave Me 1979
Lady Liberty 1979-80

Album

GREG ADAMS 1978

Agent DAVE ALLAN *(drums)* BOB SMART *(guitar)*
ANDRE KUNKEL *(bass)* CRAIG ZURBA *(keyboards)*
RICK LIVINGSTON *(vocals)*

This Vancouver quintet formed in the late 1970s when Craig Zerba and André Kunkel teamed up as music collaborators. In 1982 Bob Smart joined the duo when they backed up singer Nancy Nash on an album. The following year, Agent had begun playing one-nighters. During this time Kunkel and Zurba supplemented their income by recording advertising jingles.

In November 1983 the group signed with Vancouver manager Brian Wadsworth. They toured with Darby Mills, backup vocalist for The Headpins, in 1985. The following year, Agent had two hits: *All I Hear Is a Heartbeat* and *She Trusted Me*.

When Agent disbanded, Rick Livingston formed a new group called Montana with Dennis Driscoll, Ross Damude, and Karl Moraski. Their only hit was *Just a Minute* on the independent label, M+M Records, written by Livingston, Driscoll, and Brian MacLeod of Chilliwack.

Singles *All I Hear Is a Heartbeat* 1986 *She Trusted Me* 1986

Album AGENT 1986

Susan Aglukark Born and raised in the Arctic, Susan Aglukark made her public appearance at nine years of age as a choir member in her father's church. She grew up in the small isolated community of Arviat on the west coast of Hudson's Bay.

Through her music and personal appearances, she has become a role model for youth among Inuit. Rosemarie Kuptana, President of Inuit Tapirisat of Canada, has called her an ambassador for Inuit, a woman of wisdom, and a leader.

In 1990 she made her first video, *Searching*, which won the Top Cinematography award from MuchMusic. Her first recording was DREAMS OF YOU, an eight song cassette. Her second, ARCTIC ROSE, was released in 1992 and featured songs in her native language of Inuktitut. She was backed by the Arctic Rose Band, led by singer/songwriter Terry Tufts.

Aglukark's music is a mix of contemporary pop, folk, rock and country. Her songs deal with such social issues as teenage suicide, child abuse, drugs and alcohol, and the spiritual and cultural estrangement of Inuit.

Albums   WES DAKUS WITH THE   GOIN' PLACES 1965
              REBELS 1965   LOVEDROPS 1966

Alta Moda   STEVEN GELINEAU *(drums)*   ETRIC LYONS *(bass)*
               MOLLY JOHNSON *(vocals)*   NORMAN ORENSTEIN *(guitar,*
                                                  keyboards)

Formed in 1979, Alta Moda began as a duo — Molly Johnson and Norman Orenstein. Johnson was a child star at the The Royal Alex and O'Keefe Centre in Toronto; she later attended the National Ballet School and Banff School of Arts on a dance scholarship. At age fourteen she joined her first band.

Norman Orenstein was a professional musician for twelve years when he met Johnson. A self-taught guitarist and keyboard player, he worked with Toby Lark and Michael Jordan. He first saw Molly in 1979 when she was a singer in a club. Together they formed Alta Moda with a mutual interest in developing new sounds and musical ideas.

In 1982 Steven Gelineau joined the group to make it a trio. He always wanted to be a musician and was influenced by his uncles, Ray and Dave Davies of The Kinks. After living in Germany and France, he played with various bands, notably New York's The Nails.

Bass player Etric Lyons made it a quartet in 1983. He previously played with Liberty Silver and opened as a headliner for such acts as B.B. King, Wilson Pickett, and The Temptations. Etric also led her own band, Age of Reason, in addition to playing with Alta Moda.

Alta Moda's self-titled debut album came out on Current/Epic Records in the fall of 1987. It was produced by Colin Thurston, whose credits include Duran Duran's GIRLS ON FILM and David Bowie's HEROES. All ten tracks were written by Molly Johnson and Norman Orenstein.

Singles   *Julian* 1988

Album   ALTA MODA 1987

Tommy Ambrose

Born in 1939 in Toronto, Tommy Ambrose is a veteran of the Canadian pop music scene. When he was seventeen, he appeared regularly on CBC's *Cross-Canada Hit Parade*. After three years of singing on the road, he had his own musical/variety series, *The Tommy Ambrose Show*, on CBC, sponsored by General Motors. In 1959 he had his first big hit, *The Magic of You* on Sparton Records.

When *The Tommy Ambrose Show* was canceled in 1963, Ambrose

went on the road, but later gave it up to concentrate on studio work, which included cutting demos.

In 1965 Ambrose went to New York to work with producer Phil Ramone, who would later become Billy Joel's producer. A chance to sing with the Count Basie Orchestra brought him back to Canada.

In the late 1960s Tommy formed a partnership with Larry Trudell to create a TV and radio production company. A third partner, musician Doug Riley (of Dr. Music fame), was added in late 1979.

In 1974 Ambrose had a minor country hit with *Our Summer Song*, a self-penned tune. In 1975-76 he tried his hand at television again with the gospel music series *Celebration* on CBC. With the formation of a jazz band in 1978, Ambrose recorded two albums for Phonodisc: SWEET TIMES and AMBROSE AT LAST with the Doug Riley Band.

Today, Ambrose continues to be one of Canada's top jingle singers. He ran Jingles, his own restaurant and bar in Toronto from 1977 to 1989, where he played there occasionally with Doug Riley on keyboards, Rick Wilkins on sax, and John McLeod on trumpet.

Singles	*The Magic of You* 1959	*Our Summer Song* 1974
Albums	YOUNG TOMMY AMBROSE 1962	AMBROSE AT LAST 1980
	SWEET TIMES 1978	

Bill Amesbury

As a teenager in the late 1960s in Toronto, Bill Amesbury sang and played guitar in various bar bands. When he grew tired of singing other people's songs, he decided to become a songwriter, and later a producer and recording artist.

His first hit was *Virginia (Touch Me Like You Do)* in 1974. It became a Top Ten hit and Amesbury was able to live on the songwriting royalties. That same year he produced J.J. Barrie's *No Charge*, which was a major hit in England.

Amesbury's success as a singer/songwriter extended into Europe where he performed on every major TV variety show. In England he enjoyed further success with his self-penned songs, *Every Girl in the World Tonight, Saturday Night I'll Be Waiting*, and *I Remember* in 1976-77. By the late 1970s he had toured Western Canada, where his 1977 hit, *Can You Feel It*, was well received.

A new record deal with Capitol Records resulted in a new album in June 1977. Despite all his efforts to record new material, Amesbury has been unable to repeat the commercial success of *Virginia*.

Singles	*Virginia (Touch Me Like You Do)* 1974	*Jus' the Taste of the Kid* 1974
	Rock My Roll 1974	*I Remember* 1976
		Can You Feel It 1977

Album   CAN YOU FEEL IT   1977

Paul Anka

Born in Ottawa in 1941, Paul Anka began performing at the age of twelve as an impressionist. Two years later in 1956 he went to Hollywood where he met Ernie Freeman of Modern Records. The result was a recording of *I Confess*. When it was unsuccessful he returned to Canada.

Undaunted, in May 1957 he borrowed some money from his father and went to New York where he stayed with The Rover Boys, a Canadian group who had a recording contract with ABC-Paramount. Anka went to the label and sang some of his songs, one of which was *Diana*, for producer Don Costa. The song *Diana* was inspired by a fifteen-year-old high school student named Diana Ayoub on whom Paul had had a boyhood crush. ABC-Paramount signed Anka and released *Diana* later that summer. The single sold over eight million copies. Over the next five years Anka had several more big hits, including *You Are My Destiny*, *Lonely Boy*, and *It's Time to Cry*. He also wrote *It Doesn't Matter Anymore* for Buddy Holly in 1959.

In 1962 he switched from ABC-Paramount to RCA. He also agreed to play a small role as a soldier in the Twentieth Century Fox film, *The Longest Day*. Anka also wrote the movie's theme song. His only other major acting role has been in the police drama *Dan Raven* on NBC in the early 1960s.

In 1962 he also wrote the theme for *The Tonight Show*. It was heard five nights a week from October 1962 to May 1992 when Johnny Carson retired as host.

Anka was one of the hosts of the 1965-66 music series *Hullabaloo* and *The Midnight Special* in the early 1970s, both on NBC. In 1967 he was a guest on the 1967 comedy/variety series *Spotlight*.

In the late 1960s, he changed record companies again, this time to Buddah. *Goodnight My Love*, the Jesse Belvin hit from 1956, *Do I Love You*, and *Jubilation* put him back in the limelight. In 1968 Anka heard the French song, *Comme d'Habitude*, and bought the rights. He then wrote words to it and retitled it *My Way*. The song went on to become one of Frank Sinatra's biggest hits. Three years later, in 1971, Anka bought back the rights to all of his old songs, the same year Tom Jones recorded Anka's song *She's a Lady*.

Another turning point in his career came in 1974 when he recorded another self-penned tune, *(You're) Having My Baby*, on the United Artists label. It became a number one hit and a million seller.

By the end of the 1970s Anka had opened his own restaurant in Las Vegas and taped a television special for CBS in Monte Carlo. On September 6, 1990 Paul Anka became an American citizen. Today, he lives in Las Vegas with his wife Anne and their five daughters.

Singles

Confess/Blau-Wile Deveest Fontaine 1956
Diana 1957
I Love You Baby 1957
You Are My Destiny 1958
Just Young 1958
Crazy Love/Let the Bells Keep Ringing 1958
Midnight 1958
The Teen Commandments (with GeorgeHamilton IV &Johnny Nash) 1959
(All of a Sudden) My Heart Sings 1959
I Miss You So 1959
Lonely Boy 1959
Put Your Head on My Shoulder 1959
It's Time to Cry 1959
Puppy Love/Adam and Eve 1960
My Home Town/Something Happened 1960
Hello Young Lovers 1960
Story of My Love 1960
It's Christmas Everywhere 1960
The Story of My Love 1961
Tonight My Love, Tonight 1961
Dance on Little Girl 1961
Kissin' on the Phone/ Cinderella 1961
Loveland/The Bells at My Wedding 1961

The Fools Hall of Fame 1961-62
Love Me Warm and Tender 1962
A Steel Guitar and a Glass of Wine 1962
Every Night 1962
Eso Beso 1962
Crying in the Wind 1962
I'm Coming Home 1962
Love Me Warm and Tender 1962
I'd Rather Find Another You 1962
Love (Makes the World Go 'Round) 1963
Remember Diana 1963
Hello Jim 1963
Wondrous Are the Ways of Love 1963
Did You Have a Happy Birthday? 1963
Hurry Up and Tell Me 1963
From Rocking Horse to Rocking Chair 1963
It's Easy to Say 1964
My Baby's Comin' Home/No, No 1964
Sylvia 1964
The Loneliest Boy in the World 1965
Oh, Such a Stranger 1966
I Wish 1966
Can't Along Very Well without Her 1966
I'd Rather Be a Stranger 1966
Truly Yours 1966
Poor Old World 1966-67

But for Love 1967
That's How Love Goes 1967
Until It's Time for You to Go 1967
When We Get There 1968
Goodnight My Love 1969
In the Still of the Night 1969
Sincerely 1969
Happy 1969-70
Do I Love You 1971
Jubilation 1972
Hey Girl 1973
Let Me Get to Know You 1973-74
(You're Having) My Baby 1974
One Man Woman/ One Woman Man 1974-75
I Don't Like to Sleep Alone 1975

(I Believe) There's Nothing Stronger Than Our Love 1975-76
Anytime (I'll Be There) 1976
Happier 1976-77
Make It Up to Me in Love (with Odia Coates) 1976-77
My Best Friend's Wife 1977
Everybody Ought to Be in Love 1977
I'll Help You/Never Gonna Fall in Love 1977
This Is Love 1978
As Long as We Keep Believing 1979
You and I (Duet with Mireille Mathieu) 1979
Think I'm in Love Again 1981
I've Been Waiting for You All of My Life 1981
Hold Me 'Til the Mornin' Comes 1983

Albums/CDs

PAUL ANKA 1958
MY HEART SINGS 1959
PAUL ANKA SWINGS FOR YOUNG LOVERS 1960
ANKA AT THE COPA 1960
PAUL ANKA SINGS HIS BIG 15 1960
IT'S CHRISTMAS EVERYWHERE 1960
PAUL ANKA SINGS HIS BIG 15 VOLUME 2 1961
PAUL ANKA SINGS HIS BIG 15 VOLUME 3 1962
YOUNG, ALIVE AND IN LOVE 1962
LET'S SIT THIS ONE OUT 1962
OUR MAN AROUND THE WORLD 1963
SONGS I WISHED I'D WRITTEN 1963
PAUL ANKA AND OTHERS 1963

PAUL ANKA'S GOLDEN HITS 1963
EXCITEMENT ON PARK AVENUE 1964
STRICTLY NASHVILLE 1966
PAUL ANKA ALIVE 1967
GOODNIGHT MY LOVE 1969
LIFE GOES ON 1969
PAUL ANKA 1971
JUBILATION 1972
ANKA 1974
PAUL ANKA GOLD 1974
FEELINGS 1975
TIMES OF YOUR LIFE 1975
ESSENTIAL PAUL ANKA 1976
THE PAINTER 1976
MUSIC MAN 1977
VINTAGE YEARS 1957–61 1977
LISTEN TO YOUR HEART 1978
PAUL ANKA – HIS BEST 1980
BOTH SIDES OF LOVE 1981
WALK A FINE LINE 1983
ITALIANO 1987

30TH ANNIVERSARY
ANTHOLOGY 1989
21 GOLDEN HITS (REISSUE
OF 1963 ALBUM) 1989
DIANA & OTHER HITS 1990

FIVE DECADES OF HITS 1991
CLASSIC HITS
(WITH ODIA COATES) 1992
PAUL ANKA IN THE 70S
(REISSUE) 1993

April Wine

DAVID HENMAN *(guitar):* Replaced by GARY MOFFET
RITCHIE HENMAN *(drums):* Replaced by JERRY MERCER
MYLES GOODWYN *(guitar, lead vocals)*
JIMMY CLENCH *(bass):* Replaced by STEVE LANG
JIMMY HENMAN *(guitar):* Replaced by JIMMY CLENCH
BRIAN GREENWAY *(guitar)*

Formed in Halifax, Nova Scotia in December 1969, the original four members of April Wine moved to Montreal the following April with only $100 and their equipment. They recorded their first hit, *Fast Train*, early in 1971 in Montreal at RCA with production by Billy Hill. Their self-titled debut album, also produced by Billy Hill, was released the same year. Soon after, bassist Jimmy Henman left and was replaced by Jimmy Clench.

The popularity of April Wine began to soar in 1972 following the release of *You Could Have Been a Lady*, the group's first number one hit in Canada. The song came from the album, ON RECORD, which also featured another single, *Bad Side of the Moon*, written by Elton John and Bernie Taupin.

Two more members of the band left during the recording of the next album, ELECTRIC JEWELS. David and Ritchie Henman were replaced by Jerry Mercer and Gary Moffet prior to a live debut at Toronto's Canadian National Exhibition on Labor Day, where they opened for T. Rex.

In the spring of 1974 April Wine went on their first national tour called "The Electric Adventure." Their big hit that same year was *I'm on Fire for You Baby*, the only single not included on any album.

After their summer tour in 1975 to promote their album STAND BACK, Jimmy Clench left the group to join Bachman Turner Overdrive and later Loverboy. He was replaced by bassist Steve Lang.

In 1976 their album THE WHOLE WORLD'S GOIN' CRAZY shipped platinum (over 1,000,000 copies), the first by a Canadian group. The tour to promote the album became the first to gross one million dollars. They were joined by Heart.

The band's other achievements included being the first to sell out the Regina Stadium on April 19, 1976 and the Kinsmen Field House in Edmonton on April 23 and 24, 1976. Myles Goodwyn was the only original member of the group as of the mid-1970s. In 1977, the addition of guitarist Brian Greenway made the group a sextet.

April Wine toured for almost all of 1980 in Europe, where they impressed audiences in Germany, the United Kingdom and the Benelux countries. In 1981 their album NATURE OF THE BEAST produced the single *Just Between You and Me*, which became the biggest single ever for the group in the United States. Three years later, the group recorded their last album, ANIMAL GRACE. Their farewell tour ended on July 31, 1984 at the Kokance Bowl in Kelowna, British Columbia.

Myles Goodwyn recorded his first solo album in November 1988, which featured his first hit single, *My Girl*. He had previously moved with his family to Nassau in the Bahamas in 1983.

All the original members reunited for a cross-Canada tour in 1992. The response from the fans convinced them to stay together. Early in 1993 they released their first single in eight years, *If You Believe in Me* on the independent fre label. It was followed by an album of all new material called ATTITUDE.

Singles

Fast Train 1971
Listen Mister 1971
You Could Have Been a Lady 1972
Bad Side of the Moon 1972
Drop Your Guns 1972
Lady Run, Lady Hide 1973
Weeping Widow 1973
Just Like That 1974
Electric Jewels 1974
I'm on Fire for You Baby 1974
I Wouldn't Want to Lose Your Love 1974-75
Cum Hear the Band 1975
Oowatanite 1975
Tonight Is a Wonderful Night 1975
The Whole Town's Goin' Crazy 1976
Gimmie Love 1976
Like a Lover, Like a Song 1976

You Won't Dance with Me 1977
Rock and Roll Is a Vicious Game 1978
Comin' Right Down on Top of Me 1978
Roller 1979
Get Ready for Love 1979
Say Hello 1979-80
I Like to Rock 1980
Just Between You and Me 1981
Sign of the Gypsy Queen 1981
All Over Town 1981
Enough Is Enough 1982
Tell Me Why 1982
Rock Myself to Sleep 1985
Love Has Remembered Me 1985
If You Believe in Me 1993
That's Love 1993
Here's Looking at You Kid 1993
Voice in My Heart 1993

Albums/CDs

APRIL WINE 1971	NATURE OF THE BEAST 1981
ON RECORD 1972	POWER PLAY 1982
ELECTRIC JEWELS 1973	ANIMAL GRACE 1984
APRIL WINE LIVE 1974	ONE FOR THE ROAD 1985
STAND BACK 1975	WALKING THROUGH FIRE 1985
THE WHOLE WORLD'S GOIN'	SERIOUS BUSINESS
CRAZY 1976	(MYLES GOODWYN) 1988
FOREVER FOR NOW 1976	OVER 60 MINUTES . . . ALL THE
APRIL WINE LIVE AT THE	ROCKERS 1989
EL MOCAMBO 1977	ROCK BALLADS 1990
FIRST GLANCE 1978	GREATEST HITS 1991
HARDER . . . FASTER 1979	ATTITUDE 1993

Jann Arden

Jann Arden's musical career began in 1982 when she began writing her own songs, such as *I Just Don't Love You Anymore*, which was included in her 1993 debut album on A&M Records, TIME FOR MERCY. She was a member of several now-forgotten bands in her hometown of Calgary before she went solo in 1987. She played in lounges and bars in Calgary and at ski resorts nearby. Determined to succeed as a solo artist, she began playing at various folk festivals.

The first hit single from TIME FOR MERCY was *Will You Remember Me.*

Singles

Will You Remember Me 1993	*The Way Things Are Going* 1993
I Would Die for You 1993	*I'm Not Your Lover* 1993

CD TIME FOR MERCY 1993

Atkinson, Danko & Ford

(see Bearfoot)

B

Bachman-Turner Overdrive

CHAD ALLEN (*vocals, rhythm guitar, mandolin, piano accordion*):
Replaced by TIM BACHMAN
RANDY BACHMAN (*vocals, lead guitar, bass*): Replaced by JIM CLENCH
BLAIR THORNTON (*lead guitarist*)
FRED TURNER (*guitar*)

Bachman-Turner Overdrive began in 1970-71 when Randy Bachman, his brother Robbie, Chad Allan and Fred Turner joined together and called themselves Brave Belt. The genesis of Brave Belt was as a jam session in 1970 when Randy, who had just left the Guess Who, went over to play some songs with longtime friend Chad Allan. By the end of the year the two of them had decided to form a group. Randy's younger brother, Robbie, was asked to play drums. In 1971, Fred Turner, another old friend of Randy, made it a foursome. In April of 1971 Brave Belt signed a contract with Reprise Records and a month later their self-titled debut album came out. Another, BRAVE BELT II was released in the fall of the same year.

Success in Canada came slowly. Because the group wanted to gear itself towards a heavier sound, Chad Allen was asked to leave because his songwriting style and voice did not fit in. Chad was replaced by Randy Bachman's other brother Tim, who left college to join the band.

Reprise canceled their tour to support the release of BRAVE BELT II, but the group nevertheless went on a cross-Canada tour.

The future of the band brightened when Terry David Mulligan, then host of ROQ in Toronto, invited them to be on his show. Prior to their appearance, Randy sent a demo tape to Charley Fach at Mercury Records; he liked what he heard and immediately signed them. By now, the band had come up with a new name to fit the harder edge sound they played on stage — Bachman-Turner Overdrive. On May 1, 1973 their self-titled debut album on Mercury was released. It was the first of four successful albums.

By 1976 the group had built up a loyal following in both Canada and the United States but the following year, Randy left the group due to musical differences. He formed the groups Ironhorse and Union, both of which failed to repeat his success with The Guess Who and Bachman-Turner Overdrive.

The year 1979 marked a comeback for BTO (the acronym was adopted officially in 1978). Robbie became group leader and a new album, ROCK 'N' ROLL NIGHTS, and single, *Heartaches* (both on Mercury Records) were released. Joining the group were Jim Clench, formerly with April Wine, and Blair Thornton, who replaced Randy Bachman on bass and lead vocals.

Randy Bachman released a solo album on Polydor Records in 1978 called SURVIVOR. From it came the single, *Is the Night too Cold for Dancing?* In 1989 Randy Bachman reunited with the original members of BTO for two years. He left in 1991 and signed a solo contract with Sony Music the following year. Early in 1993 the label released his album, ANY ROAD, which contained both fast and slow versions of the single *Prairie Town*, a tribute to the artist's Winnipeg days. The video for the fast version featured Neil Young, while the slow version had both Young and Margo Timmins of The Cowboy Junkies.

Bachman released a five song mini-CD titled LIVE IN SEATTLE in the fall of 1993. It featured classic songs from his days with The Guess Who and BTO.

Chad Allan went on to have a solo career in the pop field in the 1970s and 1980s. Today, he records on his own Sea Breeze label as a Christian rock artist.

BTO has never really left the Canadian music scene. In 1993 they were playing fairs and festivals in the United States. When Randy Bachman left after signing with Sony Music, he was replaced by Randy Murray. The rest of the current group is comprised of Fred Turner, Robin Bachman, and Blair Thornton.

As Brave Belt

Singles

Rock and Roll Band 1971	*Crazy Arms, Crazy Eyes* 1971
Never Comin' Home 1972	*Dunrobin's Gone* 1972

Albums   BRAVE BELT 1971   BRAVE BELT II 1972

As Bachman-Turner Overdrive

Singles

Gimme Your Money Please 1973	*Little Candy Dancer* 1973
Blue Collar 1973	*Hold Back the Water* 1973
Takin' Care of Business 1974	*Let It Ride* 1974
Roll on Down the Highway 1975	*You Ain't Seen Nothin' Yet* 1974
Quick Change Artist 1975	*Hey You* 1975
Take It Like a Man 1976	*Down to the Line* 1976
Gimme Your Money Please 1976	*Lookin' Out for No. 1* 1976
Shotgun Rider 1977	*Life Goes On (I'm Lonely)* 1977
Heartaches 1979	*Down the Road* 1978
Wooly Bully 1989	*Jamaica* 1979

Albums/CD

BACHMAN TURNER OVERDRIVE 1973	HEAD ON 1975
BACHMAN TURNER OVERDRIVE II 1973	BEST OF BTO (SO FAR) 1976
	FREEWAYS 1977
NOT FRAGILE 1974	STREET ACTION 1978
FOUR WHEEL DRIVE 1975	ROCK AND ROLL ALL NIGHT 1979
	THE ANTHOLOGY 1993

By Chad Allan

Singles *Looking through Crystal Glass*
1969
West Coast Girl 1971
Spending My Time 1973

Dunrobin's Gone 1974
Prairietown, Midwest City 1974
Ballad of a Middle-Aged Rocker
1981

By Randy Bachman

Singles *Is the Night too Cold
for Dancing?* 1978
Prairie Town 1993

Tailspin 1993
I Wanna Shelter You 1993
Overworked and Underpaid 1994

Albums AXE 1970

SURVIVOR 1978

CD ANY ROAD 1992

**Band of
Armagh** GEORGE MAJOR (*bass*)
JIMMY RAFFERTY (*vocals,
mandolin, guitar*)

DAVE WALKER (*vocals, piano,
strings*)

This folk music group from Winnipeg was once billed as Ireland's top
variety band. They played traditional Irish music. Their debut single
on Sunshine Records in 1981 was *Black Velvet Band* with the Irish
drinking song, *Whiskey in the Jar*, on the flip side.

Single *Black Velvet Band* 1981

The Band RICK DANKO (*bass guitar*)
LEVON HELM (*drums*)
GARTH HUDSON (*organ*)

RICHARD MANUEL (*piano*)
ROBBIE ROBERTSON (*guitar*)

The origins of The Band go back to 1961 when Ronnie Hawkins
recruited them as replacements for his backup band.

All five members had experience with high-school bands: Robbie in
Thumper and The Trombones; Garth in Paul and The Captors; Richard
in The Rockin' Revols; Levon in the Jungle Bush Beaters; and Rick in
Rick and the Starliners and Rick and the Roxatones.

The Hawks played a blues/rock style of music that influenced
other Canadian bands such as Luke and The Apostles, Mandela, and
Jack London and The Sparrows. In 1965 The Hawks accompanied
Bob Dylan on a world tour. When it ended, they returned with him to
his home in the Catskill Mountains not far from Woodstock. There, in
a ranch-style house they nicknamed "Big Pink," they wrote with
Dylan, who was recovering from his celebrated motorcycle accident,

such landmark albums as THE BASEMENT TAPES, MUSIC FROM THE BIG PINK, and JOHN WESLEY HARDING.

During this time, the Hawks changed their name to The Band and made their official debut in April 1969 at San Francisco's Winterland. That summer they played at the Woodstock Festival.

Recording for Capitol Records, The Band had a huge following, and between 1968 and 1973 they had a string of successful hit singles and albums.

In 1974 The Band reunited with Dylan on a sold-out world tour which led to the release of the acclaimed concert album, BEFORE THE FLOOD. On Thanksgiving Day 1976 The Band played Winterland for the last time. Filmed by director Martin Scorsese, *The Last Waltz* is considered by many the greatest concert film ever made.

In 1983 the group reunited without Robbie Robertson, and two years later they toured with Crosby, Stills and Nash. In the fall of 1985 they played in Richard Manuel's hometown of Stratford, Ontario. He died on March 4, 1986 at age forty-two.

The band was honored with the Lifetime Achievement Award at the Juno ceremonies in 1989. In July 1990 they performed a live version of Pink Floyd's *The Wall* with Roger Waters, Van Morrison, Cyndi Lauper, Bryan Adams and Sinead O'Connor. The concert, which was taped and released on CD and home video, celebrated the tearing down of the Berlin Wall.

In the fall of 1992, The Band helped salute Bob Dylan on his thirtieth anniversary, and the following year hosted the Absolutely Unofficial Blue Jean Bash at President Clinton's Inaugural Gala in Washington, D.C.

The individual members of The Band have all been successful as single acts. Levon Helm turned to writing music and acted in the Universal film, *Coal Miner's Daughter* (1980). Robertson has acted in the film *Carny* (1980), worked as music director on Scorsese's *The King of Comedy* (1983), and released two solo albums. Garth Hudson wrote and performed an "Evening with Garth Hudson" at St. Ann's Cathedral in Brooklyn in 1989, and played on albums by such artists as Van Morrison and Marianne Faithful. Rick Danko has toured extensively throughout Europe and America as a solo performer and member of ex-Beatle Ringo Starr's All-Starr Band in 1989 (along with Helm).

In 1993, The Band finished its first album of original material since 1977. Entitled JERICHO, it was recorded at Levon Helm's studio in Woodstock, New York. The group's lineup is now comprised of original members Helm, Hudson, and Danko, along with Richard Bell, Jim Weider, and Randy Ciarlante. The Band were the first Canadian act to be inducted into the Rock and Roll Hall of Fame in Cleveland, Ohio, in January 1994.

As The Hawks
Singles *The Stone that I Throw* (as Levon and the Hawks) 1965   *Can You Please Crawl out Your Window* (with Bob Dylan) 1965
Go Go Liza Jane (as Levon and the Hawks) 1965   *Nothing Was Delivered* 1967

As The Band
Singles *Jabberwocky* 1967   *Caledonia Mission* 1972
The Weight 1968   *Ain't Got No Home* 1973-74
Up on Cripple Creek 1969   *Third Man Theme* 1974
Rag Mama Rag 1970   *Hobo Jungle* 1976
Time to Kill 1970   *Ophelia* 1976
The Shape I'm In 1971   *Acadian Driftwood* 1976
Life Is a Carnival 1971   *Georgia on My Mind* 1976
When I Paint My Masterpiece 1971   *Out of the Blue* 1978
Don't Do It 1972   *Remedy* 1993

Albums/CDs MUSIC FROM THE BIG PINK 1968   THE BEST OF THE BAND 1976
THE BAND 1969   THE LAST WALTZ 1978
STAGE FRIGHT 1970   ANTHOLOGY VOLUME I 1978
CAHOOTS 1971   ANTHOLOGY VOLUME II 1978
ROCK OF AGES 1972   TO KINGDOM COME: THE DEFINITIVE COLLECTION 1989
MOONDOG MATINEE 1973   JERICHO 1993
NORTHERN LIGHTS-SOUTHERN CROSS 1976

Barde PIERRE GUERIN (*vocals, acoustic guitar, accordion*)
TOBY CINNSEALAC (KINSELLA) (*tin flute, recorders, clarinet*)
CHRIS MacRAGHALLAIGH (*fiddle*)
ELLIOT SELICK (*fiddle*)

Formed in 1975, these four musicians from Montreal played the reels, jigs, and marches of Canada's Celtic ancestors. Their foot-stomping Celtic rock was popular at home in Quebec, Cape Breton, and in Ireland and France.

They put their music to vinyl in 1977 when they recorded their self-titled debut album, followed by IMAGES in 1979, and a third, VOYAGE, in 1983. VOYAGE included traditional latin, jazz, and country songs, as well as Celtic arrangements.

By the time Barde made their third album, only two original members remained, Pierre Guerin and Toby Kinsella, who were joined by Jacques Joubert on violin, Richard Paquette on keyboards, and Jocelyn Therrien on bass.

Albums   BARDE 1977   VOYAGE 1983
             IMAGES 1978

Barenaked Ladies   ANDY CREEGGAN (*congas, piano*) ED ROBERTSON (*vocals, guitar*)
JIM CREEGGAN (*bass*)   TYLER STEWART (*drums*)
STEVEN PAGE (*vocals, guitar*)

This Toronto-based band began when Steven Page and Ed Robertson started playing together in the fall of 1988. A year later, Andy and Jim Creeggan joined the group. In the fall of 1990, Andy Creeggan left to take part in a student exchange program in Rwanda and Uruguay. In his absence, drummer Tyler Stewart filled in. When Andy rejoined the band in 1991, Stewart stayed on as the fifth member.

The band blends the Creeggan brothers' jazz background, Robertson's country roots, Page's pop culture diet, and Stewart's hard rock to create an original, quirky sound. Their music has fascinated fans and critics since the release of their self-titled five song EP.

This Toronto-based quintet established itself as one of Canada's most unusual groups. They sold out engagements in 7000 seat venues while still unsigned, unprecedented for a band with no support from a major record company. Overseas the five member band continued to be successful. They were the first in history to perform atop the BBC Broadcasting House.

In 1991 they won Toronto radio station CFNY's CASBY (Canadian Artists Selected by You) awards for Best Overall Group and Most Promising Songwriters. The band was signed to Sire Records, distributed by Warner Music Canada, and in the summer of 1992 their first album, GORDON, went on to sell more than 500,000 copies.

Singles   *Lovers in a Dangerous Time*   *If I Had a Million Dollars*
              1992   1992-93
              Be My Yoko Ono 1992   *Brian Wilson* 1993
              Enid 1992   *What a Good Boy* 1993
              Grade Nine 1992

CD   GORDON 1992

Battered Wives

CLEVE ANDERSON: Replaced by PATRICK MOON
JOHN GIBB
JASPER KLASSEN
TOBY SWANN

In the late 1970s Battered Wives was Canada's most controversial group. Their name was not popular with women's groups, and radio programmers would not play their music for fear of public reprisals.

Despite their critics, their debut album, CIGARETTES, sold over 30,000 copies and the band had a strong following in both bar and concert venues. The controversy caused founding member Cleve Anderson to leave. He was replaced by Patrick Moon. To ease the controversy, they eventually shortened their name to The Wives when they toured with Elvis Costello.

British-born Toby Swann was a classically trained musician who changed from playing the cello and viola to the guitar after hearing a rock band play *Jumpin' Jack Flash*. He moved to England where he led a band called Streetlife. After a trip to India he returned to Canada and organized an early version of the Battered Wives with Jasper Klassen.

Another English member of the group was John Gibb. He was owner of two clothing boutiques in Toronto when he heard about the band. Before going into the fashion business he had worked with Jimmy Page and Jeff Beck in England.

In 1978 the Battered Wives' first single, *Uganda Stomp*, a satirical look at Idi Amin, was released.

Single *Uganda Stomp* 1978

Album *Cigarettes* 1979

Bearfoot

JIM ATKINSON (*vocals, guitar*)
HUGH BROCKIE (*lead and rhythm guitar, banjo*)
TERRY DANKO (*guitar*)
DWAYNE FORD (*keyboards, flute, guitar, vocals*)
MICHAEL TOMLINSON (*drums, guitar, vocals*)
CHRIS VICKERY (*bass*)

The origins of Bearfoot go back to 1970 when Ronnie Hawkins persuaded Hugh Brockie and Dwayne Ford to leave Edmonton and move to Toronto to become part of Ronnie's Rock'n'Roll Revival and Travelling Medicine Show.

When Dwayne left Hawkins he joined Terry Danko (brother of The Band's Rick Danko) and guitarist Atkinson at a farmhouse near Tillsonberg, Ontario. It was not long before they became known as Atkinson, Danko and Ford. The addition of drummer Brian Hilton and Hugh Brockie made a name change to Atkinson, Danko and Ford with Brockie and Hilton.

After more personnel changes they finally settled on the name Bearfoot. In 1974 they had two major Canadian hits, *Molly* and *Passing Time*.

Dwayne Ford had a brief solo career in the late 1970s and early 1980s. In the fall of 1979 he recorded *We'll Find a Way* as a duet with Patsy Gallant. His first solo hit was *Roll Me Away* in 1980. In 1981 he recorded the album NEEDLESS FREAKING which contained the singles *Lovin' and Losin' You* (1981) and *Hurricane* (1982).

(As Atkinson, Danko and Ford)

Single *Right On* 1972

Albums ATKINSON, DANKO & FORD WITH BROCKIE & HILTON 1972
FRIENDS 1973

(As Bearfoot)

Singles *Only a Soldier* 1973   *Passing Time* 1974
Molly 1974   *Cable to Carol* 1975

Album PASSING TIME (Dwayne Ford & Bearfoot) 1975

Beau Dommage

PIERRE BERTRAND (*vocals, bass*)   ROBERT LEGER (*keyboards*):
MARIE-MICHELE DESROSIERS   Replaced by MICHAEL HINTON
(*vocals, piano*)   MICHEL RIVARD (*vocals, guitar*)
REAL DESROSIERS (*drums*)

Beau Dommage began in 1970 as Quenouille bleue when founding member Michel Rivard and author/composer Pierre Huet were attending the University of Quebec in Montreal. At first they performed only at art shows. With the addition of Robert Leger their name changed to Theatre Sainfoin, and they began playing at theaters. During this time, Marie-Michele Desrosiers joined them on stage. By 1973 she had joined the group as a permanent member, and their name changed to Beau Dommage.

The group began practicing in Rivard's parents' basement at Boucherville. They played their first concert in October 1973 at Luducie on the campus of the University of Montreal. Two years later, Capitol Records released their self-titled debut album.

In 1977, Beau Dommage showed signs of breaking up. Rivard decided to make a solo album because he wanted to express personally his own ideas without imposing on the other members. The rest of the group had gone their separate ways by the end of the 1970s. Marie-Michele went on to enjoy a solo career, and made her first public performance in 1981.

The group reunited during the summer of 1984 for the 450th anniversary celebrations of Jacques Cartier's landing. On December 9, 1984 they played at the Montreal Forum as part of the CBC-TV's French series, *Beaux Dimanches*.

In 1985 two live albums were released from a reunion concert they gave at the Montreal Forum. The first was called AU FORUM DE MONTRÉAL, and the second, 26 ET 27 OCTOBRE 1984 AU FORUM DE MONTRÉAL.

The solo careers of both Robert Leger and Michel Rivard sparked renewed interest in the group's recordings. Polygram reissued a greatest hits album by Beau Dommage in 1988 called LEURS PLUS GRANDS SUCCÈS.

Albums

BEAU DOMMAGE 1975
OÙ EST PASSÉ LA NOCE? 1975
UN AUTRE JOUR SE LÈVE
    EN VILLE 1977
PASSAGERS 1978

LES GRANDS SUCCÈS DE BEAU
    DOMMAGE 1978
AU FORUM DE MONTRÉAL 1985
26 ET 27 OCTOBRE 1984 AU FORUM
    DE MONTRÉAL 1985
LEURS PLUS GRANDS SUCCÈS 1988

The Beau-Marks

JOEY FRECHETTE (*piano*)
RAY HUTCHINSON (*lead guitar, vocals*)

MIKE ROBITAILLE (*rhythm guitar*)
GILLES TAILLEUR (*drums*)

Formed in 1958 this Montreal quartet began as The Del Tones. After the release of *Moonlight Party* on Quality Records in April 1959, they were forced to change their name because a band in the United States had a legal right to the name.

Ray Hutchinson and Joey Frechette were the principal songwriters of the group, although credit went to all four. Frechette wrote *Clap Your Hands. Moonlight Party* and *Billy Billy Went a Walking* were written by Hutchinson.

Clap Your Hands was a number one hit in Canada and Australia and it was one of the first Canadian hits to chart in the United States when it reached number forty-two in *Cashbox Magazine*.

The Beau-Marks appeared on Dick Clark's American Bandstand and the Peppermint Lounge, where they played for two weeks. As a result of this engagement, they were asked to play at a charity show at Carnegie Hall.

The Beau-Marks broke up in 1963. Joey Frechette spent fifteen years in the music industry and currently lives in Oshawa, Ontario. Mike Robitaille is a successful businessman in Montreal. Ray Hutchinson also resides in Montreal where he has played with another group and as a solo act. Gilles Tailleur died of a cerebral hemorrhage at the age of thirty-five in the mid-1970s.

In 1968 Quality Records re-released *Clap Your Hands* as part of the label's greatest hits series. Joseph Conrad recorded his own version of this rock 'n' roll standard in 1987.

Singles

Moonlight Party 1959	*Classmate* 1961
Rockin' Blues 1959	*Little Miss Twist* 1962
Clap Your Hands 1960	*Lovely Little Lady* 1962
Billy Went a Walking 1960	*The Tender Years* 1962

Albums

HIGH FLYING BEAU-MARKS 1960

THE BEAU-MARKS IN PERSON RECORDED ON LOCATION
    AT LE COQ D'OR 1961

THE BEAU-MARKS 1962

Veronique Beliveau

Long before Veronique Beliveau (a.k.a. Nicole Monique) recorded her first English album in 1986 she was a celebrity in her native Quebec.

The rest of Canada first heard her in 1985 on the Ethiopian Hunger Relief recording of *Tears Are Not Enough*, in which she sang a French verse.

Through Francois Bernard, who had connections in the record business, she recorded for Nobel, a small Quebec independent label. In 1977 she signed with RCA and released two albums in French. Six years later she switched to A&M. At Expo 86 she sang *Toujours l'amour* before Prince Charles and Princess Diana.

Her first English album was BORDERLINE. On her English hits, *Make a Move on Me* and *I Can't Help It*, she was known simply as Veronique.

Singles

Nous partirons en univers 1977	*Je suis comme je suis* 1985
Aimer 1980	*Toute la nuit* 1985
Je suis fidele 1983	*Make a Move on Me* 1987
C'est un reveur 1983	*I Can't Help It* 1987
That Boy 1983	*Jerusalem* (Duet with
Please 1984	Marc Gabriel) 1989
Le Rock 1985	*House of Love* 1989
Cover Girl 1985	

Albums/CDs

PRENDS MOI COMME JE SUIS 1977	COVER GIRL 1985
VERONIQUE BELIVEAU 1980	BORDERLINE 1986
TRANSIT 1983	VERONIQUE 1989

The Bells CHARLIE CLARK FRANK MILLS:
ANNE EDWARDS   Replaced by DENNIS WILL
CLIFF EDWARDS MICKEY OTTIER:
JACKIE RALPH   Replaced by FRANK MILLS
DOUG GRAVELLE MICHAEL WAYE

Originally known as The Five Bells, this Montreal group formed in 1965. The original lineup consisted of Anne and Cliff Edwards, Jackie Ralph, Mickey Ottier, and Doug Gravelle.

Their first hit in late 1968 was *Moody Manitoba Morning*, written by Winnipeg singer/songwriter Rick Neufeld, who would later be a recording star in his own right, and taken from their debut album DIMENSION. Frank Mills joined the group during this period.

They changed their name to The Bells in 1970 when Cliff's wife Anne left because she was pregnant. Their next hit was *Fly Little White Dove, Fly*, written by Montrealers Marty Butler and Bob Bilyk. It was after the release of this national hit in 1970, that Mills left the group to pursue a career as a solo performer.

Another unknown singer/songwriter named Ken Tobias wrote *Stay Awhile*, the band's biggest hit and only million seller. He later became successful as a solo artist in the 1970s.

In 1971 the group's lineup consisted of Cliff and his sister-in-law Jackie, Doug Gravelle, Dennis Will, and two musicians from Halifax, Charlie Clark and Michael Waye.

Two years later, in 1973, they disbanded. Cliff Edwards had a brief solo career in 1970s and 1980s; he is currently a businessman in Ontario. Jackie lives in Vancouver. Frank Mills continues to be in demand as an international solo performer (see Frank Mills).

(As The Five Bells)

Single   *Moody Manitoba Morning* 1969

Album   DIMENSION 1969

(As The Bells)

Singles   *Fly Little White Dove, Fly* 1970   *For Better or for Worse* 1971
          Stay Awhile 1971   *Oh My Love* 1972
          Lady Dawn 1971   *Lord Don't You Think It's Time* 1972
          Sweet Sounds of Music 1971
          Easier Said than Done 1971   *Maxwell's Silver Hammer* 1972
          He Was Me, He Was You 1973   *The Singer* 1973

Albums   FLY LITTLE WHITE DOVE, FLY   LOVE, LUCK 'N LOLLIPOPS 1971
          1971   STUDIO "A" 1972

(By Cliff Edwards)

Singles		
	Hold Me 1972	*Singer of Songs* 1976
	Uncle Dad and Auntie Mom 1973	*What's Forever For* 1980
	Carry On (Cliff & Anne Edwards) 1973	*Easier Said than Done* 1981
		Grab the Money and Run 1981
	Carpenter of Wood 1973	*Keep Your Hands Off* 1982
	Love May Be the Answer 1974	*Storm* 1984
	Song for Wendy 1976	*She's My Woman* 1989
	(There's a) Fire Burning Still 1976	*Highway #1* 1989-90

Albums		
	SINGER OF SONGS 1976	WHAT'S FOREVER FOR 1981

The Bel-Vistas

MICHAEL BAXTER (*bass*)   MARK RIPP (*vocals, guitar*)
BOB HAMLYN (*guitar*)   JOHN TIFFOLI (*drums*)

Originally, this Scarborough-based band was a trio called The Game composed of Ripps, Tiffoli, and Hamlyn. In the winter of 1987 with the addition of Baxter, the group changed its name to The Bel-Vistas. Their sound is modeled after the classic two-guitar, bass and rock 'n' roll combo drum groups ranging from Buddy Holly and The Crickets to Neil Young and Crazy Horse.

In 1990, The Bel-Vistas released an independent cassette which was well received. They later signed a contract with Eureka Records, and in 1992 their debut album, SOMEWHERE ALONG THE LINE, was released.

Singles		
	Ordinary Man 1992	*A Matter of Time* 1992
	Crazy Bill 1992	

CD	
	SOMEWHERE ALONG THE LINE 1992

Barney Bentall & the Legendary Hearts

BARNEY BENTALL (*vocals, guitar*)   DOUG MCFETRIDGE (*guitar*): Replaced by COLIN NAIRN
WILL FROESE (*keyboards*): Replaced by CAM BOWMAN   BARRY MUIR (*bass*)
          JACK GUPPY (*drums*)

Formed in 1978, this Vancouver-based band began as Brandon Wolf. After the release of an independent EP, entitled PLYWOOD in 1979, the group changed its name to Barney Bentall and the Legendary Hearts. The following year they released their first independent album, LOSING CONTROL which was produced by Bob Rock and Ron Obvious.

For the next eight years they played clubs and bars until their big break came in the summer of 1987 when they made a live video performance of *Something to Live For*. Shortly after it aired on MuchMusic, various record companies came calling. Sony Music immediately signed them.

A string of hit singles, beginning with *Come Back to Me* in 1988, continued into the 1990s.

Singles

Something to Live For 1987
Come Back to Me 1988
The House of Love 1988
Something to Live For 1988
She's My Inspiration 1989
Crime Against Love 1990
Life Could Be Worse 1991
I Gotta Go 1991
Nothing Hurts Like the Words 1991
Living in the '90s 1992
Doin' Fine 1992-93
If This Is Love 1993
Belly of the Sun 1993
Family Man 1993

CDs

BARNEY BENTALL & THE LEGENDARY HEARTS 1988
LONELY AVENUE 1990
AIN'T LIFE STRANGE 1992

Bentwood Rocker

ERIC BARAGAR (*vocals, guitar, keyboards*)
MIKE GOETTLER (*vocals, bass*)
TIM CAMPBELL (*vocals, guitar*): Replaced by BARRY HAGGARTY

STEVE SMITH (*vocals, drums, keyboards*)
DAN THOMPSON (*vocals, guitar, percussion*)

Based in Belleville, Ontario, this quintet evolved from The Sands of Time. Formed in 1978, all the members held other jobs by day. Goettler and Baragar co-owned Centre Stage Music, Dan Thompson was a lawyer, and Steve Smith, a social worker. Tim Campbell was formerly a member of the group Noah. On weekends they traveled the Ontario club circuit from Ottawa and Kingston through Belleville and Peterborough.

Bentwood Rocker recorded and produced their first album, NOT TAKEN, in 1979 in Baragar's own studio. In 1981 they signed with Quality Records. That same year, the band lost Tim Campbell. He was replaced by Barry Haggarty, who had toured with Ronnie Hawkins in 1975. In 1983 the group released the album SECOND WIND under the name The Press.

Some of the people who have worked with the band include producer Jack Richardson of The Guess Who, who recorded and produced Bentwood Rocker's demo in 1988; Ian Thomas, who produced Second Wind; vocalist Louis Reny of One To One; and Ronnie Hawkins.

Today, Bentwood Rocker is still together playing for fun. They changed their name to 98.6 in the early 1980s.

Singles		
Forgive and Forget 1981		*Second Wind* 1983
Heart Says Go 1981		*Danger of Remembering* 1986
Take Me to Heaven 1982		

Albums		
NOT TAKEN 1979		TAKE ME TO HEAVEN 1982

Art Bergmann

Art Bergmann's music career began in 1977 when he played in a band called The Schmorgs in the Vancouver suburbs. He later played with such bands as The K-Tels, subsequently called The Young Canadians, who released two EPs, HAWAII and THIS IS MY LIFE.

From 1980 to 1983, Bergmann was a member of Los Popularos. They released a single, *Mystery to Me* and an EP, BORN FREE.

In 1984 Bergmann and a group of studio musicians called Poisoned released a six track EP, YEAH, I GUESS. Another EP called POISONED came out in 1985.

He signed with Duke Street Records in 1988 and recorded his first solo album, CRAWL WITH ME. His old backup group was re-christened The Showdogs and included Susann Richter, Taylor Nelson Little, and Ray Fulber. Bergmann's second solo album was called SEXUAL ROULETTE.

Turning to acting in 1991, Art played Otto in Bruce MacDonald's film, *Highway 61*. A deal with Polygram that same year resulted in his self-titled album for the label, and the single, *Faithlessly Yours*. A second hit from the album, *If She Could Sing* was released in November, 1991.

Singles		
Faithlessly Yours 1991		*If She Could Sing* 1991-92

CDs		
CRAWL WITH ME 1988		ART BERGMANN 1991
SEXUAL ROULETTE 1989		

Big House

K.B. (KEVIN) BROC *(rhythm guitar)*	CRAIG BEAKHOUSE *(bass):* Replaced by JAY SCOTT KING
JAN EK *(vocals)*	SJOR THRONDSON *(percussion, drums)*

All four members of this Edmonton-based band played with other groups before establishing themselves as one of the province's best hard rock bands. Drummer and co-founder Sjor (pronounced Shore) Throndson and lead vocalist Jan Ek were members of the punk band Down Syndrome, which released a six song EP called OTHER WAYS on their own Black Sun label. Jay Scott King was a former member of Back Street Kids, which won Pennsylvania radio station WPTA's Battle of the Bands. They opened for such groups as Helix, Twisted Sister, Talas, and Bon Jovi. King left to form his own band called Brunette and later joined Big House. Rhythm guitarist K.B. Brock played with such heavy rockers as Breaker and Hostage before joining the group. Before King and Broc made it a quartet, Jan and Sjor honed their unique brand of rock shortly after Big House formed in 1987. By 1990 the foursome had become well established in their native city. They also earned the award for Best Hard Rock Band at the Alberta Recording Industry Awards the same year.

Their first of three hit singles was *Dollar in My Pocket (Pretty Things)* in 1991.

Singles	*Dollar in My Pocket*	*All Nite* 1992
	(Pretty Things) 1991	*Baby Doll* 1992
CD	BIG HOUSE 1991	

Bim Born Roy Forbes in Dawson Creek in 1953, he was nicknamed Bim by his late father who picked it up from the song, *Bimbo, Where You Gonna Goyo*. His interest in music began in 1968 when The Beatles released their self-titled double album, known as the "White Album." He played in a rock band called Crystal Ship and played nothing but Beatles songs from THE BEATLES and RUBBER SOUL.

Bim started playing professionally in 1971 in Vancouver, where he makes his home today. His first job was with a Rita Coolidge show in Edmonton. Early in 1973, he began playing coffee houses on the west coast. Later he came east to Toronto and play at the Riverboat. Signed to A&M Records in 1975, he had a modest success on the charts in the mid-1970s.

Today, he still writes and records, and likes to try different musical styles. His seventh solo album, THE HUMAN KIND, was a tribute to his country roots. Since 1989 he has been part of the trio, UHF (Ulrich, Henderson, and Forbes).

Singles	*Me and My Baby* 1975	*Can't Catch Me* 1976
Albums/CDs	KID FULL OF DREAMS 1975	A CHRISTMAS ALBUM
	RAINCHECK ON MISERY 1976	(Roy Forbes) 1985
	THISTLES 1978	LOVE TURNS TO ICE
	ANYTHING YOU WANT 1982	(Roy Forbes) 1987
	NEW SONGS FOR AN OLD	
	CELEBRATION 1985	

Terry Black   Terry Black began singing as a teenager, and at age fifteen his solo career started with the hit *Unless You Care* in October 1964. Other hits followed in the mid-1960s, such as *Little Liar* and *Baby's Gone*. He recorded for Arc Records.

In 1970 he met Laurel Ward while performing in the Toronto production of Hair. They later married.

As Terry Black and Laurel Ward they became a popular Canadian duo. Their first hit in 1972 was *Goin' Down (On the Road to L.A.)*. They also recorded the album ALL NIGHT LONG in 1982.

(By Terry Black)

Singles	*Unless You Care* 1964	*Poor Little Fool* 1965
	Say It Again 1965	*Rainbow* 1966
	Little Liar 1965	*Baby's Gone* 1966
	Only Sixteen 1965	*Wishing Star* 1967
Albums	ONLY SIXTEEN 1965	THE BLACK PLAGUE 1966

(As Terry Black & Laurel Ward)

Singles	*Goin' Down (On the Road to L.A.)* 1972	*Love Is the Feeling* 1974
	Warm Days and Warm Nights 1972	*Back Up (Against Your Persuasion)* 1975
		Long Time 1976
Album	ALL NIGHT LONG 1982	

Blue Rodeo   CLEAVE ANDERSEN (*drums*):   MARK FRENCH (*drums*):
   Replaced by MARK FRENCH   Replaced by GLENN MILCHEM
JIM CUDDY (*vocals, guitar*)   GREG KEELOR (*vocals, guitar*)
BAZIL DONOVAN (*bass*)   BOBBY WISEMAN (*piano*):
                        Replaced by KIM DESCHAMPS

This Toronto-based band began as The HiFis when Jim Cuddy and Greg Keelor were in high school. They moved to New York City in 1981 where they tried to get a record deal. After three years they returned to Toronto, unsuccessful.

The pair then began to recruit other members to form Blue Rodeo: bassist Bazil Donovan, a friend from their New Wave days, self-taught pianist Bob Wiseman, and drummer Cleave Andersen.

In 1985 they soon began playing around Toronto and established themselves as a live act who could draw sell-out crowds. They became regulars at The Horseshoe, a local club in the city.Their debut album, OUTSKIRTS, was released in 1987 on Warner Music Canada.

After the release of their second album, DIAMOND MINE, in December

1988, the group's reputation spread south of the border. In 1990 they played at the Montreux Jazz Festival and appeared with Meryl Streep in the Columbia film, *Postcards from the Edge*. The group was honored as Best Group of the Year in 1990 and 1991 at the Juno Awards.

Their fourth album, LOST TOGETHER came out in 1992, and it was at this time the band went through two major personnel changes. Wiseman left to be replaced by Kim Deschamps and Mark French (who replaced Andersen in 1989) by Glenn Milchem, ex-Change of Heart.

In 1993 their fifth album, FIVE DAYS IN JULY was released by Warner. The first single was *Five Days in May*.

Singles

Try 1987	*What Am I Doin' Here* 1991
Day After Day 1988	*After the Rain* 1991
Rebel 1988	*Lost Together* 1992
How Long 1989	*Rain Down on Me* 1992-93
Diamond Mine 1989	*Angels* 1993
House of Dreams 1989	*Flying* 1993
Love and Understanding 1990	*Already Gone* 1993
Trust Yourself 1991	*Five Days in May* 1993
Till I Am Myself Again 1991	*Hasn't Hit Me Yet* 1994

Albums/CDs

OUTSKIRTS 1987	LOST TOGETHER 1992
DIAMOND MINE 1989	FIVE DAYS IN JULY 1993
CASINO 1990	

The Blue Shadows

BILLY COWSILL (*guitar, vocals*) JAY JOHNSTON (*drums*)
JEFFREY HATCHER (*guitar, vocals*) ELMAR SPANIER (*bass*)

Billy Cowsill, who became famous as a member of The Cowsills was instrumental in creating a band that played country music with the passion and energy of rock 'n' roll. First known as The Billy Cowsill Band when it was a duo comprised of Cowsill and Spanier, they played spellbinding renditions of classic songs by Hank Williams Sr. and Roy Orbison.

The group expanded to a quartet with the addition of Jeffrey Hatcher and Jay Johnston. The former was singer, songwriter and guitarist with such bands as The Fuse, The Six, and The Big Beat. It was Billy and Jeff's smooth harmonies that resulted in a name change to The Blue Shadows. They described their sound as "Hank goes to the Cavern Club."

Signed to Sony Music, their debut album ON THE FLOOR OF HEAVEN was released in 1993. The first single and video was *Comin' on Strong*.

Single   *Comin' On Strong* 1993

CD   ON THE FLOOR OF HEAVEN 1993

Blvd

RANDY BURGESS (*bass*)   MARK HOLDEN (*saxophone, vocals*)
DAVID FORBES (*lead vocals*) ANDREW JOHNS (*keyboards*)
RANDY GOULD (*guitar*)   RANDAL STOHL (*drums*)

Mark Holden and Randy Gould started Blvd in 1983 in Calgary. Holden had returned from Frankfurt, Germany where he worked as a sound engineer at Hotline Studios. An offer to work at Thunderhead Studios in Calgary brought him back to Canada. While working there, he assembled the group that became Blvd. When the studio closed in 1985, the band relocated to Vancouver.

In the spring of 1987, MCA released their self-titled debut album. Their first chart single was *In the Twilight* in 1988. Blvd broke up in 1990 shortly after the release of the single, *Crazy Life*.

Singles *In the Twilight* 1988   *Dream On* 1988
          Never Give Up 1988   *Lead Me On* 1990
          Far from Over 1988   *Crazy Life* 1990

Album BLVD 1987

Bond

BILL DUNN (*bass*)   JOHN ROLES (*rhythm guitar*)
JEFF HAMILTON (*drums*)   TED TRENHOLM (*keyboards*)
ALEX MacDOUGALL (*lead guitar*)

The origins of this Toronto rock band go back to 1970 when John Roles placed an ad in the trades for musicians interested in forming a band. Five years later they signed with Columbia Records. Their first hit single, *Dancin' on a Saturday Night* was a major hit. They broke up in 1979.

Singles *Dancin' on a Saturday Night*   *Hold On* 1975-76
            1975   *Back Seat Driver* 1976
          When You're Up, You're Up   *One Lives in My Life* 1976
            1975

Album BOND 1975

Mars Bonfire

As one of the original members of Jack London and the Sparrows, Mars Bonfire used his real name, Dennis Edmonton. When The

Sparrows split up in 1967, he decided to go solo and changed his name. *Ride with Me Baby* and *Faster than the Speed of Life* were his only hits.

Singles *Ride With Me Baby* 1968
Faster Than The Speed Of Life 1969

Bootsauce

ALAN BACULIS (*bass*) DREW LING (*vocals*)
PERE FUME (*guitar*) MARC VILLENEUVE (*drums*)
SONNY GREENWICH JR. (*guitar*)

Drew Ling was born in Liverpool, England and in his teens he immigrated to Calgary with his parents. There he met Pere Fume whose musical education began at age six with piano lessons. Sonny Greenwich Jr. was born in Montreal and received his first guitar on his sixteenth birthday. Soon after, he started his first band, Dog Food, later renamed Dog Star. Greenwich gave up his band and decided to travel abroad. After returning to Canada, Sonny met Steve Ship at a party. Two weeks later in Ship's office, Sonny met Drew and Pere and they became a trio with Ship as the manager.

Bootsauce ended up as a five member band when Polygram Canada signed the group six months later. On June 1, 1990, THE BROWN ALBUM was released. Their second album, BULL, came out in January 1992, their third, SLEEPING BOOTIE, in November 1993.

Singles *Masterstroke* 1990 *Whatcha Need* 1992
Scratching the Whole 1990 *Big, Bad & Groovy* 1992
Everyone's a Winner 1991 *Rollercoaster's Child* 1992-93
Play with Me 1991 *Sorry Whole* 1993
Love Monkey #9 1992 *Moanie* 1994

CDs THE BROWN ALBUM 1990 SLEEPING BOOTIE 1993
BULL 1991

The Bourbon Tabernacle Choir

GREGOR BERESFORD (*drums*) CHRIS MILLER (*guitar*)
CHRIS BROWN (*organ, clavinet,* CHRIS PLOCK (*keyboards*):
   trombone, vocals)   Replaced by DAVE WALL
KATE FENNER (*vocals*)   (*piano, vocals*)
GENE HARDY (*saxophone, vocals*) ANDREW WHITEMAN
JASON MERCER (*bass*)   (*guitar, vocals*)

The origins of The Bourbon Tabernacle Choir go back to 1985 when eight Toronto high school students joined together for a jam session later referred to as "The Sermon." Through subsequent performances they were able to smooth over the rough edges of their stage act. They eventually built up a local following in Toronto's nightclubs and bars. Chris Brown came up with the group's name in a dream.

In 1987 the group released the first of three independent cassettes, FIRST TASTE OF BOURBON. The other two were IF HELL HAD A HOUSE-BAND in 1989 and SISTER ANTHONY in 1990. Their first two singles, *As Right as They Wanna Be* and *Put Your Head On*, were produced by ex-Blue Rodeo keyboardist Bobby Wiseman. The accompanying video for *Put Your Head On*, debuted on MuchMusic in May of 1991. It was also included on the soundtrack of Bruce McDonald's feature film, *Highway 61*.

The year 1992 saw the Toronto octet record their first album, SUPE-RIOR CACKLING HEN, for Yonder Records with distribution by Sony Music. Its title comes from a Jimi Hendrix song called *Third Stone from the Sun* (from the album ARE YOU EXPERIENCED?) in which Hendrix mentions a majestic superior cackling hen. The album's first single, *Make Amends* was released in October; a second, *Afterglow*, came out in January 1993.

Singles		
As Right as They Wanna Be 1990-91	*Make Amends* 1992	
Put Your Head On 1991	*Afterglow* 1993	
	Original Grin 1993	

CD SUPERIOR CACKLING HEN 1992

Bourne and Macleod

BILL BOURNE
ALAN MACLEOD

Bill Bourne and Alan Macleod have known each other since 1980 when they were members of the Scottish band Tannahill Weavers. In 1985 Alan retired from performing to become a painter. Bill also left the band, but went back home to Alberta to pursue a songwriting career.

Alan's career as a painter was short-lived when Bill sent him a demo of songs he had written. He wanted to get Alan's professional opinion. They began talking about the songs and soon they were performing together again. Their first album, DANCE AND CELEBRATE won the 1991 Juno Award for Best Roots/Traditional Recording.

In 1992 they recorded a second album, MOONLIGHT DANCERS. Throughout the second half of 1992 and first half of 1993, they toured extensively to promote it. The Alberta-based duo is only one of three artists from the province to play at the Canada Pavilion during Expo 92 in Seville, Spain.

CDs DANCE AND CELEBRATE 1991   MOONLIGHT DANCERS 1992

The Box PHILLIPE BERNARD (*drums*)   GUY PISAPIA (*keyboards*)
JEAN-MARC PISAPIA (*vocals*)   CLAUDE THIBEAULT (*guitar*)
JEAN-PIERRE BRIE (*bass*)

Jean-Marc Pisaspia, an architecture major at the University of Montreal, dropped out of university to play keyboards for a two month tour with former classmate and friend, Ivan Doroschuk, lead singer of the band Men Without Hats. In 1982, Pisapia was invited by four other musicians to join their group to sing lead vocals. He accepted, and Montreal-based The Box was born.

Though they sang primarily in English, their early success was limited to their home province of Quebec, where their singles *Must I Always Remember* and *L'Affaire Dumoutier (Say to Me)* were popular. It was not until the release of CLOSER TOGETHER in 1987 that the group gained widespread popularity in the rest of Canada.

In 1992, Phillipe Bernand and Guy Pisapia left the group. A DECADE OF THE BOX, a retrospective of the group's music, was released the following year.

Singles *Walk Away* 1984   *Ordinary People* 1987
Must I Always Remember 1984 *Crying Out Loud for Love* 1988
L'Affaire Dumoutier 1986   *Temptation* 1990
My Dreams of You 1986   *Inside My Heart* 1990
Closer Together 1987   *Carry On* 1990

CDs THE BOX 1984   THE PLEASURE AND THE PAIN
ALL THE TIME, ALL THE TIME,   1990
   ALL THE TIME 1985   A DECADE OF THE BOX 1993
CLOSER TOGETHER 1987

Brave Belt (see Bachman-Turner Overdrive)

Brighton Rock MARK CAVARZAN (*drums*)   STEVIE SKREEBS (*bass*)
GREG FRASER (*lead guitar*)   MARTIN VICTOR (*keyboards*)
GERALD McGHEE (*vocals*)

Brighton Rock, a band in the Hamilton-Niagara region, formed in 1984 and released a self-titled independent EP a year later on Flying Fist Records, produced by Steve Vaughan and Jack Richardson.

Signed to Warner Music in 1986, they released three albums: YOUNG, WILD AND FREE (1986), TAKE A DEEP BREATH (1989), and LOVE MACHINE (1991). After a tour through Ontario and a final concert in Edmonton in July 1992, Brighton Rock disbanded.

Singles	*Can't Wait for the Night* 1987	*Hangin' High and Dry* 1989
	Can't Stop the Earth 1989	*Hollywood Shuffle* 1991
	One More Try 1989	

Albums/CDs	YOUNG, WILD AND FREE 1986	LOVE MACHINE 1991
	TAKE A DEEP BREATH 1989	

The British Modbeats

JOE COLONNA (*bass*)   ROBBIE JEFFREY (*drums*)
GREIG FOSTER (*guitar*)   FRASER LOVEMAN (*vocals*)
MIKE GORGICHUK (*guitar*)

Formed in 1964-65, this quintet from St. Catharines, Ontario played cover hits by such British rockers as The Rolling Stones, The Spencer Davis Group, and The Pretty Things. On stage they presented themselves as true Brits. Robbie Jeffrey had a Union Jack on his bass drum, and the band name was written in old English script.

Signed to Red Leaf Records, their first hit was *Whatcha Gonna Do About It* in the summer of 1966; they had three more hits in 1966-67. Their only album, MOD IS THE BRITISH MODBEATS, came out in 1967. The group disbanded in 1968.

Singles	*Whatcha Gonna Do about It* 1966	*Somebody Help Me* 1967
		Try to Understand 1967
	Love's Just a Broken Heart 1966	

Album	MOD IS THE BRITISH MODBEATS 1967

Bush

(see Mandala)

Charity Brown

At age fifteen Charity Brown started playing coffeehouses in Kitchener, Ontario. Influenced by Grace Slick of Jefferson Airplane, she sang psychedelic songs with the rock bands Landslide Mushroom and Inner Light. She later joined Rain, a commercial rock band that played mostly in Ontario high schools. For four years she displayed her exceptional vocal range.

She secured a recording contract with A&M Records in 1975 and turned her attention to such old hits such as *You Beat Me to the Punch*, *Jimmy Mack*, and *Our Day Will Come*. She had a brief but successful run on the charts in the mid-1970s.

Singles	*Jimmy Mack* 1974	*Take Me in Your Arms* 1975
	You Beat Me to the Punch 1974-75	*Our Day Will Come* 1975
		No Way to Treat a Lady 1975

Saving All My Love 1976   *No Hurt* 1977
Anyway You Want Me 1976   *Forecast* 1977
Stay with Me 1976   *Hold on Baby* 1977

Albums   CHARITY BROWN 1975   STAY WITH ME 1976
ROCK ME 1976

Brussel Sprout

JEFF BENJAMIN (*bass*)   DON PERRISH (*vocals, guitar*)
KEN LUSH (*flute*)   TOM TREECE (*vocals*)
ROGER MANNING (*vocals, harp*)   JOHN VASS (*vocals, drums*)
DANNY MOSES (*vocals, bongos, violin*)

The history of Brussel Sprout goes back to 1972 when Don Perrish and Ken Lush, who had known each other from public school, started playing with some ex-members of a jug band called Custer's Last Stand to make a demo tape. After moving to Jordan, Ontario they spent the next year-and-a-half working on their own material. They first called themselves The Amazing Vibrasonics.

After a series of personnel changes, the group was comprised of Perrish, Lush, Roger Manning, Tom Treece, John Vass, and Denny Moses; Jeff Benjamin made it a sextet in 1974. They signed a contract with MCA Records, and in the summer of 1975 their first single, *Dance She Said* was released. ONE MORE TIME was the name of their debut album. Their singles *High in the Rockies* and *Tryin' to Get Next to You* were written and arranged by Tom Treece.

Brussel Sprout has opened for Valdy, Gordon Lightfoot, and The Good Brothers.

Singles   *Dance She Said* 1975   *Tryin' to Get Next to You* 1976
High in the Rockies 1976

Album   BRUSSEL SPROUT 1976

Brutus

BRUCE GORDON (*trumpet, organ, guitar, bass*)   SANDY WHITE (*bass*)
SONNY WINGAY (*guitar*)
BILL ROBB (*sax, trombone*)   WALLY ZWOLINSKI (*organ, lead vocals*)
LEN SEMBALUK (*drums*)

Led by Walter Zwolinsky (a.k.a. Zwol), this Toronto band went through many personnel changes after its formation in 1969. Primarily a bar band, members dressed up in garish clothes co-ordinated by artist Don Norman.

Their first two hits, *Funky Roller Skates* on Quality Records and

Help Me Free Me on Yorkville Records were not successful. Signed to GRT Records in 1975, they were produced by Jack Richardson of The Guess Who fame.

When Brutus broke up, Walter Zwol had a brief solo career with the hits *New York City* (1978), *Call Out My Name* (1979), and *Shaka Shaka* (1979). He later formed a new band called Rage. Their only hit was *Darlin' I'll Be There* in 1981.

Singles	*Funky Roller Skates* 1970	*Ooo Mama Mama* 1975
	Help Me, Free Me 1971	*Who Wants to Buy a Song* 1976
	Slow and Easy 1975	
Album	BRUTUS 1975	

Bundock

PIERRE BUNDOCK (*lead vocals, saxophone*)
MARC GENDRON (*bass*)
DOMINIQUE LANOIS (*guitar, vocals*)
MARTIN PLANTE (*keyboards*)
ALAIN ROUSSEL (*drums*)

The history of this band goes back to 1979 in Grand-Mère, Quebec, when music teacher Guy Pelletier and Pierre Bundock formed the first edition of the band. Four years later, they moved to Montreal. In 1985 they decided to write and record in English.

Band members Pierre Bundock and Marc Gendron previously played in a group called Windo, an electro-pop band. They had met while studying music at College St. Laurent.

Bundock's EP, MAUVE was released in 1986 on Alert Records and contained the song *American Singer*, which was a tribute to the late Jim Morrison of The Doors. Released in 1987, it was their only national hit. They released an album, S.A. (SOCIETÉ ANONYME) in 1988.

Single	*American Singer* 1987
Album	S.A. (SOCIETÉ ANONYME) 1988

Edith Butler

Born in Paquetville, New Brunswick in 1942, Edith Butler (a.k.a. Marie Nicole Butler) was first exposed to music in her hometown where she heard country and western music on the radio. It was not until Edith left home to go to Notre-Dame-de-l'Acadie, a girl's convent, that she received her first guitar from her brother. The boarders at the convent were her first audience. There she learned all about Québecois artists and music, and later as an adult, she became interested in her Acadian past. She researched the songs, ballads, stories, legends, and tales of Acadian culture.

Although she liked to sing, her main vocation was teaching. She taught at a community school in Trudel and math and science at a secondary school in Bathurst, New Brunswick.

In 1964 she made her television debut on CBC's *Singalong Jubilee*; she performed Gordon Lightfoot's *Song for a Winter Night* in both English and French.

After two years of teaching, she went to Laval University to study for her Master of Arts degree, where she eventually realized that she could pursue a singing career. Her first album, CHANSONS D'ACADIE, came out in 1969.

Her many accomplishments include a leading role in the National Film Board production of *Les Acadiens de la dispersion* (1964) and a featured performance at the Canadian Pavilion at Expo 70 in Osaka, Japan. In 1975, she was made an Officer of the Order of Canada.

She guest starred in the CBC series *The Jubilee Years* in the fall of 1992.

Albums/CDs		
CHANSONS D'ACADIE 1969	DE PAQUETVILLE À PARIS 1984
AVANT D'ÊTRE DÉPAYSÉE 1973	UN MILLION DE FOIS
L'ACADIE S'MARIE 1975	JE T'AIME 1985
C'EST LA RÉCRÉATION 1977	LE PARTY D'EDITH 1985
EDITH BUTLER 1977	12 GRANDS SUCCÈS
L'ÉSPOIR 1978	D'EDITH BUTLER 1985
ASTEUR QU'ON EST LÀ 1979	ET LA PARTY CONTINUE 1986
A PAQUETVILLE 1981	PARTY POUR DANCER 1987
J'M'APPELLE EDITH 1981	EDITH BUTLER 1990

Marty Butler

Marty Butler started playing professionally with The Scepters for three years in the mid-1960s. Because of his vocal training as a falsetto, the group favored songs made famous by The Four Seasons. Not content to just sing in a band, Butler turned to writing songs. He and Bob Bilyk became a songwriting team. Les Sceptres (no relation to The Scepters) was the first to record one of their songs.

Their big break came in 1970 when their song *Fly Little White Dove Fly* was recorded by The Bells. Butler and Bilyk also wrote *We Gotta Make It* for Trini Lopez, *Crowded by Emptiness* for Ginette Reno, and *I Want to Be a Country Boy Again* for Tommy Hunter.

Butler won $10,000 in the Hear Canada Singing contest for his song, *Can't You Hear the Music*. He first recorded for Columbia and then switched to the independent label WAM, owned by Leon Aronson, who became Butler's arranger and producer.

Although Butler liked to record in Montreal where he used his own musicians, he moved to Toronto to be closer to Bilyk, who continued to collaborate with him on new material. Marty returned to the recording studio in 1978 to record *Lie to Myself* on WAM Records. In the fall of 1982 he released his self-titled debut album on RCA.

Singles *To a Place Near the River* 1971
We Gotta Make It Together
  1972
All the Love in My Heart 1972
Can't You Hear the Music
  1972-73
*Once-Loved Woman, Once-
Loved Man/Love Vibrations*
  1973

If You Wanna Go to New York City
  1973
Fly Little White Dove, Fly 1974
Lie to Myself 1978
Never Been in Love 1979
Saving It Up 1980

Albums WE GOTTA MAKE IT TOGETHER
  1972

LOVE VIBRATIONS 1973
MARY BUTLER 1982

Meryn Cadell

This actress/singer-songwriter from Toronto had been playing in the city's nightclubs for five years when she recorded her first independent cassette called MARE-IN KA-DELL. In 1989, she went into the recording studio to begin laying down tracks for her debut album, ANGEL FOOD FOR THOUGHT, released by Capitol Records in 1991. The first single from the album was *The Sweater*, which did not become a national hit until the spring of 1992. That same year she had two other hits, *Inventory* and *Barbie*, neither of which were as successful as her first.

Early in 1993 she recorded a single and video of the song *Courage* with The Infidels. Warner/Sire released her second solo album, BOMBAZINE. The first single was *Window of Opportunity*.

Singles	*The Sweater* 1991-92	*Johnny and Betty* 1993
	Inventory 1992	*Courage* (with The Infidels) 1993
	Barbie 1992	*Window of Opportunity* 1993

CDs	ANGEL FOOD FOR THOUGHT 1991
	BOMBAZINE 1993

John Allan Cameron

Born in 1938 at Inverness, Cape Breton, John Allan Cameron grew up in a musical family. His mother and brother played fiddle, some of his cousins stepdanced or played piano, and his Uncle Dan Rory MacDonald composed more than 2,500 fiddle tunes. When he was a teenager, John started playing jigs and reels on guitar, an F-hole type Kamico.

In 1957 he relocated from his native Inverness to Ottawa where he became a member of The Order of the Oblate Fathers. Six months before becoming a priest, he left the order and the priesthood. He ended up at St. Francis Xavier University in Antigonish, Nova Scotia, and began playing at coffeehouses and various college gatherings with a group called The Cavaliers. After he received his Bachelor of Education degree in Halifax, he taught in London, Ontario.

During the summer of 1968 he returned to performing. He appeared at the Newport and Mariposa Folk Festivals, Expo 70 in Japan, and the Grand Ole Opry in Nashville.

A contract with Apex Records in the late 1960s produced a couple of albums, HERE COMES JOHN ALLAN CAMERON and THE MINSTREL OF CRANBERRY LOVE. In the early 1970s he signed a management contract with Balmur Ltd. and released two acclaimed albums, GET THERE BY DAWN and LORD OF THE DANCE.

Cameron's repertoire consists of sixteenth and seventeenth century

Scottish and Irish ballads with some more familiar songs written by modern songwriters like Bruce Cockburn.

Since 1975, he has frequently been accompanied by four musicians who call themselves The Cape Breton Symphony: fiddlers John Donald Cameron, Winston "Scotty" Fitzgerald, and Wilfred Gilles and pianist/accordionist, Bobby Brown. With Cameron they recorded one album together in 1978 on the artist's own label, Glencoe.

On the country charts in the summer of 1976, Cameron had a hit with a song called *Tie Me Down*.

Singles		
	Streets of London 1972	*I Can't Tell You* 1973
	Sit Down, Mr. Music Man 1972	*Tie Me Down* 1976
		Overnight Success 1982

Albums/CDs		
	HERE COMES JOHN ALLEN CAMERON 1968	FIDDLE 1978
	THE MINSTREL OF CRANBERRY LANE 1969	FREEBORN MAN 1979
	GET THERE BY DAWN 1972	GOOD TIMES 1987
	LORD OF THE DANCE 1973	WIND WILLOW 1991
	WEDDING, WAKES & OTHER THINGS 1976	CLASSIC JOHN ALLEN VOLUME I 1992
		CLASSIC JOHN ALLEN VOLUME II 1992

Canada Goose

BARBRA BULLARD (*vocals*)
GARY COMEAU (*lead guitar, steel guitar*)
PAUL HUOT (*guitar, vocals*)
WAYNE LESLIE (*bass, vocals*)
JOHN MATTHEWS (*vocals*)
RICHARD PATTERSON (*drums*)

Early in 1970 three ex-members of The Esquires — Paul Huot, Gary Comeau and Richard Patterson — played at the Tabu Room of the Beacon Arms Hotel every Friday and Saturday night. They were soon joined by former Esquires Wayne Leslie, John Matthews, and Barbra Bullard, and when they were approached about a recording a single, they decided to change their name, which they considered dated. Guitarist Amos Garrett had told Patterson that The Maple Leafs or Canada Goose would be good names. After clearing the use of the latter name with Garrett, the six man band became known as Canada Goose with their first and only hit, *Higher and Higher*, on Tonsil Records, a new record label in New York. In Canada the single was distributed by Quality Records. The song was originally recorded by Jackie Wilson in 1967.

Radio airplay of the song established the group among the teen set, and they graduated from the Tabu Room to bigger venues. As the demand for appearances grew, the individual members felt they could not give up their day jobs. They disbanded at the height of their success.

Other members of the group included Lock McFadden on guitar and vocals, Daryl ("D") Wadsworth on piano and vocals, Valerie ("Val") Tuck on vocals, Derek O'Neil on guitar and vocals, and Rick Lemieux on bass guitar and vocals. Wadsworth decided to form another group under the name Canada Goose but they failed to impress fans of the old group and later disbanded.

Of the original six, Comeau went on to join James Leroy and Denim, Leslie joined Neville Wells and Wells Fargo, and Patterson became a member of several bands, including the David Wiffen Group, Sneezy Waters, Wells Fargo, Ian & Sylvia's The Great Speckled Bird, and The Radio Kings.

Single   *Higher and Higher* 1970

CANO

MARCEL AYMAR	MICHEL KENDEL
DAVID BURT	WASYL KOHUT
MICHEL DASTI	ANDRE PAIEMENT
JOHN W. DOERR	RACHEL PAIEMENT

In 1971 a group of sixty-five individuals gathered together in Sudbury, Ontario to form a society where the artistic visions of both English and French Ontarians could find expression musically under one national identity. This society took on the name of Cooperative des Artistes de Nouvel Ontario (CANO) and sponsored the creation of a unique band. By December 1975 CANO had been established with a long term contract signed with A&M Records. Although the members of the group did not enjoy commercial success on the record charts, their vision of a united Canada in song remains an important contribution to Canadian music.

Andre Paiement, the founder and co-leader of the group, committed suicide in 1978.

Singles   *Rebound* 1979-80   *Carrie* 1980
          Rendezvous 1980

Albums   TOUS DANS L'MEME BATEAU   RENDEZVOUS 1979
             1976   SPIRIT OF THE NORTH 1980
          AU NORD DE NOTRE VIE 1977   VISIBLE 1985
          ECLIPSE 1978

The Carlton Showband

GREGORY DONAGHEY
MIKE FEENEY
SEAMUS GREW
BOB LEWIS
CHRISTY MCLAUGHLIN

SEAN MCMANUS
CHRIS O'TOOLE
JOHNNY PATTERSON
FRED WHITE

The band started one night in 1963 at a St. Patrick's dance in Brampton, Ontario when Chris O'Toole, who'd recently come to Canada from Ireland, was talked into playing the drums on a few songs. Soon other Irishmen joined and they eventually formed a group that November.

They arrived at their name one night when Chris O'Toole, Seamus Grew, and Christy McLaughlin were lost in downtown Toronto. Standing outside Maple Leaf Gardens on Carlton Street, they came up with the name The Carltons Danceband, which later was changed to The Carlton Showband.

The original members consisted of Fred White, Chris O'Toole, Christy McLaughlin, Seamus Grew, and Sean McManus. Mike Feeney, Johnny Patterson and Bob Lewis joined later.

In 1966 they released two hit singles on Quality Records: *The Merry Ploughboy* and *Up Went Nelson*. Their self-titled debut album on CASL Records came out in 1966.

When CTV's *Pig and Whistle Show* went on the air in 1967, The Carlton Showband became the show's house band. They stayed for the show's entire ten-year run.

Gregory Donaghey joined the group in 1974 as lead singer. He is best known for his rendition of *Danny Boy*, one of the band's most requested songs.

After more than thirty years, The Carlton Showband remains one of Canada's most enduring concert attractions. Their current lineup is comprised of Fred White, Gregory Donaghey, Roddie Lee, Robert Benoit, Larris Benoit, and Aaron Lewis.

Singles

The Merry Ploughboy 1966
Up Went Nelson 1966
Black Velvet Band 1967
March of the Maple Leaf 1968
Westmeath Bachelor 1968
Roll It Around in Your Mind
    1972
The Leprechaun 1973
Biddy McGaw 1974
*There's Nothing like a
    Newfoundlander* 1975

Any Dream Will Do 1975
Harpers Ferry 1976
One Up on the World 1976
Sadie the Cleaning Lady 1976
More than Yesterday 1977
*Half an Hour Later in
    Newfoundland* 1978
Hard Times 1979
He Believes in Me 1979-80
What's a Nice Guy 1982
Mother 1985

Albums/CDs

THE CARLTON SHOWBAND 1966
WE'RE OFF TO DUBLIN IN THE
  GREEN 1966
THE CARLTON SHOWBAND 1967
A NIGHT AT THE PUB 1967
THE CARLTON SHOWBAND
  ON TOUR 1968
THE CARLTON SHOWBAND AT
  THE PIG AND WHISTLE 1969
TIME GENTLEMEN PLEASE 1970
CARLTON SHOWBAND SPECIAL
  1971
CARLTON COUNTRY 1972
BEST OF THE CARLTON
  SHOWBAND 1973
IF YOU'RE IRISH (CARLTON
  SHOWBAND BY REQUEST) 1973
BEST OF THE CARLTON
  SHOWBAND VOLUME II 1974

ANY DREAM WILL DO 1975
CARLTON SHOWBAND FIRST
  CHOICE 1975
ONE UP ON THE WORLD 1976
BEST OF THE CARLTON SHOWBAND
  VOLUME III 1977
HERE WE GO AGAIN 1977
20 GOSPEL FAVORITES 1977
SIXTEEN MOST REQUESTED 1978
HARD TIMES 1979
BACK TO THE SOD 1980
THREE STEPS TO HEAVEN 1982
REFLECTIONS 1985
WE WISH YOU A MERRY CHRISTMAS
  1986
CARLTON SHOWBAND'S
  25TH ANNIVERSARY 1988
CATCH THE SPIRIT 1990
25 ALL-TIME FAVORITES 1993

Andrew Cash

The music of Andrew Cash is rooted in folk and acoustic rock 'n' roll. Born in Toronto in 1962, Cash's career began in 1980 when he formed the group L'Etranger with his friend Chuck Angus. They developed a local following on Queen Street in Toronto. Their first big break was a second place finish in a band contest judged by Bob Segarini and Greg Godovitz.

When L'Etranger broke up in 1986, Cash decided to pursue a solo career. He began playing once a week for nine months as a single acoustic act at The Spadina Hotel in downtown Toronto. In 1988 Cash released his first album, TIME AND PLACE, on Island Records. Another album, BOOMTOWN followed in 1989. Cash's hit singles included *Time and Place* and *Smile Me Down*, both released in 1988 though his best known hit, *Boomtown*, was released a year later.

Signed to MCA Records in 1993, his debut album for the label was called HI. The songs on HI deal with the individual in society in a personal and abstract way. In a 1993 interview, he described the first song on the album, *John Endicott*, as "a composite of characters and ideas that floated around in the late 1980s, a last gasp of excess living." In the song *This May Be My Life, But This Is Not My Dream*, Cash reveals what he believes is the true nature of living in North America: "We have this idea that in the west we are free. . . . It's important to say that this may be my life, but this is not my dream. Our lifestyle comes with a price."

Singles		
Trail of Tears 1986		*100 Years* 1989
Time and Place 1988		*Boomtown* 1989
Smile Me Down 1988		*A Lot of Talk* 1993
What Am I Gonna Do with these Hands 1989		

Albums/CDs		
TIME AND PLACE 1988		HI 1993
BOOMTOWN 1989		

Cat

JIM CAMPBELL (*vocals*)   PHIL MULHOLLAND (*drums*)
GRAHAM FIDLER (*bass, vocals*)   GARY O'CONNOR (*guitar, vocals*)
MIKE McQUEEN (*guitar, vocals*)

This Toronto group began as The Spasstiks in 1964. After a name change to Cat four years later, they established themselves on the club circuit in the Northeastern United States.

They were part of the Festival Express train that went across Canada in 1970. Their biggest hit was *We're All in this Together* in the spring of 1970.

In 1972, Cat split up. Gary O'Connor had a brief solo career as Gary O in the early 1980s, Jim Campbell became a record executive with WEA in 1974 and later with BMG Music Canada, and the rest of the group became members of Fast Eddie.

Singles		
Doing the Best We Can 1968		*We're All in this Together* 1970
Solo Flight 1970		*Honey in the Sky* 1971

Chalk Circle

BRAD HOPKINS (*bass*)   CHRIS TAIT (*vocals, guitar*)
DERRICK MURPHY (*drums*)   TAD WINKLARZ (*keyboards*)

From Newcastle, Ontario, Chalk Circle formed in 1983. Two years later they won their first CASBY Award from Toronto radio station CFNY-FM for most promising non-recording group. They went from the indie club circuit of Toronto to a cross-Canada tour.

In 1986 they signed a contract with Duke Street Records, and the group's first EP, THE GREAT LAKE, was released, featuring two hit singles, *April Fool* and *Me, Myself and I*.

Singles		
April Fool 1986		*20th Century Boy* 1987
Me, Myself and I 1986		*Sons and Daughters* 1989
This Mourning 1987		

Albums/CDs		
THE GREAT LAKE 1986		MENDING WALL 1987

BRYAN ADAMS

Andrew Catlin

**GORDON
LIGHTFOOT**

THE RANKIN FAMILY

Peter Leverman

**JONI
MITCHELL**

Stephen Danelian

CRASH TEST DUMMIES

BARENAKED LADIES

**WILD 'T'
AND THE
SPIRIT**

The Chandells

AL GIBSON (*vocals*)
DON GOWAN (*guitar*)
NORM HESS (*drums*)

RICK HISCOX (*guitar*)
GARY STASIUK (*bass*)

This five member group was one of Calgary's first hometown rock bands. They made their first public appearance in 1962 at the Triwood Community Hall and broke up seven years later. Rick Hiscox went to Europe, and Norm Hess got married and became a lawyer.

Hess's wife, Doreen, organized the reunion of the group in 1978. A year later they recorded *One Track Mind*, the old Knickerbockers hit from 1966, produced by Danny Lowe of Painter, another Canadian band. The new Chandells was comprised of Gibson, Hess, Hiscox, and new guitarist Terry Whitford. They played oldies from the 1960s.

Single *One Track Mind* 1979

The Chantones

LARRY DESJARLAIS (*tenor*)
JACK GRENIER (*vocals*)

ROY LESPERANCE (*bass*)
JIM NANTAIS (*baritone*)

The Chantones were a popular vocal quartet from Windsor, Ontario, who played some of the top nightclub and supper clubs in Canada and the United States between 1954 and the late 1960s when they broke up.

Originally known as The Teen Tones, all four first sang together in the summer of 1953 when the Catholic Youth Organization (CYO) sponsored a Southwestern Ontario talent contest. The song they chose to sing was *Have You Talked to the Man Upstairs* by The Four Lads. When they won the contest, it was their first big break. Their second was a chance meeting with Wally Spitzig, organist at Sacred Heart Church in Windsor, who knew The Four Lads. He arranged to have them sing his arrangement of *You'll Never Walk Alone* at the Michigan State Fair.

Their next big break came from the owner and manager of the Metropole supper club in Windsor when he asked them to fill in for an act that had canceled. They were noticed by Lindsay Meehan, the nineteen-year-old leader of the house band, who encouraged them to become a professional act. From their appearance at the Metropole, they were able to play in other clubs in the Windsor area, such as the Elmwood Casino.

In 1958 singer Jack Scott, a native of Windsor, needed a backup group for the hit *My True Love,* and he chose The Chantones. Nothing happened to the song until Joe Carlton, owner of Carlton Records, bought the song and promoted it. It became a Top 5 hit in the summer of 1958. After the success of *My True Love,* the group made their own record. The A side was *Five Little Numbers*, the B side, *If I Loved You*. Although it was not a major hit, it was a big seller.

They had two other hits, *Tangerock* in 1960 on Top Rank Records, and *Stormy Weather* on Capitol Records in 1961.

During the summer of 1962 Roy Lesperance left the group to get married and raise a family. His last show was at the Michigan State Fair with Roy Orbison and The Platters. Lesperance was born with congenital cataracts and has never had more than five per cent of normal sight. Today, he is totally blind and currently works with the CNIB. Jack Grenier runs his own theatrical production company in Stirling Heights, Michigan, and Larry Desjarlais and Jim Nantais live in Detroit.

Singles *Five Little Numbers* 1959   *Stormy Weather* 1961
Tangerock 1960

Robert Charlebois A pioneer in the art of combining French Canada's joual (slang) language with rock 'n' roll, Robert Charlebois is a well-respected singer, songwriter, guitarist, and actor. Born in Montreal in 1945, he later studied piano for six years, and in his teens attended the National Theatre School in Montreal for three years (1962-65).

In 1965 he recorded his first album, MA BOULE. Three years later he recorded a song he'd written with Claude Péloquin called *Lindberg* which earned him the grand prize at the Fifth International Festival of French Song at Spa, Belgium, and, in 1969, the Prix-Leclerc at Festival du disque.

Charlebois often sang in concert and on record with Louise Forestier and Mouffe (real name Claudine Monfette).

By the late 1960s he projected the image of a "Superfrog." He wore a Montreal Canadiens hockey sweater and sang in joual with a jazz/rock group. His act became a novelty in French pop music and established his career as a performer.

Throughout his career Charlebois has turned to poets and novelists for inspiration. He has also shared the stage with The Band, Janis Joplin, The Grateful Dead, and Tom Rush.

He made his first appearance outside Quebec at the Toronto Pop Festival in Toronto in 1969. A year later, he joined other Canadian rock stars as a member of the Festival Express which traveled across Canada by train.

Charlesbois' second major hit was *Ordinaire* in 1970. He also started writing scores for Quebec's burgeoning film industry, namely *Jusqu'an coeur* (1969), *A Soir, on fait peur au monde* (1969), *Deux femmes en or* (1970) and *Bulldozer* (1971). In the early 1970s he added Cajun music to his act after he heard one of his uncles play a record called *French Chansons de la Lousianne*. Other Charlebois singles from this period include *CPR Blues, Avril Sur Mars, Le Mur Du Son,*

Fu Man Chu, California, Entre Deux Joints, Entre Dorval Et Mirabel, Que-Can Blues, and *Cauchemar*. The first single he recorded in English was *The Greatest Idea* in 1972.

In 1974, Robert took a two year sabbatical from his music to act in films: *Sombre vacances* (1975) and Italian director Sergio Leone's *Un genie, deux associés, un cloche* (1976).

He returned to the concert stage in 1976 and entertained audiences with his special brand of music. As a singer-songwriter he was arguably the first to use an electric guitar in the *chansonnier* tradition, a style of music derived from poetic expression.

In 1992 he released IMMENSEMENT, an album that earned him France's Victoire, the equivalent of the Grammy Award. He also recorded his first rock opera, *Cartier*, which was performed throughout the francophone world on the radio. In the summer of 1992 Charlebois performed with singer Claude Dubois in a rock duel at the Festival Franco-Ontarien in Ottawa.

His current style is called *musique du monde* (world beat) in France. It is an amalgam of rock, ballad, Latin rhythm, rap, and mock metal.

Singles

Lindberg 1968	*The Greatest Idea* 1972
Cent millions de gens 1968	*Conception* 1972
Ordinaire 1970	*L'Independantriste* 1992

Albums/CDs

ROBERT CHARLEBOIS VOLUME I 1965	SWING CHARLEBOIS SWING 1978
ROBERT CHARLEBOIS VOLUME II 1966	SOLIDE 1979
	EMILIE JOLIE 1979
ROBERT CHARLEBOIS (Gamma Records) 1968	HEUREUX EN AMOUR 1982
	ROBERT CHARLEBOIS (SOLUTION) 1983
CHARLEBOIS 1973	CHARLEBOIS VOLUME UN 1987
SOLIDARITUDE 1973	DENSE 1988
LONGUE DISTANCE 1976	PREMIERE PERIODE 1991
LIVE DE PARIS 1977	IMMENSEMENT 1992

Chester   MIKE ARGUE (*guitar, vocals*)
JIM MANCELL (*vocals*)
WEDGE MONROE (*drums, piano, guitar*)
GLEN MORROW (*keyboards, guitar, vocals*)

Chester was together seven months when *Make My Life a Little Better* began to climb the Canadian charts in the summer of 1973. Billed as a "Happiness Group," they recorded their hit single at Eastern Sound in Toronto.

In 1974 Mike Argue left to concentrate on a solo career. Two years later, in 1976, the group broke up.

Glen Morrow, who formed the original group, later recruited Fran Cheslo as lead singer of the reformed Chester. Their first hit was *You Give Me Strength* in 1977.

Singles	*Make My Life a Little Better* 1973	*Let the Telephone Ring* 1975
Start a Dream 1974	*You Give Me Strength* 1977

Rita Chiarelli

This Hamilton-born singer/songwriter began her music career in high school. After graduation she and her backup band Battleaxe toured North America. When they played the Nickelodeon in London, Ontario, its owner, Ronnie Hawkins, was impressed by their sound. A year later, Rita left Battleaxe to be a vocalist with Hawkins.

In 1982 Rita was unhappy with the progress of her musical career and moved to Italy for five years. Upon her return to Canada in 1987, she wrote *Have You Seen My Shoes?* which became her first single release. It also attracted attention of director Bruce McDonald who used the song for the soundtrack of his movie, *Roadkill*.

Rita went on to win the Q107 Homegrown Contest for the song *Love Overload* and received first prize in the Molson Canadian Rocks Showdown in 1991. Her other achievements include Most Deserving Artist Of a Recording Contract (1987), Toronto's Rising Star (1988), and a nomination for Female Vocalist in 1991, all at the Toronto Music Awards.

Chiarelli's debut album, ROAD ROCKETS, which is also the name of her backup band, came out in 1992 on the Stony Plain label, distributed by Warner Music.

Singles *Have You Seen My Shoes?* 1987 *Love Overload* 1992

CD ROAD ROCKETS 1992

Jane Child

A native of Toronto, Jane Child comes from a musical family. Her father is a renowned violinist and her mother a professional pianist. Her house became known affectionately as "music school." She took voice lessons from her mother, while her father taught her to play the violin. Although Jane was not allowed to play rock music at home, she did listen to an R&B station from Buffalo, New York. She had dreams of starting her own band and dropped out of the Royal Conservatory of Music to join a Toronto rock 'n' roll group.

In 1988 she completed a demo tape which she sent to Michael Ostin, Vice-President of A & R Warner Music. He was so impressed with her musical abilities that Child was immediately signed to the label.

She is one of the few Canadian artists who can write, produce, and play everything on her records. In 1990, her debut single was *Don't Wanna Fall in Love.*

Singles   *Don't Wanna Fall in Love* 1990   *Here not There* 1993
Welcome to the Real World 1990

CDs   JANE CHILD 1990   HERE AND THERE 1993

Chilliwack

HOWARD FROESE (*guitar*)   BRIAN MACLEOD (*keyboards, sax*)
BILL HENDERSON (*guitar,*   GLENN MILLER (*bass guitar*)
vocals)   ROSS TURNEY (*drums*)
CLAIRE LAWRENCE (*keyboards,*   HOWIE VICKERS (*vocals*)
sax)

First known as The Classics, this Vancouver-based band started playing together in 1964. Two years later they changed their name to The Collectors and had a string of hit records between 1967 and 1970.

The nucleus of the group was Bill Henderson, Claire Lawrence, and Ross Turney. When Howie Vickers and Glenn Miller left the group, the three original members found it difficult to replace them and, instead, stayed a trio.

In the winter of 1969-70 they changed their name to Chilliwack. By the late 1970s and early 1980s they had chalked up a string of successful singles beginning with *Lonesome Mary* (1971) and extending to *What You Gonna Do* (1982).

Brian Macleod and Howard Froese joined the group in 1977. Macleod was responsible for writing some of their hits, such as *My Girl (Gone, Gone, Gone)* in 1981. Henderson reunited with Lawrence in 1984, and together they brought Chilliwack back for a reunion concert. Two years later in 1986, Henderson and Lawrence, with drummer Jerry Adolph, bassist Brian Newcombe, guitarist John Roles, and keyboardist Robbie Gray, played as Chilliwack at the Ontario Place Forum.

Macleod died on April 25, 1992 in Vancouver after a year-long fight with cancer. He had produced such acts as The Good Brothers, Billy Newton-Davis, Chrissy Steele, and The Headpins, and wrote songs for Loverboy and Chicago, among others.

(As The Collectors)

Singles   *Looking at a Baby* 1967   *Early Morning* 1969
Fisherwoman 1967   *I Must Have Been Blind* 1970
We Can Make It 1968   *Sometimes We're Up* 1970
Lydia Purple 1968

Albums   THE COLLECTORS 1967
             GRASS AND WILD STRAWBERRIES 1968

(As Chilliwack)

Singles   *Chain Train* 1970   *Fly at Night* 1977
              Rain-O 1970   *Arms of Mary* 1978
              Sundown 1971   *Road to Paradise* 1979-80
              Everyday 1971   *Communication Breakdown*
              Lonesome Mary 1971   1980
              Groundhog 1973   *My Girl (Gone, Gone, Gone)*
              There's Something I Like   1981
                about That 1974   *I Believe* 1982
              Crazy Talk 1974-75   *What You Gonna Do* 1982-83
              Come on Over 1975   *Gettin' Better* 1983
              California Girl 1976-77   *Don't Stop* 1983
              Something Better 1977   *Don't Go* 1983
              Baby Blue 1977   *Got You on My Mind* 1984

Albums/CDs   CHILLIWACK (Parrot) 1970   LIGHTS FROM THE VALLEY 1978
                 CHILLIWACK (A&M) 1971   BREAKDOWN IN PARADISE 1979
                 MUSIC FOR A QUIET TIME 1972 WANNA BE A STAR 1981
                 ALL OVER YOU 1973   OPUS X 1982
                 RIDING HIGH 1974   SEGUE 1983
                 ROCKERBOX 1976   LOOK IN, LOOK OUT 1984
                 DREAMS, DREAMS, DREAMS 1976 CHILLIWACK'S GREATEST HITS 1988

Choya

PAUL CLINCH (*guitar*)   BRUCE LEY (*keyboards*)
JOE DINARDO (*bass*)   DEBBIE SCHALL (*viola*)
GARY GRIES (*drums*)   RICKIE YORKE (*congas*)

This sextet from Toronto was led by Paul Clinch, a former member of
Cycle and Magic Cycle. They achieved minor success in the spring of
1976 with *Linda Write Me a Letter*.

   Clinch also had minor success as a solo artist with two hits, *Don't
Take the Sun* in 1972 and *Band Bandit* in 1979. The latter was first
recorded by Tundra. (See **The Magic Cycle**)

Single   *Linda Write Me a Letter* 1976

Album   LIVING LIKE A RICH MAN 1977

Christmas

BOB BRYDEN (*vocals*)   LINDA SQUIRES (*vocals*):
TYLER REIZANNE (*bass*)   Replaced by ROBERT BULGER
RICH RICHTER (*drums*)

This four member band from Oshawa, Ontario was formed in 1969. Bob Bryden had previously been in a band called Reign Ghost. When singer Linda Squires left to star in the Toronto production of *Hair*, she was replaced by Robert Bulger. The group then changed its name to Christmas.

Although they were not successful on the charts, Christmas recorded one album called HERITAGE in the fall of 1970. When it flopped, they recorded a version of Neil Sedaka's *Sing Me (I'm a Song)* which also failed to click.

Single *Sing Me (I'm a Song)* 1971

Album HERITAGE 1970

Les Classels

MICHEL CARON
JEAN-CLEMENT DROUIN
SERGE DROUIN

GILLES GERARD
PIERRE THERRIEN

This quintet from Montreal, Quebec dyed their hair white, wore white suits, and played white instruments. The origins of the group go back to 1962 when five school friends decided to form a rock band. They called themselves The Specialtones and played small clubs, road houses, and The Windsor Hotel in St. Jean, Quebec, where they established a local following. Their material ranged from Duke Ellington and Frankie Laine to Little Richard.

In 1964 they recorded their first hit, *Avant de me dire adieu*. It went to the top of the charts in Quebec and the group was suddenly inundated by autograph seekers. The Montreal tabloids ran articles on each of the members and they soon became known as the Quebec Beatles.

They later changed their appearance by getting rid of the white hair. Outside of French Canada, their success was limited to good reviews of their hit records, but they failed to impress record buyers. In 1970 they recorded a French version of The Guess Who's 1969 international hit *These Eyes* as *Le Temps de L'Amour*.

Singles *Avant de me dire adieu* 1964   *Le temps de l'amour* 1970

David Clayton-Thomas

Best known as the lead singer of Blood, Sweat & Tears, David was born in Toronto in 1941. His first group was The Shays whose first hit was *Barbey Lee* in 1964. A year later they changed their name to The Bossmen and recorded the hit *Brainwashed* in the summer of 1966, featuring a rock guitar section with a jazz piano. Clayton-Thomas' experiment with what became known later as jazz rock paved the way for groups like Blood, Sweat & Tears and Chicago.

During his initial period with Blood, Sweat & Tears, Clayton-Thomas wrote the hits *Spinning Wheel* and *Lucretia MacEvil*. He left the group in 1972. Although he moved to the United States, he remained a Canadian citizen.

In 1980 he reformed a new Canadian version of Blood, Sweat & Tears with fellow original member Bobby Economou, who played with the group until 1977 when he left to tour with Maynard Ferguson. Signed to MCA Records in 1980, the second incarnation of Blood, Sweat & Tears first album was called NUCLEAR BLUES and featured cover versions of Jimi Hendrix's *Manic Depression* and Henry Glover's blues classic, *Drown in My Own Tears*.

(By David Clayton-Thomas)

Singles *Barbey Lee* (DC-T & the Shays) 1964
Walk that Walk (DC-T & the Shays) 1965
Take Me Back (DC-T & the Shays) 1965
Out of the Sunshine 1965
Brainwashed (DC-T & the Bossmen) 1966

This Hour Has Seven Days (DC-T & the Shays) 1966
No, No, No 1969
Sing a Song 1972
Magnificent Sanctuary Band 1972
Yesterday's Music 1972
Anytime . . . Babe 1974

Albums DAVID CLAYTON-THOMAS & THE SHAYS A GO-GO 1965
SINGS LIKE IT IS 1966
DAVID CLAYTON-THOMAS (Decca) 1969

DAVID CLAYTON-THOMAS (Columbia) 1972
DAVID CLAYTON-THOMAS (RCA) 1973

(As Blood, Sweat & Tears)

Singles *You've Made Me So Very Happy* 1969
Spinning Wheel 1969
And When I Die 1969
Hi-De-Ho 1970
Lucretia MacEvil 1970

Go Down Gamblin' 1970
Lisa, Listen to Me 1971
Got to Get You into My Life 1975
Yesterday's Music 1975
You're the One 1976

Albums/CDs CHILD IS FATHER TO THE MAN 1968
BLOOD, SWEAT & TEARS 1969
BLOOD, SWEAT & TEARS 3 1970
BLOOD, SWEAT & TEARS 4 1971
GREATEST HITS 1972

NEW CITY 1973
MIRROR IMAGE 1974
MORE THAN EVER 1976
BRAND NEW DAY 1977
NUCLEAR BLUES 1980

Bruce Cockburn

Raised on a farm outside of Pembroke, Ontario, this native Ottawan once worked as a street musician in Paris, France, and studied theory, composition, and arranging at the Berklee College of Music in Boston (1964-66).

Not until the mid-1960s did he try playing rock music when he became a member of The Esquires and The Children. By 1967 he went solo and began singing in coffeehouses. He made his first solo appearance at the Mariposa Folk Festival. Cockburn then joined the folk group Three's A Crowd in 1969-70.

In 1970 he wrote the music score for film director Don Shebib's classic film, *Goin' Down the Road.* That same year Cockburn signed a contract with True North Records and began a long association with manager Bernie Finkelstein. Success eluded Cockburn until the late 1970s when such songs as *Wondering Where the Lions Are* and *Lovers in a Dangerous Time* began to find an audience.

In the fall of 1993, he released his first Christmas album. Appropriately titled CHRISTMAS, it featured Cockburn singing in four different languages: French *(Les anges dans nos campagnes)*, Spanish *(Riu Riu Chiu)*, Huron *(The Huron Carol)*, and English (traditional Christmas songs).

Early in 1994, True North Records released an album of original material called DART TO THE HEART, produced by T-Bone Burnett.

Singles

One Day I Walk 1971
It's Goin' Down Slow 1972
Wondering Where the Lions Are 1979
Prenons la mer 1979
Tokyo 1980
Rumours of Glory 1980
Couldn't Take another Chance on Love 1981
Coldest Night of the Year 1981
I'm Okay 1981
You Pay Your Money and You Take Your Chance 1982
Lovers in a Dangerous Time 1984
Making Contact 1984

Peggy's Kitchen Wall 1985
If I Had a Rocket Launcher 1985
People See through You 1986
Call It Democracy 1986
See How I Miss You 1986
Waiting for a Miracle 1987
Don't Feel Your Touch 1989
If a Tree Falls 1989
Shipwrecked at the Stable Door 1989
A Dream like Mine 1991
Great Big Love 1992
Mighty Trucks of Midnight 1992
Somebody Touched Me 1992

Albums/CDs

BRUCE COCKBURN 1970
HIGH WINDS WHITE SKY 1971
SUNWHEEL DANCE 1972
NIGHT VISION 1973
SALT, SUN AND TIME 1974

JOY WILL FIND A WAY 1975
IN THE FALLING DARK 1976
CIRCLES IN THE STREAM 1977
FURTHER ADVENTURES OF
BRUCE COCKBURN 1978

DANCING IN THE DRAGON'S JAWS 1979
HUMANS 1980
MUMMY DUST (RÉSUMÉ IN U.S.) 1981
INNER CITY FRONT 1982
TROUBLE WITH NORMAL 1983
STEALING FIRE 1984
WORLD OF WONDERS 1986
WAITING FOR A MIRACLE (SINGLES 1970-1987) 1987
NOTHING BUT A BURNING LIGHT 1991
CHRISTMAS 1993
DART TO THE HEART 1994

Leonard Cohen

Leonard Cohen is Canada's most famous poet-songwriter.

Born in 1934 into a prosperous Jewish family in Montreal, Cohen learned to play the guitar in 1950. At age fifteen he was influenced by country and western music and played in a band called The Buckskin Cowboys. Later in the 1950s he studied at McGill University. It was there that he gave his first poetry readings accompanied by jazz in a Montreal nightclub. By March of 1966 he had a loyal following and decided to sing two of his poems, *Suzanne* and *Stranger*.

The song *Suzanne* was inspired by a woman Cohen had seen on the dance floor of a club called Le Vieux Moulin in the early 1960s. Her name was Suzanne Verdal, a dancer and artist's model.

Leonard later joined the Toronto folk group The Stormy Clovers and his songs were enthusiastically received in the local coffeehouses. He sang one of them on the soundtrack of the National Film Board production, *Angel* (1966). The following year he performed at the Mariposa Folk Festivals and Expo 67. His popularity waned in the late 1970s and early 1980s but revived in 1988 with the album I'M YOUR MAN, followed by THE FUTURE in 1992.

Cohen's songs have often been recorded by other artists like Judy Collins, Jennifer Warnes, and Joe Cocker. *Bird on a Wire* was a hit for the Neville Brothers on their CD BROTHER'S KEEPER and was included on the soundtrack of the Universal action/comedy of the same name starring Mel Gibson and Goldie Hawn.

Cohen still is active as a singer/songwriter and poet. Videos for his songs have been played regularly on MuchMusic and MusiquePlus since the late 1980s. He remains very popular in Europe.

In 1992, with the release of THE FUTURE, Cohen's career reached new heights. *Closing Time*, the single and video from the album, was a big hit.

Singles

Suzanne 1968
So Long Marianne 1968
Bird on a Wire 1969
Dress Rehearsal 1970
Passing Thru 1972
First We'll Take Manhattan 1988
Dance Me to the End of Love 1989
Closing Time 1992-93
The Future 1993

Albums/CDs	THE SONGS OF LEONARD COHEN 1967	THE BEST OF LEONARD COHEN 1975
	SONGS FROM A ROOM 1969	DEATH OF A LADIES MAN 1977
	SONGS OF LOVE AND HATE 1971	RECENT SONGS 1979
	LIVE SONGS 1973	VARIOUS POSITIONS 1984
	NEW SKIN FOR THE OLD CEREMONY 1974	I'M YOUR MAN 1988
		THE FUTURE 1992

The Collectors (see Chilliwack)

Coney Hatch

ANDY CURRAN (*vocals, bass*)   DAVE KETCHUM (*drums*)
CARL DIXON (*vocals, rhythm*   STEVE SHELSKI (*guitar*)
   guitar)

Formed in 1980, this four member Toronto-based band took its name from an English town renowned for its lunatic asylum. Carl Dixon joined the founding three members in February 1981 after playing for two years with the Montreal-based Firefly.

The turning point in their career came when Kim Mitchell, who was still with Max Webster, saw them at a Toronto club and helped Coney Hatch get a deal with Anthem Records. Mitchell produced their self-titled debut.

Critics compared their music to heavy metal rockers Deep Purple and Uriah Heep. Their commercial success was limited to one Top 40 hit, *Hey Operator* in 1982. The group reunited in July of 1992 to promote the album, BEST OF THREE.

Single	*Hey Operator* 1982	
Albums/CDs	CONEY HATCH 1982	FRICTION 1985
	OUTA HAND 1983	BEST OF THREE 1992

The Cooper Brothers

DARRYL ALGUIRE (*guitar*)   TERRY KING (*vocals, steel guitar*)
GLENN BELL (*drums*)   CHARLES ROBERTSON (*vocals,*
BRIAN COOPER (*vocals, bass*)   *reeds*)
RICHARD COOPER (*vocals,*   AL SERWA (*keyboards*)
   guitar)

In 1964, Richard Cooper saw The Beatles on The Ed Sullivan Show. From that moment he wanted to carve out a career as a musician. He and his brother Brian played in several cover bands in Eastern Canada, such as What the Cat Dragged In. They sang Paul McCartney medleys.

The sons of an Ottawa songwriter, Richard and Brian grew up listening to the music of the Big Band era and Cole Porter. The decision to form their own rock band came in 1971 when Richard was halfway through his studies for a Master's degree in English Literature at the University of Ottawa. He was eventually asked to leave because he spent too much time on the road.

In 1974 the Cooper Brothers had their own band, and put out three singles, though none was a hit. Their producer was Les Emmerson of The Five Man Electrical Band. Determined to succeed, Richard Cooper started to write his own songs. After signing with Polydor (now Polygram), they had a minor hit with *Finally with You* in 1974.

During this time, The Cooper Brothers had expanded to seven members. Their manager, Allan Katz helped the group sign a deal with Capricorn in the United States. In the summer of 1978 they had a national hit with *Rock and Roll Cowboys*, followed by *The Dream Never Dies* in the fall of the same year, which won an ASCAP award for its performance by American country singer Bill Anderson. It also charted on Billboard's Hot 100. The group also achieved success with the songs *Show Some Emotion*, and *I'll Know Her When I See Her*, which also charted on Billboard's Hot 100.

By 1980 Capricorn Records had folded, and by the end of the decade The Cooper Brothers had split up. Today, Brian Cooper and Terry King are two thirds of the trio, Cooper, King and Emmerson.

Singles

Finally (With You) 1974	*Away from You* 1979
Miss Lonely Heart 1974	*I'll Know Her When I See Her*
From Day to Day 1975	1979
Rock and Roll Cowboys 1978	*Show Some Emotion* 1979
The Dream Never Dies 1978	

Albums

COOPER BROTHERS 1978	PITFALLS OF THE BALLROOM 1979

Copperpenny

BLAKE BARRETT (*drums*)	BILL MONOMEN (*guitar*)
RON HILLER (*bass*)	RICH WAMIL (*keyboards, clavinets,*
KENNY HOLLIS (*vocals*)	*vocals*)

From Kitchener, Ontario, Copperpenny began in 1965 when original members Kenny Hollis and Rich Wamil formed their own group, first known as The Penny Farthings. In 1966 they changed their name to Copperpenny, a name taken from the song title of the B side of The Paupers hit, *If I Call You by Some Name*.

In the late 1960s Copperpenny had a hit with *Nice Girl* on Columbia Records. They switched to RCA for another hit, *Stop (Wait a Minute)*. But their big break came in the early 1970s when they signed to London Records' subsidiary label, Sweet Plum. The success of their first single and biggest hit on the new label, *You're Still the One* (1973), attracted national attention.

When it came time to record *Sittin' on a Poor Man's Throne*, they turned to Richard Becker of Pac III studios in Detroit. He helped create the R&B sound that made it their second biggest song. Backing up Copperpenny in Detroit were Joyce Vincent Wilson and Thelma Hopkins of Tony Orlando & Dawn fame. Two of their four albums were recorded in Detroit, and two at RCA studios with Jack Richardson, who also produced The Guess Who.

Copperpenny played 150 dates a year in the United States, mostly in arenas, universities, and high schools. They toured with such big names as Led Zeppelin, Uriah Heep, and Bob Seger. In Canada, they shared the same stage with The Guess Who and The Five Man Electrical Band.

In 1975 the group signed with Capitol Records, recording the hits *Disco Queen* and *Goodtime Sally*. Their last single, *Suspicious Love*, was issued under the name Rich Wamil and Copperpenny. When Copperpenny broke up in the late 1970s, Kenny Hollis had a brief solo career and recorded the hit *Goin' Hollywood* in 1979.

Singles	*Nice Girl* 1968	*Where Is the Answer* 1974
	Stop (Wait a Minute) 1970	*Summertime* 1974
	You're Still the One 1973	*Help Your Brother* 1975
	Sittin' on a Poor Man's Throne 1973	*Disco Queen* 1975
		Goodtime Sally 1975
	Rock and Roll, Boogie Woogie and Wine 1973-74	*Suspicious Love* 1976

Albums	COPPERPENNY 1970	THE FUSE ALBUM (Rich Wamil & Copperpenny) 1976
	SITTIN' ON A POOR MAN'S THRONE 1973	

Cowboy Junkies

ALAN ANTON (*bass*)   MICHAEL TIMMINS (*guitar*)
MARGO TIMMINS (*vocals*)   PETER TIMMINS (*drums*)

Cowboy Junkies have been playing since 1985. Alan Anton and Michael Timmins had been in a band called Hunger Project and played in New York and London. Margo Timmins had just graduated with a degree in social work. They had their first club date at The Rivoli in Toronto. In October 1986, they released their debut album, WHITES OFF EARTH NOW!! on an independent label.

The following year the band arranged to record live at the Church of the Holy Trinity in Toronto. Out of it came the album, THE TRINITY SESSIONS. Their first single, *Misguided Angel*, was a Top Ten hit. Their albums CAUTION HORSES and BLACK EYED MAN continued to show the band's growth as one of Canada's top bands.

Singles

Misguided Angel 1989
Sweet Jane 1989
Cause Cheap Is How I Feel 1990
Horse in the Country 1992
If You Were the Woman, I Was the Man 1992

Rock and Bird 1990
Sun Comes Up, It's Tuesday Morning 1990
Southern Rain 1992
The Post 1993-94
Hard to Explain 1993-94
Anniversary Song 1994

CDs

WHITES OFF EARTH NOW!! 1986
THE TRINITY SESSION 1988
THE CAUTION HORSES 1990

BLACK EYED MAN 1992
PALE SUN CRESCENT MOON 1993

Crack of Dawn

TREVOR DALEY (*trombone*)
GABRIEL DWIGHT (*trumpet*)
CARL HARVEY (*guitar*)
RUPERT HARVEY (*rhythm guitar*)

ALVIN JONES (*saxophone, flute*)
GLEN RICKETS (*vocals*)
JACEK SOBOTTA (*keyboards*)
ANDREE SMITH (*bass*)

In the mid-1970s Crack of Dawn, a Toronto-based group, was in demand on the disco club circuit because of its infectious and danceable beat. Signed to Columbia Records, they had two minor successes on the charts with *It's Alright I Can't Move No Mountains* and *Keep the Faith*.

Most of the group's material was written by Glen Ricketts and the two Harvey brothers, all of whom had moved from Kingston, Jamaica to Kitchener, Ontario.

Singles

It's Alright I Can't Move No Mountains 1976
Keep the Faith 1976

Album

CRACK OF DAWN 1976

Crash Test Dummies

BEN DARVELL (*harmonica, mandolin*)
MITCH DORGE (*drums, accordion*)

ELLEN REID (*keyboards*)
BRAD ROBERTS (*vocals*)
DAN ROBERTS (*bass*)

Founded by Brad Roberts, The Crash Test Dummies started as a house band at The Blue Note Cafe, owned by Roberts' friend Curtis Riddell.

Signed to Polygram Records, they achieved success in 1991 with their debut album, THE GHOSTS THAT HAUNT ME, which became the top selling Canadian album of the year. This success was due in large part to the video of the single, *Superman's Song.*

The group's second album, GOD SHUFFLED HIS FEET, was released in 1993 along with the single *Mmm Mmm Mmm Mmm.*

Singles	*Superman's Song* 1991	*Mmm Mmm Mmm Mmm* 1993
	The Ghosts that Haunt Me 1991	*Swimming in Your Ocean* 1994
	Androgynous 1992	

CDs	THE GHOSTS THAT HAUNT ME 1991
	GOD SHUFFLED HIS FEET 1993

Crash Vegas

COLIN CRIPPS (*guitar*) AMBROSE POTTIE (*drums*)
JOCELYNE LANOIS (*bass*): MICHELLE MCADOREY (*vocals*)
Replaced by DARREN WATSON

Crash Vegas is comprised of musicians who have played in other bands. Colin Cripps worked with The Spoons and The Heavenly Brothers; Ambrose Pottie with The Thin Men and White Noise; and Jocelyne Lanois with Martha and The Muffins. The group's principal songwriters are Cripps and Michelle McAdorey, whose musical career started in England where she tried to break into the British music scene. After five years she became disillusioned about a music career and returned to Toronto, giving up music altogether. Eventually, Blue Rodeo's Greg Keelor encouraged her to pursue a career as a songwriter and encouraged her to form her own group. He was an early member of Crash Vegas, and co-wrote five songs on their first album and four on their second.

Their debut album, RED EARTH, was released on Blue Rodeo's Risque Disque label. A second album called STONE was released on Polygram Records in the spring of 1993. Four of the tracks were recorded with renowned English producer John Porter who had worked with The Smiths, Bryan Ferry, and Miracle Legion. One of them, *Nothing Ever Happened*, featured an inventive mix by American garage-rock godhead Butch Vig. The only non-original song, *One Way Conversation*, was composed by Soul Asylum's Dave Pirner. Other contributors on STONE were legendary Faces keyboardist Ian McLagan and Robbie Robertson/Daniel Lanois collaborator Bill Dillon on guitar and pedal steel.

Singles	*Inside Out* 1990	*1800 Days* 1993
	Sky 1990	*My City Has a Place* 1993
	Smoke 1990	*Keep It to Myself* 1993
	You and Me 1993	

CDs	RED EARTH 1990	STONE 1993

Cream-Cheeze Goodtime Band

DAVE HARWOOD
BILLY KELL
PAT KELL

JIMI KELL
BARB PAYNE

This quintet from Stratford, Ontario had two major hits: *Uncle Jed* on Dominion Records in 1971, from the album PERTH COUNTY GREEN, and *Living Without You* in 1973 from the album of the same name.

Singles   *Uncle Jed* 1971   *Living Without You* 1973

Albums   PERTH COUNTY GREEN 1971   LIVING WITHOUT YOU 1973

The Crew Cuts

PAT BARRETT (*tenor*)
RUDI MAUGERI (*baritone*)

JOHN PERKINS (*lead*)
RAY PERKINS (*bass*)

The Crew Cuts, from Toronto, first called themselves The Canadaires. They began their musical education while attending St. Michael's Choir School in Toronto. Rudi Maugeri and John Perkins started singing in a quartet called the Jordonaires; they later joined Pat Barrett and Ray Perkins in another group called The Four Tones in March 1952.

Their big break came in 1954 when they went to Cleveland, Ohio to appear on Gene Carroll's TV show. Their manager, Fred Strauss, introduced them to Cleveland disc jockey Bill Randle, who suggested the group change its name to The Crew Cuts. He then helped them get signed to a recording contract with Mercury Records. Their first hit in April 1954, *Crazy 'Bout You Baby*, was written by Rudi and Pat. Although The Crew Cuts had more than a dozen hits between 1954 and 1956, their biggest was *Sh-Boom*, a cover of The Chords' hit. It was number one for seven weeks in 1954.

In Toronto in 1954 when the group was booked to appear at the now defunct Casino Club, the city welcomed them with a ticker tape parade up Bay Street, around the corner to the south side of Queen Street where the Sheraton Centre now stands.

They disbanded in 1963. In 1977 the original members reunited in Nashville, where they had recorded *Sh-Boom*, *Earth Angel*, and *Angels in the Sky*.

Singles   *All I Wanna Do/The Barking Dog* 1954   *The Whippenpoof Song* 1955
Crazy 'Bout You Baby 1954   *Ko Ko Mo* 1955
Sh-Boom 1954   *Earth Angel* 1955
Oop-Shoop 1954   *Chop Chop Boom* 1955
Dance Mr. Snowman Dance 1954   *A Story Untold* 1955
Gum Drop 1955
Slam Bam 1955

Angels in the Sky 1955	*Young Love* 1957
Mostly Martha 1955	*Whatever, Whenever, Whoever*
Unchained Melody 1955	1957
Seven Days 1956	*Susie Q* 1957
Tell Me Why 1956	*I Sit in My Window* 1957
Bei Mir Bist Du Schon 1956	*Be My Only Love* 1957
Love in a Home 1956	*Over the Mountain* 1959
Halls of Ivy 1956	*Legend of Gunga Din* 1959

Albums THE CREW CUTS ON THE CAMPUS 1954
THE CREW CUTS SING 1959
THE CREW CUTS HAVE A BALL 1959

Crosstown Bus

BRIAN ANDERSON (*bass, vocals*)
JEFF BOYNE (*guitar, congas, lead vocals*)
MIKE KILLEEN (*drums, vocals*)
FRANK LUDWIG (*piano, guitar, organ, vocals*)
ROB SOMMERVILLE (*organ, congas, vocals*)

Crosstown Bus, from Vancouver, had only two hits in the early 1970s which were included on their MCA album HIGH GRASS.

Singles *Rochester River* 1970   *I'm Lost without You* 1971

Album HIGH GRASS 1971

Crowbar

SONNIE BERNARDI
JOZEF CHIROWSKI
JOHN GIBBARD
ROLY GREENWAY
KELLY JAY
RHEAL LANTHIER

Formerly known as The Hawks, Ronnie Hawkins's backup group, Crowbar renamed themselves in the spring of 1970. In May of that year they recorded the album OFFICIAL MUSIC with King Biscuit Boy and later joined him on stage at the 1970 Strawberry Fields Rock Festival.

Corrina, Corrina was the first single release by King Biscuit Boy and Crowbar in September 1970. Crowbar had also released their own album, BAD MANORS, in January 1971, named after an old farmhouse outside of Hamilton.

The band developed a following on the Ontario bar circuit. By the mid-1970s they had three more albums and six singles, notably *Oh What a Feeling*.

Crowbar first split up in 1974. Jozef Chirowski went to work with the Alice Cooper Band. In November 1977 the original members (Lanthier, Jay, Gibbard, and Bernardi) reunited with new members keyboard player Ray Harrison and bassist Rick Birkett. Harrison played the organ on Del Shannon's 1961 number one hit, *Runaway*. Roly Greenway left to join Next, whose only hit was *Only a Friend* in 1976.

A new version of Crowbar toured Canada in the winter of 1977-78. The lineup consisted of Kelly Jay (a.ka. Blake Fordham), Sonny Bernardi, Rheal Lanthier, John "Ghetto" Gibbard, Roly Greenaway, and Ray Harrison. Kelly Jay had brief success in the 1970s as a solo artist with such hits as *Play Your Cards Right* (1975) and *Cherry Pie* (1977). In 1993 he returned to the recording studio to make his first solo record in ten years entitled *There's More Lovin' (Where That Came From)*, written by Denis Keldie, a longtime keyboardist and friend of Jay's.

Singles		
Oh What a Feeling 1971	*Fly Away* 1972	
Happy People 1971	*Hey Baby* 1972	
Too True Mama 1972	*Million Dollar Weekend* 1973-74	
Dreams 1972	*All the Living Things* 1974	

Albums		
OFFICIAL MUSIC (King Biscuit Boy & Crowbar) 1970	LARGER THAN LIFE 1972	
BAD MANORS 1971	HEAVY DUTY 1972	
	KE32746 1973	

Burton Cummings

Born in Winnipeg in 1947, Burton Cummings received his degree in piano in 1966 and is qualified to teach at the Royal Conservatory of Music.

In 1965 upon the invitation of Bob Burns, he joined The Guess Who, replacing Chad Allan. Prior to joining them he had been with a group called The Devrons. For the next ten years he remained with The Guess Who and reached international stardom in 1969 with the release of *These Eyes*.

After leaving The Guess Who, Cummings concentrated on a solo career. In the fall of 1976 CBS Records released his first solo album which contained the million-selling hit single, *Stand Tall*. In January 1977, he moved to Los Angeles where he played as a guest artist on albums by Leo Sayer, Bette Midler, and Randy Bachman.

One year later Cummings released his third studio album, DREAM OF A CHILD. From it came the Top 10 hit, *Break It to Them Gently*. That same year he was the only Canadian to headline a show at the Canadian National Exhibition in Toronto.

He continues to record hit albums and singles, and has become involved as a host/performer for various charitable organizations. In

1993 he produced the debut album of a new Winnipeg band called Tooth 'n Nail.

Singles

Stand Tall 1976
I'm Scared 1977
Timeless Love 1977
My Own Way to Rock 1977
Your Back Yard 1977-78
Break It to Them Gently 1978
Draggin' Them Down the Line 1979
I Will Play a Rhapsody 1979
Fine State of Affairs 1980

Mile a Second 1980
One and Only 1980
You Saved My Soul 1981
Heavenly Blue 1981
Mother Keep Your Daughter In 1981-82
One Day Soon 1990
Take One Away 1990
The Rock's Steady 1990
Free 1990

Albums/CDs

BURTON CUMMINGS 1976
MY OWN WAY TO ROCK 1977
DREAM OF A CHILD 1978

WOMAN LOVE 1980
SWEET SWEET 1981
PLUS SIGNS 1990

Bobby Curtola

Born in 1944 in Port Arthur (Thunder Bay, Ontario), Bobby Curtola was one of Canada's early teen idols. Between 1960 and 1967 he had a string of hits on his own independent Tartan Records, a company he started when no one else was interested in producing his records.

Curtola's career started with his high school band, Bobby and the Bobcats. His band made its first professional appearance at a high school assembly in 1959.

Hand in Hand with You, which Bobby wrote with Dyer Hurton, was his first hit in 1960. Other hits followed over the next seven years, such as *Don't You Sweetheart Me* in 1961 and *Three Rows Over* in 1963. His most widely known hit was *Fortune Teller* in 1962, a huge hit in both Canada and the United States.

In 1965 he was host of the CTV teenage show, *After Four.* That same year he traveled to Nashville with Kingston disc jockey Bryan Olney, who co-wrote the hit, *While I'm Away.* During Canada's Centennial year (1967) Curtola toured the country. By 1972 he began appearing regularly in Las Vegas, and in 1973 was host of his second CTV variety show, *Shake, Rock, Roll.*

In 1990 Curtola recorded two songs that entered the country charts, *Playin' in the Shadows of Glory* and *Drivin' Down a Phantom Road.* BMG Music released a special CD collection of Curtola's early recordings in 1991. In time for the holiday season in 1992 was a collection of old and new songs in an album called CHRISTMAS FLASHBACK.

Singles

Hand in Hand with You   1960
Don't You Sweetheart Me   1961
Hitchhiker   1961-62
*Fortune Teller/Johnny Take
    Your Time*   1962
You Must Belong to Me   1962
I Cry and Cry   1962
Aladdin   1962
My Christmas Tree   1962
Destination Love   1963
Indian Giver   1963
Three Rows Over   1963
Move Over   1963-64
Little Girl Blue   1964
You're Not a Goody Goody
    1964
As Long as I'm Sure of You   1964
Come Home Little Girl   1964

It's About Time   1965
Mean Woman Blues   1965
Makin' Love   1965
Forget Her   1965
While I'm Away   1966
The Real Thing   1966
Wildwood Days   1966
It's Not Funny Honey   1966-67
Give Me a Reason to Stay   1967
Quando Quando   1967
Footsteps   1967
Jean   1970
Way Down Deep   1971
Have You Ever Really Been There
    1984
Playin' in the Shadows of Glory
    1990
Drivin' Down a Phantom Road
    1990

Albums/CDs

HITCH-HIKER   1961
MR. PERSONALITY   1962
TRULY YOURS   1963
12 TICKETS TO CLOUD 9   1964
LOVE STORY IN STEREO   1965
TWELVE GOLDEN HITS   1966

CHANGES   1971
CURTOLA   1972
SHAKE, ROCK AND ROLL   1974
15 GREATEST HITS   1991
CHRISTMAS FLASHBACK ALBUM
    1992

Born in 1957, this aspiring singer/actress from Kitchener, Ontario, made her acting debut in the French musical version of *South Pacific* as Bali H'ai. She was finishing high school when David Lodge of Axe Records wanted her to sign a five-year recording contract. *Can't We Somehow*, released in February 1976, was her only chart success. She did gain fame on TV commercials, notably as the sexy lady who coos "Oooh, I love turtles" to a group of tortoises in top hats.

Gail Dahms

Singles   *Can't We Somehow*   1976   *Rescue Me* 1976

Lisa Dal Bello

Growing up in her hometown of Woodbridge, an eleven-year-old Lisa was fascinated by her neighbor's acoustic guitar. Lisa's first composition was called *Oh Why?*, which was an attempt at a protest song. At thirteen she began singing professionally and at fifteen she sang her first advertising jingle, a commercial. By her late teens Dal Bello had become a regular performer on CBC's *Music Machine*. The exposure led to a record contract with MCA and the release of her self-titled debut album in 1977. It was to be her only one with the label.

Lisa credits her success to her friend and mentor, Roy Kenner of the TV series Music Machine. He wrote the R&B influenced song *Stand in Your Way* on her debut album.

Her next two records were released by Capitol Records: PRETTY GIRLS in 1978 and DRASTIC MEASURES in 1981. The single *Pretty Girls* was a hit for Lisa in 1979; that same year, in the U.S.A., Melissa Manchester covered the song and made it a Top 40 hit.

In 1981 Dal Bello stopped her musical career to concentrate on her reading and poetry. She also took courses in Women and Law at Toronto's York University. But three years later former guitarist/producer Mick Ronson from Mott the Hoople saw Lisa in a CBC documentary and convinced her to return to the recording studio. She re-signed with Capitol Records and in 1984 WHOMANFOURSAYS (the title was a play on "human forces") was released. This album marked a change in her image and attitude from mainstream dance music to more diverse stylings. She also shortened her stage name to Dal Bello.

Five years later in 1989, she released the album SHE, featuring the single *Tango*. In between albums she wrote the lyrics for *99 Red Balloons* for Nena, and composed songs for the soundtrack of director Adrian Lyne's film *9 1/2 Weeks* (1986).

Singles   *Pretty Girls* 1979   *Gonna Get Close to You* 1984
         Never Get to Heaven 1981   *Tango* 1989
         She Wants to Know 1981

Albums	LISA DAL BELLO 1977	WHOMANFOURSAYS 1984
	PRETTY GIRLS 1978	SHE 1989
	DRASTIC MEASURES 1981	

The DeFranco Family

ANTHONY DEFRANCO
BENJAMIN DEFRANCO
NINO DEFRANCO

MARISA DEFRANCO
MERINA DEFRANCO

From Port Colborne, Ontario, The DeFranco Family was managed by Laufer Publications, who published *Tiger Beat* and *Fave*. With Tony DeFranco on lead vocals, they recorded for 20th Century Records and were considered Canada's answer to The Osmonds. However, their success on the pop charts was limited to one major hit in both Canada and the United States — *Heartbeat—It's a Lovebeat* in the fall of 1973.

Although they were Canadian citizens, their songs were written and produced in the United States. For this reason all their hits did not qualify as Canadian content as set down by the regulations of the CRTC. The DeFranco Family stopped singing in 1979. Today, they live in Southern California.

Singles
Heartbeat—It's a Lovebeat 1973
Abra-Ca-Dabra 1974
Save the Last Dance for Me 1974
Write Me a Letter 1974

Albums
HEARTBEAT—IT'S A LOVEBEAT 1973
SAVE THE LAST DANCE FOR ME
(DeFranco Family featuring Tony DeFranco) 1974

Deja Vu

BOB BONNELL (*vocals*)
WALLY CAMERON (*drums*)
CAL DODD (*vocals*)
PAUL GORDON (*vocals*)

JOHN PIMM (*guitar*)
JOHN SHEARD (*keyboards*)
TERRY WILKINS (*bass*)

Signed to Capitol Records International, Deja Vu, together since 1974, recorded one album called SONG FOR EVERYONE. Hot on the heels of its release they opened for Joe Cocker as part of his Canadian tour. *Dance* was their only hit single in the summer of 1976.

Single *Dance* 1976

Album A SONG FOR EVERYONE 1976

Deliverance DANNY JANZ   PAUL JANZ
KEN JANZ

Based in Munich, Germany but originally from Alberta, the Janz brothers began recording together after winning a contest in a German rock magazine. Their debut album TIGHTROPE produced two hit singles: *Leaving L.A.* in April, 1980 and the title track in October 1980. At the end of the year they had broken up. Paul Janz went on to have a successful solo career.

Singles *Leaving L.A.* 1980   *Tightrope* 1980

Album TIGHTROPE 1980

The Diamonds TED KOWALSKI (*tenor*): Replaced by GLEN STETSON
PHIL LEAVITT (*baritone*): Replaced by EVAN FISHER
BILL REED (*bass*): Replaced by JOHN FELTON
DAVE SOMERVILLE (*lead*): Replaced by MIKE DOUGLAS

Formed in Toronto in 1953, The Diamonds first job was in a church basement. Two years later while working at The Alpine Village Club in Cleveland, Ohio, disc jockey Bill Randle (who also helped The Crew Cuts) urged them to record and was instrumental in getting them a contract with Mercury Records. Shortly after their signing, the group made their TV debut in 1955 on CBC-TV's *Pick the Stars*.

Their hits included cover versions of *Why Do Fools Fall in Love* by Frankie Lymon and The Teenagers, *Church Bells May Ring* by The Willows, and *Little Darlin'* by The Gladiolas, which was the group's biggest hit in 1957.

Since their heyday in the 1950s and early 1960s, The Diamonds have changed personnel several times. John Felton, band leader since 1959, was killed in a plane crash in May 1982 near Mount Shasta, California.

Singles

Black Denim Trousers & Motorcycle Boots 1955	*Words of Love* 1957
Smooch Me 1955	*Zip Zip* 1957
Why Do Fools Fall in Love 1956	*Silhouettes* 1957
Church Bells May Ring 1956	*The Stroll* 1958
Love, Love, Love 1956	*High Sign* 1958
Ka-Ding-Dong 1956	*Kathy O* 1958
Soft Summer Breeze 1956	*Walking Along* 1958
My Judge and Jury 1956	*She Say (Oom Dooby Doom)* 1959
A Thousand Miles Away 1956	*Gretchen* 1959
Little Darlin' 1957	*Sneaky Alligator* 1959

Young in Years 1959
Walkin' The Stroll/Batman,
  Wolfman, Frankenstein or
  Dracula 1959-60
Tell the Truth 1960

Slave Girl 1960
You'd Be Mine 1960
Woomai-Ling 1960
One Summer Night 1961

Album THE CREW CUTS MEET PETE RUGOLO 1959

Céline Dion Céline Dion, from Charlemagne, Quebec, is the first French-Canadian singer to become a star in both the U.S.A. and Canada. Before she released her first English album, UNISON, in 1990, she was one of Quebec's most popular recording artists. She had recorded eight French language albums, sold more than 900,000 units, and had won fifteen Felix Awards, awarded annually in Quebec to honor outstanding artists. In Quebec she is known as "la petite Québécoise."

Born in 1968 into a showbusiness family, Dion's parents were traditional folk musicians who toured with Céline's four older brothers and sisters as The Dion Family. Her mother Therese played the violin, her father the accordion.

In January, 1981, Céline met Réné Angélil who became her manager after hearing her sing, *Ce n'était qu'un rêve* on cassette. Angélil signed her to his independent TBS label, and two Dion albums were released together, LA VOIX DU BON DIEU and CELINE DION CHANTE NOEL. The following year Céline represented France at the 1982 Yamaha World Popular Song Festival in Tokyo. She won a gold medal for performing *Tellement j'ai d'amour pour toi.*

Three years later, in 1985, she stopped performing to plan the next step in her career. She signed with CBS Records Canada in 1987, and her debut album INCOGNITO produced six Top Ten singles. Later that year, she sang *Just Have a Heart* in English at the Juno Awards in Toronto and received a standing ovation. A year later, she won the Eurovision Song Contest in Dublin.

For UNISON, Sony Music set aside a million dollars, the largest budget ever for a Canadian artist. Several singles were culled from the album, including the Top 5 hit, *If You Asked Me To.* Written by Diane Warren, it was first recorded in 1989 by Patti Labelle for the James Bond film, *Licence to Kill.* Labelle's rendition appeared on Billboard's Rhythm and Blues and Adult Contemporary charts, but not on the pop. Polly Anthony, head of promotion at Epic Records in the U.S.A., suggested that Céline record the song. She also had a huge success with *Beauty and the Beast*, a duet with American singer Peabo Bryson. It later went on to win an Academy Award for Best Song.

Singles

Un colombe 1985
Delivre-moi 1987
(If There Was) Any Other Way
  1990
Unison 1990
Where Does My Heart Beat
  Now 1990-91
Last to Know 1991
Ziggy 1991
Have a Heart 1991
Beauty and the Beast (with
  Peabo Bryson) 1991-92

If You Asked Me To 1992
Des mots qui sonnent 1992
Je danse dans ma tete 1992
Nothing's Broken but My Heart
  1992
Love Can Move Mountains
  1992-93
Water from the Moon 1993
When I Fall in Love
  (with Clive Griffin) 1993
Did You Give Enough Love 1993

Albums/CDs

LA VOIX DU BON DIEU 1981
TELLEMENT J'AI D'AMOUR POUR
  TOI 1982
CHANTES ET CONTES DE NOEL
  1983
LES CHEMINS DE MA MAISON
  1984
MÉLANIE 1984

C'EST POUR TOI 1985
EN CONCERT 1985
LES CHANSONS D'OR 1986
INCOGNITO 1987
DION CHANTE PLAMONDON 1991
UNISON 1990
CÉLINE DION 1992
THE COLOUR OF MY LOVE 1993

Dionysos

PHIL BECH
ERIC CLEMENT
FERN DURAND

BOB LEPAGE
PAUL-ANDRE THIBERT

Dionysos was the first Quebec band to compose and sing in both English and French. Based in Montreal they developed a local following in the Montreal-Sept-Iles-Chibogamu circuit. They also played in Toronto and New York.

In 1969 they made their first album, LE GRAND TOUR, on Jupiter Records. Their second, LE PRINCE CROULE on Zodiaque Records, followed in 1971. They composed the score for Sam Sheppard's play *The Tooth of Crime* which opened in January 1974 at the Centaur Theatre in Montreal. Dionysos also performed six songs on stage based on the lyrics from the script.

The band took a leave of absence for the balance of 1974 but reformed in the fall of 1975, recording a self-titled album on Deram Records.

Although the band sang in both languages, they still considered themselves a Quebec group. They broke up in 1978. Paul-Andre Thibert pursued a solo career and released an album on Solo Records, MUSIQUE DE MES AMIS DIONYSOS.

Albums   LE GRAND TOUR 1969   DIONYSOS 1976
             LE PRINCE CROULE 1971

The Diviners   ALAN BEARDSELL (*guitar,*   SUSAN MARIE (*bass*)
                     mandolin)   THERESA MCKAY (*vocals*)
                   ROB GREENAWAY (*drums*)   DAVID ROBERTSON (*vocals*)

The Diviners was founded as a duo in 1986 when Theresa McKay and David Robertson were watching a film adaptation of Margaret Laurence's The Diviners, directed by Anne Wheeler. Inspired by Wheeler's adaptation, they decided to write and perform together under the name of The Diviners. In 1991 they released their first independent album, FACE OF THE EARTH, which was produced by Michael Phillip-Wojoweda (Barenaked Ladies). *Listen* was the first single. Early in 1992 the group's lineup was complete, and another single, *Walk along the River*, was released.

Singles   *Listen* 1991   *Walk along the River* 1992

CD   FACE OF THE EARTH 1991

The Dorians   MIKE BETS (*drums*)   BOB NIXON (*bass*)
                  BILL LOOP (*guitar*)   JOHN UNGER (*vocals*)

The Dorians hailed from the small town of Kingsville, Ontario, which is about 30 miles from Windsor. John Unger was the lead singer and songwriter. He had worked with two local bands, The Small Town Boys and The Living Ends, before he and bass player Bob Nixon formed The Dorians in 1968.

When Floyd James, a member of Ray Charles's backup band, heard The Dorians, he arranged for them to record *Psychedelic Lipstick* which became a hit overseas. Their first North American hit was *Help for My Waiting* in 1971.

Singles   *If I Were 21 and You Were 24*   *Pyschedelic Lipstick* 1970
                1969   *Help for My Waiting* 1970

Doucette   Montreal-born Jerry Doucette was raised in Hamilton. When he was eight years old he took up the guitar, and by the time he was eleven, he was in a Hamilton band called The Reefers. When they split up, he moved to Toronto where he worked as a backup guitarist and singer for the bands Brutus, Trybe, and Southco. When a record deal fell through, Jerry worked with more groups, such as The Seeds of Time and Rocket Norton. The latter became known as Prism.

He was living in Vancouver when he and four other musicians used his last name as a moniker for a new band who recorded for Mushroom Records. In February 1978 the label released their first album, MAMA LET HIM PLAY. Doucette's backup band was comprised of Duris Maxwell on drums, Don Cummings on bass, Brent Shindel and Jimmy Butler on guitar, and Mark Olson on keyboards. Doucette is best known for the song, *Nobody* which was a major hit in the summer of 1979.

Singles		
Down the Road 1978		*Nobody* 1979
Mama Let Him Play 1978		*Run Buddy Run* 1979
All I Wanna Do 1978		*Some Day* 1979-80

Albums/CDs		
MAMA LET HIM PLAY 1978		THE DEUCE IS LOOSE 1979

Doug and the Slugs

RICK BAKER (*guitar*)   STEVE BOSLEY (*bass*)
DOUG BENNETT (*vocals, guitar*)   SIMON KENDALL (*keyboards*)
JOHN BURTON (*guitar*)   WALLY WATSON (*drums*)

Formed in 1977 by Doug Bennett, this Vancouver basement band developed a loyal club following in Toronto's El Mocambo and Kingston's Prince George Hotel. The band's name referred to the slimy, black creatures found on Vancouver's lawns and sidewalks. Despite their success on the club circuit, they could not get a record deal until 1979. Signed to RCA, they released their first hit single *Too Bad* in 1980. Other hits followed throughout the 1980s.

Leader Doug Bennett decided to leave music temporarily and try his hand at acting. He starred in John Gray's hit play, *Rock and Roll*, but re-joined the band in 1992 to record TALES FROM TERMINAL CITY.

Singles		
Too Bad 1980		*I'll Be Waiting for You* 1985
Chinatown Calculation 1980		*It's Got to be Monday* 1986
Drifting Away 1981		*(I Don't Want To) Walk Away*
Real Enough 1981		1988
Who Knows How to Make Love Stay 1983		*Tomcat Prowl* 1988
		It's a Powerful Thing 1989
Makin' It Work 1983		*Terminal City* 1992
Day by Day 1984-85		*Rusty Bus* 1993

Albums/CDs		
COGNAC AND BOLOGNA 1980		ANIMATO! (Doug Bennett) 1986
WRAP IT 1981		TOMCAT PROWL 1988
MUSIC FOR THE HARD OF THINKING 1983		TERMINAL CITY 1992
TEN BIG ONES 1983		SLUCOLOGY 101: A DECADE OF DOUG AND THE SLUGS 1993
POPAGANDA 1984		

The Doughboys   JOHN BONHEAD (*bass, vocals*): Replaced by PETER ARSENAULT
JOHNATHON CUMMINS (*guitar, vocals*)
JOHN KASTNER (*lead vocals, guitar*)
BROCK PYTEL (*drums, vocals*): Replaced by PAUL NEWMAN

Formed in Montreal in late 1986, this Montreal quartet practiced for six months, recorded a demo tape, and signed immediately with Pipeline Records. Although primarily a rock band, The Doughboys made forays into heavy metal, too. Their first album, WHATEVER, came out in late 1987. In February of 1988 they made a video of the song, *You're Related*, which was included in the soundtrack of the film *Hit and Run*.

Between 1988 and 1991 they toured extensively. In 1992 they signed a major deal with A&M Records. They also took the year off to write new material and to plan the group's future. In 1993 the group released CRUSH, their first album on A&M Records.

Singles   *You're Related* 1988   *Neighbourhood Villain* 1994
Shine 1993

Albums/CDs   WHATEVER 1987   SOMETHING'S GONE WRONG
HOME AGAIN 1988   AGAIN 1992
HAPPY ACCIDENTS 1990   CRUSH 1993

Downchild Blues Band   BILL BRYANS (*drums*)   DON WALSH (*guitar*)
TONY FAIM (*vocals*)   RICK WALSH (*vocals*)
WAYNE JACKSON (*trumpet*)   JAMES WARBURTON (*alto sax*)
JIM MILNE (*bass*)   VIC WILSON (*baritone*)
PAUL NIXON (*drums*)   DAVE WOODWARD (*tenor sax*)
JANE VASEY (*piano*)

The origins of Downchild go back to 1969 in Toronto when Donnie Walsh and five of his friends worked for scale at various clubs on Spadina Avenue. Their name came from a song by blues legend Sonny Boy Williamson. As their influences, Downchild list such blues greats as Willie Dixon, B.B. King, Muddy Waters, and Elmore James.

Although they had few chart hits, they had a huge following. *Flip, Flop and Fly*, off their 1973 album STRAIGHT UP, remains their only major hit. It was released twice, in the summer of 1973 and in the spring of 1974.

The Downchild Blues Band disbanded in 1978 and re-emerged as a three-piece band called Mister Downchild comprised of Jane Vasey, Don and Rick Walsh. Rick Walsh had returned to Downchild after a brief stint with his own band. He also worked as a solo act at the

Toronto club, The Cameo Lounge.

In 1982 Jane Vasey passed away after a nine year association with the group. John Witmer, formerly with Whiskey Howl, joined the group as a replacement for seven-year veteran Tony Faim, who joined the Scuffers Blues Band.

The band, now known as Downchild, returned to the recording studio in 1987 to record a new album. After many personnel changes the band is still performing in the 1990s.

Singles

Flip, Flop and Fly 1973
Flip, Flop and Fly (Re-release) 1974
I've Got Everything I Need (Almost) 1974
Tell Your Mother 1975

Goin' Dancin' 1975
Old Ma Belle 1976
Tryin' to Keep Her 88's Straight 1980
Hey Hey Little Girl 1981

Albums/CDs

BOOTLEG 1972
STRAIGHT UP 1973
DANCING 1974
WE DELIVER 1980
ROAD FEVER 1981
BLOOD RUN HOT 1981
GONE FISHING 1989

DOWNCHILD BLUES BAND
(Reissue of STRAIGHT UP and WE DELIVER) 1988
DOWNCHILD BLUES BAND
(Reissue of DANCING and ROAD FEVER) 1992

Dr. Music

Douglas Riley had been playing music since his teens when he was with the R&B group The Silhouettes. They built up a local following at the Toronto nightclub, The Blue Note.

By the late 1960s, he had worked with Ray Charles as his arranger and keyboard player. Riley was also arranger and pianist for *The Ray Stevens Show* (CTV, 1969-70) and *Rolling on the River* (CTV, 1970-72). He was also music director for three CBC shows: *Music Machine* (1973-74), *Tommy Ambrose's Celebration* (1975-76), and *The Wolfman Jack Show* (1976-77).

Dr. Music was created by Riley as background singers for *The Ray Stevens Show*. When the show was cancelled, the group toured Western Canada and became the leading jazz exponent in Toronto through the 1970s.

Signed to the now defunct GRT Record label, they had several hits, notably *Sun Goes By* in the summer of 1972. *Try a Little Harder* was written by Steve Kennedy of Motherlode fame and *One More Mountain to Climb* by Neil Sedaka.

Doug Riley remains active as a songwriter and performer today.

Singles	*Try a Little Harder* 1971	*Sun Goes By* 1972
	One More Mountain to Climb 1971	*Long Time Comin' Home* 1972
	Gospel Rock 1972	*Tryin' Times* 1973

Albums	DR. MUSIC 1972	DR. MUSIC CIRCA 1984 1985
	DR. MUSIC II 1973	FREEDOM (Doug Riley) 1990

Annette Ducharme

After playing in Vancouver for almost ten years, Windsor native Annette Ducharme finally received her due when Capitol Records released her debut album BLUE GIRL in June 1989.

Her musical career had begun in the 1970s, and in 1981 she released an EP called IN REAL LIFE while a member of the Bower Ducharme Duo. Four years later, she earned the 1985 West Coast Music Award for Most Promising Artist, which led to a recording session with John Webster, the keyboard player for Red Rider. The result was BLUE GIRL, an album comprised mostly of ballads.

Singles	*No Such Thing* 1989	*Sanctuary* 1994
	Slavery 1989	

CDs	BLUE GIRL 1989	SANCTUARY 1994

**Edward
Bear**

Larry Evoy (*drums, vocals*)
Danny Marks (*guitar*): Replaced by Roger Ellis
Paul Weldon (*organ*): Replaced by Bob Kendall

Edward Bear started out as a five piece band in 1967. They have the distinction of being the first Canadian act to have an album released without a prior hit single. Released on Capitol Records it was called BEARINGS. Reaction to their debut album was strong and radio stations began playing *You, Me & Mexico*. Capitol was soon forced to make it a single release and it was an instant Top Ten hit across Canada.

Originally classed as a rock and blues band, the success of *Mexico* made them a commercial hit. It paved the way for their second album, ECLIPSE. Evoy's vocalizing was recognized by critics as the main reason for Edward Bear's instant success. In September 1972 came another hit single, *Last Song*. Written and sung by Evoy, it went to become a smash in both Canada and the United States, selling over a million copies.

The group's success took its toll in the personnel changes. Danny Marks (who was replaced by Roger Ellis) left after the completion of ECLIPSE. Paul Weldon left in 1972 to concentrate on his graphic arts business and was replaced by Bob Kendall. Ellis left in 1973 to start his own band in Los Angeles. Then Kendall left after the release of *Walking on Back*, in 1974 and was replaced by Barry Best.

The original backup group for Edward Bear was Potatoes who played with the band until 1975 when they went out on their own. They were comprised of Randy Gulliver, Tim Wynveen, Denny Deporter, Carl Pamminger, and Bill Loop. Evoy continued to perform as Edward Bear with the backup group Horizon, but in 1978 he recorded under his own name and had minor success as a solo artist.

In 1984 Capitol released THE BEST OF BEAR. From it was released the single, *God Bless Us Now* which was only serviced to radio stations.

Singles

You, Me & Mexico 1970	*Same Old Feeling* 1974
You Can't Deny It 1970-71	*Freedom for the Stallion* 1974
Spirit Song 1971	*On and On* 1975
Fly Across the Sea 1972	*Perfect Strangers* (Larry Evoy) 1976
Masquerade 1972	
Last Song 1972-73	*Here I Go Again* (Larry Evoy) 1978
Close Your Eyes 1973	
Walking on Back 1973	*God Bless Us Now* 1984

Albums/CD

BEARINGS 1969	THE BEST OF THE BEAR (1969-1984) 1984
ECLIPSE 1970	
EDWARD BEAR 1972	THE EDWARD BEAR COLLECTION 1991
CLOSE YOUR EYES 1973	

Eight Seconds   DEL CASTILLO (*vocals*)   SCOTT MILKS (*drums*)
MARCH CESARE (*bass*)   MARC PARENT (*guitar*)
FRANK LEVIN (*keyboards*)

Formed in 1982 in Ottawa, Eight Seconds first made their mark the following year when they won a local talent contest sponsored by CHEZ radio. First prize was a chance to make a video, and Eight Seconds recorded a video for *Where's Bula?*.

In May 1985 they made an mini-album called OTTAVA RIMA on Apprentice Records. A year later, Rupert Hines, CHEZ-FM's music director, was impressed by the video and arranged for the group to sign with Polygram Records. Their debut album ALMACANTAR was released in November 1986. From it came their first single, *Kiss You (When It's Dangerous)*, which was a hit in 1986-87.

Singles   *Kiss You (When It's Dangerous)* 1986-87
Tell Diane 1990

Albums   ALMACANTAR 1987   BIG HOUSES 1990

Shirley Eikhard   At age thirteen, Sackville, New Brunswick native Shirley Eikhard was a hit at the Mariposa Folk Festival. She had her first recording contract at fourteen, and at seventeen played in Las Vegas. Early in her musical career she demonstrated an ability to write songs, notably *It Takes Time*, recorded by Anne Murray in 1971. She also wrote *Something in Your Face*, recorded in 1971 by Donna Ramsey, and *Don't Try To Please*, recorded in 1971 by The Sanderlings, a teenaged singing group from Newfoundland.

Eikhard's first single as a recording artist was *Smiling Wine* in the spring of 1972. Her biggest hit was *Say You Love Me* in the summer of 1976. The following year she stopped recording and concentrated on writing more of her own music, and for the next ten years she experimented on her own record label, Eika Records. Two singles, *It's Understood* (her first bilingual record) and *Someone Else* came out in 1986, and the album TAKING CHARGE in 1987.

More recently, Eikhard won a 1991 Grammy Award for her song *Something to Talk About* which Bonnie Raitt recorded on her 1989 Grammy winning album, NICK OF TIME. She also wrote *Kick Start My Heart* for Alannah Myles on her debut album.

Singles   *Smiling Wine* 1972   *Say You Love Me* 1976
Rescue Me 1974   *It's Understood* 1986
Play a Little Longer 1975   *Someone Else* 1986
I Just Wanted You to Know 1976

Albums   SHIRLEY EIKHARD 1972   HORIZONS 1977
             CHILD OF THE PRESENT 1975 GREATEST HITS 1978
             LET ME DOWN EASY 1976   TAKING CHARGE 1987

Rik Emmett

For twelve years Rik Emmett was a member of the Toronto rock band Triumph. When he left in 1987, he was offered the chance to play guitar in such groups as Asia and Damn Yankees. However, he turned them all down because he liked the freedoms associated with being a solo performer.

In 1990 Duke Street Records released his debut solo album, ABSOLUTELY. IPSO FACTO, his second solo effort on Duke Street, was released in 1992. The song *Out of the Blue* was written with Stevie Ray Vaughn in mind, while *Rainbow Man* was Emmett's tribute to blues legend Robert Johnson and the impact his music had on Muddy Waters, Howlin' Wolf, T. Bone Walker, B.B. King, and Chuck Berry.

Emmett is a guitar aficionado and a regular contributor to *Guitar Player* magazine. He is often invited to guitar seminars and workshops where he sits beside some of the greatest guitarists around today, such as Steve Morse, Steve Vai, Mike Stern, and Frank Gambale.

Singles   *Big Lie* 1990   *The Way that You Love Me* 1991
              When a Heart Breaks 1990-91   *Dig a Little Deeper* 1992
              Saved by Love 1991   *Heaven in Your Heart* 1993
              World of Wonder 1991

CDs   ABSOLUTELY 1990   IPSO FACTO 1992

Ensemble Claude-Gervaise

MARCEL BENOIT   DIANE PLANTE
PHILIPPE GELINAS   GILLES PLANTE
JEAN-MARC GRAS   DANIEL THONON
ISABELLE MARCHAND

The history of this Quebec folk group goes back to 1967 when they were known as the Ensemble Pierre-Attaingnant. The original members were flutists Francois Barre, Jean Gagné, Joseph Guilmette, and Gilles Plante. They later renamed themselves Ensemble Claude-Gervaise in honor of the late French musician whose songs and dances inspired the band.

The Ensemble aimed to bridge old and new music styles, original sixteenth-century songs and music with the recent work of Felix Leclerc, Gilles Vigneault, and Claude Léveillée. Their 1982 album LA RENCONTRE featured adaptations of songs from the modern chansonniers to the airs of the Renaissance.

On stage, each member performed in costume. All eight played several traditional instruments, including the recorder, cervelat, reed-pipes, krumm horn, whistles, lute, cittern, theorbo, rebeck, sackbutt, spinett, and harpsichord. They played throughout Canada, the United States, Mexico, and Europe.

Albums TOUT L'MONDE EST MALHEUREUX 1976
CHANTE L'AMOUR ET LA GUERRE 1977
JOUISSANCE VOUS DONNERAY 1981
LA RENCONTRE 1982
MUSIQUE AU TEMPS DE LÉONARD DA VINCI 1987
NOELS DE LA RENAISSANCE 1988

Karl Erikson A landed immigrant in Canada since 1969, Karl Erikson was born in Port Washington, Wisconsin, and earned a bachelor's degree in history and anthropology from the University of Wisconsin.

When he moved to Canada, he worked as a solo singer at Whistler Mountain, north of Vancouver, then relocated to Australia for a short period before returning to Toronto, where he laid down tracks for his first album for United Artists. Titled AEROGRAMME, it featured six songs penned by Erikson, three by Gene MacLellan, and one each from Shirley Eikhard and Joan Guenther. Erikson's first hit single was *Midnight Road* in the spring of 1973.

Singles *Midnight Road* 1973　　　*It's Gonna Be Alright* 1974
Carnival Town 1973

Album AEROGRAMME 1973

Eritage MARC BENOIT (*bass, guitar*)　　RAYNALD OUELLET (*accordion*)
BENOIT BOURQUE (*jig-dancer*　VINCENT OUELLET (*fiddle*)
　extraordinaire)　　　　　RAYMOND PHILIPPE (*percussion,*
YVAN BRAULT (*piano*)　　　　　*flute*)

This six-member bilingual folk group from Quebec formed in 1977 with the aim of bringing the color and spirit of Québécois folk music to life. They began their musical career at the Télé-Capitale television network in Quebec City, where they taped shows for two folk-based music shows, *Gentil' Alouette* and *Folklore en Tête*. On stage Eritage specialized in a program of songs, dances, jigs, reels, rags and cakewalks.

Eritage played at many folk festivals throughout Canada and the United States, and toured Ontario, Nova Scotia, Greece, Bulgaria, and Washington, D.C. They recorded five albums, three of which were produced for the Catholic School of Quebec: LA POULETTE GRISE, L'ALOUETTE CHANTE ENCORE, and CHANSONS DE TOUTES LES COULEURS.

Their first non-children's album was their 1979 self-titled debut on Son-D'Or Records, ERITAGE. In 1983 they recorded LA RONDE DES VOYAGEURS, which was produced by the late Stan Rogers.

Albums		
ERITAGE 1979		CHANSONS DE TOUTES LES
LA POULETTE GRISE 1980		COULEURS 1982
L'ALOUETTE CHANTE ENCORE		LA RONDE DES VOYAGEURS 1983
1981		

The Esquires

GARY COMEAU (*lead guitar*)   CLINT HIERLIHY (*bass*)
BOB HARRINGTON (*vocals*):   PAUL HUOT (*rhythm guitar*)
   Replaced by DON NORMAN   RICHARD PATTERSON (*drums*)
DON NORMAN (*vocals*):
   Replaced by BRIAN LEWIS

Formed in 1962, the Ottawa-based Esquires played their first public performance at the Rockcliffe Air Base Teen Club. After joining the Musician's Union in 1963, they signed a full-time contract to play every Friday and Saturday night at the Pineland Dance Pavilion.

The major influence of the original members (Harrington, Comeau, Hierlihy, Huot, and Patterson) was Cliff Richard and The Shadows; on stage they were a carbon copy of the English group.

Managed by Sandy Gardner, a columnist for *The Ottawa Journal*, The Esquires played with many rock 'n' roll stars of the early and mid-1960s. On July 18, 1963 they were among the Canadian acts featured on *The Dick Clark Show* at Faucher Stadium with Gene Pitney, The Dovells, Paul and Paula, and The Tymes. At the Montreal Forum and Maple Leaf Gardens they played with The Dave Clark Five. The Esquires also shared the same stage with The Beach Boys, Roy Orbison, and The Rolling Stones.

Their first single was *Atlantis* in 1963 on the Capital Records of Canada label; the second was the instrumental smash, *Man from Adano*. Their biggest hit, written by Don Norman, was *So Many Other Boys* in late 1964 and early 1965. After two more hits on Capitol, they switched to Columbia Records. At Bell Studios in New York City they recorded two hits for the label, *It's a Dirty Shame* and *Love's a Multitude of Sins*. Their only Capitol album, INTRODUCING THE ESQUIRES, was released in 1964 and featured a Buddy Holly tribute and *Man from Adano*.

In 1967 the Esquires disbanded. They reunited in 1987 for the 25th anniversary of the group. The lineup was comprised of Don Norman,

Gary Comeau, Paul Huot, Brian Lewicki, and Richard Patterson. Through the years 1962-66 the members of the group included Gail Thompson, Bert Hart, Ted Gerow, John Cassidy, Bernie Jessome, Doug Orr, Bruce Cockburn, Robert Coulthart, and Mike Argue.

In 1993 two music videos made by The Esquires were discovered. According to Richard Patterson, *The Man from Adano* is the first music video made in Canada. The other was *Gee Whiz It's You*, which featured Bob Harrington on lead vocals.

Singles   *Atlantis/I've Lost My Girl* 1963
Man from Adano/Gee Whiz It's You 1964
So Many Other Ways/The Oldest Story 1964-65
Cry Is All I Do/We've Got a Future 1965
Love's Made a Fool of You/Summertime 1965
It's a Dirty Shame/The Sea Rushes to the Shore 1966
Love Hides a Multitude of Sins/Why Should I Care? 1966-67

Album   INTRODUCING THE ESQUIRES 1964

The Eternals   The Eternals made a name for themselves in their native Winnipeg by recording covers of old and established hits, such as the Del Vikings' *Come Go with Me* and Buddy Holly's *Raining in My Heart*. Group members Ron Paley and Harry Hildebrand wrote some of the band's original material, including *Girl in the Window*, which the group recorded on Quality Records.

Their 1968 hit, *Falling Trees*, was written by Ottawan Dave Britten and featured string and horn arrangements by CBC musical director Bob McMullin. Randy Bachman, then a member of The Guess Who, wrote their next hit, *The Real World of Marianne*.

Singles   *Girl in the Window* 1967   *Falling Tears* 1968
Come Go with Me 1967   *Real World of Marianne* 1968
Raining in My Heart 1967

Everyday People   DAVID HARE (*keyboards*)   CHRIST PAPUTTS (*guitar*)
PAMELA MARSH (*vocals*)   CARSON RICHARDS (*bass guitar*)
ALAN MUGGERIDGE (*drums*)   BRUCE WHEATON (*vocals, guitar*)

Three members of Everyday People were from Ontario, the other three from the Maritimes. Founded by Bruce Wheaton of Stitch in Tyme in 1970, Everyday People, based in Toronto, was one of those bands that found it difficult to make it in the city. Their first single, *You Make Me*

Wonder, was not the hit the band expected. With their second, *I Get That Feelin'*, a U.S. deal was made, but after two more releases they faded into obscurity.

Singles

You Make Me Wonder 1971	*Don't Wait for Tomorrow* 1972
I Get That Feeling 1971	*Feelin' Better Already* 1972
You Make Me Wonder 1971	*Memories* 1972
I Like What I Like 1972	

Percy Faith

Born in Toronto on April 17, 1908, Percy was a promising pianist as a teenager, but he severely wounded his hands putting out a fire, and turned to composing, arranging, and orchestrating for the CBC in the 1930s.

After moving to the United States in 1940 he became prominent on radio there, too. Ten years later he became musical director of Columbia Records' popular music division and made over forty-five albums. During his tenure as musical director he was responsible for arranging three of Tony Bennett's early hits: *Because of You*, *Rags to Riches*, and *Cold, Cold Heart*. Guy Mitchell's *My Heart Cries for You* was another example of Faith's work. Faith also composed film scores: his first for *Love Me or Leave Me* earned him an Academy Award nomination in 1955.

Beginning in May 1950 with *I Cross My Finger*, Faith had a string of hits at home and in the U.S. His biggest success was *The Theme from a Summer Place* which was the number one song of 1960. He died in 1976 at his home in Los Angeles.

Singles

Valley Valaparaiso 1956	*Theme from a Summer Place* 1960
We All Need Love 1956	*Theme for Young Lovers* 1960
With a Little Bit of Luck 1956	*Theme from Chinatown* 1974
Till 1957	

Albums

MUSIC FROM HOLLYWOOD 1953	LEAVING ON A JET PLANE 1970
VIVA — THE MUSIC OF MEXICO 1957	HELD OVER! TODAY'S GREAT MOVIE THEMES 1970
BOUQUET 1959	PERCY FAITH PLAYS THE BEATLES 1970
THEME FROM A SUMMER PLACE 1959	TIME FOR LOVE 1971
THEMES FOR YOUNG LOVERS 1963	I THINK I LOVE YOU 1971
FOR THOSE IN LOVE 1968	BLACK MAGIC WOMAN 1971
ANGEL OF THE MORNING 1968	JESUS CHRIST SUPERSTAR 1971
THOSE WERE THE DAYS 1969	JOY 1972
WINDMILLS OF YOUR MIND 1969	DAY BY DAY 1972
LOVE THEME FROM ROMEO AND JULIET 1969	

Tim Feehan

Tim Feehan of Toronto was the principal writer of Footloose but left the group to go solo after their first album came out in 1981.

Recording for Mushroom Records, his first solo hit was *Backseat-Backseat* in 1981. His second, *Go Ahead and Break My Heart*, was released in 1982. His career as a solo artist was short-lived.

Singles *Backseat-Backseat* 1981
Go Ahead and Break My Heart 1981-82

Album FOOTLOOSE 1981   SNEAK PREVIEW (Tim Feehan) 1981

Ferron   From Vancouver, Ferron (a.k.a. Debbie Foisy) learned to play the guitar at age eleven. She made her professional debut in 1974 at a benefit for the Women's Press Gang with the song *Who Loses*. At Tom Lavin's (of Powder Blues Band) studio she recorded her first self-titled album for Lucy Records, her own label.

Single *Who Loses* 1974

Albums/CDs   FERRON 1977   PHANTOM CENTER 1990
FERRON BACKED UP 1978   NOT A STILL LIFE 1992
TESTIMONY 1980   RESTING WITH THE QUESTION 1992
SHADOW ON A DIME 1984   DRIVER 1993

The Fifth   This Winnipeg-based group came from the northern Manitoban town of Gimli. Their first hit single, *Yesterday's Today*, was written by bassist Melvyn C. Ksionzek on London Records and received the Lloyd C. Moffat Award in 1968 as the year's best Canadian produced rock recording. The Fifth had one more national hit in December 1967 and early 1968 with *Tears*, also on London Records.

Singles *Yesterday's Today* 1967   *Caprice* 1968
Tears 1967-68

54-40   PHIL COMPARELLI (*guitar,*   DARRYL NEUDORF (*drums*):
trumpet, vocals)   Replaced by MATT JOHNSON
BRAD MERRITT (*bass*)   NEIL OSBORNE (*vocals*)

Formed in 1981, 54-40 first got together in a studio to record four songs for the EP THINGS ARE STILL COMING ASHORE which was released by the pioneer Mo Da Mu, a group who recognized the need to promote the aspiring musicians of Canada's West Coast.

Early in 1982 54-40 toured the West Coast for the first time. Originally the group was a trio comprised of Neil Osborne, Brad Merritt, and Darryl Neudorf. In 1984 Camparelli was added to complement the band's sound and, a year later, Neudorf left to be replaced by Matt Johnson, formerly of the group French Letters.

The name 54-40 comes from a U.S. presidential slogan used by James Polk, "54-40 or Fight", who wanted to expand the U.S. border north past the 49th parallel. The numbers "54-40" indicate the precise geographical reference where the stars and stripes were supposed to fly.

The music of 54-40 has been compared to such groups as R.E.M. Their album SET THE FIRE and the popularity of the song *The Sound of Truth* established the group.

Warner Music signed the group after label executives Felix Chamberlain and Kevin Laffey saw them perform live. In the 1990s they switched to Sony Music. Their third album, DEAR DEAR, was released in May 1992.

Singles

What to Do Now 1984	*Baby Have Some Faith* 1990
The Sound of Truth 1984	*Nice To Luv You* 1992
Christmas Time 1984	*She La* 1992
One Day in Your Life 1988	*Music Man* 1992
Walk in Line 1988	*You Don't Get Away (That Easy)* 1993
One Gun 1988	
2000 Years of Love 1988	*We Are, We Pretend* 1993
Miss You 1989	*Train of Dreams* 1993-94
Baby Ran 1989	*Blame Your Parents* 1994
I Go Blind 1990	

CDs

SET THE FIRE 1984	DEAR DEAR 1992
SHOW ME 1987	SMILIN' BUDDHA CABARET 1994
FIGHT FOR LOVE 1989	

Figgy Duff

NOEL DINN	DAVID PANTING
PHILIP DINN	ARTHUR STOYLES
PAMELA MORGAN	

Formed in the mid-1970s by Noel Dinn, Figgy Duff developed a style of traditional songs and dance tunes that has now become popular with other Canadian folk/traditional groups, such as The Rankin Family and The Barra MacNeils.

Pamela Morgan's classical background and Noel Dinn's rock and R&B influences combined to help make the group's music take shape. Although their music is rooted primarily in folk, they try to incorporate a few elements of rock, especially in their jigs and reels.

They recorded their self-titled debut on Phonodisc Records in 1981. In 1990 they began writing their own songs on their album WEATHER OUT THE STORM. Their third album, AFTER THE TEMPEST, continued in the traditional vein. And their 1993 album DOWNSTREAM contained all original material written by Noel and Pamela. The first single, and accompanying video, was *Freedom*.

Noel Dinn died of cancer in St. John's Hospital on Monday, July 26, 1993. He was 45.

Single   *Freedom* 1993

Albums   FIGGY DUFF (Phonodisc) 1981   AFTER THE TEMPEST 1991
WEATHER OUT THE STORM 1990   DOWNSTREAM 1993
FIGGY DUFF (Hypnotic/A&M)
   1991

The Five D

JACK ARSENAULT   BRAD CAMPBELL (*bass, vocals*)
   (*rhythm guitar, vocals*)   DAVE POULIN (*lead vocals*)
BRIAN BRADFIELD (*drums*)   KEITH RICHARDSON (*vocals, guitar*)

From Ottawa, Ontario, The Five D were a pop/rock group who recorded for the Sir John A label. They started out in 1965 as The Fifth Dimension but had to change their name to avoid conflict with the American group of the same name. Their first hit was *Bady Bay* in 1967.

That year Mark Corbin and Jim Pagliaro joined the group when two members left. The band appeared on a live broadcast of the Centennial Celebrations on Parliament Hill with Queen Elizabeth II and Prince Philip. The group's farewell concert was also in July 1967 when they played with The Who, The Troggs, and Ohio Express as a backup orchestra.

The Five D's biggest hit was *Runnin' Around in Circles* which went to number one on the Ottawa TV show *The Swing Set* and reached number three in Regina, Saskatchewan.

Singles   *Bady Bay* 1967   *She Can't Be My Girl* 1968
Runnin' Round in Circles 1967

Gary Fjellgaard

Gary Fjellgaard (pronounced Fell-gard) is one of Canada's most prolific singer-songwriters. His songs reflect his folk-country roots.

Born in Rose Valley, Saskatchewan in 1937, he began singing at an early age in the town's church choir. In his teens he moved with his family to Prince George, British Columbia, where he worked as a logger during the day and played music at night. A back injury forced him to abandon logging as a career in 1973, and he concentrated full time on his music, playing at various coffeehouses and bars throughout the west coast.

In 1976 he recorded ME AND MARTIN, the first of two albums on the independent Royalty label. BALLADS AND BEER was released in 1979.

Fjellgaard received a British Columbia Country Music Award Song of the Year for *Ten Years Old and Barefoot* in 1982. His success brought him to the attention of Savannah Music and its president, Brian Ferriman, who signed Gary in the mid-1980s. In 1986 NO TIME TO LOSE was the first album to be released by the label.

Fjellgaard has won countless awards for his music from the Canadian Country Music Association (CCMA), Country Music News, *RPM Magazine*'s Big Country Awards, The Canadian Music Publishers Association (CMPA), British Columbia Country Music Association (BCCMA), and the Dutch Country Music Awards. In 1990 the TMI Fender Humanitarian Award was presented to Gary by the CCMA in recognition of his outstanding contribution to increased environmental awareness through his composition *Somewhere on the Island*.

The year 1988 saw him try his turn as an actor in *The Ranch*. Directed by actress Stella Stevens, he starred as Cody Brewster, a crippled and aging rodeo-cowboy/singer who lives at a ramshackle Canadian ranch inherited by a U.S. businessman. *The Ranch* was filmed entirely on location in Calgary.

Singles

Ride Away to the Country 1977
Old Fashioned Cowboy Song 1977
How Much of Me 1978
Me and Martin 1979
Ballads and Beer 1979-80
Real Contender 1981
Too Much of a Lady 1983
Never Leave the Farm 1983
Finest Dancer 1984
Ten Years Old and Bearfoot 1984
Running Back to Your Heart 1984
Riding on the Wind 1985
She Can Survive 1985
Too Much of a Lady 1985
Dancing in the Ring 1986
Heroes 1987
As Rivers Run Saskatchewan 1987
Walk in the Rain Tonight 1988
Tears on Mainstreet 1988
Once Upon a Time 1988

The Moon Is Out to Get Me (Duet with Linda Kidder) 1989
Cowboy in Your Heart 1990
Cry in the Wilderness 1990
The Color of Your Collar 1990
Somewhere on the Island 1990
In My Heart (Duet with Linda Kidder) 1990
Dance with This Old Cowboy 1991
Heart of a Dream 1991
Drifting Cowboy 1991
Fire and Lace (Duet with Linda Kidder) 1991
The Last Hurrah 1992
Two Gun Kid 1992
The Winds of October 1992
Remember When 1993
Never Say Goodbye 1993
Shaganippi Hick 1993
Train of Dreams 1993-94
Islanders 1994

Albums/CDs	ME AND MARTIN 1976	HEART OF A DREAM 1989
	BALLADS AND BEER 1979	WINDS OF OCTOBER 1991
	NO TIME TO LOSE 1986	BELIEVE IN FOREVER 1994
	TIME AND INNOCENCE 1987	

Fludd

JOHN ANDERSON	BRIAN PILLING
PETER CZANKEY	ED PILLING
GREG GODOVITZ	GORD WASZEK

Fludd was formed in 1969 by brothers Brian and Ed Pilling who previously had played in the band The Wages of Sin and had backed up Cat Stevens.

Originally a quartet, Peter Czankey made it a five man band in 1972. In 1974, Gord Waszek was added as a replacement for Brian Pilling who left because of ill health. When he returned, Gord remained with the group.

Their first two singles, *Turned 21* and *Get Up, Get Out and Move On*, were on the Warner Brothers label and were big hits. Success continued to follow when they had a contract with Daffodil Records (1972-74) and the independent Attic label (1974-76).

The band broke up when Brian Pilling died of cancer in 1978. Godovitz went on to form the group Goddo.

Attic Records released a retrospective collection of the group's hits in 1977 called FROM THE ATTIC '71-'77.

Singles	*Turned 21* 1971	*Cousin Mary* 1973
	Get Up, Get Out and Move On 1972	*I Held Out* 1974
		Brother and Me 1974
	Always Be Thinking of You 1972-73	*Dance Gypsy Dance* 1974
		What an Animal 1975
	Yes 1973	*I'm on My Way* 1976
	C'Mon C'Mon 1973	

Albums	FLUDD 1972	GREAT EXPECTATIONS 1975
	ON! 1972	FROM THE ATTIC '71 TO '77 1977

Flying Circus

Originally from Australia, Flying Circus had a hit in 1969 with *Hay Ride* in their home country and in the Maritimes, where it became a pick hit on CFNB's Top 40 chart.

In 1971 Flying Circus won top honors in San Francisco at a "Battle of Sounds" competition. They eventually relocated to Toronto, but after three months they went back home to Australia. Later, though, they returned to Canada as immigrants. Rather than record right away, they toured the Ontario high school circuit and played in some bars. They signed a contract with Capitol Records in 1972, and *Maple Lady* was their first single with the label, taken from their debut album, GYPSY ROAD. Their biggest hit was *Old Enough to Break My Heart* in 1972.

Singles   *Hay Ride* 1969   *Old Enough to Break My Heart*
              Maple Lady 1972   1972

Albums   PREPARED IN PEACE 1971   GYPSY ROAD 1972

Peter Foldy

This Hungarian-born singer/songwriter moved to Sydney, Australia with his parents in 1956, and arrived in Toronto, Ontario, nine years later. In 1976 Peter Foldy became a Canadian citizen.

He scored a major hit in both Canada and the United States with the self-penned hit *Bondi Junction* in 1973, which was written about a place in Australia.

Following the success of *Bondi Junction*, he went to Hollywood where he played bit parts in The Last Detail (1973) and The Paper Chase (1973). In the late 1970s he moved to Los Angeles, and in 1980 he starred in *Roadie* with Alice Cooper, Meatloaf and Blondie.

The early 1980s saw Foldy co-write with fellow Canadian David Daniels the hit *Let's Start Again* for Australian singer Samantha Sang. In 1981 he performed in the Los Angeles production of *Hair*.

Today, he is now a writer/director of films. His first, *Midnight Madness* stars Maxwell Caulfield (*Grease 2*), Jan-Michael Vincent, and veteran actress Virginia Mayo (*White Heat*). Produced by Menahem Golan, it also features original songs by Foldy.

Singles   *Bondi Junction* 1973   *Roxanne* 1976
              I'll Never Know 1973   *Julie Ann* 1977
              When I Am So in Love 1974   *Love City* 1979
              Christmas Eve with You 1974   *School of Love* 1981

A Foot in Coldwater

(See The Lords of London)

49th Parallel

BARRY ALLAN   DANNY LOWE
DORIN BEATTIE   WAYNE MORICE
BOB EGO

From Calgary Alberta, this band evolved in 1966 from a group called The Shades of Blonde. The original lineup was comprised of Barry Allan, Dorrin Beattie, Bob Ego, Danny Lowe and Wayne Morice. Other members included Denny Abbot, Robby Carlson, Dave Petch, Terry Bare, and Mick Woodhouse. They went through three name changes: Painter, Hammersmith, and 451 Degrees.

(As 49th Parallel)
Singles *Labourer* 1967
She Says 1968
Blue Bonnie Blue 1968

Twilight Woman 1969
Now That I'm a Man 1970
I Need You 1970

(As Painter)
Singles *West Coast Woman* 1973
Going Home to Rock and Roll 1974

Crazy Feelin' 1974

(As Hammersmith)
Singles *Feelin' Better* 1976

Late Night Lovin' Man 1976

Fosterchild BARRY BOOTHMAN (*bass*)
JIM FOSTER (*guitar, vocals*)
GERRY WAND (*drums*)

VERN WILLS (*guitar, vocals*)
PETER SWEETZIR (*keyboards*)

Jim Foster, a native of Victoria, British Columbia, was a radio addict and began playing guitar at thirteen. Vern Wills was an army brat born in Calgary who joined his first band at the age of twelve. Foster and Wills first met when their respective bands played at a local teen hangout, The Haunted House, in Calgary. Not content to remain with a bar band, Wills left Canada for New York where he became a member of the group The Walkers. When he had problems renewing his work visa, Wills returned to Calgary and joined Foster.

After a number of personnel changes the group Fosterchild was born in 1976. The following year they signed a record deal with CBS Records. They only had two hit singles; an album ON THE PROWL, was released in 1980.

Singles *Until We Meet Again* 1977

I Need Somebody Tonight 1978

Albums FOSTERCHILD 1977
TROUBLED CHILD 1978

ON THE PROWL 1980

The Four Lads

JAMES ARNOLD (*first tenor*) CONNIE CODARINI (*bass*)
FRANK BUSSERI (*baritone*) BERNARD TOORISH (*second tenor*)

The Four Lads originally called themselves The Four Dukes; however, a Detroit quartet owned the name so they changed it. Julius Monk, the group's Master of Ceremonies, suggested The Four Lads.

Growing up in their native Toronto, the four were choirboys. Signed to a recording contract with Columbia Records in the early 1950s, they backed up Johnny Ray on his hits *Cry, Little White Cloud Cried, Brokenhearted,* and *Please Mister Sun* before branching out on their own.

They made their American TV debut on *The Ransom Sherman Show* on NBC in 1950. Other TV appearances included *The Pat Boone-Chevy Showroom* on ABC and *Perry Presents* on NBC in 1959. The Four Lads were also one of the guest hosts of the summer music series *Upbeat* on CBS in 1955.

In 1952 Columbia released their first hit, *The Mockingbird.* Among their others were *Moments to Remember* and *No, Not Much* written by the songwriting team of Bob Allen and Al Stillman, who wrote Johnny Mathis's big hit *Chances Are,* among others.

Singles

The Mockingbird 1952
Istanbul 1953
Down by the River Side 1953
Skokiaan 1954
Gilly Gilly Ossenfeffer Katenellen Bogen by the Sea 1954
Moments to Remember 1955
No, Not Much 1956
I'll Never Know 1956
Standing on the Corner/My Little Angel 1956
The Bus Stop Song (A Paper of Pins) 1956
A House with Love in It 1956
Who Needs You 1957
I Just Don't Know 1957
Put a Light in the Window 1957
There's only One of You 1958
Enchanted Island 1958
The Girl on Page 44 1959
The Fountain of Youth 1959
Happy Anniversary 1959

Albums

STAGE SHOW 1954
ON THE SUNNY SIDE 1956
THE FOUR LADS SING FRANK LOESSER 1957
FOUR ON THE AISLE 1958
BREEZIN' ALONG 1958
GREATEST HITS 1958

Frozen Ghost

SAMMY D. BARTEL (*keyboards*) WOLF HASSEL (*bass*)
JOHN BOUVETTE (*drums*) ARNOLD LANNI (*vocals, guitar*)

Formed in 1985 by Arnold Lanni and Wolf Hassel, both former members of Sheriff, Frozen Ghost released their self-titled debut album in

1987 with Warner Music Canada.

Lanni is the singer, songwriter, producer, and leader. As a member of Sheriff, he wrote *When I'm with You*, which was a hit in 1983 and 1989. The second time around it went to number one on Billboard's Hot 100.

Their second album, NICE PLACE TO VISIT, came out in 1988, and their third, SHAKE YOUR SPIRIT in 1992. In the four years between albums, Lanni worked on new material and produced other artists such as Wild 'T' and The Spirit.

Singles		
Should I See 1987	*Dream Come True* 1989
Round and Round 1988	*Head over Heels* 1992
Yum Bai Ya 1988	*Shake Your Spirit* 1992
Pauper in Paradise 1989	*Shine on Me* 1992

Albums		
FROZEN GHOST 1987	NICE PLACE TO VISIT 1988

B.B. Gabor

B.B. Gabor (Gabor Hegedus), a refugee from Hungary and a talented singer/songwriter/producer, built up a loyal following in Toronto in the early 1970s. By 1980 he had formed his own backup group, The Instabands. He signed a contract with Anthem Records, and his first single was the two-sided *Nyet, Nyet Soviet (Soviet Jewellery)* and *Moscow Drug Club*, a Russian folk song that describes an underground location where people escaped from the KGB. As a producer, he has worked with the female new wave group, True Confessions. In 1987, he formed a new band in British Columbia.

Singles	*Nyet Nyet Soviet (Soviet Jewellery)* 1980	*Jealous Guy* 1981
Albums	B.B. GABOR 1980	GIRLS OF THE FUTURE 1981

Andre Gagnon

Although Andre Gagnon's achievements have been mostly in the classical field, his 1976 album NEIGES became a best seller and earned him a Juno Award. His subsequent recordings, such as *Smah*, *Chevauchee*, *Surprise*, *Donna*, and *Mouvements*, quickly established him in the disco and pop fields.

Born in 1942 and raised in St. Pacôme-de-Kamouraska, Quebec, he learned to play the piano as a child and began writing short pieces at the age of six. In 1961 he went to study in Paris on a grant from the Quebec government. A year later, he returned to Canada and worked with Claude Leveillee until 1969. That same year Gagnon turned solo and traveled to London to record with the London Baroque Orchestra, and in 1972 with the Hamburg Philharmonic Orchestra. He has recorded over twenty albums, and in 1993 Star Records released two new works, LES JOURS TRANQUILLES and PRESQUE BLEU.

Singles	*Don't Ask Why* 1968	*Surprise* 1976-77
	Song for Petula 1969	*Weekend* 1977
	Rainbow 1971	*A Ride to Ville Emard* 1980
	Wow 1976	

Albums/CDs	ANDRE GAGNON – PIANO ET ORCHESTRE 1964	LET IT BE ME 1971
	LEVEILLEE-GAGNON 1965	LES GRANDS SUCCES D'ANDRE GAGNON 1971
	UNE VOIX, DEUX PIANOS 1966	LES TURLUTERIES 1972
	POUR LES AMANTS/DON'T ASK ME WHY 1968	ENCORE 1972
	NOTRE AMOUR 1969	PROJECTION 1973
	MES QUATRES SAISONS 1969	SAGA 1974
		NEIGES 1976

LE ST. LAURENT 1978
MOUVEMENTS 1980
VIRAGE A GAUCHE 1981
GREATEST HITS 1982
IMPRESSIONS 1983

COMME DANS UN FILM 1986
DES DAMES DE COEUR 1989
NOEL 1992
LES JOURS TRANQUILLES 1993
PRESQUE BLUE 1993

Patsy Gallant

From Campbellton, New Brunswick, Patsy Gallant was born in 1950. At a very young age her mother insisted she join her three older sisters and perform at fairs. Billed as The Gallant Sisters, they also performed on radio and TV.

In 1967, Patsy decided to go solo and released a single which led to TV appearances on *Music Hop, Discotheque, Jeunesse Oblige,* and *Smash.* She was able to sing in both English and French and appeared on stage with Charles Aznavour at Montreal's Place des Arts.

In 1969, Patsy met songwriter Yves Lapierre and became involved in the commercial jingle business. Her most famous jingle was for the Ford Motor Co. Her group was dubbed Ford-A-Maniacs. This experience led her to Ian MacDonald who later became her manager. In Quebec she began singing movie themes, notably *Theme from L'Initiaton* and *Theme from Ya Pas De Trou A Perce.*

Her English debut came in 1972 with the album UPON MY OWN and the single *Get that Ball.* While she enjoyed success with *Are You Ready for Love* in English Canada in 1977, she also recorded her first French language album, BESOIN D'AMOUR which yielded three hit singles: *Libre pour l'amour,* the French version of *Sugar Daddy,* and the title track. Her hit single *From New York to L.A.* was only played in English Canada and was a disco version of Gilles Vigneault's *Mon Pays.*

In 1993 she played the leading role in a musical about French singer Edith Piaf that toured only in Quebec.

Singles

Get That Ball 1972
Power 1973
Save the Last Dance for Me
  1974
Make My Living 1974
Doctor's Orders 1974-75
Makin' Love in My Mind 1975
From New York to L.A. 1976
Are You Ready for Love 1977
Sugar Daddy 1977

Back to the City 1977-78
Will You Give Me Your Love 1978
Stay awhile with Me 1978
Best of the Woman in Me 1979
We'll Find a Way
  (with Dwayne Ford) 1979
It's Got to Be You 1979-80
How Many Lonely Nights? 1980
Don't Forget about Me 1981
Hit the Streets Tonight 1984

Albums UPON MY OWN 1972
ARE YOU READY FOR LOVE 1977
BESOIN D'AMOUR 1977

WILL YOU GIVE ME YOUR LOVE? 1978
GREATEST HITS 1979
AMOUREUSE 1981

Garfield Band

DENNIS FRENCH (*drums, percussion*)
JACQUES FILLION (*keyboards*)
GARFIELD FRENCH (*lead vocals*)

WALTER LAWRENCE (*guitar, electric cello*)
PAUL O'DONNELL (*guitar, harmonica, banjo*)
CHIP YARWOOD (*flute, synthesizer*)

Fronted by Garfield French, The Garfield Band got its start playing university pubs, their English-style sound making them unique for a Canadian group. However, the sextet had so much equipment that it was hard to book the band in small clubs. In October 1976, Garfield made a debut at the National Arts Centre in Ottawa as the opening act for 10 C.C. In the audience that night were several Mercury Record executives who were impressed enough to sign the band right away.

Their first album was STRANGE STREETS, and their first hit single was *Old Time Movies* in 1976. Other hits were charted in the late 1970s and early 1980s.

Singles *Old Time Movies* 1976
Give My Love to Anne 1976
All Alone Again 1978

Buffalo to Boston 1980
Like I Love You 1981
High Class 1981

Albums STRANGE STREETS 1976
OUT THERE TONIGHT 1977

COLD ON THE STREETS 1978

Gary and Dave

GARY WEEKS
DAVE BECKETT

This duo from London, Ontario, began performing together in 1966 when they auditioned at a United Appeal concert and came in fourth. Both were psychology majors at the University of Western Ontario.

On stage, Gary was the straight man, while Dave played the clown. They sang original compositions, comedy numbers, and hits by such artists as Creedence Clearwater Revival and Three Dog Night. Dave would add his own funny imitations of *Stay Awhile* (The Bells hit) as a fourteen-year-old Viennese choirboy, and an a-capella song called *Linoleum* in which Dave used his own absurd lyrics. Together they would perform Lighthouse's *One Fine Morning* with a kazoo. Their act was widely acclaimed throughout Europe, especially in Holland.

Gary and Dave was one of the first acts signed to Greg Hambleton's Axe Records in April 1972. Their first single was *You Can't Do It Now*, and their biggest hit was *Could You Ever Love Me Again* in 1973. Twelve-year-old Michel Lesage from Montreal recorded a French version of the song in 1974.

After a few more hits, the duo decided to stop recording and began working as pilots for Air Canada in 1975. A year later, they realized that music meant more to them than flying and returned to music on a full-time basis performing again with their new backup group, the Stewart Brothers Band. In 1977 Axe released the album 14 GREATEST HITS. Two years later, they left the music business.

Singles		
Tender Woman 1970		*It Might as Well Rain Until September* 1974
You Send Me 1971		*I May Never See You Again* 1974
Can't You Do It Now 1972		*What Can You Do about It?* 1975
Here It Comes Again 1973		*All in the Past Now* 1975
Could You Ever Love Me Again 1973		*I Can't Find the Words* 1975
I Fell in Love with You Sometime 1974		*It's Alright My Darling* 1977

Albums		
TOGETHER 1973		14 GREATEST HITS 1977
ALL IN THE PAST 1974		

Gary O

Gary O is the son of Billy O'Connor, who had one of the first Canadian music series on Canadian television.

Gary O's musical career goes back to the 1960s when he was a member of the groups Synics, Cat, Liverpool, and Aerial. In Liverpool he and the rest of the group played covers of Beatles songs and released one single, *Dolly*, produced by Ian Thomas. When they grew tired of playing covers, they played under the name of Aerial and had two hit singles, *Easy Love* and *Tears that You Cry*.

After Aerial split up, Gary spent four years on the executive board of the Toronto Musicians's Association and formed the band Kid Rainbow, where he tested his skills as a songwriter. In January of 1981 Gary decided on a solo career and shortened his last name. From his self-titled debut album came a cover of the old Hollies hit, *Pay You Back with Interest*. For Gary O, it was not a hit.

(As Liverpool)
Single *Dolly* 1976

(As Aerial)

Singles	*Easy Love* 1978	*Tears that You Cry* 1980
Albums	IN THE MIDDLE OF THE NIGHT 1978	MANEUVERS 1980

(By Gary O)

Singles	*Pay You Back with Interest* 1981 *I Believe in You* 1981	*Get It While You Can* 1984 *Shades of 45* 1985
Albums	GARY O 1981	PRETTY BOY 1984

Gettysburg Address Led by Mike Hanford, this Winnipeg group began as The Shondells (no relation to the American group fronted by Tommy James). Their first recording on the Winnipeg-based label Eagle Records was *Another Man* in 1965, which was later recorded on Columbia Records in 1966. That same year they had another hit with *I Take It Back*.

In 1967 they changed their name to Gettysburg Address and began recording on the Winnipeg based Franklin label which was distributed by Caravan. The band also changed their singing styles from Hanford's British-influenced lyrics to the Motown sound. *Come Back Baby* was their last hit in February 1968.

(As The Shondells)

Singles	*Another Man* 1966	*I Take It Back* 1967

(As Gettysburg Address)

Singles	*Love Is a Beautiful Thing* 1967 *My Girl* 1967	*Come Back Baby* 1968

Nick Gilder Nick Gilder first gained prominence as a member of the Vancouver quintet Sweeney Todd. After two albums and four singles, they broke up in 1977 when Gilder and Jimmy McCullouch, another member of the group, moved to Los Angeles. Their biggest hit was *Roxy Roller* in 1976, which was written by Gilder and McCullouch.

In 1977 Gilder went on to enjoy a successful solo career. Signed to Chrysalis Records, his debut album was YOU KNOW WHO YOU ARE in 1977.

Not until his second album, CITY NIGHTS did he finally experience success with the song *Hot Child in the City*. It reached number one on Billboard's Hot 100 chart on October 28, 1978.

Gilder went on to record other albums and hit singles but was unable to duplicate the success of his only number one hit.

(As Sweeney Todd)

Singles	*Sweeney Todd Folder* 1976	*Say Hello Say Goodbye* 1976
	Roxy Roller 1976	*If Wishes Were Horses* 1977
Albums	SWEENEY TODD 1975	IF WISHES WERE HORSES 1977

(By Nick Gilder)

Singles	*She's a Star (In Her Own Right)* 1975-76	*Metro Jets* 1980
		Catch 22 1981
	Hot Child in the City 1978	*Prove It* 1981
	Here Comes the Night 1978-79	*Let Me In* 1985
	(You Really) Rock Me 1979	*Footsteps* 1986
Albums	YOU KNOW WHO YOU ARE 1977	FREQUENCY 1979
	CITY NIGHTS 1978	BODY TALK MUZAK 1981

Gilmore Singers

The Gilmore Singers were thirty-nine elementary school students who attended James Gilmore School in Richmond, British Columbia. In 1971 they recorded the song *The Answer Rests upon You* on Rada Records.

The school project was the brainchild of schoolteacher Robert Waugh who started it as a centennial project. Schools and churches immediately requested copies of sheet music to the song when it was aired locally. Rada Records distributed the single nationwide when several radio stations in British Columbia began playing it.

Single *The Answer Rests upon You* 1971

Bobby Gimby

From Cabri, Saskatchewan, Bobby Gimby was born in 1919. His greatest contribution to pop music was *Canada: A Centennial Song*.

Gimby first achieved fame as a member of radio's *Happy Gang*, and between 1958 and 1961 he was a regular on the *Juliette* show on CBC television. During a world tour, he composed *Malaysia Forever*, which later became Malaysia's national anthem. Back in Canada, he was referred to as "The Pied Piper of Canada." The cape he wore as The Pied Piper of Canada was designed by Gimby's daughter Lynn. She also decorated the heraldic trumpet he used when marching with children in each place he visited. Gimby's centennial song united young Canadians from coast to coast. There are more than thirty recorded versions of the song. All the royalties were donated to the

Boy Scouts of Canada.

Today, he leads the band at the Leisure World Retirement Home in North Bay, Ontario.

Singles	*Canada* (with The Young Canada Singers) 1967	*Manitoba Hundred* 1970 *Go British Columbia* 1971

Glass Tiger

AL CONNELLY (*guitarist*) WAYNE PARKER (*bass*)
ALAN FREW (*vocals*) SAM REID (*keyboards*)
MICHAEL HANSON (*drums*)

From Newmarket, Ontario, Glass Tiger was first known as Tokyo, a bar band that toured Southern Ontario for three years before they went through a name change and signed with Capitol Records. Their debut album, THE THIN RED LINE, produced the number one hit single, *Don't Forget Me (When I'm Gone)* in the summer of 1986. Their second single, *Someday*, was also well received.

In 1988, Michael Hanson left the band, and the rest of the group broke up in 1993.

Singles	*Don't Forget Me (When I'm Gone)* 1986 *Someday* 1986 *The Thin Red Line* 1986 *You're What I Look For* 1987 *I Will Be There* 1987 *I'm Still Searching* 1988 *Diamond Sun* 1988 *My Song* 1988	*Send Your Love* 1989 *Watching Worlds Crumble* 1989 *Animal Heart* 1991 *The Rhythm of Your Love* 1991 *My Town* 1991 *Rescued (By the Arms of Love)* 1991-92 *Touch of Your Hand* 1993
Albums/CDs	THE THIN RED LINE 1986 DIAMOND SUN 1988	SIMPLE MISSION 1991 BEST OF THE BEST 1993

Goddo

GREG GODOVITZ (*vocals, bass*) MARTY MORIN (*drums*):
GINO SCARPELLI (*guitar*) Replaced by DOUG INGLIS

Formed in the mid-1970s by former Fludd member Greg Godovitz, this trio from Toronto played for ten years before breaking up in the mid-1980s. Godovitz first worked in a band called Mushroom Castle in 1967 with Buzz Sherman, who later joined Moxy. Godovitz later joined Fludd but left in 1975 to form Goddo.

By 1983 the band had shortened its name by one "d" to Godo and the members were all new: J.F. Leary (guitar), Matt Meehan O'Leary (drums), and Tommy Mack Simpson (bass).

Their only chart success was a remake of the Kingsmen's 1963 hit *Louie Louie* in the summer of 1975. Six years later, they recorded *Pretty Bad Boy* but it was not a national hit. In 1989 the original group reunited to do some concert dates.

Singles	*Louie Louie* 1975	*Pretty Bad Boy* 1981-82
	Fortune in Men's Eyes 1980-81	
Albums/CDs	GODDO 1977	KING OF BROKEN HEARTS 1992
	PRETTY BAD BOYS 1981	

Gogh Van Go   SANDRA LUCIANTONIO   DAN TIERNEY

Daniel Tierney and Sandra Luciantonio first met in 1980 when they were students at the University of Guelph. Tierney, from Montreal, studied biology, while Luciantonia, from Sarnia, the fine arts. It was not until 1985 when they both moved to Montreal that they decided to form a musical group called The Hodads. For the next four years they played the club circuits in Montreal and Toronto. They also opened for such diverse acts as Los Lobos, Chris Isaak, John Hiatt, and The Tragically Hip.

In 1989 The Hodads recorded a two-song, twelve-inch disc featuring *Routine* and *Quand le soleil dit bonjour aux montagnes*. The independent release was charted at many college radio stations across Canada.

In 1991 Sandra and Dan changed their moniker to Gogh Van Go. Signed to Audiogram Records in Montreal, their self-titled debut album was released in February, 1993, produced by Pierre Marchand, whose credits include Sarah McLachlan's *Solace* and The McGarrigle Sisters' *Heartbeats Accelerating*. *Bed Where We Hide* was the first single from Gogh Van Go; the accompanying video was directed by James Di Salvio.

(As The Hodads)
| Singles | *Routine* 1989 |
| | *Quand le soleil dit bonjour aux montagnes* 1989 |

(As Gogh Van Go)
Singles	*Bed Where We Hide* 1993	*Call It Romance* 1994
	Say You Will 1993	
CD	GOGH VAN GO 1993	

Robert Goulet

Born in 1933 in Lawrence, Massachussets, Robert Goulet moved to Edmonton, Alberta, at age ten. His first job was at radio station CKUA in Edmonton as a radio announcer. In 1953 he earned a scholarship to

The Royal Conservatory of Music, but by the late 1950s he had left the Conservatory to pursue other work in radio and TV.

While on vacation in Bermuda in 1958, he was invited by Abe Newborn, agent for Lerner and Lowe, to play the part of Lancelot in *Camelot*. *Camelot* opened at the O'Keefe Centre in November 1958. In 1993 he returned to the O'Keefe to star in *Camelot* as King Arthur.

His other major acting role was in the ABC spy series *Blue Light* in 1966, in which he played David March. He also made guest appearances on the CBS comedy/variety show *Spotlight* in 1967, and ABC's music/comedy series *That's Life* (1968-69).

What Kind of Fool Am I? was his first and biggest hit. Goulet was made a honorary fellow of The Royal Conservatory of Music in Toronto in 1993.

Singles		
What Kind of Fool Am I? 1962	*Summer Sounds* 1965	
My Love Forgive Me 1964		

Albums		
SINCERELY YOURS 1963	ROBERT GOULET'S WONDERFUL
THIS CHRISTMAS I SPEND WITH	WORLD OF CHRISTMAS 1968
YOU 1963	BOTH SIDES NOW 1969
MY LOVE FORGIVE ME 1964	SOUVENIR D'ITALIE 1969
WOMAN WOMAN 1968	I WISH YOU LOVE 1970

Gowan

Before going solo, Gowan formed the group Rheingold when he was seventeen years old. Gowan's first big break came when he was introduced to producer David Tickle, who took him to Ringo Starr's recording studios in England. His self-titled debut album in 1982 was not a big seller but it did receive critical acclaim. His second, STRANGE ANIMAL in 1985, sold well and from it came the singles *A Criminal Mind* and the title track. GREAT DIRTY WORLD, his third, outdid his previous efforts.

Gowan took a three year break from recording before releasing his fourth album, LOST BROTHERHOOD, in 1990. His next album, entitled BUT YOU CAN CALL ME LARRY!, featured a duet with Jann Arden on *Last Laugh* and King Crimson's Robert Fripp on *Last Face*.

Singles	
A Criminal Mind 1985	*Living in the Golden Age* 1987
Strange Animal 1985	*All the Lovers in the World* 1990
Guerilla Soldier 1985	*Lost Brotherhood* 1990
Cosmetics 1986	*Out of a Deeper Hunger* 1990-91
Moonlight Desires 1987	*When There's Time for Love* 1993
Awake the Giant 1987	*Dancing on My Own Ground* 1994

Albums/CDs	LARRY GOWAN 1982	LOST BROTHERHOOD 1990
	STRANGE ANIMAL 1985	BUT YOU CAN CALL ME LARRY! 1993
	GREAT DIRTY WORLD 1987	

Grace Under Pressure

LINDA ELDER (*vocals*) NANCY POWELL (*vocals*)
STEVE HOY (*drums*) VAN WILMOTT (*keyboards*)
BRAD PACK (*guitar*)

This Edmonton quintet became known through the recording of *Belli-To-Belli* which won a local radio contest in 1988. The group was founded in 1985 when British born Van Wilmott recruited Linda Elder and Nancy Powell for a recording session. With the addition of Brad Pack and Steve Hoy, the band established itself on the local Alberta scene with a funky electro-acoustic sound which musical pundits compared to ABBA and Eurthymics.

Single *Belli-To-Belli* 1988

Tommy Graham

Tommy Graham first became involved in the Toronto music scene in 1958 with his high school band. After playing at the Blue Note Club when it opened in 1960, he moved to Los Angeles. In 1963 he returned to Toronto and joined The Big Town Boys who backed up Shirley Matthews on such hits as *Big Town Boy* (1963-64) and *Private Property* (1964). Five years later the group broke up, and Graham began a journey around the world, stopping in India where he became interested in the country's music and took lessons from Ravi Shankar's sarode player, Ali Akbar Kahn.

In 1970 he returned to Canada where he worked with his friend and leading record producer, Brian Aherne. Graham backed up Anne Murray on her international hit *Snowbird*. Paul White, executive producer at Capitol Records, asked Graham if he would like to make a record. His solo debut album, PLANET EARTH, was released in December 1970. Backing him up were studio musicians Skip Beckwith (bass), Ron Rully (drums), Bill Speer (piano), and Buddy Gage (steel guitar). Graham's solo career was short-lived.

(As Big Town Boys)

Singles	*Put You Down* 1965	*Hey Girl Go It Alone* 1966
	It Was I 1965	*My Babe* 1966

(As B.T.B-4)

Singles	*Do It to 'Em* 1967	*Jack Rabbit* 1967

(By Tommy Graham)

Singles	*Things You Say* 1971	*My Happy Song* 1973
	Sahajiya 1971	*Sea Cruise* 1974
	After the Goldrush 1972	

Album   PLANET EARTH 1970

Grapes of Wrath

CHRIS HOOPER (*drums*)   VINCENT JONES (*keyboards*)
TOM HOOPER (*bass*)   KEVIN KANE (*vocals, guitar*)

This quartet began as a punk band called Kill Pigs in Kelowna, British Columbia. When it split up, the Hooper brothers joined another punk band, Gentlemen of Horror, while Kevin Kane played in the group Empty Set. In the spring of 1983, Chris, Tom, and Vincent reunited for a one night engagement and decided to stay together. They named themselves after a John Ford movie, *Grapes of Wrath*, based on the John Steinbeck novel, because Chris was a film buff.

The band moved to Vancouver, where they signed to the independent Nettwerk label and released a self-titled four song EP in 1984; a year later they released the independent album SEPTEMBER BOWL OF GREEN nationwide when Capitol Records inked a distribution deal with Nettwerk.

Their next album, TREE HOUSE, was produced by Tom Cochrane and released in October 1987. Two years later, their album NOW AND AGAIN featured guest performances by Chuck Leavell of the Allman Brothers and "Sneaky" Pete Kleinor of Flying Burrito Brothers and Byrds fame. In August of 1991 their fourth album, THESE DAYS, was recorded at Vancouver's Mushroom Studio and mixed at Abbey Road Studios in London, England.

Their first of several hit singles, *Peace of Mind*, was released in 1987. They continued to have hits until early 1992 when Kevin Kane left the group. Due to legal problems over their name Grapes of Wrath, the remaining members became known as Ginger.

Singles	*Backward Town* 1985	*Do You Want to Tell Me* 1990
	Misunderstanding 1986	*What Was Going through My*
	Peace of Mind 1987	*Head* 1990
	O Lucky Man 1987	*I Am Here* 1991
	All the Things I Wasn't 1989	*You May Be Right* 1991-92

Albums/CDs	SEPTEMBER BOWL OF GREEN 1985	NOW AND AGAIN 1989
	TREEHOUSE 1987	THESE DAYS 1991

The Gravelberrys

ROB GREENWOOD (*drums*) PAUL MEYERS (*vocals, guitar*)
RAY MONTFORD (*guitar*) GLENN OLIVE (*bass*)

Founded by Paul Meyers, brother of Mike Myers, in mid-1991, The Gravelberrys was an offshoot of The Paul Meyers Band. The band's debut independent CD, BOWL OF GLOBES, released in January 1993, produced by Michael-Phillip Wojewoda (Barenaked Ladies). *Wonder Where You Are Tonight* was the first single from the album.

Singles *Wonder Where You Are Tonight* 1993
Rocks and Bones 1993

CD BOWL OF GLOBES 1993

Greaseball Boogie Band

Formed in 1971 in Toronto by Duncan White (a.k.a. King Grease), Greaseball Boogie Band played 1950s rock 'n' roll. They first became famous in the city's downtown clubs, such as the El Mocambo. On stage, King Grease wore a sleeveless T-shirt, spattered jeans, biker boots, and a chain-link belt. As the band started to play Gene Vincent's *Be Bop A Lula*, he squeezed a tube of Brylcreem over his head and belched out loud.

The sextet built up a loyal following on the Southern Ontario club circuit. Their only album was the self-titled GREASEBALL BOOGIE BAND on GRT Records in 1973. The main members of the group were White on vocals, Ray Harrison on keyboards, Wayne Mills on saxophone, John Bride on guitar, and Tommy Frew on drums. Their last show as Greaseball Boogie Band was a Liberal campaign rally with Pierre Trudeau in the spring of 1974.

In 1974 the Greaseball Boogie Band changed its image and name when the nostalgia craze of the early 1970s gave way to disco. They became known as Shooter Review and added The Murphy Sisters, a trio from Winnipeg. The act now played the music of the 1940s and 1950s, such as *Boogie Woogie Bugle Boy* by The Andrews Sisters and *Caldonia* by Louis Jordan.

Their new name was shortened to Shooter, and GRT released their first hit *I Can Dance (Long Tall Glasses)* in 1975, which Leo Sayer also recorded.

Shooter broke up in the late 1970s. Harrison, Mills, and Bride joined Toronto's Cameo Blues Band.

Singles *I Can Dance*   *Hard Times* 1976
 (Long Tall Glasses) 1975   *Standing on the Inside* 1976
Train 1975

Album GREASEBALL BOOGIE BAND 1973

Lorne Greene   Born in Ottawa in 1915, Lorne Greene was best known as Ben Cartwright in the long-running Western TV series *Bonanza* (1959-73). Greene started his radio career in the 1930s at radio station CBO in Ottawa. During World War II he was the "voice of doom" reading the news on the national network. Greene made his first Broadway appearance in 1953 in *The Prescott Proposals* opposite Katherine Cornell.

After starring in a few movies — *The Silver Chalice* (1954), *Peyton Place* (1957), and *The Buccaneer* (1958) — he was offered the part of Ben Cartwright.

In the 1960s he turned to recording, with his best known hit, *Ringo*, charting number one on Billboard's Hot 100 in 1964. When *Bonanza* went off the air, he worked on CTV's Lorne Greene's New Wilderness for five years. He later starred in two short-lived TV series, *Battlestar Galactica* and *Code Red*.

Greene died on September 11, 1987 of complications from an operation for a perforated ulcer.

Singles   *Ringo* 1964   *An Old Tin Cup* 1965
          The Man 1965

Joey Gregorash   This native of Winnipeg started out in music as a teenager when he learned to play the drums. In 1967 he formed his own group, The Mongrels, and went on to host a weekly TV show called *Young as You Are*, while the group had minor success with the hit *Ivy in Her Eyes* in October 1970.

Gregorash was twenty years old when he signed a record contract with Polydor Records. He went to Minneapolis in the spring of 1970 to record two of his own songs, *Stay* and *Tomorrow Tomorrow*, the first of several hits he would have with the label in the early 1970s. He made an unsuccessful comeback in 1987 with the song *Together*.

Singles   *Stay* 1970   *Take the Blindness* 1972
          Tomorrow Tomorrow 1970   *Tell the People* 1972-73
          Jodie 1971   *Liza* 1973
          Don't Let Your Pride Get You   *You've Been Wrong* 1974
             Girl 1971   *Love Is Gonna Bring Us*
          Down by the River 1971   *Together* 1984
          My Love Sings 1972   *Together* 1987
          Bye Bye Love 1972

Albums   NORTH COUNTRY FUNK 1971   TOGETHER 1987

Bobby G. Griffith

Shortly after the release of Bobby G. Griffith's first album, LIVING ON A WISHBONE, on MTCC Records, the label folded. Winnipeg-based Griffith and his manager Jules Rabkin went to the United States and negotiated a single release on Polydor Records in 1971. The song was *709*.

In 1972 Rabkin signed a deal for Griffith with Ranwood Records, which also recorded Lawrence Welk. In Canada, Quality Records distributed Griffith. At the time Bobby's backup group consisted of George Dearling on drums, Lou Fortin on bass, Valentine Bent on lead guitar, and Jimmy Carver on electric piano. His biggest hit was *The Badger's Song* in the fall of 1973.

Singles

Living on a Wishbone 1970
709 1971
The Badger's Song 1973
The Sound of Peace 1973
You Can't Get It All 1974

Give My Love to Lady Canada 1975
Keep an Eye on Your Friends 1975-76

The Guess Who

CHAD ALLAN
BOB ASHLEY
RANDY BACHMAN
BURTON CUMMINGS
JIM KALE
GREG LESKIW
VINCE MASTERS

DON MCDOUGALL
GARY PETERSON
ALLEN SUFOE
DOMENIC TROIANO
BILL WALLACE
KURT WINTER

The story of The Guess Who begins in Winnipeg, Manitoba, in 1957 when original members Jim Kale and Allen Sufoe and two of their friends formed Al and the Silvertones. When Al and another member left in 1958, they were replaced by Randy Bachman and Gary Peterson. The group's first record was *We'll Always Remember*, dedicated to the late Buddy Holly. Bob Burns, who was responsible for getting them on Channel 17 in Winnipeg, became the group's manager.

In 1962 the group changed its name to Chad Allan and the Reflections. But they had to change it again two years later when an American group called The Reflections had a huge hit with *Just like Romeo and Juliet*. The band was then known as Chad Allan and the Expressions. *Shy Guy* was their next single. The year 1964 saw the band sign a contract with Quality Records and record *Till We Kissed* as a first single in January 1965.

Quality Records executive George Struth gave the band the name The Guess Who. Although the group felt that The Guess Who might be confused with The Who from England, the Winnipeg group began to experience a loyal following in the U.S.A. on Scepter Records as well as at home, especially with the release of *Shakin' All Over*, an international hit, in 1965.

Following the release of this song, Chad Allan left to go back to school. He was replaced by Burton Cummings, who at that time was a member of the Devrons, a local Winnipeg band. With a new lead singer The Guess Who continued to make hit records, including Neil Young's *Flying on the Ground Is Wrong* in 1967. *His Girl*, also released in 1967, was a bigger hit in England than at home.

In 1968 Jack Richardson became their new producer and manager. He signed them to his label, Nimbus 9 Productions. In November, *Of a Dropping Pin* was released and in the new year The Guess Who rose to international stardom with the song *These Eyes*, their first million seller.

The Guess Who continued to have more hits, notably *Laughing/Undun* and *No Time*. The spring of 1970 saw *American Woman* become a number one hit on Billboard's Hot 100. It remained there for three weeks. And in 1970 the band played at the White House. For the next five years they toured throughout North America, New Zealand and Australia.

Shortly after the success of the album AMERICAN WOMAN, Bachman left to form Brave Belt. He was replaced by two guitarists, Kurt Winter and Greg Leskiw. Three years later, Kale was replaced by Bill Wallace, and Leskiw by Don McDougall; and in 1974 Winter and MacDougall were replaced by Domenic Troiano.

The Guess Who with Burton Cummings gave its final concert at the Montreal Forum on September 13, 1975. Cummings went on to have a successful solo career in the late 1970s and 1980s. Kale, McDougall, Winter, and drummer Vince Masters began touring as The Guess Who in 1978.

The Guess Who were inducted into the Juno Hall of Fame in 1987.

(As Chad Allan & the Expressions)

Singles   *Tossin' & Turnin'* 1965   *Hey Ho* 1965

(As The Guess Who)

Singles   *Till We Kissed* 1965   *Flying on the Ground Is Wrong*
              Shakin' All Over 1965   1967
              Hurting Each Other 1966   *When Friends Fall Out* 1968
              Believe Me 1966   *Of a Dropping Pin* 1968
              Clock on the Wall 1966   *These Eyes* 1969
              And She's Mine 1966   *Laughing/Undun* 1969
              His Girl 1967   *No Time* 1969-70
              Pretty Blue Eyes 1967   *American Woman/No Sugar*
              This Time Long Ago 1967   *Tonight* 1970

Hand Me Down World 1970
Share the Land 1970
Running Down the Street 1970
Hang On to Your Life 1970-71
Broken-Albert Flasher 1971
Rain Dance 1971
Sour Suite 1971
Life in the Bloodstream 1972
Heartbroken Bopper 1972
Guns Guns Guns 1972
Heaven Only Moved Once Yesterday 1972
Running Back to Saskatoon 1972
Follow Your Daughter Home 1972-73

Bye Bye Babe 1973
Orly 1973
Glamour Boy 1973
Star Baby 1974
Clap for the Wolfman 1974
Dancin' Fool 1974-75
Loves Me like a Brother 1975
I Can't Live without You 1975
Rosanne 1975
When The Band Was Singin' 1975-76
Silver Bird 1976
C'Mon Little Mama 1978
Love Lite 1981
What a Feeling 1981

Albums/CD

SHAKIN' ALL OVER 1965
HEY HO (WHAT YOU DO FOR ME) 1966
IT'S TIME 1966
WHEATFIELD SOUL 1969
SUPER GOLDEN GOODIES 1969
CANNED WHEAT 1969
AMERICAN WOMAN 1970
SHARE THE LAND 1970
BEST OF THE GUESS WHO VOLUME I 1971
SO LONG BANNATYNE 1971
ROCKIN' 1972
LIVE AT THE PARAMOUNT 1972
ARTIFICIAL PARADISE 1973
NUMBER TEN 1973

BEST OF THE GUESS WHO VOLUME II 1973
ROAD FOOD 1974
FLAVOURS 1975
POWER IN THE MUSIC 1975
THE WAY THEY WERE 1976
GREATEST OF THE GUESS WHO 1977
GUESS WHO'S BACK 1978
ALL THIS FOR A SONG 1978
NOW AND NOT THEN 1981
TOGETHER AGAIN 1983
REUNION 1983
GUESS WHO '87 1987
TRACK RECORD: THE GUESS WHO COLLECTION 1988

Keith Hampshire

Born in London, England, in 1945, Keith Hampshire moved with his parents to New York, where they acted in stage and theater, then on to Toronto and Calgary. While growing in Calgary, Keith sang in the local Anglican church choir and took weekly vocal lessons. At age seventeen he performed at a local coffeehouse called The Depression, which attracted such folk talent as David Wiffen, Donna Warner, Will Millar, and Joni Mitchell.

When rock'n'roll became more and more popular, Hampshire decided to form his own group called The Intruders. When it folded, he started another one, Keith and The Bristols. It, too, quickly disbanded. A third group, Keith and The Variations, lasted three years on the club circuit.

After graduating from high school, Hampshire worked at CFCN Radio and Television as a cameraman, then became a disc jockey playing British rock on an after-midnight show, introducing listeners to Brian Poole and The Tremeloes, The Swinging Blue Jeans, The Animals, and The Searchers. In 1966 he applied for a job on Radio Caroline, Amsterdam's 50-kilowatt pirate radio station in the North Sea. For thirteen months he became an English idol with *Keefer's Uprising* morning show and later *Keefer's Commotion* in the afternoon. A year later, radio station CKFH in Toronto hired him as a disc jockey, where he remained for three years.

Through a friend he met producer Bill Misener (ex-Paupers) at RCA and recorded *I Wish I Could Wish Away* which was retitled *Ebenezer*. *Daytime Night-time*, written by Mike Hugg of Manfred Mann, was an immediate smash, along with the follow-up hit, *First Cut Is the Deepest*. In 1974 Hampshire recorded *Hallelujah Freedom*, a hit for Junior Campbell in England.

Since the late 1970s, Keith has made a living singing commercials for a variety of products, such as Aquafresh, Miss Mew, Imperial Margarine, Seven-Up, and Elk's Clothing on radio and television. He returned to the recording studio in 1982 to record his debut album, VARIATIONS, on Freedom Records. The first single from the album, *I Can't Wait too Long*, was not a national hit.

Singles

Ebenezer 1971
Daytime, Night-time 1972
First Cut Is the Deepest 1973
Big Time Operator 1973-74

Forever and Ever (Baby I'm Gonna Be Yours) 1974
Hallelujah Freedom 1974
I Can't Wait too Long 1982

Album THE FIRST CUT 1973

VARIATIONS 1981

Hagood Hardy Born in Indiana in 1937, Hagood Hardy became a professional musician at eighteen years of age, and played in Toronto's House of Hambourg jazz club while attending the University of Toronto. In the early 1950s he played with a group called The Montage.

For the majority of Canadians, vibraphonist and composer Hardy is best known for his international hit *The Homecoming* in 1975, which was originally written in 1972 and produced for a Salada Tea commercial. The song was number one smash instrumental hit in Canada and was charted on Billboard's Hot 100. In 1976 the Canadian Talent Library included *The Homecoming* with other songs on a special disc of Canadian music. Capitol-EMI, which held the world distribution rights, released *The Homecoming* in France and Japan in 1977, where it became an instant hit.

On the heels of this success, Hardy went on to compose music for many TV programs, notably his award-winning score for CBC's *Anne of Green Gables*. In 1992 he performed at the Ottawa International Jazz Festival. He frequently plays at various jazz clubs in Toronto, backed up by Mark Crawford (guitar), Rick Homme (bass), and Barry Holmes.

Singles

Just a Little Lovin' 1971
The Homecoming 1975
Wintertime/Jennifer's Song 1975
Love Theme from Missouri Breaks 1976

The Harlequin Theme (A Time for Love) 1978
Love Song/Sonny's Ragtime 1979
The Birdwalk 1979-80
Working in L.A. 1981

Albums/CDs

STOP 33 1967
HAGOOD HARDY AND MONTAGE (CBC) 1970
HAGOOD HARDY AND MONTAGE (Canadian Talent Library) 1972
THE HOMECOMING 1975
MAYBE TOMORROW 1976
TELL ME MY NAME 1977
REFLECTIONS 1978
THE HAGOOD HARDY COLLECTION 1979

THE CHRISTMAS ALBUM 1979
AS TIME GOES BY 1980
LOVE ME CLOSER 1982
CHASING A DREAM 1983
NIGHT MAGIC 1985
HAGOOD HARDY 1986
ALL MY BEST 1988
ALL MY BEST VOLUME II 1989
MOROCCO 1989

Harem Scarem

MIKE GIONET (*bass*)
HAROLD HESS (*vocals*)

PETE LESPERANCE (*guitars*)
DARREN SMITH (*drums*)

Harem Scarem has been together since 1987. Each member of the band comes from a different musical background. Harold Hess began his career at the age of twelve playing and singing in various bands before he joined a heavy metal group when he was fifteen. Pete Lesperance started playing the guitar at eight and seven years later also joined a heavy metal band that opened for Anvil. He joined Harem Scarem in 1988 after trying to make a living as a guitarist on the road. Mike Gionet has had conservatory training in piano and guitar; he spent his teens playing bass in polka bands and show bands. Darren Smith is an accomplished musician who first met Hess when the two of them were in the band Blind Vengeance. Before Smith joined Harem Scarem, he sang lead vocals and played guitar in various groups. In 1989 Harem Scarem put together an eleven song demo CD and spent the following year writing and recording new material. In 1990 the group negotiated a recording contract with Warner Music Canada, after finishing second in Toronto radio station Q-107's Homegrown Competition. Their self-titled debut album for Warner and first hit single, *Slowly Slippin' Away*, were released in 1991.

| **Singles** | *Slowly Slippin' Away* 1991 | *No Justice* 1993 |
| | *Something to Say* 1992 | *Change Comes Around* 1993 |

| **CDs** | HAREM SCAREM 1991 | MOOD SWINGS 1993 |

Harlequin   GEORGE BELANGER (*vocals*)   JOHN WHITE (*keyboards*):
       JOHN HANNAH (*guitar*):   Replaced by GARY GOLDEN
           Replaced by GLEN WILLOWS   DENTON YOUNG (*drums*):
       RALPH JAMES (*bass*)   Replaced by DAVID BUDZAK

From Winnipeg, Harlequin was formed in 1975 by bassist Ralph James. Signed to Epic Records in 1979, their debut album, VICTIM OF A SONG, was first issued on the now defunct Inter Global Music label. All of the songs were written by Belanger and Glen Willows. Harlequin had a string of hits in the 1980s.

Singles	*Survive* 1979	*Superstitious Feeling* 1982
	You Are the Light 1980	*I Did It for Love* 1982
	Innocence 1981	*Take this Heart* 1984
	Thinking of You 1981	*It's No Mystery* 1986

| **Albums/CDs** | VICTIM OF A SONG 1979 | HARLEQUIN'S GREATEST HITS 1986 |
| | LOVE CRIMES 1980 | |

Michael Tighe

Andrew Catlin

Jann Arden
The Bells
Bryan Adams
April Wine

The Box
Paul Anka
Alanis
The Band

Andrew MacNaughtan

Elliott Landy

Victoria Pearson

Chick Rice

Joseph Ciancio

Céline Dion
Bruce Cockburn
Barney Bentall
 and the
 Legendary Hearts
Ronnie Hawkins
Bobby Curtola

Graham Kennedy

Andrew MacNaughtan

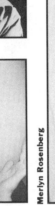

Merlyn Rosenberg

Andrew Cash
Meryn Cadell
Jane Child
Bootsauce
John Allan Cameron
Shirley Eikhard

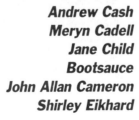

Kevin Westenberg

Andrew MacNaughtan

Andrew MacNaughtan

Lincoln Clarkes

Mitsou
The Grapes of Wrath
The Boomers
Doughboys
54-40

Denise Grant

Chris Chapman

Glass Tiger
Rik Emmett
Canada Goose
Gogh Van Go
Gowan

The Guess Who
Figgy Duff
Corey Hart
Spirit of the West

Denise Grant

Peggy Sirota

Raeanne Holoboff

Moshe Brakha

Denise Grant

Rick MacInnis

Albert Sanchez

Sass Jordan
Paul Janz
Haywire
k. d. lang

Harmonium

PIERRE DAIGNEAULT (*flute, piccolo, soprano sax, clarinet*)
SERGE FIORI (*guitar, flute, zither harp, bass drum, vocals*)
SERGE LOCAT (*piano, mellotron, synthesizer*)
MICHEL NORMANDEAU (*guitar, accordion, vocals*)
LOUIS VALOIS (*bass guitar, electric piano, vocals*)

The origins of Montreal's Harmonium go back to 1973 when Serge Fiori, Michel Normandeau and Louis Valois formed a trio. Like most groups in Quebec in the early 1970s, their popularity began on the coffeehouse circuit of Old Montreal and university campuses. During the summer of 1974, they played to packed houses at Place des Arts and the Sports Centre of the University of Montreal. Quality Records eventually signed them, releasing two albums, HARMONIUM and LES CINQ SAISONS, in 1974 and 1975.

The band broke up in 1980. Six years later, Serge Fiori went solo, and in 1986 Polygram Records released his self-titled debut album. Michel Normandeau also had a brief solo career in 1979 with the release of his album JOUER on Polydor Records.

Albums

HARMONIUM 1974	L'HEPTADE D'HARMONIUM 1977
LES CINQ SAISONS 1975	EN TOURNEE 1980

Corey Hart

Born in 1957, Corey Hart grew up in his native Quebec, Spain, Mexico, and Florida. When he was a teenager, he approached Montreal record companies with cassettes of his songs without success. At seventeen, he ran away from home to live in New York, where he became friends with members of Billy Joel's backup band. He later returned to Montreal, and in 1983 signed a contract with Aquarius Records.

Sunglasses at Night was his debut hit single in the spring of 1984. In 1985 *Never Surrender* became his biggest chart hit. Hart appeared on the cover of the December 12, 1987 issue of *TV Guide* to promote his first CBC concert special.

Singles

Sunglasses at Night 1984	*Can't Help Falling in Love* 1986-87
It Ain't Enough 1984	
She Got the Radio 1984	*Take My Heart* 1987
Lamp at Midnight 1985	*Too Good to Be Enough* 1987
Never Surrender 1985	*Dancing with My Mirror* 1987
Boy in the Box 1985	*In My Soul* 1988
Everything in My Heart 1985	*Spot You in a Coalmine* 1988
Eurasian Eyes 1986	*Still in Love* 1989
I Am By Your Side 1986	*A Little Love* 1990

Bang! (Starting Over) 1990
Rain on Me 1990
92 Days of Rain 1992

Baby When I Call Your Name
  1992
Always 1992
I Want (Cool Cool Love) 1993

CDs FIRST OFFENSE 1984
BOY IN THE BOX 1985
FIELDS OF FIRE 1986
YOUNG MAN RUNNING 1988

BANG 1990
THE SINGLES COLLECTION
  (1983-1990) 1991
ATTITUDE & VIRTUE 1992

The Haunted BOB BURGESS (*bass, vocals*)
PIERRE FAUBERT (*guitar*):
  Replaced by
  ALLAN BIRMINGHAM
TIM FORSYTHE (*organ*)
GLEN HOLMES (*bass*):
  Replaced by MASON SHEA,
MICHAEL ST. GERMAIN

JURGEN PETER (*guitar*)
JIM ROBERTSON (*vocals*)
PETER SYMES (*drums*):
  Replaced by BRIAN ROBERTS,
DAVE WYNNE

Formed in 1963 in Montreal as The Blue Jays, an instrumental group whose style of music was similar to The Ventures, the band soon changed its name to The Haunted.

Jurgen Peter founded the band at his home in Chateauguy, a suburb of Montreal, and over a decade members came and went. Allan Birmingham replaced Pierre Faubert on lead guitar. Drummer Peter Symes was replaced by Brian Roberts, who in turn left to join The Raving Madd, replaced by Dave Wynne. Michael St. Germain, formerly from The Beat Boys, joined on bass but left with Bob Burgess to join The Esquires in Ottawa. Burgess later returned to The Haunted; St. Germain formed his own band, The Cavemen. Pierre Faubert and his brother Gilbert later formed their own band, Sir Bradley and the Screams, with Glen Holmes and Greg Tomlinson

On January 3, 1966, The Haunted won a battle of the bands contest at the Montreal Forum. First prize was a contract with Quality Records. Their first hit single for the label was *1-2-5* in the summer of 1966; their second, *I Can Only Give You Everything*, followed in the fall. The Haunted broke up in 1970.

Singles *1-2-5* 1966
I Can Only Give You Everything 1966

Album THE HAUNTED 1967

The Hawks (See The Band)

Ronnie Hawkins

This Arkansas-born singer has left an indelible mark on the Canadian music scene. Born in 1935, he first came to Canada in 1958 and adopted it as his new home three years later when he married a Canadian woman in Toronto. He then brought his band up from Memphis, Tennessee and formed his own label, Hawk, to promote Canadian talent.

Many Canadian artists and groups have received their big break with Hawkins, including Bobby Curtola, The Four Fables, Ray Hutchinson, Larry Lee, King Biscuit Boy, and Toby Lark. His influence has been felt by John Kay (Sparrows and later Steppenwolf), Robbie Lane, and of course, The Band.

Hawkins himself had several hits in the late 1950s and early 1960s with his backup band The Hawks, later Levon & The Hawks. Ronnie Hawkins remains one of Canada's most sought after performers.

Singles

Forty Days 1959
Mary Lou 1959
Southern Love 1960
The Ballad of Cheryl Chessman 1960
Clara/Lonely Hours 1960
Summertime/Mister & Mississippi 1961
Ruby Baby/Hay Ride 1961
Cold Cold Heart 1961
I Feel Good/Come Love 1961
Bo Diddley/Who Do You Love 1963
High Blood Pressure 1963

Get My Mojo Working 1964
Goin' to the River 1965
The Stones I Throw 1965
Home from the Forest 1967-68
Reason to Believe 1968
Go Go Lisa Jane 1968
Down in the Alley 1970
Bitter Green 1970
Patricia 1971
Cora Mae 1972
Lonesome Town 1972
Lady Came from Baltimore 1976
(Stuck In) Lodi 1981

Albums/CDs

RONNIE HAWKINS 1959
MR. DYNAMO 1960
FOLK BALLADS 1960
SONGS OF HANK WILLIAMS 1960
THE RETURN OF THE HAWK
  (reissued in 1976) 1967
RONNIE HAWKINS 1967
RONNIE HAWKINS 1969
BEST OF RONNIE HAWKINS 1970
RONNIE HAWKINS 1970
THE HAWK 1971

ROCK AND ROLL RESURRECTION
  1972
THE GIANT OF ROCK AND ROLL
  1974
THE HAWK 1979
SOLD OUT 1979
LEGEND IN HIS SPARE TIME 1981
THE HAWK AND ROCK 1983
MAKING IT AGAIN 1984
HELLO AGAIN...MARY LOU 1987

Haywire MARVIN BIRT (*guitar*)   DAVID RASHED (*keyboards*)
SEAN KILBRIDE (*drums*)   RON SWITZER (*bass*)
PAUL MACAUSLAND (*vocals*)

This band from Charlottetown, P.E.I. was originally a quartet when they formed in 1982. They later added Sean Kilbride on drums to make it a five man band. Constant touring tightened their sound and they quickly became one of the most popular acts in the Atlantic Provinces.

In 1984 they won Q104 Halifax's homegrown contest which resulted in the release of a five-song EP in June 1985. Signed to Attic Records in January 1986, their debut album BAD BOYS went on to sell more than 100,000 copies. The group's popularity was acknowledged by the readers of *Music Express* magazine who voted them Best New Group of 1986.

The group's producer, Brian Allen, was a composer and guitarist for five years with the band Toronto.

In 1987 they represented the nation at the Yamaha World Popular Song Festival in Tokyo and won the Golden Award for Best Song.

By the end of 1987, their second album JUST DON'T STAND THERE had been released. Attic Records released a greatest hits album by the group in the fall of 1993. Haywire's biggest hit was *Buzz* in 1992.

Singles *Bad Bad Boy* 1986   *Fire* 1988
Standing in Line 1986   *Operator Central* 1989-90
Shot in the Dark 1986   *Short End of a Wishbone* 1990
Dance Desire 1987   *Taken the Pain* 1991
Black and Blue 1987-88   *Buzz* 1992
Thinkin' about the Years 1988 *Wanna Be the One* 1992

Albums/CDs BAD BOYS 1986   GET OFF 1992
DON'T JUST STAND THERE 1987 WIRED: THE BEST OF HAYWIRE 1993
NUTHOUSE 1991

The Headpins AB BRYANT   BRIAN MACLEOD
MATT FRENETTE   DENISE MCCANN:
Replaced by DARBY MILLS

Founded in 1980 by Chilliwack's Brian MacLeod and Ab Bryant, The Headpins was a Vancouver quartet who first played part-time for fun. Between live performances, they went through six drummers, two guitarists, three bassists, and two vocalists. On stage, they were backed up by Scott Reid, Dave Reimer, and Bernie Aubin. When Denise McCann did not work out as the band's vocalist, she was replaced by Darby Mills, a twenty-two-year-old from Vernon, British Columbia. During this time, MacLeod and Bryant remained members of Chilliwack and did double duty until the group's last album, OPUS X, came out in 1983.

The Headpins' debut album TURN IT LOUD on Solid Gold Records sold well when it was released in 1982, as did the follow-up, LINE OF FIRE, in 1983. Their third, HEAD OVER HEELS, was released in the fall of 1985 on MCA Records. The Headpins broke up in 1986.

Singles		
Don't It Make Ya Feel 1982		*Just One More Time* 1984
Celebration 1983		*Staying All Night* 1985

Albums/CD		
TURN IT LOUD 1982		HEAD OVER HEELS 1985
LINE OF FIRE 1983		GREATEST HITS 1988

Jeff Healey Band

JEFF HEALEY (*guitar, vocals*)   JOE ROCKMAN (*bass, keyboards*)
MISCHKE MATTHEWS (*vocals*)   WASHINGTON SAVAGE (*keyboards*)
TUKU MATTHEWS (*vocals*)   TOM STEPHEN (*drums*)

Blind at the age of one, Jeff Healey has been playing the lap top guitar since he was three years old. His virtuoso technique has been acknowledged by blues guitarist B.B. King when he and Healey played together at a Vancouver music festival in 1986. The late Stevie Ray Vaughn, who was also a close friend, said that Healy would revolutionize guitar playing.

In 1982 Healey recorded an independent video called *Adriana* which was played on MuchMusic. Three years later at Grossman's, a small Toronto nightclub, the Jeff Healey Band came together when bassist Joe Rockman and drummer Tom Stephen decided to join forces. After signing a record deal with BMG Music Canada Inc. and releasing their debut album SEE THE LIGHT, in 1988, they soon established themselves as a hot new Canadian group.

MGM/UA in Hollywood invited Healey to star in the film *Road House* opposite Patrick Swayze. Its box office success helped draw international attention to Healey and his band.

In 1990 came their second album, HELL TO PAY, featuring a guest appearance by ex-Beatle George Harrison on a cover version of *While My Guitar Gently Weeps*. The first single, *I Think I Love You too Much*, featured Mark Knopfler of Dire Straits. The Jeff Healey Band's biggest hit was the pop ballad, *Angel Eyes*.

Their third album, FEEL THIS, marked a new beginning for the band with the addition of keyboardist Washington Savage and vocalists Mischke and Tuku Matthews.

In addition to writing music, Jeff Healey hosts his own radio show on the CBC network called *My Kinda Jazz*, featuring songs from the artist's own collection of 78s and CD reissues.

Singles

Adrianna 1982
See the Light 1988
Confidence Man 1988
My Little Girl 1988
Angel Eyes 1989
While My Guitar Gently Weeps 1989

I Think I Love You too Much 1990
Cruel Little Number 1992-93
Heart of an Angel 1993
Lost in Your Eyes 1993
It Could All Get Blown Away 1993
Leave the Light On 1993
You're Coming Home 1994

CDs

SEE THE LIGHT 1988
HELL TO PAY 1990

FEEL THIS 1992

Heart

ANN WILSON (*vocals*)
NANCY WILSON (*vocals*)

ROGER FISHER (*guitarist*)
STEVE FOSSEN (*bass*)

Fronted by Ann and Nancy Wilson, Heart established themselves in 1976 with the album DREAMBOAT ANNIE and the single *Crazy on You* on Mushroom Records. By 1979, the band had sold in excess of 10 million copies of their albums. Although the two sisters were born in Seattle, Washington, they adopted Canada as their new home and were given landed immigrant status. They are widely acknowledged, though, as progenitors of the Seattle "grunge" scene.

Their music continued to draw sell-out crowds throughout the 1980s. In 1993 the Wilson sisters became members of a new group called The Lovemongers. Their first hit, *Battle of Evermore*, on Capitol Records was written by veteran rockers Jimmy Page and Robert Plant. That same year they released the album DESIRE WALKS ON as Heart.

Singles

Magic Man 1975
Crazy on You 1976
Magic Man 1976
Dreamboat Annie 1977
Barracuda 1977
Tell It Like It Is 1981
This Man Is Mine 1982
What about Love 1985
Never 1985
These Dreams 1986

Nothin' at All 1986
If Looks Could Kill 1986
Alone 1987
Who Will You Run To 1987
There's the Girl 1987
I Want You So Bad 1988
All I Wanna Do Is to Make Love to You 1990
I Didn't Want to Need You 1990

Albums/CDs

DREAMBOAT ANNIE 1976
LITTLE QUEEN 1977
MAGAZINE 1978
DOG & BUTTERFLY 1978
BEBE LE STRANGE 1980
GREATEST HITS LIVE 1980

PRIVATE AUDITION 1982
PASSIONWORKS 1983
HEART 1985
BAD ANIMALS 1987
BRIGADE 1990
DESIRE WALKS ON 1993

Helix   DARYL GRAY (*bass, keyboards*)   GREG "FRITZ" HINZ (*drums*):
PAUL HACKMAN (*guitar*)   Replaced by BRENT and
BRIAN VOLLNER (*vocals*)   BRIAN DOERNER

This London-Kitchener based heavy metal group has released several albums on Capitol Records since they organized in 1975. Their eighth, BACK FOR ANOTHER TASTE featured songs that reflected the band's roots.

After the release of this album, Greg "Fritz" Hinz left and was replaced by two new members, Brent and Brian Doerner. In July 1992, lead guitarist Paul Hackman died of injuries suffered in an accident when the group's van flipped on the Coquihalla Highway in British Columbia.

In 1993, Helix released a new album on Aquarius Records called IT'S A BUSINESS DOING PLEASURE, featuring Kim Mitchell on *Sleeping in the Doghouse Again* and a duet with Lee Aaron called *Look Me Straight in the Heart*. The first single from the album was *That Day Is Gonna Come*, a tribute to the late Paul Hackman. The accompanying video for the song was comprised of Super 8 home movies that were shot on the road between 1976 and 1982.

Singles   *Don't Hide Your Love* 1980   *Wild in the Streets* 1987
It's too Late 1981   *The Storm* 1990
Rock You 1984   *Runnin' Wild in the 21st Century*
(Make Me Do) Anything You   1990
   Want 1985   *Good to the Last Drop* 1991
Deep Cuts the Knife 1985   *That Day Is Gonna Come* 1993
The Kids Are All Shakin' 1985   *Tug of War* 1993

Albums/CDs   BREAKING LOOSE 1980   WILD IN THE STREETS 1987
WHITE LACE AND BLACK   OVER 60 MINUTES WITH . . . HELIX
   LEATHER 1981   1989
NO REST FOR THE WICKED 1983   BACK FOR ANOTHER TASTE 1990
WALKIN' THE RAZOR'S EDGE   IT'S A BUSINESS DOING PLEASURE
   1984   1993
LONG WAY TO HEAVEN 1985

Hemingway Corner   JOHNNY DOUGLAS (*bass, lead guitar, percussion, background vocals*)
DAVID MARTIN (*rhythm guitar, lead vocals*)

Because of the sound of their acoustic guitars, Hemingway Corner has been compared to Crosby, Stills, Nash and Young, America, the Indigo Girls, and R.E.M.

David Martin hails from Atlanta, Georgia. He lived in Nashville for several years where he honed his craft as a songwriter before moving to Los Angeles. Johnny Douglas is from Toronto. He left Los Angeles to set up roots in Nashville to concentrate on his songwriting. The two met while writing songs for Sony Music and began working together in December 1992.

Their self-titled debut album on Epic/Sony came out in 1993. The first single was *Man on a Mission*.

Singles	*Man on a Mission* 1993	*Love Love Love* 1994
	So Long JFK 1993	

CD	HEMINGWAY CORNER 1993

Pat Hervey

Pat Hervey was one of Canada's first successful female singing stars. She grew up in Toronto and sang as a hobby through her high school years. It was not until she performed at an amateur rock 'n' roll show with disc jockey Al Boliska that success began to come her way. Boliska put her in touch with the local CBC-TV station, which signed her as a regular on the network shows *Holiday Ranch* and *Country Hoedown*.

Producer Art Snider was instrumental in getting her to record on his own label, Chateau Records. The result was her first hit, *Mr. Heartache*, in 1962. In the mid-1960s she gave up show business to raise a family.

Singles	*Mr. Heartache* 1962	*Walking in Bonnie's Footsteps* 1964
	A Mother's Love/Heaven for Awhile 1962	*Think about Me* 1965
	Tears of Misery 1963	*He Belongs to Yesterday* 1965

Dan Hill

Born in 1954, Dan Hill, from Don Mills, Ontario, got his start in the music business when he finished Grade 12. He had been writing songs since he was fourteen and sent a tape of six of them to RCA. A month later at age eighteen he signed his first record contract but success did not come him until 1975 when he recorded *You Make Me Want to Be* for GRT Records.

His biggest hit to date is *Sometimes When We Touch*, recorded in 1977. Written by Hill and American songwriter Barry Mann, it was number one in Canada, Australia, and ten other countries. Hill's next big success came in 1987 when he recorded a duet called *Can't We Try* with Vonda Sheppard. After its success he took a break from recording to concentrate on his songwriting. He wrote songs for such artists as Jeffrey Osborne, George Benson, Tina Turner, and Céline Dion.

In the fall of 1991 Hill reunited with his old friend Russ Regan, co-founder of Quality Records. The result of their new collaboration was the album DANCE OF LOVE and its first single *I Fall All Over Again*.

Singles		
You Make Me Want to Be 1975	*I'm Just a Man* 1982
Growing Up 1975	*Can't We Try* (with
You Say You're Free 1976	Vonda Sheppard) 1987
Hold On 1976	*Never Thought (That I Could*
Sometimes When We Touch 1977	*Love)* 1988
Let the Song Last Forever 1978	*Carmelia* 1988
All I See Is Your Face 1978	*Unborn Heart* 1989
Dark Side of Atlanta 1978	*I Fall All Over Again* 1991-92
Hold On to the Night 1979	*Is It Really Love* 1992
When You Smile 1979-80	*Hold Me Now* 1992
I Still Reach for You 1980	*Flirting with a Heartache* 1993
Don't Give Up on Love 1981	*Healing Power of Love* 1993

Albums/CDs		
DAN HILL 1975	LOVE IN THE SHADOWS 1983
HOLD ON 1976	DAN HILL 1987
LONGER FUSE 1977	REAL LOVE 1989
FROZEN IN THE NIGHT 1978	THE DAN HILL COLLECTION 1989
IF DREAMS HAD WINGS 1980	DANCE OF LOVE 1991
PARTIAL SURRENDER 1981	

Honeymoon Suite

DAVE BETTS	DERRY GREHAN
RAY COBURN	GARY LALONDE
JOHNNY DEE	

From Niagara Falls, Ontario, Honeymoon Suite signed with WEA in 1984 and within two years established themselves as one of Canada's most popular rock groups. Their first hit single was *New Girl Now*.

In 1986 they achieved success simultaneously in U.S.A. and Canada when their hit single *Feel It Again* started climbing up the charts. Their next hit, *What Does It Take*, was featured in an episode of NBC's *Miami Vice* and the soundtrack of the Warner Bros. movie, *One Crazy Summer*.

After fifteen hit singles, the group changed management and Dave Betts and Gary LaLonde left. In 1991 they released MONSTERS UNDER

THE BED and in 1992 HONEYMOON SUITE: THE SINGLES.

Singles		
New Girl Now 1984		*It's Over Now* 1988
Burning in Love 1985		*Love Changes Everything* 1988
Stay in the Light 1985		*Lookin' Out for Number One* 1988
Wave Babies 1985		*Still Lovin' You* 1989
Feel It Again 1986		*Long Way* 1990
What Does It Take 1986		*Say You Don't Love Me* 1990-91
All Along You Knew 1987		*The Road* 1991-92
Lethal Weapon 1987		

Albums/CDs HONEYMOON SUITE 1984   MONSTERS UNDER THE BED 1991
THE BIG PRIZE 1986   HONEYMOON SUITE: THE SINGLES
RACING AFTER MIDNIGHT 1988   1992

Gregory Hoskins and the Stick People COLEEN ALLEN (*saxophones*) GEORGE CIVELLO (*keyboards, vocals*) MIKE FABELLO (*bass*) GREGORY HOSKINS (*guitars, vocals*) LYNN SIMMONS (*voice*) MICHAEL SPENCER-ARSCOTT (*drums*)

Gregory Hoskins was born in Chateauguay, Quebec, in 1964, and moved with his family to a small town outside Newmarket, Ontario when he was nine. At fifteen he formed his first group which played Harry Chapin and Valdy songs at a high school coffeehouse. Hoskins moved to Toronto and with his musician friends founded Gregory Hoskins and the Stick People.

In 1990 they became the first act to sign with True North Records in six years. Their debut album MOON COME UP, was released in February 1991. From it came the Top Ten single *Neighbourhood*. On the road, they have opened for The Indigo Girls, The Neville Brothers, and Sarah McLachlan.

Sony released their second album, RAIDS ON THE UNSPEAKABLE in 1993. *Dance of the Vulnerable* and *Let the World Call You Crazy* were the first two singles.

Singles	
Neighbourhood 1991	*Dance of the Vulnerable* 1993
Let Her Go 1991	*Let the World Call You Crazy* 1993
Labelling Blues 1991	

CDs MOON COME UP 1991   RAIDS ON THE UNSPEAKABLE 1993

Lorence Hud An accomplished guitar player and pianist, Lorence Hud studied music at the University of Saskatchewan and signed a contract with A&M Records in 1972. He enjoyed success with *Sign of the Gypsy*

Queen which reached number 16 on RPM's Top 100 singles chart.

Singles	*Sign of the Gypsy Queen* 1972-73	*Out on the Road (Rollin' Home)* 1974-75
	Master of Pantomime 1973	*Love You All Night Long* 1975
	Guilty of Rock'n'Roll 1974	*(Belly Up to the Bar) Flashing Signs & Neon Lights* 1975
Albums	LORENCE HUD 1972	DANCIN' IN MY HEAD 1973

Humphrey & the Dumptrucks

HUMPHREY DUMPTRUCK
MICHAEL TAYLOR

MICHAEL ("BEAR") MILLER

Humphrey and the Dumptrucks were formed in 1967 and soon established themselves as one of Canada's best country, folk, and bluegrass groups. They hailed from Saskatoon, Saskatchewan.

In 1975 they wrote a country and western opera called *Cruel Tears*, a modern version of Shakespeare's *Othello*. Music and lyrics were written by poet and playwright Ken Mitchell and the members of the group. The opera opened in Saskatchewan in 1975 and finished in Toronto two-and-a-half years later.

Humphrey and the Dumptrucks made inroads on the pop charts with two hits in 1971: *Man from the City* and *Six Days of Paper Ladies*. A third, *Snowball*, was charted as a country hit.

Singles	*Man from the City* 1971	*Snowball* 1973
	Six Days of Paper Ladies 1971	
Albums	SIX DAYS OF PAPER LADIES 1971	GOPHER SUITE 1975
	HOT SPIT 1972	SONGS FROM CRUEL TEARS 1978
	SASKATOON 1973	

Ian and Sylvia

Ian Tyson
Sylvia Fricker

Ian and Sylvia have been an integral part of the Canadian music scene since the late 1950s. They were also one of the first duos to make it big in the U.S.A. with their songs. Born in 1933, Ian Tyson's career goes back to 1956 when he performed at the Heidelberg Café in Vancouver. He also played guitar in a rock band called The Seasonal Stripes in southern British Columbia before moving to Toronto in 1959. There he sang blues with actor Don Francks and folk music with Sylvia Fricker, his future wife. Born in 1940, Sylvia Fricker left her hometown of Chatham, Ontario, in 1949 with aspirations of becoming a singer. She ended up in Toronto where her repertoire included traditional ballads.

Ian and Sylvia became a team in 1959 and five years later they were married. They performed at the Mariposa Folk Festival for the first time in 1961 and later toured folk clubs in New York and Chicago. Their second single, *Four Strong Winds*, was released in 1964 and was an instant hit. By 1967 they had become one of the nation's top folk duos. During Canada's centennial year they played to packed houses when they toured Canadian Army bases.

In 1968 they decided to form their own backup group, The Great Speckled Bird. For the next eight years they played country rock instead of traditional folk. Ian and Sylvia made their last public appearance together in 1975, and The Great Speckled Bird split up a year later.

In 1986 they were reunited at the Kingswood Music Theatre for one concert which was taped by the CBC network for broadcast. Their unique harmonies were in evidence once again as both old and new fans heard what was once one of the most influential folk acts in Canada.

Since their breakup, they have each carved out successful careers in the country field.

Singles

House of Cards 1962	*Creators of Rain* 1971
Four Strong Winds 1963	*More Often than Not* 1971
You Were on My Mind 1964	*Salmon in the Sea* 1972
Lovin' Sound 1967	*Calgary* 1973

Albums/CDs

IAN & SYLVIA 1962	NASHVILLE 1968
FOUR STRONG WINDS 1963	FULL CIRCLE 1968
NORTHERN JOURNEY 1964	GREAT SPECKLED BIRD 1969
EARLY MORNIN' RAIN 1965	IAN & SYLVIA'S GREATEST HITS
PLAY ONE MORE 1966	VOLUME I 1969
SO MUCH FOR DREAMING 1967	IAN & SYLVIA'S GREATEST HITS
LOVIN' SOUND 1967	VOLUME II 1970
BEST OF IAN & SYLVIA 1968	IAN & SYLVIA 1971

YOU WERE ON MY MIND 1972   THE BEST OF IAN & SYLVIA 1973

Idle Eyes

TAD CAMPBELL (*vocals*)   GLENN R. SMITH (*guitar*):
MILES FOX HILL (*bass*)   Replaced by SCOTTY HALL
PHIL ROBERTSON (*drums*)   JOHN WEBSTER (*keyboards*)
                                                    Replaced by BRUCE MACKENZIE

Vancouver-based Idle Eyes joined together in the early 1980s. Bruce Mackenzie joined the group in 1986 as a replacement for John Webster, while Scotty Hall replaced Glenn Smith. Tad Campbell had once played professional hockey and performed in Australia with an early incarnation of Idle Eyes.

Their self-titled debut album came out in 1985 featuring the first single *Tokyo Rose*.

Singles   *Tokyo Rose* 1985   *Blue Train* 1989
                    All Day 1985   *Midnight Sun* 1993
                    Sandra 1986

Albums   IDLE EYES 1985   STANDING AT THE EDGE 1988
                    LOVE'S IMPERFECTION 1986

Idyl Tea

HENRY ENGEL (*bass, vocals*)   IAN MARTIN (*guitar*)
EVERETT LAROI (*guitar, vocals*)   CRAIG METCALFE (*drums, percussion*)

The origins of this Edmonton-based group go back to the early 1980s when the original three members were part of the band Route 66, an alternative rock group that developed a following on the campus circuit. In 1986 they recorded their first EP, HOW I SEE THIS TABLE, featuring the underground hit, *Awfully Nice Eyes*. Three years later came their self-titled album, IDYL TEA. *Oh Brother* was its first single and video.

Singles   *Awfully Nice Eyes* 1987   *Oh Brother* 1990

Album   IDYL TEA 1990

I Mother Earth

EDWIN (*vocals*)   CHRISTIAN TANNA (*drums*)
BRUCE GORDON (*bass*)   JAGORI TANNA (*guitar*)

From Toronto, I Mother Earth formed in September 1990 to play 1960s rock inspired by the music of Pink Floyd, Santana, and Led Zeppelin.

Brothers Christian and Jagori Tanna began playing in their parents' basement and graduated to a number of garage bands until mid-1989 when they met Edwin, who became vocalist for the group. Bruce Gordon made it a foursome when his previous band Roctopus broke up. Signed to EMI, their first album, DIG, was released in 1993. The first single and video was *Rain Will Fall.*

Singles   *Rain Will Fall* 1993   *So Gently We Go* 1994

CD   DIG 1993

The Infidels   MOLLY JOHNSON (*vocals*)
NORMAN ORENSTEIN (*guitar*)

This Toronto band, fronted by Molly Johnson, have been together since 1980 when they were first known as Alta Moda. The group's sound is a combination of rock, funk, rhythm and blues, and jazz. The name Infidels refers to the various musical influences that comprise their sound.

Molly Johnson and Norman Orenstein have known each other since high school. Johnson lived above the infamous Cameron House Pub and sang jazz and rhythm and blues to help pay the bills, while Orenstein played guitar in various local bands.

As Alta Moda they had minor success in 1988 with the hit *Julian*. As The Infidels, their self-titled debut album on I.R.S. Canada was released in 1991. From it came their first single, *100 Watt Bulb*. In January 1993 the duo joined Meryn Cadell in a video of the funk/dance/rock song *Courage*. Written by the Infidels, it was part of a campaign to promote sustainable development and the responsible use of our resources.

Singles   *100 Watt Bulb* 1991   *Without Love* 1992
          Celebrate 1991-92

CD   THE INFIDELS 1991

Influence   JACK GEISINGER (*bass*)   ANDREW KEILER (*vocals*)
BOBO ISLAND (*organ, piano*)   WALTER ROSSI (*guitar*)
LOUIS CAMPBELL MCKELVEY   DAVE WYNNE (*drums*)
   (*guitar*)

Walter Rossi, a member of Influence, began his career as as one of the Soul Mates in 1965 and then toured as a sideman with Wilson Pickett. In 1967-68 Rossi joined Influence, a Montreal-based band that played in Toronto and New York.

During the short time that Influence was together, they made one album which featured the mini-opera *Man Birds of Prey*. It was released in 1968, the same year the band broke up. Rossi went on to play in the Buddy Miles Express and Luke and The Apostles before forming his own short-lived band, Charlee, in 1972.

Album	INFLUENCE	1968

The Irish Descendants

D'ARCY BRODERICK   CON O'BRIEN
LARRY MARTIN   RONNIE POWER

The Irish Descendants, a Celtic band from from St. John's, Newfoundland, has a large following in Atlantic Canada. Their first independent album, MISTY MORNING SHORE, was released in July 1991.

During the next two years, the Irish Descendants performed to a sold out show at St. John's Arts and Culture Centre; participated in Canada's Greatest Party on July 1, 1992 which was televised nationally by MuchMusic; and appeared at the International Celtic Festival (1992) in Halifax as well as the Mariposa Folk Festival (1993) in Toronto.

They signed an international recording deal with Warner Music Canada in August 1993, and the first single from their album LOOK TO THE STARS was *Useta Love Her*, written by the Irish band The Saw Doctors.

Single *Useta Love Her* 1993

Albums/CDs MISTY MORNING SHORE 1991   LOOK TO THE STARS 1993

The Irish Rovers

JIMMY FERGUSON (*vocals*)   JOE MILLAR (*accordion, bass*)
WILCIL MCDOWELL (*accordion*) WILL MILLAR (*vocals, guitar,*
GEORGE MILLAR (*guitar*)   *banjo*)

The Irish Rovers formed in Calgary, Alberta, in 1964. The band was comprised of brothers Will and George Millar, their cousin Joe Millar, and Jimmy Ferguson. All were born in Northern Ireland.

They started performing at The Depression coffeehouse in Calgary. Four years later they signed a recording contract with Decca Records (now MCA). Their first single penned by Shel Silverstein was *The Unicorn*, which became an international hit and sold over 8 million copies.

The group earned a loyal following when they toured Canada and around the world. From 1971-74 they were hosts of their own weekly variety show on CBC. Other hits by the band ranged from the cute novelty number *The Biplane Evermore* to the whimsical *Lily the Pink*, which was also recorded by the English group The Scaffold.

They did not have another major hit until 1980 with *Wasn't that a Party*. Attic Records released the album PARTY WITH THE ROVERS in 1985. In 1989 they celebrated their 25th anniversary.

Singles

The Unicorn 1968
Whiskey on a Sunday 1968
The Puppet Song 1968
The Biplane Evermore 1968
Lily the Pink 1969
Peter Knight 1969
Did She Mention My Name
   1969
Rhymes and Reasons 1970

*Years May Come, Years
   May Go* 1970
Morning Town Ride 1973
Wasn't that a Party 1980
Mexican Girl 1981
Chattanooga Shoe Shine Boy
   1981
No More Bread and Butter
   1982

Albums/CDs

FIRST OF THE IRISH ROVERS
   1967
THE UNICORN 1968
ALL HUNG UP 1968
TALES TO WARM YOUR MIND
   1969
ON THE SHORES OF AMERICAY
   1971
IRISH ROVERS LIVE 1972
GREATEST HITS 1974

TALL SHIPS AND SALTY DOGS 1979
THE ROVERS 1980
NO MORE BREAD AND BUTTER
   1982
IT WAS A NIGHT LIKE THIS 1982
PARTY WITH THE ROVERS 1985
SILVER ANNIVERSARY 1989
HARDSTUFF 1989
WHEN THE BOYS COME ROLLIN'
   HOME 1993

Ironhorse

RANDY BACHMAN (*guitar*)
CHRIS LEIGHTON (*drums*)

TOM SPARKS (*guitar*):
   Replaced by FRANK LUDWIG

Established in 1979 by Randy Bachman, Ironhorse was comprised of Bachman and guitarist Tom Sparks. The duo released their self-titled debut album on the Scotti Brothers label and had a minor hit with *Sweet Lui-Louise*. In 1980, Frank Ludwig, formerly with Trooper, replaced Sparks.

After the release of the second album, EVERYTHING IS GREY, and the single, *What's the Hurry Darlin?*, Ironhorse left Scotti Brothers because of musical differences. The band later broke up.

Singles

Sweet Lui-Louise 1979
He's a Joker 1979-80

What's the Hurry Darlin? 1980
Symphony 1980

Albums

IRONHORSE 1979

EVERYTHING IS GREY 1980

Jackson Hawke

CHRIS CASTLE
BOB "CROW" CLARKE:
 Replaced by BUCKY BERGER
GENE FALBO

GARRY HOLT
TIM RYAN
BOB YEOMANS

Tim Ryan and Bob Yeomans first started working together in 1963, in a band called Amen. Their manager was Bernie Finkelstein, who also looked after Kensington Market at the time. When Amen split up in mid-1965, Ryan went to work at the steel mills in Sault Ste. Marie, his hometown.

In 1973 he moved to Montreal after Andre Perry, who had worked with John Lennon and Yoko Ono, heard some demos that Ryan and Yeomans had put together. Perry suggested that they get together to put out an album, produced by Frazer Mohawk. When Bob left the project, the result was a solo album by Tim Ryan.

Back in Toronto in 1973, Tim and Bob met again. This time they decided to form their own band called Hero. They later represented Canada at the World Popular Song Festival in Tokyo with the song *Sweet December*. Ryan left to concentrate on his writing and became a solo performer.

In August 1975, Ryan, Yeomans, and Gene Falbo became a trio. Again, they were called Hero. But when they signed to CBS Records Canada in April 1976, they changed their name to Jackson Hawke, and added Bob "Crow" Clarke on drums. They later added Chris Castle on keyboards.

Jackson Hawke's first single, *You Can't Dance*, was an immediate success. Radio programmers turned it into a double-sided hit when they played the flip side, *Into the Mystic*, written by Van Morrison.

In 1977 the group added two more new members, Gary Holt on guitar and Bucky Berger on drums. The latter replaced Bob Clarke.

Singles *You Can't Dance/Into the Mystic* 1976
   Set Me Free 1977

Album JACKSON HAWKE 1976

J.B. and the Playboys

BILL HILL
ANDY KAYE
ALLAN NICHOLLS

DOUG WEST
LOUIS YACHNIN

This Montreal-based band started out as J.B. and the Playboys in the early 1960s. After establishing themselves with the local club scene, they signed with RCA Records. In 1965 their first single, *Don't Ask*

Me to Be True, was released.

After a name change to The Jaybees, they continued to have more hits in the mid-1960s. In 1968 their name changed again, this time to The Carnival Connection. They had only one hit, *Poster Man*, on Capitol Records in 1968.

(As J.B. & the Playboys)

Single   *Don't Ask Me to Be True* 1965

Album   J.B. & THE PLAYBOYS 1965

(As The Jaybees)

Singles   *Poor Anne* 1965   *I Think of Her* 1967
I'm a Loner 1966

(As Carnival Connection)

Single   *Poster Man* 1968

Shawne Jackson

Shawne Jackson began singing at the age of nine when she joined the British Methodist Episcopal Church in Toronto. Her first group was The Tierras, a rhythm and blues group that played Yonge Street in a club called The Blue Note for three years.

Shawne later played in such R&B groups as The Silhouettes and The Majestics, a showband that liked to wear flashy clothes. When Shawne's brother Jay joined The Majestics, they became known as Shawne and Jay and The Majestics. In the late 1960s they disbanded.

In 1973, Shawne Jackson returned to the recording studio, and the following year her first solo hit, *Just as Bad as You*, was released on Playboy Records. It was a national hit. After enjoying brief success as a solo artist, she sang backup for other Canadian acts, such as Luba. In the 1980s she turned to acting and had a small role on CTV's *Night Heat*.

Singles   *Just as Bad as You* 1974   *Come Back Boy* 1980
Get Out of the Kitchen 1976

Album   SHAWNE JACKSON 1976

Susan Jacks   (See The Poppy Family)

Terry Jacks   (See The Poppy Family)

Colin James Born in Regina, Saskatchewan, in 1964, Colin Munn grew up listening to folk music and The Staple Singers, but was most drawn to the blues. In his early teens he learned the penny whistle and mandolin, and in his mid-teens he quit school and later formed his own trio, The Hoo Doo Men. They played the Winnipeg Folk Festival and opened at clubs for such artists as Mississippi bluesman John Lee Hooker and Delaware rocker George Thorogood.

The year 1983 was a turning point in his career. He moved to Vancouver and joined David Burgin in the group The Night Shades. They were the opening act for Stevie Ray Vaughan's show in Saskatoon. James ended up opening for Vaughn for the rest of his Canadian tour.

Because his last name, Munn, was the subject of too many jokes, Colin decided to change it. Vaughn is responsible for changing it to James and encouraging him to start his own band.

Back in Vancouver, James and his manager Stephen Macklam put a band together. In 1988 James's self-titled debut album on Virgin/EMI was released, and it became the fastest selling debut in the Canadian music industry. Two years later, the label released his second album, SUDDEN STOP. James has had a string of hit singles, including *Voodoo Thing* in 1988 and *Cadillac Baby* in 1993.

Singles
Voodoo Thing 1988
Dream of Satin 1989
Chicks in Cars 1989
Five Long Years 1989
Why'd You Lie 1989
Back in My Arms Again 1990

Keep on Loving Me Baby 1990
Just Came Back 1990
If You Lean on Me 1990
Love Thang 1992
Cadillac Baby 1993
Surely (I Love You) 1994

CDs COLIN JAMES 1988
SUDDEN STOP 1990

COLIN JAMES AND THE LITTLE BIG BAND 1993

Paul Janz Born in Three Hills, Alberta, 50 miles northeast of Calgary, Paul Janz's formal music training took place in Basil, Switzerland. In the 1970s he was a member of the German group Deliverance, formed by Paul and his brother Ken. In the U.S.A., they enjoyed brief success with the hit song *Leaving L.A.* in 1980 on CBS Records (now Sony Music). A lawsuit over the band's name, which came from the banjo duo in the film *Deliverance*, resulted in the breakup of the German group.

Paul decided to go back to school and enrolled at Simon Fraser University in Vancouver. He also worked on jingles to keep his hand in the business. In 1983 he decided to record an eight song demo which resulted in a deal with A&M Records. His debut album, HIGH STRUNG, and hit single, *Go to Pieces*, came out in 1985. The artist's other accomplishments include writing, producing, and performing *Something Special*, the theme of the CTV show Neon Rider and writing *Enemies like You and Me*, the love theme for the film *Iron Eagle II*. As well, he was media spokesman in 1992 for World Vision, a non-profit organization that appeals for funds to help the Third World. A string of hit singles continued to keep Janz in the spotlight, and in 1992 A&M released a "best of" compilation called PRESENCE. That same year he switched to Attic Records who released his album TRUST.

Singles		
Go to Pieces 1985	*Every Little Tear* 1990	
Don't Cry Tonight 1985	*Rocket to My Heart* 1990	
High Strung 1985	*Stand* 1990	
Close My Eyes 1985	*Hold Me Tender* 1990-91	
One Night (Is All It Takes) 1987	*Wind Me Up* 1992	
Believe in Me 1987-88	*Amazon Rain* 1993	
I Won't Cry 1988	*Calling My Personal Angel* 1993	
Send Me a Miracle 1988		

CDs		
HIGH STRUNG 1985	PRESENCE: A COLLECTION OF	
ELECTRICITY 1987	HIT SINGLES 1992	
RENEGADE ROMANTIC 1990	TRUST 1992	

Sheree Jeacocke

Sheree Jeacocke started out as a session musician in 1981 singing background vocals on albums by Gordon Lightfoot, Rita MacNeil, Eye Eye, Glass Tiger, and Kim Mitchell. In 1986 Jeacocke had her first taste of success as a solo artist with the hit *Feel It*, on the independent Factor label from the album SHAKIN' IN STEREO.

Three years later, she signed with BMG Music. In the fall of 1989, *Woman's Work* was released. Her debut album, simply entitled SHEREE, came out in 1990. Other singles from the album were *Before We Fall* and *Bang On*. Her next album, MISS MY GIRL, came out in 1993. The title track was the first single.

Singles		
Feel It 1986	*Miss My Girl* 1993	
Woman's Work 1989	*Serious* 1993	
Before We Fall 1990	*Everybody Needs a Love* 1994	
Bang On 1990		

Album/CDs		
SHAKIN' IN STEREO 1986	MISS MY LOVE 1993	
SHEREE 1989		

Jenson Interceptor

ALBERT BLAINE (*bass*)
DOUG JENSON (*guitar, vocals*)
KENNEDY JENSON (*woodwinds, synthesizer, vocals*)

ED JOHNSON (*guitar, vocals*)
CHARLOTTE WIEBE (*keyboards, vocals*)

Formed in 1976 by the brother and sister team of Kennedy and Doug Jenson, this Edmonton rock group combined the art rock sound of Procol Harum with their own unique raw-edged flavor. Ed Johnson, who had his own band called Valhalla, joined the Jensons, and they became known for a short time as Dickens. After more personnel changes, they changed their name to Jenson Interceptor in late 1979. Charlotte Wiebe and Doug Jenson wrote most of the band's material.

Singles
Crazy Monkey 1979-80
Tiny Thing 1980

Heavenly Angels 1980
Fine Man 1981

Albums
JENSON INTERCEPTOR 1980

COSMETICS 1983

Jericho

FRANK DE FELICE
GORD FLEMING

DANNY GERARD
FRED KEELER

This Toronto-based had one hit record with *Make It Better* in 1971 on Bearsville Records, distributed by Ampex Records in Canada and United States. *Make It Better* and its flipside, *Cheater Man*, were written by Fred Keeler.

Single
Make It Better 1971

Album
JERICHO 1971

The Jitters

DANNY LEVY (*guitar, vocals*)
GLENN MARTIN (*drums*)

BLAIR PACKHAM (*vocals, guitar*)

The origins of The Jitters go back to 1981 when they spent several years performing on the Toronto college club circuit. Three years later, they recorded their first hit single, *Take Me as I Am*. In 1986 they earned finalist honors in Q-107's Homegrown contest with an early version of *Last of the Red Hot Fools*.

In 1987, Toronto producer Paul Gross heard some of the band's early demo tapes and offered to record them. A new four song tape was then sent to Capitol Records, who later signed the group. *Last of the Red Hot Fools* was their first of several hits.

Singles	*Take Me as I Am* 1984		*Go Ahead 'n' Love Me* 1988
	Last of the Red Hot Fools 1987		*The Bridge Is Burning* 1989-90
	Closer Every Day 1987-88		*'Til the Fever Breaks* 1990
	That's When I Need You 1988		*I Love Her Now* 1991
Album	THE JITTERS 1987		LOUDER THAN WORDS 1990

France Joli A teenaged pop sensation from the Montreal suburb of Dorion, France Joli began singing at the age of four when she lip-synched to records and performed in front of relatives with a piece of skipping rope for a microphone. In 1974 at eleven years of age, France began singing on amateur talent shows and commercials. Her first hit in 1979 was the song *Come to Me*, written by Tony Green. That same year it reached number thirteen on Billboard's Hot 100. Managed by her mother Michelle Joli, France later performed on American television, where she appeared on The Bob Hope Special in 1979, The Merv Griffin Show, Dinah Shore, and Midnight Special. France also played two shows a night for a week at the Riviera Hotel in Las Vegas with Peaches and Herb and Tuxedo Junction. In 1982 she played with The Commodores at Radio City Music Hall.

Singles	*Come to Me* 1979		*Dumb Blonde* 1984
	This Time 1980		
Albums	FRANCE JOLI 1979		FRANCE JOLI NOW 1982
	TONIGHT 1981		ATTITUDE 1983

Jon and Lee and the Checkmates
JEFF CUTLER (*drums*)
JOHN FINLEY (*vocals*)
PETER HODGSON (*bass*)

LEE JACKSON (*lead vocals*)
LARRY LEISHMAN (*guitar*)

Formed in Toronto in the early 1960s, this band started out as a sextet comprised of Lee Jackson (Michael Ferry), Larry Leishman, Michael Fontara, Dave McDevitt, and Al Dorsey. In 1964, after some personnel changes, they adopted the name Jon and Lee and the Checkmates. Three years later, they released their only hit, *Bring It Down Front*, on Sparton Records. Finley, Hodgson, and Leishman later became members of the American group Rhinoceros, which had a major hit in 1969 with *Apricot Brandy*.

Single	*Bring It Down Front* 1967

Marc Jordan   Marc Jordan left his film studies at Brock University in 1970 to become a professional musician. He first tried out for a part in the Toronto musical production of *Hair* but ended up getting an understudy's role. During that time he played in a bar band and worked as a backup singer for Bobby Vee.

Jordan returned to university briefly, then formed a duo that sang Burt Bacharach songs in cocktail lounges, before leaving Canada to travel. When Jordan returned to Toronto, Edmonton publisher Doug Hutton signed him to a publishing, recording, and management contract. Jordan then became involved in two unsuccessful music projects: a song-saga double album called CANTATA CANADA (Capitol), and an album that paid tribute to the RCMP on its golden anniversary. Soon after, he was backed by Bernard Schaeffer, a former store owner who quit his business and mortgaged his house so he could support his new discovery.

By 1978 Warner Bros. had signed Jordan and released his debut album, MANNEQUIN. Schaeffer also managed to get Jordan billed as an opening act for Jimmy Buffett on a U.S. tour. Jordan also signed a publishing deal with Almo Music. Success finally came with the song *Marina Del Ray*.

In 1990, after a ten year absence, Jordan returned to the charts with *Burning Down the Amazon* and *Edge of the World*. He recorded *'Til the Last Teardrop Falls* with Exchange and Amy Sky in 1993. That same year, Warner Music released his solo album, RECKLESS VALENTINE, and the first single, *Waiting for a Miracle*.

Singles

It's a Fine Line 1973	*You Found Out* 1981
New York Kids 1975	*Burning Down the Amazon* 1990
Marina Del Ray 1978	*Edge of the World* 1990
Survival 1978	*'Til the Last Teardrop Falls*
I'm a Camera 1979	(with Exchange and Amy Sky)
Release Yourself 1979-80	1993
Twilight 1979-80	*Waiting for a Miracle* 1993
Generalities 1980	*Back Street Boy* 1994
New York New York 1980	

Albums/CDs

MANNEQUIN 1978	TALKING THROUGH PICTURES 1987
BLUE DESERT 1979	RECKLESS VALENTINE 1993

Sass Jordan   Born in 1962, this vocalist from Montreal captured the country by storm with her first hit single, *Tell Somebody*, in 1988. When she was seventeen years old, she learned the bass guitar and later joined a group called The News, which later became known as The Pin Ups.

She left the group when she was twenty-one to work as a television interviewer, a house painter, and a backup singer for The Box, a Montreal band.

In 1985 she struck out on her own, and Aquarius Records in Montreal liked her enough to groom her for stardom working with guitarist, arranger, and composer Bill Beaudoin. Her first two songs were *Steel on Steel* and *No More*, both included on her debut album, TELL SOMEBODY, in 1988. Her album RACINE (1992) was a tribute to the artists she listened to when she was a teenager: The Rolling Stones, David Bowie, Bad Company, Free, and Faces.

Singles	*Tell Somebody* 1988-89	*I Want To Believe* 1992
So Hard 1989	*You Don't Have to Remind Me* 1992
Double Trouble 1989	*Goin' Back Again* 1992-93
Stranger than Paradise 1989	*Who Do You Think You Are* 1993
Rescue Me 1990	*High Road Easy* 1994
Make You a Believer 1992

CDs	TELL SOMEBODY 1988	RATS 1994
RACINE 1992

Joshua BILL BROADHURST   PAT GAMBLE
CARL BURGESS   AL FETH
DON DUNLOP

This gospel/rock quintet from Woodstock, Ontario, had five hits on GRT Records in the early 1970s.

Singles	*Thoughts* 1971	*Poor Folks* 1972
Throw a Rope 1971	*Come on Home* 1972
Bow Down (To the Dollar) 1971

Album JOSHUA 1972

Diane Juster Diane Juster began her musical training at age five, and in her teens at College André-Grasset she sang under the name of Marie Octobre. She started writing her own songs at seventeen, and in the mid-1970s newcomer Julie Arel made her famous when she recorded seven of Juster's original compositions.

At twenty-five years of age a record company executive convinced her to record the single *Ce Matin*, which became a hit after she introduced it on the TV show *Jeunesse*. Her other hits included *Ma maison, c'est une île* and *Quands tu partiras*.

In 1975, after the release of her second album, Juster announced that she was quitting the stage to concentrate on writing songs for other artists, such as Robert Charlebois, Céline Dion, and Ginette Reno. Juster's 1980 composition, *Je ne suis qu'une chanson*, recorded by Reno, won the Felix Award as best song of 1980. By 1991 it had become the best selling song in Quebec. In 1981 Diane became a founding member of the Société Professionelle des Auteurs-Compositeurs du Quebec (SPACQ).

In addition to writing songs, she has composed film scores for Jean-Claude's *Éclair au chocolat*, Danièlle Suissa's *The Morning Man*, and the music of *Monsieur Amilcar* for the Eddy Tousaint Ballet. More recently, she has become a crusader for songwriter's rights, and is a vice-president of Quebec's songwriter's association. In 1993 she released a self-titled album of sixteen songs.

Singles	*Ce matin* 1974	*Quands tu partiras* 1975
	Ma maison, c'est une île 1974-75	

Albums	MELANCOLIE 1974	RIEN QU'AMOUREUSE 1984
	M'AIMERAS-TU DEMAIN 1975	J'AI BESOIN DE PARLER 1987
	REGARDE EN MOI 1977	DIANE JUSTER 1993
	TU AS LAISEE PASSER L'AMOUR 1981	

Justin Tyme

DON GUNTER	GARNET SCHNEIDER
JIM MAXWELL	JOHN WITTMAN

Winnipeg-based Justin Tyme signed a three-year recording contract with Warner Brothers-Seven Arts in 1969. Garnet Schneider, the principle songwriter of the group wrote *Nonsense Child* and its flipside, *Miss Felicity Grey*. Their only national hit was *Child of Dawn* in 1970.

Singles	*Nonsense Child* 1969	*Child of Dawn* 1970

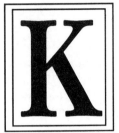

Kashtin

CLAUDE MCKENZIE
FLORENT VOLLANT

This popular Montagnais duo started singing together in 1984. The name "Kashtin" means tornado in the Montagnais Innu Aionum language. Their first performances were at the Innu Nikamu festival at Maliotenam and other native communities along the Lower North Shore of the St. Lawrence River.

Montreal composer/producer Guy Trepanier saw potential in this duo, and he encouraged them to record their self-titled debut album in 1989, which featured the hits *E Uassiuian* (*Mon enfance* in French and *My Childhood* in English), *Tipatshimun* (*Chanson du diable* in French and *Song of the Devil* in English), and *Tshinanu* (*Nous Autres* in French and *Ourselves* in English).

1989 marked the duo's debut in Paris, France, at the Theatre de la Ville and La Cigalle. A year later, they played at the New Music Seminar in New York.

CDs KASHTIN 1989 INNU 1991

Christopher Kearney

Born in Toronto in 1947, Christopher Kearney was four years old when he moved with his parents to Lindsay, Ontario. His musical career started in the mid-to-late 1960s when he lived and worked on the American West Coast. He later met Gordon Lightfoot who encouraged him to be a singer/songwriter.

In 1970 Kearney recorded *Theme for Jody* on Apex Records. He returned to Toronto in mid-1971 and published a number of songs with Lightfoot's Early Morning Music. Capitol Records released his self-titled debut album in 1972. The first single was *Loosen Up*.

Kearney played at various folk clubs throughout the United States, such as the Bitter End in New York. He also toured with Anne Murray. He represented Canada, along with The Stampeders, at the Seventh Rio International Pop Song Festival in Rio de Janeiro, Brazil in 1972. The following year Capitol released Kearney's second album, PEMMICAN STASH. Although he never achieved the same success as Lightfoot, he was one of Canada's most popular singer/songwriters in the early 1970s.

In 1993 he wrote (with Scott Lane and Neil Dobson) *A Letter from Sarajevo*, a public awareness video which featured Tom Cochrane, Rik Emmett, Molly Johnson, Murray McLauchlan, and Ian Thomas. Directed by John Grierson, the namesake and grandson of the National Film Board founder, it showed footage of the Niagara Children's

Chorus singing with children on the streets of Toronto set against war footage from Bosnia.

Singles   *Theme for Jody* 1970   *Loosen Up* 1972
      Rocking Chair Ride 1971

Albums   CHRISTOPHER KEARNEY 1972   SWEETWATER 1975
      PEMMICAN STASH 1973

James Keelaghan

Singer/songwriter James Keelaghan's musical career began in 1983 when he played guitar with Scottish folksinger Margaret Crystal in his hometown of Calgary. He also played in several groups, notably Ernie the Band, an acoustic punk/folk group that played everything from the late Stan Rogers to the Talking Heads.

In 1985 folksinger/songwriter Garnet Rogers heard him sing *Jenny Bryce* and encouraged James to make music a full-time career. In 1987 he released his first independent cassette, TIMELINES; a second, SMALL REBELLIONS, came out in 1989.

Keelaghan has played at many folk festivals around the world, such as the Australia National Festival, Ann Arbor Folk Festival, Lunenberg Folk Harbour Festival, Santa Monica Festival, and the Vancouver, Edmonton, and Winnipeg Folk Festivals. Until 1992 he toured with Bill Eaglesham (bass, background vocals) and Gary Bird (six string and steel guitars). Oscar Lopez toured with James in 1993. Signed to Green Linnet Records out of Minneapolis, Minnesota, in 1993, his first release on that label was MY SKIES.

Albums/CDs   TIMELINES 1987   MY SKIES 1993
       SMALL REBELLIONS 1989

Kensington Market

ALEX DAROU   KEITH MCKIE
LUKE GIBSON   JOHN MILLS-COCKELL
EUGENE MARTYNEC   JIMMY WATSON

Named after a downtown neighborhood in Toronto, the group was founded in 1967 by Bernie Finkelstein who later guided the careers of Bruce Cockburn and Murray McLauchlan in the 1970s. At first they were a quartet. Gibson, leader of Luke and the Apostles (1964-67) joined in 1967, and John Mills-Cockell in 1969. They recorded for Stone Records and had some success with *Mr. John* and *Bobby's Birthday* in 1967. After one more hit and a second U.S. tour, the group disbanded in 1969.

Singles	*Mr. John* 1967	*I Would Be the One* 1968
	Bobby's Birthday 1967	
Albums	AVENUE ROAD 1968	AARDVARK 1969

Kilowatt

BOB BRETT   GREG LESKIW
STEVE HEGYI   BILL WALLACE

Kilowatt, from Winnipeg, was formed by Greg Leskiw from The Guess Who and Steve Hegyi when Les Q, the group in which they both played began breaking up in 1988. The addition of bassist Bill Wallace, another former member of The Guess Who, and drummer Bob Brett rounded out the quartet. They were the first act sign with RCA's independent Dallcorte label. Their self-titled debut album contained the two singles, *Lovers on the Run* and *Kids Are Krazy*, and was produced by Domenic Troiano, another former member of The Guess Who.

Singles	*Lovers on the Run* 1982	*Not a Kid Anymore* 1983
	Kids Are Krazy 1983	
Albums	KILOWATT 1983	CURRENTS 1983

Andy Kim

Born in 1946 as Andrew Youakim, this Montreal-based singer grew up listening to Elvis Presley and Buddy Holly while attending Pius X High School in Montreal. Determined to become a recording star, Kim went to New York in 1962 and talked to various executives, and was told to make a demo. Not knowing what a demo was, he returned home to Montreal but soon quit school and returned to New York where he recorded a couple of songs: *I Loved You Once* for United Artists in 1963 and *I Hear You Say I Love You* for Red Bird in 1965. They were not successful.

Eventually he caught the attention of songwriter Jeff Barry, who, along with his wife and partner Ellie Greenwich, wrote classic hit songs for Paul Peterson, Lesley Gore, The Exciters, The Shirelles, and The Dixie Cups, among others. With Kim, the three of them became a songwriting team. Kim, Barry, and Greenwich went on to write songs for the cartoon series *The Archies*, including *Bang Shang A Lang*, *Sugar, Sugar*, and *Jingle Jangle*.

Barry produced Kim's first big hit, *How'd We Ever Get this Way*, released in March 1968.

In 1969, he recorded *So Good Together* and *Baby, I Love You*, which sold a million-and-a-half copies. Other hits followed in the

1970s, the biggest of which was *Rock Me Gently,* in 1974.

Two years after the success of *Gently*, Kim's father died; he was hit hard by his death and withdrew from the music business for two years. By the 1980s he began recording under the name of Baron Longfellow, a name given to him by Gordon Mills (who managed Engelbert Humperdinck and Tom Jones). Under the moniker of Baron Longfellow, he recorded *Go It Slow* and *Amour*, one of the top five selling singles in Canada and a Juno Award nominee for Single of the Year. He continues to record today under the name of Longfellow. He dropped "Baron" in the 1990s.

(As Andy Kim)

Singles		
I Loved You Once 1963	*Be My Baby* 1970
I Hear You Say (I Love You) 1965	*I Wish I Were* 1971
	I Been Moved 1971
How'd We Ever Get this Way 1968	*Shady Hollow Dreamer* 1972
	Who Has the Answers 1972
Shoot'em Up Baby 1968	*Love the Poor Boy* 1972-73
Rainbow Ride 1968-69	*Oh What a Day* 1973
Tricia Tell Your Daddy 1969	*Rock Me Gently* 1974
Baby I Love You 1969	*Fire, Baby I'm on Fire* 1974
So Good Together 1969	*The Essence of Joan* 1975
A Friend in the City 1970	*Mary Ann* 1975
It's Your Life 1970	*Baby You're All I Got* 1975
You 1970	*Harlem* (as Andy Kimm) 1976

Albums RAINBOW RIDE 1969   ROCK ME GENTLY 1974
BABY I LOVE YOU 1969   ANDY KIM'S GREATEST HITS 1974

(As Baron Longfellow)

Singles		
Go It Slow 1980	*Hold Me* 1984
Amour 1980	*In the Night Machine* 1985
I'm Gonna Need a Miracle Tonight 1984	*Powerdrive* (as Longfellow) 1991-92

Albums BARON LONGFELLOW 1980   PRISONER BY DESIGN 1984

Bill King

Bill King left the U.S. Army and fled to Canada in the early 1970s. Once he was settled here, he became involved in a campaign to have the U.S. government grant amnesty to so-called draft dodgers and deserters.

In the late 1960s, King had worked with such artists as Janis Joplin, Chuck Berry, and Linda Ronstadt. After getting his own band together in Toronto, he began playing charities. Signed to Capitol Records, he had a string of hits beginning with *Goodbye Superdad* in 1973. In 1982 he formed a new group called China with Christopher Kearney and Danny McBride.

The 1980s also saw King change musical direction from rock to jazz, and form his own record label, Night Passage Records. He also was editor and publisher of *Jazz Magazine*. King recorded several other albums, including AVENUE B (1984) and CITY OF DREAMS (1985), as The Bill King Quintet. Today, Bill King's latest group is The Jazz Report All-Stars, comprised of some of Toronto's jazz elite: tenor saxists Pat LaBarbera and Kirk MacDonald, altoist Campbell Ryga, guitarist Ted Quinlan, vibist Don Thompson, and conductor/arranger John Cheesman.

Singles	*Goodbye Superdad* 1973	*Wheel of Good Fortune* 1974
	Canada 1973	*Blue Skies* 1974
	Give Me Love 1973	*Love and Affection* 1980

Albums	GOODBYE SUPERDAD 1973	BLUE SKIES 1974

King Biscuit Boy

Born in 1944, Richard Newell grew up in Hamilton listening to the blues on American radio shows. In his teens he began playing harmonica, and between 1961 and 1965 worked with the blues/rock band The Barons. They made one record in 1961 called *Bottleneck*.

In the early 1960s, The Barons changed their name to Son Richard and The Chessmen. By 1966 Richard had left the Chessmen for the Midknights. Two years later he joined Ronnie Hawkins, who nicknamed him King Biscuit Boy after a radio show at KFFA in Helena, Arkansas.

Newell left Hawkins to play with Crowbar in 1970 he recorded OFFICIAL MUSIC with the group. From the early to mid-1970s, King Biscuit Boy went solo and recorded a few songs but commercial success eluded him.

Singles	*Corrina Corrina*	*Barefoot Rock* 1972-73
	(with Crowbar) 1970	*29 Ways/Boom Boom* 1972
	Biscuit's Boogie 1971	*New Orleans* 1975

Albums	OFFICIAL MUSIC (King Biscuit Boy & Crowbar) 1970
	MOUTH OF STEEL 1982
	RICHARD NEWELL A.K.A. KING BISCUIT BOY 1988

The Kings DAVID DIAMOND (*vocals, bass*) MAX STYLES (*drums*)
SONNY KEYES (*keyboards*) ARYAN ZERO (*guitar*)

Formed in 1979 in Hamilton, Ontario, The Kings captured Canadian and American audiences with their first hit, *Switchin' to Glide*, in 1980. On stage they projected the image of a new wave group, but were a rock 'n' roll band. Their debut album, THE KINGS ARE HERE, was produced by Bob Ezrin (Pink Floyd, Alice Cooper, Kiss). From it came the singles *Switchin' to Glide* and *Don't Let Me Know*.

The original members reunited to record the album UNSTOPPABLE in 1993.

Singles *Switchin' to Glide* 1980   *Lesson to Learn* 1993
Don't Let Me Know 1981   *Tonight I Got You* 1994
Unstoppable 1993

Albums THE KINGS ARE HERE 1980   UNSTOPPABLE 1993

Klaatu TERRY DRAPER (*drums*)   JOHN WOLOSCHUK (*keyboards*)
DEE LONG (*guitar*)

Named after a character in the 1951 RKO science fiction classic *The Day the Earth Stood Still*, this trio from Toronto formed in 1973. They prided themselves on their anonymity until 1982 when they publicly identified themselves through radio and print interviews.

Klaatu recorded six albums between 1973 and 1982. The Carpenters recorded a remake of their song *Calling All Occupants* in 1977. For their first album, Klaatu chose the title *3:47 E.S.T.*, the time when Michael Rennie arrived in Washington in *The Day the Earth Stood Still*. When the album was released in 1976, it was the subject of much talk in both the United States and Canada because Klaatu sounded a lot like The Beatles. A rock music writer for the *Providence Journal* in Rhode Island started the controversy with an article he wrote called "Is Klaatu Band The Beatles?" Their first album was a smashing success because of the controversy. However, their albums sold less as the controversy faded.

In 1981 the group released their fifth album, MAGENTALANE, recorded from their first live performances. They also added three new members: Gary McCracken on drums, Michael Gingrich on bass, and Gerald O'Brien on keyboards.

Klaatu broke up in the mid-1980s, but in 1988 the trio reunited to record *Tatort*, a song for West German television.

Singles	*Hanus Of Uranus* 1973	*Routine Day* 1979
	California Jam 1975	*Knee Deep in Love* 1980
	Calling All Occupants/Sub-Rosa	*I Can't Help It* 1980
	Subway 1977	*The Love of a Woman* 1981
Albums/CDs	KLAATU 1976	ENDANGERED SPECIES 1980
	3:47 E.S.T. 1976	MAGENTALANE 1981
	(re-issued in 1994)	PEAKS 1993
	HOPE 1977	KLAATU CLASSICS 1982
	SIR ARMY SUIT 1978	

Richie Knight & the Mid-Knights

MIKE BROUGH   BARRY LLOYD
DOUG CHAPPELL   GEORGE SEMKIW
RICHIE KNIGHT   BARRIE STEIN

Led by Richard Hubbard, alias Richie Knight, this band recorded for Arc Records and had a major success with the hit, *Charlena*, in 1963.

(As Richie Knight & the Mid-Knights)
Single *Charlena* 1963

(As Richie Knight)
Singles *One Good Reason* 1965   *That's Alright* 1966

Moe Koffman

Morris "Moe" Koffman's contribution to Canadian rock music in Canada is his self-penned composition, *Swinging Shepherd Blues*, which established his reputation as a flutist in the field of jazz. *Shepherd Blues* was released in 1958 and again in 1973.

Born in 1928, Koffman studied violin and the alto saxaphone as a child. He quickly gained notoriety as one of Canada's best jazzmen and was among the first to adopt the New York be-bop style in the 1940s. He won a CBC Jazz Unlimited poll as best alto saxophonist.

His first recordings were 78s made in Buffalo, N.Y. In 1950 he moved to the United States where he played in such big bands as Jimmy Dorsey and Sonny Dunham. Five years passed before he decided to return to Toronto to stay. He made his first appearance in the city at House of Hamburg. The following year, in 1956, he became a booking agent for George's Spaghetti House, a position he held for the next twenty years.

With his acceptance as a top jazzmen, Koffman joined Doug Riley (of Dr. Music fame) and made several popular recordings. He later turned solo and made several recordings of his own music. He has also played in several jazz-oriented TV orchestras led by Guido Basso, Jimmy Dale, Rob McConnell and The Boss Brass, among others. In

1972, he led his own band for Global TV's *Everything Goes.*

Moe Koffman was appointed to the Order of Canada on July 6, 1993 in recognition of his outstanding achievement and service to the arts and music community.

Singles   *Swinging Shepherd Blues* 1958   *Little Pixie* 1958
(reissued in 1973)

Albums/CDs

HOT AND COOL SAX 1957	LIVE AT GEORGE'S 1975
THE SHEPHERD SWINGS AGAIN 1958	JUNGLE MAN 1976
	MUSEUM PIECES 1977
MOE KOFFMAN THE SWINGING SHEPHERD PLAYS FOR TEENS 1962	THINGS ARE LOOKING UP 1978
	BACK TO BACH 1979
TALES OF KOFFMAN 1962	BEST OF MOE KOFFMAN VOLUME I 1983
THE MOE KOFFMAN QUARTET 1963	BEST OF MOE KOFFMAN VOLUME II 1983
MOE KOFFMAN GOES ELECTRIC 1967	IF YOU DON'T KNOW ME BY NOW 1983
TURNED ON MOE KOFFMAN 1968	THE MAGIC FLUTE 1985
	ONE MOE TIME 1986
MOE'S CURRIED SOUL 1970	MOE-MENTUM 1987
MOE KOFFMAN PLAYS BACH 1971	OOP-POP-A-DA 1988
THE FOUR SEASONS 1972	MOE KOFFMAN QUINTET PLAYS 1990
MASTER SESSION 1973	
SORCERER'S DANCE 1973	MUSIC FOR THE NIGHT: A TRIBUTE TO ANDREW LLOYD-WEBBER 1991
SOLAR EXPLORATIONS 1974	
BEST OF MOE KOFFMAN 1975	

Tony Kosinec

Tony Kosinec gained an international reputation as an actor and as an opening act for such diverse acts as Seals and Crofts, Poco, Laura Nyro, Procol Harum, and Blood, Sweat and Tears. His first two albums were produced by Peter Asher of Peter and Gordon fame. In 1971 he had a major success with the song *48 DeSoto.*

In 1973 Smile Records, an independent label in Toronto, released the album CONSIDER THE HEART, which included the hit single *All Things Come from God.* The following year, Kosinec switched to GRT Records. His first single with the label was *Love Hurts* in 1974.

Singles   *48 DeSoto* 1971   *A Little Road and a Stone to Roll*
All Things Come from God 1973   1974
Love Hurts 1974   *So Long* 1974

Album   CONSIDER THE HEART 1973

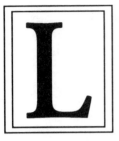

Diane Landry

A former Miss Canada, Diane Landry signed a recording contract with Columbia Records in 1971. She was completely bilingual and recorded in both English and French. Both sides of her first English recording *A Corner of Your Heart/I'm Gonna Get Out* were written by Marty Butler and Bob Bilyk, who had composed The Bells' *Fly Little White Dove, Fly.*

Single   *A Corner of Your Heart*   1971

Robbie Lane & the Disciples

TERRY BUSH (*guitar*)
DOUG COPELAND (*drums*)
WILLIAM CUDMORE
 (*harmonica, sax*)
PAUL DENYEF (*keyboards*):
 Replaced by BILL DAVIS

ROBBIE LANE (*vocals*)
PAUL MIFSUD (*tenor sax*)
GENE TRACK (*bass*)

Formed in the mid-1960s in Toronto, Robbie Lane and the Disciples started out as a backup group for Ronnie Hawkins and later became the host band on CBC-TV's *It's Happening.* In 1965, The Disciples recorded *Baby Ruth* under a different name, The Butterfingers. The band played in and around Toronto and developed a local following. By the end of the decade the group broke up.

Robbie Lane (Robin Curry) had an unsuccessful solo career. Terry Bush continued to write and record, recording the theme song for CTV's *The Littlest Hobo.* Lane and the Disciples reunited in the mid-1980s. Today, they are active on the club circuit.

(As Robbie Lane and the Disciples)
Singles   *Fannie Mae*   1964
Ain't Love a Funny Thing   1965
Sandy   1965
Baby Ruth (The Butterfingers)
 1965

What Am I Gonna Do   1966
You Gotta Have Love   1966
It's Happening   1967

(As Robbie Lane)
Singles   *M'Lady*   1974

Missing You   1975

k.d. lang

Born in 1961 in Consort, Alberta, k.d. (Katherine Dawn) lang is one of Canada's most controversial recording artists. Until 1988 when *Crying*, a duet with Roy Orbison from the soundtrack of the film *Hiding Out*, became a hit, her music was largely unknown to a majority of Canadians and rarely played on Canadian radio stations. Her second album, ANGEL WITH A LARIAT, leaned more toward rural folk or country than pop. Her first single release in 1983, entitled *Friday Dance Promenade*, was pressed on white vinyl and is now considered a collector's item.

Her singing style has been deliberately modeled on Patsy Cline's recordings. Owen Bradley, Cline's producer, came out of retirement to produce Lang's 1988 album, SHADOWLAND.

In concert she wowed audiences with her frenetic performance and vocal stylings. At the closing ceremonies of Calgary's Winter Olympics in 1988 she led a rousing square dance. That same year, *Chatelaine* magazine chose her as their woman of the year. In 1989 she made her sixth appearance on *The Tonight Show Starring Johnny Carson* and performed at New York's Radio City Music Hall at the invitation of Barbara Orbison, Roy Orbison's widow.

In the early 1990s she admitted publicly that she was a lesbian and offended her critics when she became a spokesperson in a "Meat Stinks" campaign.

In 1992 her single, *Constant Craving* reached Billboard's Hot 100.

Singles		
Hanky Panky 1984		*Pulling Back the Reins* 1989
Crying (with Roy Orbison) 1987-88		*Big Boned Gal* 1990
I'm Down to My Last Cigarette 1988		*Constant Craving* 1992
Lock, Stock and Teardrops 1988		*Miss Chatelaine* 1992
Full Moon Full of Love 1989		*The Mind of Love (Where Is Your Head Kathryn?)* 1992
Three Days 1989		*Just Keep Me Moving* 1993
		Hush Sweet Lover 1994

Albums/CDs		
A TRULY WESTERN EXPERIENCE 1984		ABSOLUTE TORCH AND TWANG 1989
ANGEL WITH A LARIAT 1986		INGENUE 1992
SHADOWLAND 1988		EVEN COWGIRLS GET THE BLUES 1993

Daniel Lanois

Daniel Lanois is known more for his work as one of the recording industry's most influential producers than as a singer/songwriter. Since the 1980s he has produced such acts as Martha and the Muffins, The Parachute Club, Luba, Ian Tyson, Willie P. Bennett, Sylvia Tyson, Bob Dylan, Peter Gabriel, Robbie Robertson, The Neville Brothers, and U2.

Born in Ottawa, he moved with his parents to Hamilton at the age of ten. By the time he was in his twenties, he was operating his first studio in the basement of his parents' house.

It was not until 1989 that Lanois had the urge to record his own material. The resulting album, ACADIE, was praised by music critics in both Canada and the United States. One of the songs on ACADIE, *Jolie Louise* was featured on the hit CBS-TV series *Northern Exposure*. It was also included in an album of music from the series in 1992.

Early in 1993 Lanois released his second solo album, FOR THE BEAUTY OF WYNONA. Both albums trace the singer's roots from his French-Canadian ancestors to the Louisiana Delta to his own personal experiences.

Today, he continues to be in demand as a record producer. After the release of WYNONA, he collaborated with his sister Jocelyne on the music for the Canadian production of *Camille*.

Singles	*The Maker* 1989	*Jolie Louise* 1990
	Still Water 1990	*Lotta Love to Give* 1993

CDs	ACADIE 1989
	FOR THE BEAUTY OF WYNONA 1993

Brent Lee & the Outsiders

RON DESJARLAIS (*guitar*)	MIKE LYNCH (*bass*)
BRENT LEE (*vocals, guitar*)	NAOISE SHERIDAN (*guitar*)

From Vancouver, Brent Lee & the Outsiders started playing together in 1990 and relocated to Toronto in the summer of 1991, where they released their debut album, ROSE TATTOO. Signed in 1992 to Justin Entertainment, a small label distributed by MCA, the group's first single was *Would You Love Me*. By the fall of 1992, the group had broken up.

Singles	*Would You Love Me* 1992	*Mexican Bandits* 1992
	Where I'm Going 1992	*Take It to the Mountain* 1992

Album	ROSE TATTOO 1992

Lee Aaron

LEE AARON (*vocals*)	KIMIO OKI (*drums*)
JOHN ALBANI (*guitar*)	CHAS ROTUNDA (*bass*)
GREG DOYLE (*guitar*)	

This hard rock band from Toronto took its name from their female lead singer whose powerful vocals have made them one of the most respected groups on the international rock scene. Born in Belleville, Ontario and raised in Brampton, Lee Aaron (Karen Sue Greening) studied the alto saxophone in high school. She grew up listening to her mother's Anne Murray and Supremes records. Lee's first exposure to heavy metal music occurred in Grade 10 when she was introduced to Deep Purple, Led Zeppelin, and other heavy rockers.

In 1983 the band made its English debut at the Marquee Club. They later played at various European rock festivals, notably the Reading Festival in England.

Lead singer Aaron has graced the covers of many English and European music magazines, and has ranked in the Top 10 Vocalist of the Year Reader's Polls in *Kerrang!* and *Sounds Female* (two British publications). Aaron has also been voted as the second Best Instrumental Vocalist by the German magazine *Metal Hammer*.

Although the band has had little commercial success on the charts, Lee Aaron continue to do well with their albums and concerts. In 1992 the group left Attic Records after releasing POWERLINE: THE BEST OF LEE AARON and its first single, *Peace on Earth*.

Singles		
	Shake It Up 1984	*Sweet Talk* 1990
	Only Human 1987	*Hands On* 1990
	Goin' Off the Deep End 1987	*Sex with Love* 1991
	Whatcha Do to My Body 1989	*Peace on Earth* 1992

Albums/CDs		
	LEE AARON PROJECT 1983	BODYROCK 1989
	METAL QUEEN 1984	SOME GIRLS DO 1991
	CALL OF THE WILD 1985	POWERLINE: THE BEST OF
	LEE AARON 1986	LEE AARON 1992

Leigh Ashford

JOE AGNELLO (*bass*)	NEWTON GERARD (*keyboards*)
WALLY CAMERON (*drums*)	BUZZ SHERMAN (*vocals*)
DON ELLIOT (*bass*)	GORD WASZEK (*guitar*)

Leigh Ashford was formed in 1966 in Toronto while all the members were in their last year of high school. Named after a sixteenth-century English prostitute, they were together for a year. They later joined another Toronto group, The Spirit, and became known as The Spirit Revue. When they disbanded in 1968, the original members of Leigh Ashford reunited and began playing in Yorkville.

In the fall of 1969 they signed a record contract with Nimbus 9 and went to New York to make their first album. *Dickens* was the group's first hit single on Revolver Records, which was distributed by RCA. They split up in 1971.

Singles		
	Dickens 1970-71	*Never Give Myself* 1971

Album	
	LEIGH ASHFORD 1971

James Leroy Born in 1946, James Leroy grew up in Martintown, Ontario, and later moved to Ottawa where he started out as a folksinger in the mid-1960s. In 1970 he turned his attention to the contemporary field and gathered together a backup group that would serve his musical tastes. They called themselves Denim, after the song *You Look Good in Denim*, which was written by Leroy during a lunch break while rehearsing for a new album.

In 1976 Leroy joined Major Hoople's Boarding House as its new leader. On May 10, 1979 he died in Ottawa at the age of 32.

Singles *Touch of Magic* 1973   *Some Kind of Fool* 1974
You Look Good in Denim 1973 *Lady Ellen* 1974
Make It All Worthwhile 1973

Album DENIM 1973

Les Bel Air Benoit Guimonds   Andre Theaume
Andre Roy   Bernard Vallee

From Quebec City, this quartet had one major hit in 1970 with a song called *Caroline*. In the fall of 1970, they changed their name to Canadian Pea Soup.

Single *Caroline* 1970

Leslie Spit Treeo Laura Hubert (vocals)   Jack Nicholsen (vocals)
Pat Langner (vocals)

This folk/rock group began on the streets of Toronto where founders Laura Hubert, Jack Nicholsen, and Pat Langner were buskers at the Leslie Street Spit, a lakefront site that bears the group's name. After winning the 1991 Juno Award for Most Promising Group, the trio quickly became one of the nation's hottest new bands.

In 1992, they added keyboardist Jason Sniderman and bassist Frank Randazzo to their lineup to create the group's new rock 'n' roll sound, heard on their second album, BOOK OF REJECTION. The first single, *In Your Eyes*, features Randy Bachman on guitar. Bachman also contributed to *Redirected*, another track on the album.

The group changed its name in 1993 to Leslie Spit when Jack Nicholsen left to play a role in *The Civilization of a Shoe Shine Boy* at the Buddies in Bad Times Theatre in Toronto.

Singles	*Angel from Montgomery* 1991	*Sometimes I Wish* 1992-93
	Heat 1991	*Happy* 1993
	In Your Eyes 1992	
CDs	DON'T CRY TOO HARD 1990	BOOK OF REJECTION 1992

Leyden Zar

SERGE GRATTON (*drums*) JACQUES NOEL (*rhythm guitar*)
PAUL GRONDIN (*bass*) BRIAN WILSON (*lead guitar*)
PASCAL MAILLOUX (*keyboards*)

The five members of Leyden Zar met in 1976 when they backed up French singer Robert Leroux. With the exception of Brian Wilson, who was born in Scotland, the rest of the group was Quebecois.

Leyden Zar named themselves after an electrical condenser invented by George Leyden. On stage they played American rock and sang in English. Their first hit was *Back Street Girl* in 1981.

Single	*Back Street Girl* 1981	*It's Alright* 1985
Album	LEYDEN ZAR 1985	

Monique Leyrac

Born in 1928, Monique Leyrac studied with Jeanne Mauberg and in 1943 took the role of Bernadette in Frank Werfel's *Le Chant de Bernadette*. She also sang and played a few songs in the film, *Lumieres de ma ville* (1949). Her popularity as a singer grew in Quebec, and by the early 1960s she started to put some of her material on vinyl. Her debut album in 1963 included songs by Vigneault and Leveillee.

Two years later, she was chosen by the CBC to sing at the International Song Festival in Sopot, Poland, and won the Grand Prix of International Day for her rendition of Vigneault's *Mon Pays*. In 1967 she played Toronto's Massey Hall and New York's Carnegie Hall. The following year she was named an Officer of the Order of Canada. In 1978 she received the prestigious Prix de musique Calixa-Lavallee.

Albums MONIQUE LEYRAC CHANTE VIGNEAULT ET LEVEILLEE 1963
PLEINS FEUX SUR MONIQUE LEYRAC 1964
  (Re-released as MES PREMIERES CHANSONS in 1973)
MONIQUE LEYRAC EN CONCERT 1965
MONIQUE LEYRAC 1967
MONIQUE LEYRAC A PARIS 1967
BEAUTIFUL MORNING 1968
MONIQUE LEYRAC CHANTE LA JOIE DE VIVRE 1969

LES GRANDS SUCCES DE MONIQUE LEYRAC 1971
MONIQUE LEYRAC (1968-1972) 1972
QUI ETES-VOUS MONIQUE LEYRAC? 1972
MONIQUE LEYRAC CHANTE NELLIGAN 1975
MONIQUE LEYRAC CHANTE FELIX LECLERC 1977

Lick 'n Stick

BOB HANCOCK (*drums*)   MARTIN SOLDAT (*keyboards*):
RICK LAW (*bass*)   Replaced by BRIAN FRASER
                               PAUL VIGNA (*guitar, vocals*)

Lick 'n Stick had been playing dance music on the Yonge Street strip and in Richmond Hill when Columbia Records signed them in 1975. Their first hit single was *Take It Easy*.

Prior to signing with Columbia, Paul Vigna had written three children's plays which were performed by the Young People's Theatre Company in Toronto.

Singles   *Take It Easy* 1975   *Mary Ann*   1976
           Under My Thumb 1976

Gordon Lightfoot

Gordon Lightfoot is one of Canada's top folksingers. In the 1960s he wrote songs that are now pop standards and have been recorded by other artists, including *Ribbon of Darkness* (Marty Robbins), *For Lovin' Me* (Peter, Paul & Mary), and *Early Mornin' Rain* (Johnny Cash).

At eight years of age he took piano lessons and later sang in the local United Church junior choir. He played at civic centers and local radio shows in his teens. Jazz was another kind of music that influenced him, and he played in various jazz groups. In junior high, he gave up the piano for the guitar and drums.

In 1955 Lightfoot placed second in a province-wide competition of barbershop quartets. Two years later when he left high school, he still wanted to be a performer and wrote *The Hula Hoop Song*. On CBC's *Country Hoedown*, he was one of the Swinging Singing Eight. Country music inspired him to learn more about other types of music. When he heard the Weavers's Carnegie Hall album, he turned to traditional folk music.

In the early 1960s Lightfoot recorded for Chateau Records, owned by Norman Snider, who was instrumental in launching the young singer's recording career. Lightfoot and Terry Whelan (ex-barbershopper) formed a duo called The Two Tones and recorded a live album in

January 1962 on Chateau Records. By 1965 Lightfoot was becoming well known: he frequently played at Toronto's Riverboat and appeared on *The Tonight Show Starring Johnny Carson*. Lightfoot signed a contract with United Artists in 1966 and his self-titled debut album was released. His hit songs around this time were *Spin Spin*, *Go Go Round*, and *The Way I Feel*, which all made the Canadian Top Ten. In 1969 he signed a million dollar deal with Reprise/Warner which was unheard of for an artist at that time. In 1970 he received the Order of Canada.

Lightfoot became an international star in the 1970s. The song *If You Could Read My Mind* was a smash in both Canada and the U.S. In 1974 *Sundown* became his first U.S. gold single. The end of the decade saw Lightfoot tour more of the U.S.A., Canada, and the British Isles.

In the 1980s Lightfoot recorded infrequently. He lives in Toronto, where he continues to perform annually at Massey Hall. In the spring of 1993, Warner Music released his first album in seven years, WAITING FOR YOU.

Singles		
(Remember Me) I'm the One 1962	*Same Old Obsession/You Are What I Am* 1972	
It's too Late, He Wins/ Negotiations 1962-63	*10 Degrees and Gettin' Colder* 1972	
I'm Not Sayin' 1965	*High and Dry* 1974	
Just like Tom Thumb's Blues 1965	*Sundown* 1974	
Spin Spin 1966	*Carefree Highway* 1974	
Go Go Round 1967	*Rainy Day People* 1975	
The Way I Feel 1967	*The Wreck of the Edmund Fitzgerald* 1976	
Black Day in July 1968	*Race Among the Ruins* 1977	
Bitter Green 1968	*The Circle Is Small* 1978	
Me and Bobby McGee 1970	*Daylight Katy* 1978	
If You Could Read My Mind 1970-71	*Dream Street Rose* 1980	
	If You Need Me 1980	
This Is My Song 1971	*Baby Step Back* 1982	
Talking in Your Sleep 1971	*Blackberry Wine* 1982	
Summer Side of Life 1971	*Anything for Love* 1986	
	Stay Loose 1986	
Beautiful 1972	*I'll Prove My Love* 1993	

Albums/CDs		
TWO TONES AT THE VILLAGE CORNER 1962	SUNDAY CONCERT 1969	
LIGHTFOOT 1965	IF YOU COULD READ MY MIND 1970	
THE WAY I FEEL 1967	EARLY LIGHTFOOT 1971	
DID SHE MENTION MY NAME 1968	SUMMER SIDE OF LIFE 1971	
	DON QUIXOTE 1972	
	OLD DAN'S RECORDS 1972	
BACK HERE ON EARTH 1968	SUNDOWN 1973	

COLD ON THE SHOULDER 1975
GORD'S GOLD VOLUME I 1975
SUMMERTIME DREAM 1976
ENDLESS WIRE 1978
DREAM STREET ROSE 1980
SHADOWS 1982
SALUTE 1983
EAST SIDE OF MIDNIGHT 1986

OVER 60 MINUTES WITH...
   GORDON LIGHTFOOT 1987
GORD'S GOLD VOLUME II 1988
EARLY MORNING RAIN — BEST OF
   GORDON LIGHTFOOT 1990
BEST OF GORDON LIGHTFOOT
   1991
WAITING FOR YOU 1993

Lighthouse

DICK ARMIN (*cello*)
RALPH COLE (*guitar*)
DON DiNOVO (*violin*)
PAUL HOFFERT (*keyboards, vibes*)
KEITH JOLLIMORE (*sax, flute*)
BOB McBRIDE (*vocals*)

PETER PANTALUK (*trumpet*)
SKIP PROKOP (*drums*)
HOWARD SHORE (*sax, flute*)
LARRY SMITH (*trombone*)
LOUIS YACKNIW (*bass*)

Founded by drummer Skip Prokop in 1968, Lighthouse remains one of the more prominent groups to emerge on the Canadian rock music scene. Prokop started on drums in 1963 when he played with small bands in legion halls in Toronto. His first group was the Riverside Three. Six months later they broke up and he ended up playing in other city bands. In the mid-1960s he met Bill Misener, Chuck Beale, and Danny Gerard and together they became The Paupers. In 1968 Prokop left the band to organize a thirteen-piece group called Lighthouse.

The first musician asked to join the group was Ralph Cole, whom Prokop had met while still a member of The Paupers. Signed to MGM Records in the United States, Lighthouse was managed by Vinnie Fusco, a music publisher in New York, who was impressed by their demo tape. Prokop began recruiting other members for the group: Grant Fullerton and Pinky Dauvin from Toronto's Stitch in Tyme; and saxophonist Howard Shore, a composer friend of Paul Hoffert's.

When Al Kooper and Mike Bloomfield canceled their May 1969 show at The Rockpile, a club in Toronto, Lighthouse was added as a last-minute replacement. They were introduced by Duke Ellington. Later that same year, they signed a contract with RCA Records. Their only two singles with the label were *Feels So Good* in November 1969 and *The Chant* in March 1970.

They played at the Newport, Monterey, and Boston Globe jazz festivals, the Atlantic City Pop Festival, and the Isle of Wight Festival in England. They were invited to play at Woodstock, but the group backed out because they feared it would turn into a horror show. They were also one of the first rock acts who refused to tour South Africa.

By the end of 1970 they had signed with GRT Records and Jimmy Ienner became their producer. The beginning of the end came in 1973 when Paul Hoffert left the group, followed by Bob McBride, who had already recorded his first solo album on Capitol Records. In 1974, Skip Prokop left. Ralph Cole replaced him as leader until the rest of the group disbanded in 1976.

In September 1982, the original members of Lighthouse reunited again for four shows at the Ontario Place Forum and in 1993 Lighthouse reunited again for a concert in Toronto's City Hall Square. Original members Hoffert, Prokop, and Cole were joined by Danny Clancy as lead singer and Donald Quan on keyboards. Bob McBride was unable to join due to ill health.

Today, Prokop is a successful Christian rock singer and host of his own weekly radio program of Christian rock and gospel music called *Rock in the Hard Place*.

Singles		
Feels So Good 1969		*Sunny Days* 1972
The Chant 1970		*You Girl* 1973
Hats Off (To the Stranger) 1971		*Broken Guitar Blues* 1973
One Fine Morning 1971		*Pretty Lady* 1973
Take It Slow 1971-72		*Can You Feel It* 1974
I Just Wanna Be Your Friend 1972		*Good Day* 1974

Albums/CD		
PEACING IT ALL TOGETHER 1970		CAN YOU FEEL IT 1973
ONE FINE MORNING 1971		GOOD DAY 1974
THOUGHTS OF MOVIN' ON 1971		THE BEST OF LIGHTHOUSE 1975
LIGHTHOUSE LIVE! 1972		THE BEST OF LIGHTHOUSE —
SUNNY DAYS 1972		SUNNY DAYS AGAIN 1989

(By Bob McBride)

Singles		
Pretty City Lady 1972		*Treasure Song* 1973
Butterfly Days 1973		*Do It Right* 1974

Album	
BUTTERFLY DAYS 1973	

Lisa Hartt Band

RAY BLAKE (*guitar*)   LISA HARTT (*vocals*)
MARTY CORDRAY (*drums*)   RICHARD YUEN (*keyboards*)
DENNY GERARD (*bass*)

Lisa Hartt has been performing since she was fifteen years old and has toured the world. With her band she made her debut in the fall of 1973 in Montreal. A former member of the Gino Vannelli band, Hartt has worked with Ken Tobias and Cliff Jones in New York. In the fall of 1975, Hartt and her band released their first single, *The Last Blues I'll Ever Sing*.

| Singles | *The Last Blues I'll Ever Sing* 1975 | *Old Time Movie* 1976 *All Over The World* 1977 |

Little Caesar and the Consuls

BRUCE MORSHEAD
    (*vocals, keyboards*)
KEN PERNOKIS (*guitar*)
NORM SHERRAT (*sax*)

TOM WILSON (*bass*)
GARY WRIGHT (*drums*):
    Replaced by WAYNE CONNORS

Little Caesar and the Consuls first formed in 1957 in Toronto and were named after a British sedan. The original lineup consisted of Bruce Morshead, Norm Sherrat, Peter Deremiccious, Ken Pernokis, and Gene MacLellan, who would later write *Snowbird* for Anne Murray. Robbie Robertson was with the group for a brief time but left because he did not like the style of music the group was playing.

In 1963 Little Caesar and the Consuls had their first hit, *If I Found a New Girl*, on Columbia Records. Two years later, they recorded *My Girl Sloopy* on the Red Leaf label, which was distributed by Raleigh Records and Caravan Records. *Sloopy* was also recorded by The McCoys, a group from Union City, Indiana. Both versions charted in the United States and Canada. In the U.S., the American version reached number one, while the Canadian version reached number fifty, selling over 140,000 copies, and leading to offers to tour with the Beach Boys, to appear on American Bandstand, and to play in Los Angeles. But The Consuls declined because all but of one of them were committed to day jobs.

On December 13, 1965, the band's version of The Miracles' *You Really Got a Hold on Me* was number one on RPM's singles chart. The Consuls returned to Columbia for their last two hits, *Mercy Mr. Perry* and *My Love for You*. That same year, Morshead left the band to return to Kodak where he worked while attending night school in the 1950s. He was replaced by Steve Macko. Tom Wilson left in 1969 to become an agent, later handling such Canadian acts as April Wine, Ronnie Hawkins, and Bachman-Turner Overdrive.

The group broke up in 1971, but reunited in 1973 for a six week tour. The lineup was comprised of originals Norm Sherrat (vocals), Gary Wright (drums) and Tom Wilson (bass), with new members Paul Denyes (keyboards) and Tommy Graham (guitar). In 1976 they reunited again, this time with new members John Bradley on guitar and Bob Oliffe on bass. Under the leadership of Steve Macko, they opened for The Bay City Rollers on their Canadian tour. They also recorded a new up-tempo version of *Sloopy* retitled *Hang on Sloopy*.

With a different lineup, Little Caesar and the Consuls were back in 1993. This time the members were Sherrat, Wright, Macko, and Wilson, along with Tony Crivaro and Vic Wilson who had co-managed Rush with Ray Danniels.

Their reunion also marked a return to the recording studio where they made the album SINCE 1956, featuring cover versions of such rock 'n' roll favorites as Hank Ballard's *Annie Had a Baby*, The Coasters' *Love Potion #9* and The Four Seasons' *Let's Hang On*.

Singles

If I Found a New Girl 1963	*One Thousand Miles Away* 1966
My Girl Sloopy 1965	
You Really Got a Hold on Me 1965	*Mercy Mr. Perry* 1966
You Laugh Too Much 1966	*My Love for You* 1967
	Hang on Sloopy 1976

Albums/CDs   LITTLE CAESAR AND THE CONSULS 1965
SINCE 1956 1993

The Lords of London

GREG FITZPATRICK (*bass guitar, vocals*): Replaced by Alex Machin	HUGHIE LEGGAT (*guitar*)
	JOHN RICHARDSON (*guitar, vocals*): Replaced by Paul Naumann
BOB HORNE (*organ*)	DANNY TAYLOR (*drums*)

This band began in 1966 when five teenagers from the east end of Toronto formed a group called Nucleus. Eventually, Nucleus changed their name to The Lords of London when the music they were playing changed from hard rock to more mainstream pop. The Lords' first hit was *Cornflakes and Ice Cream* in 1967 on the independent Canadian Ampex label.

Another group that evolved out of The Lords of London was Leather, whose music was similar to that of Nucleus.

In 1971 the group changed its name to A Foot in Coldwater and signed a contract with Daffodil Records. That same year Greg Fitzpatrick left to concentrate on a solo career. Two of his hits were *Tuneful Spoonful* and *We're All Singing the Same Song*, both released in 1971. A Foot in Coldwater had two major hits for Daffodil Records: *(Make Me Do) Anything You Want* and *(Isn't Love Unkind) In My Life*.

When the band split up in 1977, Scottish-born Hughie Leggat went on to form the bands Thunder Road and Private Eyes. He also joined his brother Gordon as a duo, and in 1982, they recorded their debut album, ILLUMINATIONS, on Capitol Records. Another group that evolved from The Lords of London was Leather.

A Foot In Coldwater reunited for a series of concerts in 1988.

(As The Lords of London)

Singles   *Cornflakes and Ice Cream* 1967
The Popcorn Man/21,000 Dreams 1968
Candy Rainbow 1968

(As A Foot in Coldwater)

Singles   *(Make Me Do) Anything You Want* 1972
(Isn't Life Unkind) In My Life 1973
Lady True 1973

Love Is Coming 1973
Para-Dice 1975
I Know What You Need 1975
Midnight Lady 1976

Albums/CDs   A FOOT IN COLDWATER 1972
THE SECOND FOOT IN COLDWATER 1973
ALL AROUND US 1974

BREAKING THROUGH 1977
FOOTPRINTS 1 1983
FOOTPRINTS 2 1983

Lost and Profound

LISA BOUDREAU *(vocals)*
TERRY TOMPKINS *(vocals)*

The history of this Toronto-based duo began in Calgary where Lisa Boudreau and Terry Tompkins met. Both were members of local bands — Lisa in The Now Feeling and Tery in The Left Book Club. They eventually teamed up as The Psychedelic Folk Virgins, and moved from Calgary to Toronto.

Lisa began her musical career while still in high school in Moncton, New Brunswick, where she occasionally played back up for The Nerves. After the members split up in search of separate careers, they coincidentally all ended up in Calgary and formed The Left Book Club.

Born in Hamilton, Terry became interested in music when he received a Beatles compilation album. He spent much of his youth in Hamilton and then Calgary writing songs. When he talked to groups like The Sex Pistols and The Ramones about music, they convinced him to join a band. Before joining The Now Feeling he was a member of The Snots, The Deceitful Concubines, and Hamilton's The False Idols.

Boudreau and Tompkins added Allan Baekeland and Bartok Guitarsplat to the group and released an independent cassette called *The Bottled Romance of Nowhere*. When Guitarsplat left, he was replaced by

Curtis Driedger of The Ceedees. Then Driedger and Baekeland left to pursue solo work. Terry and Lisa eventually signed a contract with Polygram Records under the name of Lost and Profound.

Their self-titled debut album was released in the spring of 1992. The first single, *Brand New Set of Lies*, went Top 20 in *The Record's* Power Trax chart. Terry and Lisa are backed up by Alan Beardsell on mandolin and guitar, Vic D'Arsie on keyboards, Anton Evans on bass, and David Quinton-Steinberg on drums.

Singles		
Brand New Set of Lies 1992		*All Consuming Mistress* 1993
Curb the Angels 1992		*Miracles Happen* 1994
Winter Raging 1992		

CDs		
LOST AND PROFOUND 1992		MEMORY THIEF 1994

Lost Dakotas

PAUL DAKOTA (*vocals*)	ADAM FAUX (*guitar*):
RON DUFFY (*drums*)	Replaced by RICK O'BRIEN
	GREG MCCONNELL (*bass*)

The Lost Dakotas began in 1989 as the street busking duo of Paul Dakota and Greg McConnell. Prior to their partnership, Paul was a solo act, while Greg was bassist for the group Absolute Whores.

Dakota and McConnell first started playing on the corner of Yonge and Dundas Streets and later in the Toronto subway system, where they were rated number one at the 1991 subway auditions.

Adam Faux of the punk band Pig Farmer was a member of the group until October 1992, joining the other members in the recording of the Lost Dakota's independent cassette, LOVE TO PLAY, in December 1990. In 1991 they released their independent album LAST TRAIN TO KIPLING, which included Faux's song, *Sugar Shaker*. When Faux left, he was replaced by Rick O'Brien from Wolfville, Nova Scotia. To promote their debut album, they hired Toronto artist Erella Vent who was also responsible for the group's colorful stage and video sets.

Singles	*To Love Someone* 1992	*Over You* 1993
CDs	LAST TRAIN TO KIPLING 1991	SUN MACHINE 1993

Lisa Lougheed

Lisa Lougheed grew up listening to her brother Danny's record collection, which included the O'Jays and Rose Royce. She attended Etobicoke's School of the Performing Arts for four years, and her first professional job was part of Canada's Wonderland's stage troupe as a singer and dancer. At seventeen she was one of the featured voices on the soundtrack of the animated series *The Raccoons*. Her performances gained her a 1988 Juno nomination as Most Promising Female Vocalist. That same year she enjoyed minor success with the hit, *Run with Us*.

Lougheed signed a recording contract with Warner Music Canada in 1991. Her debut album, WORLD LOVE came out in March 1992. *Love Vibe* and the title track were the first two singles. In 1993 she released her second album, PEACE AND HARMONY. The first single and video was *Won't Give up My Music*.

Singles		
Run with Us 1988		*World Love* 1992
Running Out of Love		*Love You by Heart* 1992
(with Acosta Russell) 1992		*Won't Give up My Music* 1993
Love Vibe 1992		

CDs	WORLD LOVE 1992	PEACE AND HARMONY 1993

Love and Sas   LOVENA FOX
SASKIA GAREL

This Toronto based duo's sound combines silky soul, hip hop, and reggae. With their first hit single, *I Don't Need Your Kiss* in 1991, they became an overnight sensation.

Lovena Fox (a.k.a. Love) was blessed with a strong voice. Her professional career began as lead singer for various funk and R&B groups. She also appeared on stage in Vancouver, including one thousand performances as part of the cast of the hit musical *Ain't Misbehavin'*. She gained recognition as a featured solo performer when she backed up Bon Jovi, Loverboy, The Payola$, and Colin James.

Saskia Garel (a.k.a. Sas) was born in Kingston, Jamaica. At the age of six she moved to Canada with her parents. She developed a smooth and sensual voice and went on to study jazz and classical voice at York University, where she earned the Oscar Petersen Award for high artistic standards. She signed on as a vocalist with the Toronto funk, reggae, and salsa band Coconut Groove.

Love & Sas is one of Canada's most popular dance acts.

Singles		
I Don't Need Your Kiss 1991		*Don't Stop Now* 1992
Call My Name 1991		*Once in a Lifetime* 1992

CD	CALL MY NAME 1992

Loverboy   PAUL DEAN (*guitar*)   MIKE RENO (*vocals*)
MATT FRENETTE (*drums*)   SCOTT SMITH (*bass*)
DOUG JOHNSON (*keyboards*)

Formed in Calgary by Paul Dean and Mike Reno, then relocated to Vancouver in 1979, Loverboy became one of Canada's hottest rock bands. Discovered by a CBS talent scout during a club appearance, the band recorded a self-titled debut album and released the single *The Kid Is Hot Tonite* in the summer of 1980.

They broke up in 1987 after one last show in Europe with Def Leppard. But in 1991 they reunited for a benefit concert for the late Brian Macleod. They reunited again in 1993 for a series of dates in British Columbia, Alberta, and Saskatchewan.

Singles		
The Kid Is Hot Tonite 1980	*Gangs in the Street* 1984	
Lady of the '80s 1981	*Lovin' Every Minute of It* 1985	
Working for the Weekend 1981-82	*Dangerous* 1985	
Hot Girls in Love 1983	*This Could Be The Night* 1986	
Queen of the Broken Hearts 1983	*Heaven in Your Eyes* 1986	
	Notorius 1987	
	Too Hot 1989	

Albums/CDs		
LOVERBOY 1980	LOVIN' EVERY MINUTE OF IT 1985
GET LUCKY 1981	WILDSIDE 1987
KEEP IT UP 1983	BIG ONES 1989

Luba Luba Kowalchyk was born in 1958 and, as a teenager, traveled across Canada to sing traditional folk tunes in Canadian Ukrainian communities. She had begun taking vocal lessons as a child and learned to play the guitar, flute, and piano by the time she was in her teens.

In 1979 Luba, drummer Peter Marunzak, and guitarist Mark Lyman formed a rock group and released a mini-album featuring *Every Time I See Your Picture*, a song dedicated to Luba's late father. She later married Marunzak.

In 1984 Luba recorded her first album, and two years later came her second, BETWEEN EARTH AND SKY, which contained her first chart hit, *How Many (Rivers to Cross)*. Its soul-stirring sound made it one of the most popular songs of the year.

Singles		
Let It Go 1984	*Strength in Numbers* 1986	
Storm Before the Calm 1985	*Act of Mercy* 1987	
Secrets and Sins 1985	*When a Man Loves a Woman* 1987-88	
How Many (Rivers to Cross) 1986	*Giving Away a Miracle* 1989	
Innocent (With an Explanation) 1986	*No More Words* 1990	
	Little Salvation 1990	

Albums/CDs   SECRETS AND SINS 1984   60 MINUTES WITH . . . LUBA 1987
BETWEEN EARTH AND SKY 1986   ALL OR NOTHING 1989

Luke & the Apostles

LUKE GIBSON   PAT LITTLE
PETER JERMYN   MIKE MCKENNA
JIM JONES

Luke & the Apostles began playing in Toronto's Yorkville Village where they performed to sold out audiences on the coffeehouse circuit. In 1967 they released their first hit single, *Been Burnt*, which was also played in the U.S.A. In August of that year, the group broke up.

Luke Gibson joined Kensington Market; Mike McKenna became one of the Ugly Ducklings and later McKenna Mendelson Mainline; and Pat Little started with Tranfusion which later became known as Crazy Horse. The original members of the band reunited in 1970 and had success with the hit, *You Make Me High*. By the end of the year they had disbanded again.

Gibson enjoyed brief success as a solo artist in 1972. He also turned to film and starred opposite Genevieve Bujold in *Journey* (1972), directed by Paul Almond. Gibson sang several of his own songs on the soundtrack. That same year, True North Records released his first solo album.

(As Luke & the Apostles)
Singles   *Been Burnt* 1967   *You Make Me High* 1970

(By Luke Gibson)
Single   *Another Perfect Day* 1972

Album   ANOTHER PERFECT DAY 1972

Ray Lyell

From Hamilton, Ontario, Ray Lyell and his back-up band The Storm released their self-titled debut album in 1989. To help prepare him for his second album, DESERT WINDS, Lyell lived in a tent in the desert 30 miles from Phoenix in 1991. The band recorded the album in the Bearsville studio in New York, Winfield Studios in Hamilton, and The Metal Works in Mississauga.

Between recording albums Lyell learned about another band who called themselves The Storm. To avoid a legal suit, they dropped the name and became known simply as Ray Lyell.

Singles *Another Man's Gun* 1989   *Desert Nights* 1993
        Cruel Life 1990   *Don't Let Go* 1993
        Carry Me 1990   *Bitter Creek* 1993
        Gypsy Wind 1993

  CDs   RAY LYELL AND THE STORM 1989
        DESERT WINDS 1993

Gisele Mackenzie

Gisele Lefleche was born in 1927 and adopted her husband's surname. She learned to play the piano and violin while growing up in her hometown of Winnipeg. Her first professional job was with the Bob Shuttelworth Band. Shuttelworth later became her manager.

During the late 1940s she had her own radio show on the CBC. In the mid-1950s she recorded three songs that were minor hits, and she hosted her own TV series on the NBC network during the 1957-58 season. Her first two albums, both entitled GISELE, were released by RCA in 1958.

Singles *Hard To Get* 1955   *The Star You Wished upon*
        Pepper-Hot Baby 1955   *Last Night* 1956

Albums GISELE 1958
        GISELE 1958
        GISELE MACKENZIE AT THE EMPIRE ROOM OF
           THE WALDORF ASTORIA 1960
        GISELE MACKENZIE SINGS LULLABY AND GOODNIGHT 1963

Rita MacNeil

Born in 1944, this Maritime folksinger from Big Pond, Cape Breton, has been making music since 1971, when she wrote her first song. At seventeen, Rita MacNeil moved to Toronto, married, and had two children. Divorced in 1978, she moved to Ottawa, where she scrubbed floors for a living. She later returned to Big Pond where she formed a trio. Her big break came at Expo 86 in Vancouver where she played at the Canadian Pavilion for a six-week run.

She recorded her first album, BORN A WOMAN, in 1975, the first of three recorded independently. Her major label debut came in 1987 with *Flying on Her Own* on Virgin Records.

Her accomplishments are many. She is the only female singer ever to have three albums in Australia's Top 100 in the same year. In 1990 she sold more records in Canada than Garth Brooks and Clint Black. In 1991 she was invited to play at Royal Albert Hall in London, England. In 1992 she was named a member of the Order of Canada by Governor-General Ray Hnatyshyn.

Singles *Flying on Your Own* 1987   *When Love Surrounded You and I*
        Fast Train to Tokyo 1987   1990
        Used to You 1987   *You Taught Me Well* 1990-91
        Leave Her to Memory 1988   *Call Me and I'll Be There* 1991
        Walk on Through 1988   *Bring It on Home to Me* 1992
        We'll Reach for the Sky Tonight   *Moment in Time* 1993
          1990   *Shining Strong* 1993

Albums/CDs BORN A WOMAN 1975 RITA 1989
PART OF THE MYSTERY 1981 NOW THE BELLS RING 1989
I'M NOT WHAT I SEEM 1983 HOME I'LL BE 1990
FLYING ON YOUR OWN 1987 THINKING OF YOU 1992
REASON TO BELIEVE 1988 ONCE UPON A CHRISTMAS 1993

Madrigal PETER BOYNTON (*piano, organ, bass, vocals, keyboards*) DON SIMPSON (*drums, vocals*)
JOHN SWAINSON (*guitar, bass, vocals*)
RICK HENDERSON (*guitar, vocals*)
ARVO LEPP (*lead guitar*)

Formed in 1968, the original members of Madrigal met while still students at Willowdale Junior High School. They were formed as a studio group by producer Greg Hambleton of Tuesday Records. Their first hit on the Tuesday label was *I Believe in Sunshine* in October 1970. In 1971 they had one more hit with *Hallelujah*.

Madrigal broke up in 1973, but two years later, they reunited with many membership changes.

Singles *I Believe in Sunshine* 1970 *Hallelujah* 1971

Album SUNSHINE AND BAKED BEANS 1970

The Magic Cycle KEVIN BARRY (*drums, vocals*) JOEY ROME (*bass, vocals*)
PAUL CRAIG (*rhythm guitar, vocals*) STAN THERIAULT (*lead guitar, vocals*)
PETER GOODALE (*organ*) PETE YOUNG (*guitar*)

Formed in Toronto in 1966, The Magic Cycle recorded their first hit *Let's Run Away* on Red Leaf Records in early 1967. The original lineup was comprised of Paul Clinch (a.k.a. Paul Craig), Stan Theriault, Pete Young, Joey Rome, and Kevin Barry. In the spring of 1970 they became a sextet with the addition of Peter Goodale. The principle songwriters of the group were Rome and Craig.

The Magic Cycle later became known as The Cycle in 1970 when they recorded on Tamarac Records. The release of their 1973 single *Magic Music* marked the tenth anniversary of the label. In 1976 The Cycle had changed personnel and became known as Choya. Paul Clinch died on November 8, 1988.

Singles *Let's Run Away* 1967 *Gimme Some Time* 1971
Doctor Lollipop 1968 *All I Really Need Is You* (The Cycle) 1972
Groovy Things 1970
Wait for the Miracle (The Cycle) 1971 *If You Call Out My Name* 1973
Magic Music 1973

Albums SATURDAY AFTERNOON RUMMAGE SALE 1970
MAGIC MUSIC 1973

Mahogany Rush

JIM AYOUB (*drums*)   FRANK MARINO (*guitar*)
PAUL HARWOOD (*bass*)

Mahogany Rush, from Montreal, was more famous in the United States than in their native Canada. Their heavy metal sound can be attributed to leader Frank Marino's affection for the late Jimi Hendrix's music. In the U.S., Mahogany Rush headlined shows with The Chambers Brothers, Graham Central Station, Ted Nugent, and The Amboy Dukes. Their first single *Buddy* was recorded at the Little Coyote Studio in Quebec City, and their debut album was called MAXOOM.

Singles *Buddy* 1972   *Satisfy Your Soul* 1975
A New Rock and Roll 1974

Albums MAXOOM 1972   MAHOGANY RUSH IV 1976
CHILD OF THE NOVELTY 1974   WORLD ANTHEM 1977
STRANGE UNIVERSE 1975   TALES OF THE UNEXPECTED 1979

Major Hoople's Boarding House

PETER BEACOCK (*keyboards*)   ROCKY HOWELL (*lead guitar*)
DAVID GOODING   ED MILLER (*drums*)
    (*alto, tenor sax, flute*)   KEITH STAHLBAUM (*bass*)
DAVID GREGG (*slide trombone*)

Major Hoople's Boarding House began as an amateur Galt High School trio called The Shan-de-leers. In mid-1967 three of its members (Rockey Howell, Peter Pandalino, Rick Riddell) decided to turn professional and added a new member, David Lodge, on bass. By November of that year the group changed its name to Major Hoople's Boarding House; the creator of the *Major Hoople* comic strip allowed the group to use the name.

Until their success with the hit *I'm Running After You* in the summer of 1975, the group worked in nightclubs between Kitchener and Kingston, Ontario. In 1976 James Leroy joined the group as its new leader, and the group's name was shortened to Boarding House. Leroy died three years later. David Lodge died in late 1986. Rocky Howell remains the only original member from the days at Galt High.

Early in 1982, Major Hoople performed with the Kitchener-Waterloo Symphony. Howell gathered together a new group called Boardinghouse in 1988 in honor of the group's twentieth anniversary.

Besides Howell on vocals and guitar, it was comprised of Grant Heywood on vocals and drums, Gary Hintz on bass, and Ralph Hetke on keyboards.

Singles

All of My Body 1971	*You Girl* 1976
Lady 1971	*Someone* 1980
I Believe in You 1972	*This Song Reminds Me of You*
Everything's the Same 1972-73	1981
I'm Running after You 1975	*You're Hurtin' Everyone* 1983

Albums   THE HOOPLES ALBUM 1981

THE NEW ADVENTURES OF HOOPLES 1986

Mandala

WHITEY GLEN (*drums*)   PRAKASH (*bass*)
GEORGE OLLIVER (*vocals*):   DOMENIC TROIANO (*guitar*)
    Replaced by ROY KENNER

Domenic Troiano was the driving force behind one of Canada's best rock groups of the mid-1960s, Mandala. He first came to Canada from Italy at age fifteen and in 1961 started playing the guitar. He was first a member of Robbie Lane's The Disciples before he formed his first group, The Rogues.

In 1966 they changed their name to Mandala, and the following year they released their first hit single, *Opportunity*. The following year, George Olliver left to form his own group called George and the Children. He was replaced by Roy Kenner. The group added Prakash in 1969 as bass player and the group's name changed to Bush. Their only hit was *I Can Hear You Calling* in 1970. A year later they disbanded.

When George and the Children broke up in 1968, Olliver formed a new band called Natural Gas in 1969. Their first single was *All Powerful Man* in 1970 from their self-titled debut album on the Firebird label. In 1973, Olliver went solo. His first hit single was *I May Never Get to See You Again* on Much Records.

(As Mandala)

Singles

Opportunity 1967	*Love-Itis* 1968
Give and Take 1967	*You Got Me* 1968

Albums   SOUL CRUSADE 1968   MANDALA CLASSICS 1986

(As Bush)

Single   *I Can Hear You Calling* 1970

Album   BUSH 1970

Maneige

ALAIN BERGERON
JEROME LANGLOIS
VINCENT LANGLOIS
DENIS LAPIERRE

YVES LEONARD
PAUL PICARD
GILLES SCHETAGNE

A jazz/rock fusion band from Montreal, Maneige formed in 1972. Denis Lapierre and Yves Leonard had known each other since they were thirteen, and together with Alain Bergeron, Vincent Langlois, and Jerome Langlois, they were members of the rock band Lasting Weep.

After building up a local following in their native province, Maneige decided to break into the English market where they were well received in Western Canada and Northern Ontario. Their self-titled debut album on Capitol Records was released in 1975, followed by a second that same year, LES PORCHES DE NOTRE-DAME. Following their 1981 album, MONTREAL, 6 A.M., Maneige took a three year break, but returned in 1984 to make the last album IMAGES.

Album

MANEIGE 1975
LES PORCHES DE NOTRE-DAME
  1975
NI VENT...NI NOUVELLE 1977

LIBRE SERVICE 1978
COMPOSITE 1980
MONTREAL, 6 A.M. 1981
IMAGES 1984

The Marshmallow Soup Group

TIM COTTINI
TIM EATON
JOHN LEMMON

RON "SMACK" SMITH
WAYNE SWEET

This Ottawa-based band had one major Canadian hit in November 1969 called *I Love Candy*. That same month they represented Canada at the International Trade Fair in Lima, Peru.

Tim Eaton later had success as a solo artist with his own backup group called Timothy. His hits were *Riverboat Ladies* (1972), *Brotherhood* (1972), and *Rock and Roll Music* (1972-73). In 1974, he recorded the hit *Falling Out of Love* as Buster Brown.

Single *I Love Candy* 1969-70

Martha and the Muffins

CARL FINKLE (*bass*)
MARK GANE (*guitar*)
TIM GANE (*drums*)
ANDY HAAS (*sax*)

MARTHA JOHNSON (*vocals, keyboards*)
MARTHA LADLY (*vocals, keyboards, trombone*):
  Replaced by JOCELYNE LANOIS

The history of Martha and the Muffins goes back to 1975 when all of the members lived in the same neighborhood in Thornhill, in the north end of Toronto. By 1975 they all had moved to downtown Toronto. Martha Johnson was in a band called The Doncasters. In 1977 Mark Gane, David Millar, and Carl Finkle asked her to play keyboards in their new band, which also included Mark's brother Tim, and Martha Ladley. They called themselves Martha and the Muffins.

After they made their first independent single, *Insect Love/Suburban Dream*, in 1979, they were offered an eight album deal with Virgin Records in the United Kingdom. During 1979 and 1980 they toured England. They played at the New York City New Wave club, Hurrah. Martha and the Muffins were the first Canadian act to perform there.

Their debut single on Virgin in the United States was *Echo Beach*. It was their only major hit. They later changed their name to M+M. *Song in My Head* was their first effort under the new name in 1986.

In 1984, Martha Johnson and Mark Ganz moved to Bath, England. After the release of *Song in My Head*, they were not heard from again until 1992 when their next album, MODERN LULLABY, was released. The first single was *Rainbow Sign*. They also reverted back to their original name, Martha and the Muffins.

Singles

Insect Love/Suburban Dream 1979
Echo Beach 1980
Paint by Number Heart 1980
About Insomnia 1980-81
Women around the World at Work 1981-82

Mystery Walk (as M+M) 1984
Cooling the Medium (as M+M) 1984
Song in My Head (as M+M) 1986
Rainbow Sign 1992

Albums/CDs

METRO MUSIC 1980
THIS IS THE ICE AGE 1981
DANSEPARC 1983

MYSTERY WALK 1984
THE WORLD IS A BALL 1986
MODERN LULLABY 1992

Mashmakhan

RAY BLAKE (*guitar*)
BRIAN EDWARDS (*bass, vocals*)
PIERRE SENECAL (*flute*)
JERRY MERCER (*drums*)

The origins of Mashmakhan go back to 1960 when all four members were a backup group for a Montreal R&B singer. In 1965 they formed The Triangle, a backup group for R&B singer Trevor Payne.

Tired of playing backup, they left Payne and signed a contract with Columbia Records. They also changed their name to Mashmakhan, the name of a drug. *As the Years Go By* was their first hit in the spring of 1970. It became an international smash. In Japan they were presented with the Hit Disc Award for having the third largest selling foreign record ever released in Japan.

Pierre Senecal, who left the band in the early 1970s, resurfaced as a solo artist in 1979 with the song called *The Gypsy* on Nova Scotia's Black Bear Records. In 1983, he recorded a solo album called VOICI MON AMOUR.

Singles   *As the Years Go By* 1970   *Ride Johnny Ride* 1972
          Days When We Are Free 1970   *Dance a Little Step* 1973
          Start All Over 1971

Album   MASHMAKHAN 1970

Ray Materick

Ray Materick developed an interest in poetry and music while growing up in Brantford. In the late 1960s he traveled across Canada and performed as a solo act and as a member of a duo.

In 1972 Materick signed with Kanata Records. After one album, SIDE STREETS, the label folded, and he switched to Asylum Records. *Linda Put the Coffee On* was his only national hit.

Singles   *Season of Plenty* 1972   *Northbound Plane* 1975
          Linda Put the Coffee On 1975

Albums   SIDESTREETS 1972   DAYS OF THE HEART 1975
         RAY MATERICK 1974   BEST FRIEND OVERNIGHT 1976
         NEON RAIN 1975   FEVER IN RIO 1978

Shirley Matthews

From Harrow, Ontario, Shirley Matthews started singing in church and school. At age nineteen she played at the Club Blue Note. Discovered by an associate of Bob Crewe, who managed the Four Seasons, Matthews went to New York and signed a record deal. Her first single was *Big Town Boy*, which sold a million copies in late 1963 and early 1964.

Singles   *Big Town Boy* 1963-64   *Private Property* 1964
         He Makes Me Feel So Pretty   *Stop the Clock* 1965
          1964

Max Webster

PAUL KERSEY (*drums*): Replaced   MIKE TILKA (*bass*)
    by GARY MCCRACKEN   TERRY WATKINSON (*keyboards*):
KIM MITCHELL (*guitar, vocals*)   Replaced by DAVE STONE

Formed in Sarnia in 1973 by Kim Mitchell, the group moved to Toronto three years later where they signed a contract with Anthem Records. They remained with the label during the band's eight years together.

Known for their unpredictable musical progressions and abstract lyrics, half of the group's name comes from a band Mike Tilka once played in, the other half from a song that band used to play. The band's self-titled debut album came out in May 1976, and in January 1977 they signed an international record deal with Mercury Records.

In the spring of 1981 the group broke up and Mitchell went on to pursue a successful solo career.

Singles *Let Go the Line* 1979   *Check* 1980
Paradise Skies 1980   *Blue River Liquor Store* 1981

Albums/CDs MAX WEBSTER 1976   A MILLION VACATIONS 1979
HIGH CLASS IN BORROWED   LIVE MAGNETIC AIR 1980
SHOES 1977   UNIVERSAL JUVENILES 1980
MUTINY UP MY SLEEVE 1978   BEST OF MAX WEBSTER 1989

Denise McCann Hailed as Canada's Disco Queen because of her 1977 hit, *Tattoo Man*, Denise McCann was born in 1950 and grew up in a musical family in Clinton, Ohio. Her father played guitar, while the rest of the family all played the piano. As a young girl she participated in the local church choir and high school musicals. In 1967 she moved to California where she bought her first guitar and attended the first Monterey Pop Festival. For the next five years she was a folksinger on the coffeehouse circuit.

In 1972 she joined her first rock band; two years later she moved to Vancouver where she worked as a folksinger at the Egress. It was there, in 1974, that she wrote *Tattoo Man*.

McCann also worked on a number of jingles and toured with the Vancouver band Hot Crackers. *Tattoo Man* finally became a hit in 1977 when a Polydor sales rep from Montreal recognized the song's potential. Its follow-up, *I Don't Want to Forget You*, was also successful.

Singles *It Still Hurts* 1976   *I Don't Want to Forget You* 1977
Tattoo Man 1977

Albums DENISE MCCANN 1977   MIDNIGHT MAN 1979

Bob McCord and the Vibrations TOM BENNETT (*drums*)   AL DUFF (*rhythm guitar*)
PAT BRYNES (*organ*)   KEITH MCDONNELL (*bass*)
ROGER COOKE (*lead guitar, vocals*)   BOB MCCORD (*lead vocals*)

Bob McCord and the Vibrations were one of Kingston, Ontario's top bands. Formed in late 1961 and early 1962, they performed mostly in high schools in the Kingston-Brockville area and in Alexandria Bay, New York. Pat Byrnes, Al Duff, and Roger Cooke were all from Kingston. Tom Bennett and Keith McDonnell lived on Wolfe Island.

One of the highlights of their musical career was sharing the same stage on one of their Wednesday night shows with Roy Orbison. They played show tunes and covers of the Top 40 hits of the day. In 1964 John Bermingham, who was then program director of CKLC Radio in Kingston, wrote two original songs that the band recorded in Toronto on the Star label, a subsidiary of Arc Records. It was the first disc pressed by the new record company. The "A" side was *I Missed My Year*, while *Grain of Sand* was the "B" side. During the summer of 1964, it was a Top 5 hit in Kingston.

McCord left the band in 1965, and The Vibrations broke up later that same year.

Single *I Missed My Year/Grain of Sand* 1964

Kate and Anna McGarrigle Born of French-Canadian and Irish parents in St.-Sauveurs-des-Monts, Kate and Anna McGarrigle have been singing together since 1959. They both sing in English and French, and they both can play piano, banjo, guitar, and button accordion.

In 1963 Kate and Anna began playing in Montreal's coffeehouses as part of the Mountain City Four, a folk group completed by Jack Nissenson and Peter Weldon. By the 1970s they gained international recognition as songwriters with *Heart Like a Wheel*, first recorded in 1972 by McKendree Spring, then in 1975 by Linda Ronstadt.

Signed to Warner Brothers, the McGarrigle Sisters' self-titled debut album was released in 1975. It was followed by DANCER WITH BRUISED KNEES and PRONTO MONTO. In addition to recording, the sisters appeared at the 1976 Charley Wakes Folk Festival in Lancashire, England and made their London debut at Victoria Palace that same year.

The McGarrigles's repertoire includes songs inspired by the various styles of popular music and French-Canadian folk music.

In 1992 BMG Music released an album of new material which included *Mother Mother*, the album's first video.

Albums/CDs

KATE AND ANNA MCGARRIGLE 1976

DANCER WITH BRUISED KNEES 1977

PRONTO MONTO 1978

ENTRE LA JEUNESSE ET LA SAGRESSE 1980

LOVE OVER AND OVER 1982

HEARTBEATS ACCELERATING 1992

MCJ & Cool G

MCJ
Cool G

MCJ (James McQuaid) and Cool G (Richard Gray) were the first dance/rap act in Canada to be signed to a major domestic label, Capitol Records. The duo hail from Halifax, Nova Scotia, but in 1988, they moved to Montreal. They call their music "double R&B" for "rap, rhythm and blues." The first single from their self-titled debut album in 1990 was *So Listen*.

Singles	*So Listen* 1990	*Smooth as Silk* 1993
	No Sexx with My Sister 1993	
CDs	SO LISTEN 1990	DIMENSIONS OF DOUBLE R&B 1993

McKenna Mendelson Mainline

MICHAEL MCKENNA (*vocals, guitar*)
JOE MENDELSON (*vocals, guitar, bass, harmonica*)
TONY NOLASCO (*vocals, drums*)
FRANK "ZEKE" SHEPPARD (*vocals, bass, mandolin, harmonica*)

In 1970, when Joe Mendelson and Michael McKenna put an ad in a Toronto newspaper to form a band, Danny Gerard, the former bass player of The Paupers, joined them but left after three months. Previously McKenna had played with Luke and the Apostles in 1963 and in 1967-68 with The Ugly Ducklings. In 1968 the group went to England to record their first album, STINK, and returned to Canada the following year. The name of the group was shortened to Mainline in mid-1971, and the band broke up in 1972.

Joe Mendelson recorded his first solo album that same year, *Mr. Middle of the Road*. He wrote all the music and played all the instruments. In 1975 he became known as Mendelson Joe and began a career as a painter. He released two albums, SOPHISTO, and a reunion album with Mike McKenna called NO SUBSTITUTE. From 1979 to 1981 he recorded three more albums on Boot Records. By 1988 he had acquired a reputation as a producer. In 1991 he released the hard-edged bluesy album ADDICTED, which was supported by the video of *Passion*. In 1992 Mendelson Joe released his first cassette independently. Entitled *Friendly Cookies*, each one was signed.

Tony Nolasco and McKenna went on to form the group Diamond-back. They had only one hit in 1974, *Just My Way of Loving You*.

(As McKenna Mendelson Mainline)

Singles	*Better Watch Out* 1969	*One Way Ticket* 1970

Albums/CDs	STINK 1969	THE MAINLINE BUMP AND GRIND
	CANADA, OUR HOME AND	REVUE — LIVE AT THE VICTORY
	NATIVE LAND 1971	THEATRE 1972

(As Mainline)

Singles	*Get Down To* 1972	*Games of Love* 1972
Album	BISCUIT MEETS MAINLINE (Mainline & King Biscuit Boy) 1973

Loreena McKennitt

Born in 1957, Loreena McKennitt grew up in Morden, Manitoba, and dreamed of becoming a veterinarian. She loved music, too, and studied piano with Olga Friesen and voice with Elma Gislason. In her teens, Loreena switched from classical to folk music. At seventeen years of age, she played in a folk club in Winnipeg down the street from the girls' school she attended.

By the late 1970s when she started university, she had been introduced to Celtic music. Her love for harp music came from hearing Alan Stivell, a harpist from Brittany. She liked his recording of *The Celtic Harp Renaissance*. In 1984 she bought a second-hand harp that she uses to this day. McKennitt has used Celtic-style folk instruments, such as the harp, fiddle, tin whistle, the Russian balalaika, the Indian sitar and tamboura. She has also made use of synthesizers and electric guitars.

In 1981 she moved to Stratford, Ontario where she worked as a composer, actor, and singer in the Stratford Festival. Using Diane Rapaport's book, *How to Make Your Own Recordings*, she recorded ELEMENTAL, her first of three independent recordings. Her other independent releases were TO DRIVE THE COLD WINTER AWAY and PARALLEL DREAMS.

Signed to Warner Music Canada, her first record with the label was THE VISIT. McKennitt also has written film scores for *Bayo* (1985), the TV movie *Heaven on Earth* (1986), and several National Film Board productions: *The Burning Times, Goddess Revisited, To a Safer Place*, and *Full Circle*.

CDs	ELEMENTAL 1985	PARALLEL DREAMS 1989
	TO DRIVE THE COLD WINTER	THE VISIT 1991
	AWAY 1987	THE MASK AND THE MIRROR 1994

Catherine McKinnon

Born in 1944, Catherine McKinnon made her radio debut in her hometown of Saint John, New Brunswick, at age eight and at twelve her TV debut in London, Ontario. She studied music at Mount Saint

k. d. lang

THE WALTONS

**SPIRIT OF
THE WEST**

**ALANNAH
MYLES**

**THE COWBOY
JUNKIES**

DANIEL LANOIS

JANN ARDEN

**MICHELLE
WRIGHT**

David Gray

BLUE RODEO

JANE SIBERRY

Vincent College in Halifax, and after graduating in 1963, she spent the next seven years as a regular on the CBC television show *Singalong Jubilee*. She also sang on *Don Messer's Jubilee* for two years and on *Music Hop*. The singer also had her own CBC show called *That McKinnon Girl*.

Her first album was *Voice of An Angel* on Arc Records. In 1966 she had a major success with *Until It's Time for You to Go*, a song written by Buffy Sainte-Marie. One of the highlights of her career was her Command Performance for Her Majesty Queen Elizabeth in Halifax in 1976.

Another of McKinnon's talents is acting. She has starred in several musical stage productions, notably *Spring Thaw, Rainbow Stage, The Wizard of Oz*, and *My Fair Lady*. Her first film acting role was in *Same Time Next Year* in the summer of 1976. On television McKinnon also became well known in the "Come Back to Ireland" commercial and as the Florida "Sunshine Girl" in the orange juice commercials.

She returned to the studio in 1980 to make her self-titled debut album on Pickwick's Intercan label featuring the single *That's When You Know*. In December 1992 she recorded her second Christmas album. The year 1993 saw McKinnon perform at benefit concerts for the Multiple Sclerosis Society of Canada, of which she was its national spokesperson.

Singles

Until It's Time for You to Go 1966
Everybody's Got the Right to Love 1970
Peaceful Mountain 1970
This World of Mine 1976-77
That's When You Know 1980
Give Yourself Up 1980
Sail On 1984

Albums

VOICE OF AN ANGEL 1964
VOICE OF AN ANGEL II 1965
THE CATHERINE MCKINNON CHRISTMAS ALBUM 1966
BOTH SIDES NOW 1968
EVERYBODY'S TALKIN' 1969
CATHERINE MCKINNON 1980
EXPLOSIVE 1980
PATRICIAN ANNE 1984

Sarah McLachlan

Sarah MacLachlan received classical training at the Nova Scotia Royal Conservatory, where she studied the classical guitar and piano. She first gained notice in the band October Game. When Nettwerk Records executives saw her, they immediately offered her a record contract.

Relocating to Vancouver, she signed a multi-record deal with Nettwerk, and accompanied by After All's keyboardist Darren Phillips and ex-54-40 drummer Darryl Neudorf, she recorded her first album,

TOUCH, in 1989. Her second album, SOLACE, came out in 1991. FUM-BLING TOWARD ECSTASY, her third, was released in 1993.

Sarah MacLachlan's classical training and strong songwriting skills have distinguished her as one of Canada's best known singer/song-writers.

Singles		
Vox 1989		*Drawn to the Rhythm* 1992
The Path of Thorns 1991		*Possession* 1993
Into the Fire 1991		*Hold On* 1994

CDs		
TOUCH 1989		FUMBLING TOWARDS ECSTASY 1993
SOLACE 1991		

Murray McLauchlan

Born in 1948 in Paisley, Scotland, Murray McLauchlan moved to Toronto when he was five. At age twelve he began playing the guitar, and in school he demonstrated an aptitude for art, winning a $250 scholarship from Hallmark Cards to attend art school. After graduating, he decided to pursue a career in music, and it was not long before he started performing at the Village Corner Club in Yorkville. In the mid-1960s he left Toronto for New York's Greenwich Village but in 1968 returned to Toronto, where he made his first appearance at The Riverboat, owned by Bernie Finkelstein, who managed such Canadian groups as The Paupers and Kensington Market.

During this period, two of MacLauchlan's songs, *Child's Song* and *Old Man*, were recorded by American folksinger Tom Rush on a Columbia album which drew attention to Rush's ability to discover promising new songwriters.

Finkelstein became Murray's manager in 1970, and in 1971, McLauchlan recorded his debut album, SONGS FROM THE STREET, on Finkelstein's True North label.

Throughout the 1970s McLauchlan had such hits as *The Farmer's Song*, *Little Dreamer*, *The Shoeshine Working Song*, *Down by the Henry Moore*, *On the Boulevard*, and *Whispering Rain*. The 1980s saw him become a CBC radio host, first with his *Timberline* series and currently with *Swingin' on a Star*.

The Canadian Rehabilitation Council for the Disabled chose *If the Wind Could Blow My Troubles Away* as its theme song for the 1981 International Year of Disabled Persons. That same year, Murray wrote *Alligator Shoes*, the theme for the film of the same name which was written, co-produced, and directed by Clay Borris. His other humanitarian efforts were Christmas Seals Chairman for the Canadian Lung Association in 1984, participation in several benefits for the Barrie tornado victims, and joining the Northern Lights for African Relief Aid in 1985 on *Tears Are Not Enough*.

In 1988, he switched from True North to Capitol Records. His first release was SWINGIN' ON A STAR in November. Three years later came the second album THE MODERN AGE.

Singles

Jesus Please Don't Save Me 1972
Farmer's Song 1973
Hurricane of Change 1973
Linda Won't You Take Me In 1974
Shoeshine Working Song 1974
Do You Dream of Being Somebody 1975
Down by the Henry Moore 1975
Little Dreamer 1975
On the Boulevard 1976
Love Comes and Grows 1977

Straight Outta Midnight 1978
You Can't Win 1979
Whispering Rain 1979
Try Walkin' Away 1980
Into a Mystery 1980
If the Wind Could Blow My Troubles Away 1981
Never Did like that Train 1985
Imaginary Tree 1988
Love with a Capital L 1989
The Modern Age 1991
So I Lost Your Love 1991

Albums/CDs

SONGS FROM THE STREET 1971
MURRAY MCLAUCHLAN 1972
DAY TO DAY DUST 1973
SWEEPING THE SPOTLIGHT AWAY 1974
ONLY THE SILENCE REMAINS 1975
BOULEVARD 1976
HARD ROCK TOWN 1977
GREATEST HITS 1978

WHISPERING RAIN 1979
INTO A MYSTERY 1980
STORM WARNING 1981
WINDOWS 1982
TIMBERLINE 1983
HEROES 1984
MIDNIGHT BREAK 1985
SWINGING ON A STAR 1988
THE MODERN AGE 1991

McManus Brothers

From Ireland, The McManus Brothers settled in Toronto in 1971 and established themselves by touring major cities in Canada, the United States, and the West Indies. In Toronto, they performed at various clubs and worked in both theater and television. Their first Canadian release on Boot Records was *Everyday* in 1974.

Single *Everyday* 1974

Sue Medley

Born in 1962, Courtenay, British Columbia, Sue Medley first became interested in music when she was given a drum set at the age of nine.

Four years later, she acquired a guitar and soon began writing songs. At fifteen she turned professional and became half of a folk/country duo. In June 1987 she recorded the independent hit *Cryin' over You*, which was well received by critics in Western Canada. A second independent release followed in 1989 called *Angel Tonight*. That same year she made an appearance at the Big Valley Jamboree in Saskatchewan. She was nominated for the Vista (Rising Star) Award at the 1989 Canadian Country Music Awards.

Polygram signed her to a contract in 1989, and in 1990 her self-titled debut album was released, produced by Medley and John Cougar Mellencamp's guitarist Michael Wanchic. Supplying background vocals on that album was John Hiatt's backup group The Goners, comprised of slide guitarist Sonny Landreth, guitarist Robbie Steininger, drummer Kenneth Bevins, bassist David Ranson, and keyboardist Steve Todd. Throughout 1990 she toured Canada and the United States, opening for Bob Dylan on some dates.

Medley's first hit was *Dangerous Times*, inspired by the events in Tienanmen Square. Her second album, INSIDE OUT, was released in 1992.

Singles		
Dangerous Times 1990	*When the Stars Fall* 1992	
That's Life 1990	*Inside Out* 1992	
Love Thing 1990	*Jane's House* 1992-93	
Maybe the Next Time 1991	*Forget You* 1993	
Queen of the Underground 1991		

CDs		
SUE MEDLEY 1990	INSIDE OUT 1992	

Men Without Hats

STEFAN DOROSCHUK   IVAN DOROSCHUK
COLIN DOROSCHUK

From Montreal, Men Without Hats was founded by the three Doroschuk brothers in 1977. They spent the next six years playing in clubs and establishing themselves as a simple rock 'n' roll band. They were jokingly called Men Without Surnames because they didn't want anyone to know three of the members were brothers.

Their first single release in 1983 was THE SAFETY DANCE, which was a Top Ten hit in twenty countries and was nominated for a Grammy Award. *Pop Goes the World* was their next hit in 1988, which also went Top Ten in Canada and the United States.

Singles		
The Safety Dance 1983	*Hey Men* 1989	
Where Do the Boys Go 1984	*In the 21st Century* 1990	
Pop Goes The World 1988	*Sideways* 1991	
Moonbeam 1988		

Albums/CDs RHYTHM OF YOUTH 1983   THE ADVENTURES OF WOMEN AND
FOLK OF THE 80S PART III 1984   MEN WITHOUT HATE IN THE
FREEWAYS 1985   21ST CENTURY 1989
POP GOES THE WORLD 1987   SIDEWAYS 1991

The Mercey Brothers

LARRY MERCEY (*guitar, vocals*)   RAY MERCEY (*guitar, vocals*)
LLOYD MERCEY (*drums, vocals*)

The Mercey Brothers, from Hanover, Ontario, first got together in 1957 and began recording for Chateau Records in their early days. Their first single, *Just the Snap of Your Fingers*, was a pop hit in 1961-62.

For almost twenty-five years The Mercey Brothers have continued to entertain audiences with their vocal harmonies. After recording with RCA and Columbia they decided to form their own label, Mercey Brothers Records (MBS). They moved to Elmira, Ontario, where they set up their own recording studios. Although their music was played mostly on country stations, some MOR (Middle of the Road) and Adult Contemporary stations played their songs as well.

Ray left the group in 1980 to devote more time to his family but he stayed on as manager. Gordon Ogilvie and Darrell Scott were added to the line up soon after The Mercey Brothers broke up in 1989. That same year they were inducted into the Canadian Country Music Hall of Fame. Lloyd started his own rock group, Larry pursued a solo career as a country artist, and Ray retired.

Singles *Just the Snap of Your Fingers* 1961-62
Whistle on the River 1966
Uncle Tom 1968
The Great Snowman 1968
What's a Guy to Do 1968
Who Drinks My Beer When I'm Gone 1969
Ordinary Peeping Tom 1969
My Song for You 1970
Pickin' Up the Pieces 1970
Goodbye 1970
Old Bill Jones 1970
Hello Mom 1971
Who Wrote the Words 1971
The Day of Love 1972
Kentucky Turn Your Back 1972

It's So Easy to Please Me 1973
Anytime Down 1983
Meant to Be with Me 1973
I Heard Bells 1973
California Lady 1974
Did You Hear My Song 1975
Loving You from a Distance 1975
Old Loves Never Die 1976
If I Believed in Myself 1976
Jamie 1977
You Know It Felt Good 1977
Home Along the Highway 1978
Comin' on Stronger 1978
Stranger 1978
Hell Bent for Mexico 1979
I Wish You Could Have Turned My Head 1979

Your Eyes Don't Lie to Me 1980
Makin' the Night the Best Part of My Day 1980
Sweet Harmony 1981
The Same Eyes that Drove Me Crazy 1981
Maybe It's Love this Time 1982
Starting All Over Again 1982
I've Already Left You in My Mind 1982
The Day That You Walked In 1983
The Leader of the Band 1984
Love at Last Sight 1984
You Lifted Me High Enough 1985
Love Is the Reason 1985
Take a Little Chance on Love 1986
Pretty Diamond Ring 1986
Heroes 1986-87
Raised by the Radio 1987
Straight to Your Heart 1988

Albums/CDs

THE MERCEY BROTHERS (Columbia) 1968
MY SONG FOR YOU 1969
THE MERCEY BROTHERS (Harmony) 1969
NATURALLY 1970
THE MERCEY BROTHERS (CTL/Columbia) 1970
HAVE MERCEY 1971
MERCEY BROTHERS COUNTRY 1972
THE MERCEY BROTHERS (RCA) 1973
DID YOU HEAR MY SONG 1975
BEST OF THE MERCEY BROTHERS 1975

HOMEMADE 1976
MERCEY BROTHERS RADIO SHOW 1976
COMIN' ON STRONGER 1977
COMMAND PERFORMANCE 1980
THE MERCEY BROTHERS (MBS) 1982
LATEST AND GREATEST VOLUME 1 1984
LOVE IS THE REASON 1985
LATEST AND GREATEST VOLUME 2 1988
THE MERCEY BROTHERS 30 GREATEST: THEIR HITS AND MORE 1990
FULL SPEED AHEAD (Larry Mercey) 1991

Messenjah

ERROL BLACKWOOD (*vocals, bass*)
HAL DUGGAN (*keyboards, bass, vocals*)
RUPERT "OJIJI" HARVEY (*vocals, guitar*)
TONY KING (*percussion*)
CRASH MORGAN (*drums*)
RAYMOND RUDDOCK (*drums, keyboards, percussion, vocals*)
CHARLES SINCLAIR (*bass*)
ERIC WALSH (*guitar, vocals*)
HAILE YATES (*percussion*)

The origins of one of Canada's first reggae band go back to 1980 in Kitchener, Ontario, where Errol Blackwood and Rupert Harvey enjoyed playing together and decided to form a band. Brought up by Jamaican parents, Blackwood was tired of playing in rock bands and wanted to get back to his roots. Harvey was a Toronto musician and producer of such groups as Crack of Dawn. Together, Blackwood and Harvey developed a strong following in the United States, particularly

California, Texas, and New Mexico.

After a year of touring, they recorded an independent album called ROCK YOU HIGH in California. In 1982 they signed with WEA Records of Canada (now Warner Music) who reissued ROCK YOU HIGH as their first release. They became the first Canadian reggae band to sign with a major label.

With their second album JAM SESSION in 1984, the group added Tony King on percussion. Between their second and third albums, the group went through a major personnel change. Errol Blackwood left in 1986 to pursue a solo career, and seven years later he recorded the independent hit *Unforeign Dub*.

Messenjah's next album was COOL OPERATOR in 1987. The group played themselves in the movie *Cocktail* (1988). In 1990 came their fourth album, ROCK AND SWAY.

Albums	ROCK YOU HIGH 1982	COOL OPERATOR 1987
	JAM SESSION 1984	ROCK & SWAY 1990

Mighty Pope

As a child Jamaican-born Earl "Mighty Pope" Heedram sang in church choirs, but after graduation from high school in Toronto, he lost interest in music and became an accountant.

In 1966 some of his friends encouraged him to sing on stage. He abandoned accountancy and for the next twelve years he worked hard at perfecting his disco act, adopting Pope as his first stage name, then Mighty Pope. In the late 1970s he got his big break when he was asked to open for Natalie Cole at Ontario Place. In 1977 he had his first and only major hit, *Heaven on the Seventh Floor*.

Singles	*Heaven on the Seventh Floor*	*Can't Get by Without You* 1977
	1977	*Sweet Blindness* 1979-80
Albums	MIGHTY POPE 1977	

Frank Mills

Frank Mills was born in 1942 and grew up in Verdun, Quebec. As a child he could play the piano by ear and in high school he played the trombone.

Mills attended McGill University but left in 1965. After pursuing different careers, he joined the Sirocco Singers which disbanded after three months. From 1968 to 1970 he was a member of The Five Bells, later The Bells.

In 1971 he released his first solo album, *Seven of My Songs (Plus Some Others)*. The following year he had a big hit with the song *Love Me Love Me Love*. In 1978 *Music Box Dancer* was released on Polydor (now Polygram) and became an international hit. His follow-up, *Peter Piper*, was also well received. Today, he continues to perform his easy listening hits throughout Canada and around the world.

Singles

Love Me Love Me Love 1972
Poor Little Fool 1972
Sunshine Morning 1972
Reflections of My Childhood 1972
How Can I Be Sure 1973
When Summer Is Gone 1976

Look at Me Real 1976
Music Box Dancer 1979
Peter Piper 1979
Most People Are Nice 1979
Breakaway 1980
Happy Song 1981
Plaisir d'amour 1981

Albums/CDs

SEVEN OF MY SONGS 1971
REFLECTIONS OF MY CHILDHOOD 1972
FRANK MILLS 1974 (reissued in 1978 as THE POET AND I)
LOOK AT ME REAL 1976
SUNDAY MORNING SUITE 1978
MUSIC BOX DANCER 1979
PRELUDE TO ROMANCE 1981

RONDO 1983
FRANK MILLS — A SPECIAL CHRISTMAS 1983
TRAVELLER 1984
TRANSITIONS 1986
60 MINUTES WITH FRANK MILLS 1987
MY PIANO 1988
CHRISTMAS WITH FRANK MILLS & FRIENDS 1992

Minglewood Band

PAUL DUNN (*vocals*)
PAUL HANN (*bass, violin, vocals*)
MARK McMILLAN (*guitar*)

MATT MINGLEWOOD (*vocals, guitar*)
ENVER SAMPSON JR. (*vocals*)
BOB WOODS (*drums, percussion*)

The history of the Minglewood Band goes back to the late 1960s when Matt Minglewood joined Caper Sam Moon in a band called Moon, Minglewood and the Universal Power. When they broke up, Matt went on to form his own band. In 1976 the Minglewood band released their self-titled independent album. Three years later, they signed to RCA Records.

Enver Sampson Jr., who joined the band in the early 1970s died in a motorcycle accident in 1985. By the mid-1980s the Minglewood Band had disbanded. Matt went on to a solo career, and signed a contract with Savannah Records. In 1986 the label released the single *Far Side of Town*. Four years later his debut album, THE PROMISE, came out. Early the following year he had a minor hit with *You're Not Drinking Enough*.

Singles

Ain't What It Used to Be 1979
Counting on You 1980
Me and My Baby 1980
Rocket Fuel 1981

Highway to Your Heart 1981
I'm Gonna Forgive You Again 1981
Me and the Boys 1985

Albums/CDs	MINGLEWOOD BAND 1976	ME AND THE BOYS 1986
	MINGLEWOOD BAND (RCA) 1979	THE PROMISE (Matt Minglewood) 1988
	MOVING 1980	THE BEST OF THE MINGLEWOOD
	SMOKERS — BEST OF 1982	BAND 1992
	OUT ON A LIMB 1983	

Joni Mitchell Joni Mitchell is one of Canada's most revered singer/songwriters. Born Roberta Joan Anderson in Fort MacLeod near Lethbridge, Alberta in 1943 and raised in Saskatoon, Saskatchewan, she studied piano as a child. She later learned the ukelele and guitar, and started singing when she contracted polio at the age of nine.

For one year she studied art at the Alberta College of Art in Calgary. During this time she made her professional debut at The Depression, a local coffeehouse. She then moved to Toronto and performed in Yorkville as Penny Farthing. In 1965 she married American folksinger Chuck Mitchell. A year later they were divorced.

In 1968 Joni Mitchell recorded a self-titled album, and during the next few years she performed throughout the northern United States and Ontario before settling down in Vancouver.

Her hits began with *Big Yellow Taxi* in 1970 and lasted for the next six years. In the late 1970s she switched from pop to jazz. She released an all jazz album, MINGUS, in memory of the legendary Charles Mingus. In 1982 she released her first album on Geffen Records, WILD THINGS RUN FAST. Nine years later, she released her sixteenth album, NIGHT RIDE HOME. She now lives in southern California.

Singles	*Big Yellow Taxi* 1970	*Help Me* 1974
	Carey 1971	*Free Man in Paris* 1974
	California 1971	*Big Yellow Taxi* (live version) 1975
	You Turn Me On (I'm a Radio) 1972	*In France They Kiss on Main Street* 1976
	Raised on Robbery 1974	

Albums/CDs	JONI MITCHELL 1968	HEJIRA 1976
	CLOUDS 1969	DON JUAN'S RECKLESS DAUGHTER 1977
	LADIES OF THE CANYON 1971	
	BLUE 1971	MINGUS 1979
	FOR THE ROSES 1972	SHADOWS AND LIGHT 1980
	COURT AND SPARK 1974	WILD THINGS RUN FAST 1982
	MYLES OF AISLES 1974	DOG EAT DOG 1985
	THE HISSING OF SUMMER LAWNS 1975	CHALK MARK IN A RAIN STORM 1988
		NIGHT RIDE HOME 1991

Kim Mitchell

Kim Mitchell was born in 1952 in Sarnia, Ontario. His music career began as the leader, singer/songwriter, and guitarist for the art rock band Max Webster. In 1984 he released his debut album, AKIMBO ALOGO, which went double platinum in Canada (over 200,000 copies). From it came the hit single *Go for Soda*, which went Top Five in the summer of 1984. It was endorsed by the 60,000 member strong organization Mothers Against Drunk Driving (or MADD) in the United States as its 1985 summer theme. Written by Mitchell and lyricist Pye Dubois, it was not meant to be an anti-alcohol statement. However, the chorus was perfect for MADD: "Might as well go for a soda/Nobody hurts and nobody cries/Might as well go for a soda/Nobody drowns and nobody dies."

In 1986 Mitchell continued to enjoy success with *Patio Lanterns*, the first of three hits from the album SHAKIN' LIKE A HUMAN BEING. That same year, *Music Express* honored him with the title "Working Class Hero." The Kingswood Music Theatre north of Toronto awarded Kim the first ever Platinum Ticket Award in 1988 to celebrate the 100,000th Kim Mitchell ticket sold over a five-year period. He also performed three sold out concerts at the park, surpassing his previous attendance record and those of such acts as David Lee Roth, ZZ Top, and Sting.

The early 1990s saw Mitchell's solo career soar. He performed his hit *Rock 'n' Roll Duty* at the 1990 Juno Awards Show. The following year he had his biggest tour ever, and in 1992 he released his fourth album, ORAL FIXATIONS, which contained the single *America*.

Singles

Go for Soda 1984	*Lost Lovers Found* 1990
All We Are 1984	*All We Are* (Live) 1990
Patio Lanterns 1986	*Expedition Sailor* 1990
Alana Loves Me 1986	*I Am a Wild Party* 1990
Easy to Love 1987	*Find the Will* 1992
In Your Arms 1987	*America* 1992
Rock 'n' Roll Duty 1989	*Pure as Gold* 1992
Rockland Wonderland 1989	*Some Folks* 1992-93

Albums/CDs

KIM MITCHELL 1982	ROCKLAND 1989
AKIMBO ALOGO 1984	I AM A WILD PARTY 1990
SHAKIN' LIKE A HUMAN BEING 1986	AURAL FIXATIONS 1992

Mitsou

Pop siren Mitsou Gelinas from Montreal captured audiences in her native Quebec with her hit *Bye Bye Mon Cowboy* in 1989. A year earlier, she received the Quebec Felix Award for Most Promising Artist.

Mitsou comes from one of Quebec's most famous families. Her

grandfather was the renowned writer/actor Gratien Gelinas and her father, Alain Gelinas, is also an actor. As a teenager she concentrated on acting, and appeared in TV ads, French theatrical productions in arts school, and had a role in a French TV series.

The success of *Bye Bye Mon Cowboy* in 1988 made her a French superstar in North America and in Europe.

In 1991 the video for *Dis-Moi, Dis-Moi (Tell Me, Tell Me)* featured nudity. The controversy over the video led to a multi-million dollar deal with Disney's Hollywood Records.

In 1992 she recorded her first English language album, HEADING WEST, featuring the single *Deep Kiss*. She co-wrote the title song with Cyndi Lauper. Her second English album, TEMPTED, came out in 1993. Its first single was *Everybody Say Love*.

Singles		
Bye Bye Mon Cowboy 1988	*A Funny Place The World Is* 1991	
Les Chinois 1989	*Deep Kiss* 1992	
La Corrida 1989	*Heading West* 1992	
Mademoiselle Anne 1990	*Everybody Say Love* 1993	
Dis-Moi, Dis-Moi 1991		

Albums/CDs		
LE MUNDO 1988	HEADING WEST 1992	
TERRE DES HOMMES 1990	TEMPTED 1993	

Jackie Mittoo

Jamaican-born Jackie Mittoo was born in 1948 and moved to Toronto in 1968. He was an influential keyboardist who played regularly with the late Bob Marley, Jimmy Cliff, and Johnny Nash. He worked with Nash on his albums HOLD ME TIGHT and CUPID. In 1971, Jackie had his only major success as a solo artist with *Wishbone*. He died of cancer in Toronto on December 16, 1990.

Singles   *Soul Bird* 1971   *Wishbone* 1971

Album   JACKIE MITTOO 1978

Monkeywalk

ANDREW FRANK (*bass*)
BIL RINGGENBERG (*vocals*)

The origins of the Montreal duo Monkeywalk go back to 1982 when they were members of the "Brit-funk" band Seven Sinners. They left in 1987 to pursue a different kind of sound, rhythm and blues. Their self-titled debut album was released in 1992. *Tear It All Down* was the band's first single.

Single	*Tear It All Down* 1992
CD	MONKEYWALK 1992

Mae Moore

This singer/songwriter from Brandon, Manitoba relocated to Vancouver to work the coffeehouse circuit with a trio. She played acoustic guitar and dulcimer while her two bandmates played cello and electric guitar. Mae later joined Foreign Legion, a rock band, as an electric guitarist. While working at the Railway Club in Vancouver, she met songwriter John Dexter. Together they wrote a number of songs, including *Heaven in Your Eyes*, which was recorded by Loverboy for the Paramount film *Top Gun* (1986).

Her friendship with Barney Bentall and his lead guitarist Colin Nairn resulted in a contract with CBS Records (now Sony Music). She began making demos with Bentall, Nairn, and Geoff Kelly of Spirit of the West. Her debut album, OCEANVIEW MOTEL, was released in 1990. Her second album, BOHEMIA, was released in the fall of 1992.

Singles	*I'll Watch over You* 1990	*Because of Love* 1993
	Where Loneliness Lives 1991	*Coat of Shame* 1993
	Red Clay Hills 1991	*The Wish* 1993
	Bohemia 1992	
CDs	OCEANVIEW MOTEL 1990	BOHEMIA 1992

Morse Code Transmission

JOCEYLN JULIEN (*guitar*)
RAYMOND ROY (*drums*)

CHRISTIAN SIMARD (*vocals, keyboards*)
MICHEL VALLEE (*guitar*)

Morse Code Transmission from Quebec was first known as Les Maitres. Founded by Michel Vallee and Raymond Roy in 1967, they played the club circuit in Quebec as a cover band who sang songs by The Beatles, The Bee Gees, Tom Jones, Robert Charlebois, Peter and Gordon, and Claude Léveillee.

Les Maitres recorded three singles without success. By the early 1970s they had changed their name to Morse Code Transmission and had also signed a record contract with RCA. The label released their self-titled debut album and the single *Oh Lord* in 1971. Produced by Bill Misener of Sun Bar Productions, the French group did not know English well enough to write lyrics. They used the talents of Misener, Graeme Box, John de Nottbeck, and Stan Rogers.

Morse Code Transmission gave its final performance in October

1990 at the Anglicane in Levis near Quebec City.

Singles		
Oh Lord 1971	*Ceremonie de nuit* 1977
Cocktail 1975	*Sommeil* 1977
Punch 1975	*Je suis le temps* 1977

Albums MORSE CODE TRANSMISSION 1971 JE SUIS LE TEMPS 1977
LA MARCHE DES HOMMES 1975   CODE BREAKER 1983

Motherlode

STEVE KENNEDY (*tenor sax, harmonica*)
KEN MARCO (*guitar*)
WILLIAM "SMITTY" SMITH (*keyboards*)
WAYNE "STONEY" STONE (*drums*)

From London, Ontario, these musicians began playing together in 1968 as part of Grant Smith and the Power, a nine-piece soul band from Toronto that enjoyed success with a cover of the Spencer Davis Group hit, *Keep on Running*. Steve Kennedy, Ken Marco, William Smith, and Wayne Stone grew tired of playing hits by other artists and left the group in 1969 to form Motherlode.

Steve Kennedy, who hails from Windsor, began playing guitar and later studied the saxophone under the direction of noted saxophonist Bill Sparling. In 1965 he formed a group called The Silhouettes with Doug Riley (Dr. Music), Terry Bush, Howard Glen, and Fred Theriault. After some personnel changes, they called themselves Eric Mercury, Dianne Brooks and The Soul Searchers. They disbanded in 1968. After playing in other groups, Kennedy went to the Image Club in London, Ontario, and convinced Marco, Stone, and Smith to form Motherlode.

Kenny Marco began playing in various local groups in his native Brantford. At seventeen he toured with The Bar-Kays in Northern Ontario. He later moved to Chicago and joined the Upset. He returned to Canada and played lead guitar for Grant Smith and the Power.

William Smith was the only non-Canadian member. Born in Belleville, Virginia, he began his musical career with The Belltones when he was nine-years old. He emigrated to Canada in 1964 and played with The Soul Searchers, David Clayton-Thomas, Grant Smith and The Power, and Lenny Breau.

Wayne Stone played drums with various local rock groups while growing up in London. After graduating from high school, he moved to Toronto and became the drummer for Grant Smith and the Power.

RPM Magazine heralded Motherlode as Canada's first supergroup. In 1969 producer Mort Ross was impressed enough to sign the band to a contract with Revolver/Compo in Canada and Buddah in the U.S.A. Their first of three hit singles was *When I Die* in the summer of 1969. At the end of 1971, Motherlode disbanded.

(As Grant Smith and the Power)
Single *Keep On Running* 1968

(As Motherlode)
Singles *When I Die* 1969   *Dear Old Daddy Bill* 1970
Memories of a Broken Heart   *All That's Necessary* 1971
1969

Album WHEN I DIE 1969

Mother Tucker's Yellow Duck
PAT CALDWELL (*mouth harp, vocals*)   HUGH LOCKHEAD (*drums*)
CHARLES FAULKNER (*bass*)   DONNY MCDOUGALL (*guitar, vocals*)
ROGER LAW (*guitar*):
     Replaced by LES LAW

Formed by Hugh Lockwood and Roger Law in 1967, this quintet from the West Coast had its first hit *One Ring Jane* on London Records in 1969. Pat Caldwell was responsible for coming up with the group's name. After they broke up in 1971, Donny McDougall went on to join The Guess Who in 1972.

Singles *One Ring Jane* 1969   *I/Funny Feeling* 1969
Little Pony 1969   *Starting a New Day* 1970

Moxy
BUDDY CAINE   BUZZ SHERMAN:
EARL JOHNSON   Replaced by MIKE RYNOSKI
TERRY JURIC   BILL WADE

From Toronto, Moxy was one of Canada's best hard rock bar bands. Like Mahogany Rush, they enjoyed a strong following in the United States. Moxy had only one hit, *Take It or Leave It*, in the fall of 1976. Buzz Sherman died in a motorcycle accident on June 16, 1983. He was thirty-three years old.

Singles *Take It or Leave It* 1976   *Cause there's Another* 1977
Albums MOXY 1976   RIDIN' HIGH 1977
MOXY II 1976   A TRIBUTE TO BUZZ SHEARMAN
TAKE IT OR LEAVE IT 1977   1984

Moxy Früvous
MICHAEL FORD (*guitar, percussion, vocals*)
MURRAY FOSTER (*bass, guitar, vocals*)
JEAN GHOMESHI (*drums, percussion, vocals*)
DAVID MATHESON (*guitar, accordion, vocals*)

This quasi-a capella group began as buskers at Toronto's Harbourfront in 1990. In 1992 they released an independent cassette of six songs, featuring *King of Spain,* which became their first video.

Signed to Warner Music, Moxy Früvous's debut album BARGAINVILLE was released early in 1993.

Singles	*King of Spain* 1993	*My Baby Loves a Bunch of Authors*
	Stuck in the 90s 1993	1993
		Fell in Love 1994

CD BARGAINVILLE 1993

Anne Murray

Anne Murray was Canada's first international female singing star. Since 1970 she has sold over twenty-two million albums, earned four Grammys, and almost thirty Junos. In 1980 the Canadian Recording Industry Association honored her as the Female Recording Artist of the Decade. In addition to her numerous awards in both the pop and country fields, her 1988 CBC-TV Christmas Special was the most widely viewed program of the decade. In September of 1991, Capitol Records released her thirtieth album, and early in 1992 a greatest hits album came out.

The story of Anne Murray's rise to the top of the music charts began in Springhill, Nova Scotia, where her parents had her take piano and vocal lessons. She made her first TV appearance on Moncton's CKCW-TV's *Supper Club* where she sang *Moon River.* Her first professional audition was in 1966 for the CBC show *Singalong Jubilee;* there she met her future husband, Bill Langstroth, whom she married in 1975. She became a regular on CBC-TV's *Let's Go* in Halifax and later returned to *Singalong Jubilee.*

Brian Ahern, the musical director of *Singalong,* invited Anne to record an album for Arc Records, and in 1968 *What about Me* was released. She later signed a contract with Capitol Records, where she stayed for the next twenty-two years. Anne's first major hit on Capitol was Gene McLellan's *Snowbird.* On *The Merv Griffin Show* in November 1970 she became the first female artist from Canada to receive a U.S. gold record, for *Snowbird.* In 1992 Anne appeared on American PBS television's *Evening at the Pops* with host conductor John Williams.

Her image as the girl next door has endeared her to millions of fans, and she continues to draw sell-out crowds to her concerts in both Canada and the U.S.

Anne returned to EMI Records in 1993. Her first album for the label was CROONIN', a collection of 1950s torch songs.

Singles

What about Me 1968
Bidin' My Time 1970
Snowbird 1970
Sing Hi, Sing Low 1970
A Stranger in My Place 1971
It Takes Time 1971
Talk It Over in the Morning
    1971
*I Say a Little Prayer/By the
    Time I Get to Phoenix
    (with Glen Campbell)* 1971
Cotton Jenny 1972
Robbie's Song for Jesus 1972
Danny's Song 1972-73
What about Me 1973
Send a Little Love My Way 1973
Love Song 1973-74
You Won't See Me 1974
Children of My Mind 1974
Just One Look 1974
Day Tripper 1974-75
Uproar 1975
Sunday Sunrise 1975
The Call 1976
Things 1976
You Needed Me 1978
I Just Fall in Love Again 1979
Shadows in the Moonlight 1979
Broken Hearted Me 1979
Daydream Believer 1979
Why Don't You Stick Around
    1979-80
Lucky Me 1980
*I'm Happy Just to Dance
    With You* 1980

Could I Have this Dance 1980
Blessed Are the Believers 1981
It's All I Can Do 1981
We Don't Have to Hold Out 1981
Another Sleepless Night 1982
A Little Good News 1983
*That's Not the Way It's
    Supposed to Be* 1984
Just Another Woman in Love 1984
Nobody Loves Me Like You Do
    1984
I Don't Think I'm Ready for You
    1985
Time Don't Run Out on Me 1985
Who's Leaving Who 1986
Now and Forever (You and Me)
    1986
Are You Still in Love With Me
    1987
Anyone Can Do the Heartbreak
    1987
*Perfect Strangers
    (with Doug Mallory)* 1988
Flying on Your Own 1988
Slow Passin' Time 1988
Who But You 1989
If I Ever Fall in Love Again (Duet
    with Kenny Rogers) 1989
Feed This Fire 1990
Bluebird 1990
Everyday 1991
I Can See Arkansas 1992
Are You Still in Love with Me 1992
Make Love to Me 1993
The Wayward Wind 1994

Albums/CDs

WHAT ABOUT ME 1968
THIS WAY IS MY WAY 1969
SNOWBIRD 1970
HONEY, WHEAT & LAUGHTER
    1970
STRAIGHT, CLEAN & SIMPLE 1971
TALK IT OVER IN THE MORNING
    1971

ANNE MURRAY/GLEN CAMPBELL
    1971
ANNIE 1972
DANNY'S SONG 1973
LOVE SONG 1974
COUNTRY 1974
HIGHLY PRIZED POSSESSION
    1974

TOGETHER 1975	HOTTEST NIGHT OF THE YEAR 1982
KEEPING IN TOUCH 1976	A LITTLE GOOD NEWS 1983
THERE'S A HIPPO IN MY TUB 1977	HEART OVER MIND 1984
LET'S KEEP IT THAT WAY 1978	SOMETHING TO TALK ABOUT 1986
NEW KIND OF FEELING 1979	HARMONY 1987
I'LL ALWAYS LOVE YOU 1979	ANNE MURRAY'S COUNTRY HITS 1987
A COUNTRY COLLECTION 1980	AS I AM 1988
SOMEBODY'S WAITING 1980	CHRISTMAS 1988
GREATEST HITS 1980	GREATEST HITS VOLUME II 1989
WHERE DO YOU GO WHEN YOU DREAM? 1981	YOU WILL 1990
CHRISTMAS WISHES 1981	YES I DO 1991
	FIFTEEN OF THE BEST 1992
	CROONIN' 1993

Bruce Murray

Growing up in the mining town of Springhill, Nova Scotia, Bruce Murray was the youngest of six children. As Anne Murray's younger brother, he carried on the family's musical tradition. He took piano lessons as a boy and became a church organist at age eleven. He attended St. Francis Xavier University, and after graduation he auditioned unsuccessfully for *Singalong Jubilee*. He studied at the University of Victoria before moving to Toronto, where he signed with Anne's management company, Balmur.

Between 1976 and 1978 Bruce Murray toured with Olivia Newton-John and developed his own sound. He sang backup vocals on Anne's album, CROONIN', in 1993.

Singles *We're All Alone* 1977   *In the Still of the Night* 1979
Who, What, When, Where, Why 1978

Album BRUCE MURRAY 1976   BRUCE MURRAY 1984

Alannah Myles

Alannah Myles' self-titled debut album has sold over one million copies in both the U.S.A. and Canada, where it holds the record for being the biggest selling debut album by a Canadian artist.

Alannah, who changed her surname when she became a performer, spent her childhood in both Toronto and the town of Buckhorn, north of Peterborough. At age five she had aspirations to become a singer and started playing the guitar at eleven. At nineteen she found an agent and began performing solo in various clubs in and around Toronto. Two years later, she opened for the Christopher Ward Band and used them as her backup band on a tour of Canada's East Coast. It later became known as the Alannah Myles Band.

Love Is was the first single to be released from Alannah's debut album in 1989, followed by *Black Velvet*, a number one hit in Canada in 1989, and number one on Billboard's Hot 100 for two weeks in 1990. In the fall of 1992 Warner Music released her second album, ROCKINGHORSE.

Singles	*Love Is* 1989	*Tumbleweed* 1992
	Black Velvet 1989	*Our World Our Times* 1993
	Still Got this Thing 1990	*Livin' on a Memory* 1993
	Lover of Mine 1990	*Sonny Say You Will* 1993
	Song Instead of a Kiss 1992	
Albums/CDs	ALANNAH MYLES 1989	ROCKINGHORSE 1992

Myles & Lenny

MYLES COHEN
LENNY SOLOMON

Myles Cohen was born in Montreal and began writing music when he was thirteen. A self-taught guitarist, he began playing with bands around Toronto while still in his teens. The son of Stanley Solomon, the Toronto Symphony Orchestra's principal violist, Lenny began studying the piano at age six and playing the violin at seven. He later studied music at McGill University, and has played violin in the National Youth Orchestra. He was a featured soloist on albums by Flying Circus and Luke Gibson.

Myles and Lenny Solomon first met while attending high school in Toronto. When they discovered their musical styles were compatible, they became a duo in 1969. Based in Toronto, they were part of the Canadian music scene for seven years. Their first real engagement was the 1969 Mariposa Songwriters Conference. A contract with GRT Records in 1972 allowed them to make their very first record, *Time To Know Your Friends*. Two years later they joined Columbia, where they experienced major success. While promoting their self-titled debut album in 1974, they toured with Ivan Boudreau on bass, Bill MacKay on drums, and Rick Doyle on guitar.

In 1976 Myles dissolved his partnership with Lenny, forming his own band which later became known as Ambush. In 1978 Myles went solo and signed with the Toronto independent label, Change Records. His debut album, TAKE A RIDE WITH ME, and the single *Hold on Lovers*, a remake of the old Myles & Lenny hit, were released that same year. He also recorded *Holiday*, a Bee Gees hit from 1967.

Lenny Solomon went on to form a jazz quintet.

(As Myles & Lenny)

Singles *Time to Know Your Friends* *Hold on Lovers* 1975
1972 *I Care Enough* 1976
Can You Give It all to Me
1974-75

Albums MYLES AND LENNY 1975 IT ISN'T THE SAME 1975

(By Myles Cohen)

Singles *Hold on Lovers* 1978 *Jamaica* 1979
Holiday 1979

Albums TAKE A RIDE WITH ME 1978 STARTING ALL OVER AGAIN 1979

National Velvet

MARIA DEL MAR (*vocals*)   MARK STORM (*bass*)
MARK CROSSLEY (*guitar*)   TIM WELCH (*guitar*)
GARY FLINT (*drums*)

Maria Del Mar first met Mark Storm in a Toronto alley during a party in the mid-1980s. They soon formed a band and released the independent single *Pacifist at Risk/Equus* in 1987. Their self-titled debut album on Capitol Records in 1988 was released in eight countries, including Germany and Scandinavia. In March 1990 Capitol released their second album, COURAGE, which was produced by Zeus B. Held at his Eastcote Studio in London, England.

Singles	*Pacifist at Risk* 1987	*68 Hours* 1989
	Flesh under the Skin 1988	*Shine On* 1990
	Bam Bam 1988-89	*Sex Gorilla* 1990

Albums/CDs	NATIONAL VELVET 1988	COURAGE 1990

NEOA4

JOEL ANDERSON (*drums*)   JOHN TIDSWELL (*bass*)
RIC JOHNSTON (*guitar*)

Formed in 1981, this trio from Edmonton, Alberta was a cover band that sounded like King Crimson. Later on, they decided to write their own material and, in 1985, recorded their first independent album, THE WARMER SIDE OF YOU, which led to a contract with Duke Street Records. Their commercial success was limited to four single releases, beginning with *Desire* in 1987.

Singles	*Desire* 1987	*Say This to Me* 1988
	Only a Fool 1988	*That's the Way* 1989

Albums	THE WARMER SIDE OF YOU 1985	DESIRE 1987
		NEOA4 1988

Rick Neufeld

Born in 1947, Rick Neufeld grew up in the Mennonite farming community of Boissevain. After studying architecture at the University of Manitoba and traveling throughout Europe and North America, he decided to concentrate on a new career as a singer/songwriter.

Neufeld played at coffeehouses throughout North America, performing at the Regina Folk Festival and the Mariposa Folk Festival. Many appearances on CBC television followed, and in the early 1970s he hosted his own series called *The Songsingers*.

Of all the songs he wrote, his most famous is *Moody Manitoba*

Morning, which The Bells recorded in 1969. Neufeld recorded the song in 1971 on his debut album, HIWAY CHILD, on Astra Records. Throughout the 1970s Neufeld made two more albums, co-hosted the TV series *On the Road* on CBC with Colleen Peterson, and played at the Grand Old Opry in Nashville.

Singles		
Moody Manitoba Morning 1970	*Hiway Child* 1971	
The Christmas Song 1970	*A Love Worth Living For* 1974	
Country Princess 1971	*Morning Song* 1974	

Albums		
HIWAY CHILD 1971	MANITOBA SONGS 1978	
PRAIRIE DOG 1975		

Dave Nicol

Dave Nicol's first hit was *Goodbye Mama* in June of 1973 on Columbia Records. A second single, *Mexico*, was released in the summer of 1974 but did not equal the success of his first. He continued to write new material and perform in nightclubs throughout the 1970s and 1980s.

Today, he lives in Kelowna, British Columbia, where he has become a part of the nightclub scene there. In 1993 he released an independent CD called NIGHT CROSSING, which was dedicated to his late friend Brian MacLeod of Chilliwack fame.

Singles		
No One Ever Told Me 1972	*Salvation* 1975	
Goodbye Mama 1973	*Jeannie* 1975	
Mexico 1974		

Album/CDs		
ALL THE WILD BIRDS 1975	NIGHT CROSSING 1993	

Ron Nigrini

Born in 1948, Ron Nigrini started playing as a teenager in 1965 with a duo called The Coachmen from Toronto. Two years later, he was a member of Dan's Heard. In 1970, Nigrini went solo, touring the coffeehouse circuit through the American Midwest, Texas, New Mexico, Connecticut, New Hampshire, and Massachusetts. Back in Canada in 1972 he wrote commercials for TV and radio with Michael Hasek, a singer on A&M Records.

In July 1974 Nigrini signed a contract with Attic Records and recorded his first single, *Letters*. Two years later, he recorded his own version of the Oscar-winning song *I'm Easy* from the movie *Nashville*.

After a long absence he returned to the recording studio in 1983 and formed his own label, Oasis Records. His first single, *Baby I'm a Lot Like You*, was not a national hit.

Singles	*Letters* 1974	*I'm Easy* 1976
	Lost in Colorado 1974	*Baby I'm a Lot like You* 1983
	Horses 1975	*Thin Line* 1987
Albums	RON NIGRINI 1975	THE DRIFT 1987
	RICH THINGS 1976	

Noah

PAUL CLAPPER: MARINUS VANDERTOGT
  Replaced by RON NEILSON   PETER VANDERTOGT
BARRY "BUZZ" VANDERSEL

Noah, a Toronto-based band formed in late 1960s as Tyme and a Half, had a minor hit with *It's Been a Long Time* in 1969. Al MacMillan at Nimbus 9 Productions gave the group their name Noah. They had another minor success in 1972 with the album PEACEMAN'S FARM. The title track charted at CKLW in Windsor, where it received a major push, and received good reviews in *Billboard*, *Cash Box*, and *Record World*, the three major US trade magazines.

Singles	*Summer Sun* 1971	*Peaceman's Farm* 1972
Album	PEACEMAN'S FARM 1972	

Don Norman and the Other Four

GARY COMEAU (*guitar, vocals*)   BILL HELMAN (*bass, vocals*)
BRIAN DEWHURST (*drums*)   DON NORMAN (*vocals, guitar*)
RON GREENE (*guitar, keyboards, vocals*)

The history of Don Norman and the Other Four began in the summer of 1965 in Ottawa, where Gary Comeau, Ron Greene, Bill Helman, and Paul Huot met. Don Norman was invited to join, and with the addition of Brian Dewhurst, the band called themselves Don Norman and the Esquires. Since another Ottawa group was called The Esquires, they were taken to court over the use of the name. Norman signed an out-of-court settlement and changed the name. John Matthews was then added as second lead vocalist and sax player. They were managed by John Pozer, a local radio and television personality.

The band recorded *All of My Life* at the RCA Victor Studios in Toronto in 1966. The B side was *The Bounce*, a song originally recorded by The Olympics in 1963. The record was distributed in Canada by Quality Records, and in the United States by MGM Records. Both songs were re-recorded in French as *Je T'ai Cherche* and *Le Bounce* on the Sol Pege label.

In 1966, Comeau left to join The Townsmen, another Ottawa group, and was replaced by Art Kirkby on guitar and flute. Early in 1967, they made their second record, *Low Man*, another Norman original, at Stereo Sound Studios in Montreal on the Sir John A label, distributed by RCA. That same year, the group lost Bill Helman, Brian Dewhurst, and John Matthews, who were replaced by John Winskol, Rick Pandis, and Skip Layton. They played together until the summer of 1967.

Singles *All of My Life* 1966   *Low Man* 1967

Tom Northcott

Tom Northcott, born in 1943, began singing in 1963 at Vancouver's coffeehouses, notably The Inquisition. With two other musicians he performed as The Tom Northcott Trio in San Francisco at The Matrix and The Avalon in the summer of 1966.

Northcott later signed as a solo artist with Warner Brothers and had three minor hits: *1941*, *Girl from the North Country*, and *The Rainmaker*. In 1969 he formed a partnership to build a studio in Vancouver to produce such acts as Crosstown Bus, The Irish Rovers, and Anne Attenborrow.

By the time Northcott stopped performing in 1973, he had several hit singles and a distinguished career that included a stint with the Vancouver Symphony Orchestra in 1970, which premiered his twelve-minute symphony, *And God Created Woman*. He resurfaced on the country charts with a song called *The Trouble with Love* in 1990. He is still best known for his 1970-71 hit, *I Think It's Gonna Rain Today*.

Singles
Going Down 1966
Sunny Goodge Street 1967
1941 1968
Girl from the North Country 1968
The Rainmaker 1970

Crazy Jane 1970
Suzanne 1971
I Think It's Gonna Rain Today 1970-71
Spaceship Races 1971
The Trouble with Love 1990

Albums UPSIDE DOWNSIDE 1971

Northern Lights

For the first time in history, an all-star lineup of Canadian artists gathered together in 1985 under one roof to record *Tears Are Not Enough* for Ethiopian famine relief. David Foster wrote the music, while Bryan Adams and his songwriting partner Jim Vallance wrote the lyrics. Rachel Paiement (of CANO fame) wrote the French translation of the words. The video of *Tears Are Not Enough* was directed by Stephen Surjik.

Tears Are Not Enough was Canada's answer to British pop star Bob Geldof's Band Aid benefit recording of *Do They Know It's Christmas?* and the American recording *We Are the World* by USA For Africa.

The following Canadian performers participated in *Tears Are Not Enough*:

Bryan Adams	Geddy Lee
Paul Anka	Eugene Levy
Carroll Baker	Gordon Lightfoot
Veronique Beliveau	Murray McLauchlan
Doug Bennett	Frank Mills
Salome Bey	Joni Mitchell
Liona Boyd	Kim Mitchell
John Candy	Anne Murray
Robert Charlebois	Bruce Murray
Tom Cochrane	Aldo Nova
Bruce Cockburn	Catherine O'Hara
Burton Cummings	Oscar Petersen
Lisa Dal Bello	Carole Pope
Claude Dubois	Lorraine Segato
Rik Emmett	Paul Shaffer
Wayne Gretzky	Graham Shaw
Corey Hart	Jane Siberry
Ronnie Hawkins	Liberty Silver
Dan Hill	Wayne St. John
Honeymoon Suite	Ian Thomas
Tommy Hunter	Jim Vallance
Paul Hyde	Neil Young
Martha Johnson	Alfie Zappacosta

Northern Pikes

MERYL BRYCK (*vocals, guitar*) JAY SEMBO (*vocals, bass*)
BRYAN POTVIN (*vocals, guitar*) DON SCHMID (*drums*)

From Saskatoon, Saskatchewan, Northern Pikes formed in 1984. The band has opened for David Bowie, The Fixx, The Alarm, and Andy Summers. Their albums BIG BLUE SKY, SECRETS OF THE ALIBI, and SNOW IN JUNE have been certified gold and platinum. The band broke into the U.S. market in January 1992 when their hit, *She Ain't Pretty*, entered Billboard's Hot 100.

Northern Pikes broke up in 1993.

Single	Teenland 1987	Dream Away 1991
	Things I Do for Money 1987	*Kiss Me You Fool* 1991
	Wait for Me 1988	*Twister* 1992
	One Good Reason 1988	*Believe* 1993
	Hopes Go Astray 1989	*Everything* 1993
	Let's Pretend 1989	*Worlds Away*
	She Ain't Pretty 1990	(with Margo Timmins) 1993
	Girl with a Problem 1990	

Albums/CDs	SCENE IN NORTH AMERICA 1985	SNOW IN JUNE 1990
	BIG BLUE SKY 1987	NEPTUNE 1992
	SECRETS OF THE ALIBI 1989	GIG 1993

Aldo Nova

Aldo Nova (a.k.a. Aldo Scarporuscio), a Montreal-born musician, producer, singer, and songwriter, honed his craft writing jingles and commercials. His first hit single was *Fantasy* in 1982.

After playing guitar for Jon Bon Jovi on *Blaze of Glory* in 1990, Nova signed to Jon Bon Jovi's JAMBCO Records, distributed by Polygram. His first single release on Polydor was *Blood on the Bricks* in 1991.

Singles	Fantasy 1982	Blood on the Bricks 1991
	Foolin' Yourself 1982	*Medicine Man* 1991
	Always Be Mine 1984	*Someday* 1992

Albums/CDs	FANTASY 1982	TWITCH 1985
	SUBJECT 1983	BLOOD ON THE BRICKS 1991

The Nylons

RALPH COLE: Replaced by   CLAUDE MORRISON
   ARNOLD ROBINSON   BILLY NEWTON-DAVIS
MARC CONNORS   DENIS SIMPSON: Replaced by
PAUL COOPER: RALPH COLE
   Replaced by MICAH BARNES

This a cappella quartet from Toronto was organized in 1979. The four original members were Marc Connors, Paul Cooper, Claude Morrison, and Denis Simpson. Simpson left the group in April, 1979 and was replaced by Ralph Cole, who in turn left in November 1980. Arnold Robinson joined the three original members in March 1981.

After establishing themselves on the club circuit, they caught the attention of Attic Records, who signed them to a record contract in 1981. They recorded cover versions of old rock classics such as

Silhouettes by The Rays, *The Lion Sleeps Tonight* by The Tokens, and *One Fine Day* by The Chiffons. International recognition followed six years later when they released the album HAPPY TOGETHER and the single *Kiss Him Goodbye*, a revival of Steam's 1969 smash hit, *Na Na Hey Hey Kiss Him Goodbye* and a Top 30 hit on Billboard's Hot 100.

In 1986 they won the best singer award at the 15th Annual Tokyo Music Festival for the song *Up the Ladder to the Roof*, the old Supremes hit. They opened for such acts as Pointer Sisters and Hall and Oates before headlining their own U.S. tour in 1987.

Paul Cooper decided to leave the group in 1990. He was replaced by Micah Barnes, who convinced the group to sing cover songs by Prince and Labelle. On March 25, 1991 Marc Connors died of viral pneumonia at age forty-three. Billy Newton-Davis ably filled Connor's shoes when he joined the group in 1991. A three-time Juno Award-winning vocalist for his albums LOVE IS A CONTACT SPORT and SPELLBOUND, Newton-Davis became part of the group's new sound. In 1992 they signed with BMG Music and released the album LIVE TO LOVE. *Don't Look Any Further* was the first single.

Singles

The Lion Sleeps Tonight 1982	*Happy Together* 1987
Silhouettes 1983	*Chain Gang* 1987
That Kind of Man 1983	*Wild Fire* 1989
Take Me to Your Heart 1984	*Drift Away* 1989
Perpetual Emotion 1984	*Call My Name* 1991
Stepping Stone 1984	*One Fine Day* 1991
Combat Zone 1984	*Don't Look Any Further* 1992
Kiss Him Goodbye 1987	

Albums/CDs

THE NYLONS 1982	ROCKAPELLA 1989
ONE SIZE FITS ALL 1982	FOUR ON THE FLOOR 1991
SEAMLESS 1984	LIVE TO LOVE 1992
HAPPY TOGETHER 1987	

JANICE BROWN (*lead guitar*)   JEFF JONES (*bass, vocals*)
GREG BROWN (*vocals,*   CHUCK SLATER (*drums*)
   keyboards)   DAVE TAMBLYN (*guitar*)

Ocean

This Toronto group achieved success with their first hit, *Put Your Hand in the Hand*. Written by Gene MacLellan, the song was a gospel rock song promoted by the CHUM radio network in Canada and distributed in the United States by Kama Sutra Records. The song was a million seller as well as a Top Five hit.

    Ocean was not able to duplicate the success of their first hit south of the border. In Canada, they had other songs but none of them a national hit. They broke up in 1975.

Singles

Put Your Hand in the Hand   *Make the Sun Shine* 1972
   1971   *One More Chance* 1972
Deep Enough for Me 1971   *I Have a Following* 1973
We've Got a Dream 1971

Album   PUT YOUR HAND IN THE HAND 1971

Octavian

DARYL ALGUIRE (*vocals*)   RAY LESSARD (*bass*)
WARREN BARBOUR (*guitar*)   ROB MCDONALD (*keyboards*)
KIRK DARROW (*drums*)   JOHN PULKINEN (*vocals*)
BILL GAVREAU (*lead guitar*)

Octavian has been together since 1969 when they were all in high school and known as Octavius. Their first engagement was at the Green Door room of The Chaudiere Club in Aylmer, Quebec, before an audience of members of Satan's Choice. The name of the group changed to "Octavian" when it was misspelled on a marquee at the Woodstock, Ontario, Rock Club. It took six years before the group was signed to MCA Records.

    Their first single release was *Good Feeling (To Know)* in 1974, but it failed to crack the Top 10. Their second, *Round and Round*, fared better when it came out in 1975. That same year they also drew a sell-out crowd at the Forum in Ontario Place. Mismanagement and communication problems with their record company forced an end to Octavian in 1979.

Singles

Good Feeling (To Know) 1974   *You Can't Do That* 1976
Round and Round 1975   *Some Kinda People* 1976
Hold Me, Touch Me 1975-76   *Can't Stop Myself from Lovin' You*
                                  1979

Album   SIMPLE KINDA PEOPLE 1975

The Odds   PAUL BRENNAN (*drums*)   DOUG ELLIOT (*bass*)
STEVEN DRAKE (*guitar, vocals*)   CRAIG NORTHEY (*vocals, guitar*)

Originally a cover band from Vancouver called Dawn Patrol, these four musicians began playing original material and changed their name to The Odds in 1987. Disappointed by the poor response to their music in Canada, The Odds moved to Los Angeles, where they played at Coconut Teasers, a local nightclub, an engagement that led to a contract with Zoo Records and a tour with Warren Zevon.

NEAPOLITAN, the first album by The Odds, was released in 1991. From it came the single *Wendy Under the Stars*. Two years later, their second album, BEDBUGS, was released. The first single, *Heterosexual Man*, sparked controversy because of its suggestive lyrics. Its accompanying video featured The Odds in drag performing with The Kids in the Hall, a Toronto comedy troupe, as crazy drunks.

Singles   *Wendy Under the Stars* 1992   *Jack Hammer* 1994
Heterosexual Man 1993   *Yes (Means It's Hard to Say No)*
It Falls Apart 1993   1994

CDs   NEOPOLITAN 1991   BEDBUGS 1993

Offenbach   GERRY BOULET   WEZO: Replaced by PIERRE
JOHNNY GRAVEL   LAVOIE, ROBERT HARRISON
MICHAEL LAMONTHE JR.:   JOHN MCVALE
   Replaced by NORMAN KERR   JEAN MILLAIRE
BREEN LEBOEUF

Formed in 1969 by Gerry Boulet, Michael Lamonthe, Jr., and Wezo (Roger Belval), Offenbach was one of the more original rock bands to emerge in Quebec after the heyday of American imitators like Les Classels, Les Houlops, and Les Sultans. In the early 1970s, the group played *A Mass for the Dead* at St. Joseph's Oratory in Montreal. This performance gave Offembach much needed publicity and led to a recording contract with the independent Barclay label. Their debut French album in 1972 was called OFFENBACH SOAP OPERA. They released their first English album, NEVER TOO TENDER (A&M Records) in 1977.

Bassist Lamonthe and drummer Wezo left the group in 1977, and were replaced by Norman Kerr and Pierre Lavoie, respectively. Both Kerr and Jean Milliare left in 1978. The former joined a jazz rock group, while the latter joined Francois Guy. In 1979, Breen LeBoeuf and John McVale were added. Two years later, the group took a year off, and in 1982, they were back on tour in Quebec. During this time, drummer Robert Harrison left the band. He was replaced by Paul Martel. Offenbach broke up in 1986. Their last album, LE DERNIER SHOW, was recorded at the Montreal Forum in November 1985.

In 1984, Gerry Boulet had recorded a solo album called PRESQUE 40S ANS DE BLUES. His first album after Offenbach disbanded was RENDEZVOUS DOUX, which came out in late 1988. About this time he learned that he had colon cancer. He died on July 16, 1990.

Albums	OFFENBACH 1977	TONNEDEBRICK 1983
	NEVER TOO TENDER 1977	LIVE À FOND D'TRAIN 1984
	OFFENBACH 1977	ROCKORAMA 1985
	TRAVERSION 1979	LE DERNIER SHOW 1986
	EN FUSION 1980	

Mary Margaret O'Hara

Mary Margaret O'Hara's first band was Songship, and when it disbanded she joined Go Deo (Gaelic for "eternal") Chorus until they split up in 1983. A year later she signed a solo recording contract with Virgin Records. Four years later, her debut album MISS AMERICA was released. The first single, *Body in Trouble*, came out in February 1989.

Single *Body in Trouble* 1989

CD MISS AMERICA 1988

One Horse Blue

GORD MAXWELL (*vocals, bass*)
LARRY PINK (*keyboards*)
MICHAEL SHELLARD (*vocals, guitar, harmonica*)
ROCKO VAUGEOIS (*vocals, drums, percussion, guitar*)

Originally based in Edmonton, Alberta, One Horse Blue began as a commercial rock band comprised of Gord Maxwell from Saskatoon, Rocko Vaugeois and Michael Shellard from Edmonton, and Larry Pink from Winnipeg. In the late 1970s and early 1980s, they scored with such Top 40 hits as *Cry Out for the Sun, Deliver Me, Bring My Love Around,* and *Crazy Fool.*

By the early 1990s they had changed their musical direction and moved to Vancouver. In 1991, 1992, and 1993 they won Group of The Year honors at the BCCMA Awards. Signed to Savannah Records in 1993, their first release was the CD single, *Starting All Over Again,* previously recorded in 1979.

Singles	*Cry Out for the Sun* 1978	*Crazy Fool* 1980
	Deliver Me 1979	*Starting All Over Again* 1993
	Bring My Love Around 1979-80	*Love's Looking for Me* 1994

Albums	ONE HORSE BLUE 1979	ONE HORSE BLUE 1993
	BITE THE BULLET 1980	

One to One

LESLIE HOWE
LOUISE RENY

One to One evolved from the group Mainstream which was together from 1975-1983 and played versions of hit songs from artists such as Pat Benatar and Van Halen. Late in 1984 the duo of Leslie Howe and Louise Remy sent demo tapes to various record companies. They eventually signed to Bonaire Records, distributed by WEA Canada. Their debut album FORWARD YOUR EMOTIONS produced the single *There Was a Time* in late 1985. Their first American single was *Angel in My Pocket* in 1986.

Singles	*There Was a Time* 1985-86	*We've Got the Power* 1989
	Angel in My Pocket 1986	*Peace of Mind (Love Goes On)*
	Black on White 1986	1992
	Hold Me Now 1987-88	*Memory Lane* 1992
	Love Child 1989	*Friends* 1992
	Do You Believe 1989	

Albums/CDs	FORWARD YOUR EMOTIONS 1985
	IMAGINE IT 1992

Original Caste

GRAHAM BRUCE
JOSEPH CAVENDER
BRUCE INNES

DIXIE LEE INNES
BLISS MACKIE

Formerly known as the North Country Singers, a Canadian version of the New Christy Minstrels, the name of the band was changed to Original Caste in 1966 after Dixie Innis Stone joined the group. Dixie's strong lead vocals helped the band achieve popular success in their stage act as well as in the recording studio. Born in Moose Jaw, Saskatchewan, she started her professional career at age eleven with a local rock group. In 1964 she was voted "The Finest Young Talent on Television," in Canada.

The Original Caste's first single with Dot Records was *I Can't Make It Anymore* in July 1968. It was not until they switched to Bell

Records and recorded *One Tin Soldier* that success finally came. Released in November 1969, this song became a huge hit in Canada and the U.S.A. and was used in the film *Billy Jack*, sung by Jinx Dawson of the group Coven.

Although The Original Caste did not repeat their initial success south of the border, they continued to have hits in Canada with such songs as *Nothing Can Touch Me* and *Ain't That Tellin' You People*. In the early 1970s the band broke up. Dixie Lee Innis and her husband Bruce Innis, formerly a member of the Big Sky Singers, later toured as a duo and recorded separately and together on Bell Records.

Singles   *I Can't Make It Anymore* 1968   *Nothing Can Touch Me* 1970
One Tin Soldier 1969   *Ain't that Tellin' You People* 1970
Mr. Monday 1970   *Sault Ste. Marie* 1971
Country Song 1970

Album   ONE TIN SOLDIER   1970

(By Dixie Lee Innes)
Singles   *Black Paper Roses* 1972   *Queen of Colby Kansas* 1977

Michel Pagliaro

Born in 1948, Michel Pagliaro began playing the guitar at the age of eleven. By the time he reached fifteen, he had mastered the instrument and started playing with Montreal's Les Stringmen. He later joined Les Bluebirds and Les Merseys. By his eighteenth birthday he had organized his first group, Les Chancelliers. Their first hit single was *Le P'tit Poppy* in 1966. With producer George Lagios he left Les Chancelliers to pursue a solo career. He had several hits in Quebec, including *Comme d'habitude* and *Avec la tete*.

In 1970 he started recording for CHUM's Much Records and released his first hit single in English, *Give Us One More Chance*. Three years later he had a huge hit with *J'entends frapper*, which became the biggest selling single in the history of the Quebec music industry. Its impact in English Canada was felt in Kingston where it became number one at both CKWS (now CFFX) and CKLC.

Pagliaro was backed up three musicians who called themselves Moonquake (Jack August, Hovanes Hagopian, Derek Kendrick). They would later achieve minor success on their own in the summer of 1975 with the hit *Wild Little Story*. Their debut album, STARSTRUCK, on Aquarius Records, was released in 1975.

By 1975 Pagliaro had switched to Columbia Records and in February of that year he scored a hit with *What the Hell I Got*. He was still performing in both languages in the late 1970s and 1980s. More recently, he has recorded only in French.

Singles

Le p'tit poppy 1966
Comme d'habitude 1966
Avec la tete 1966
Give Us One More Chance 1970
Lovin' You Ain't Easy 1971
Rainshowers 1972
Some Sing, Some Dance 1972

J'entends frapper 1972-73
Run Along Baby 1973
Sure, Maybe 1974
What The Hell I Got 1975
I Don't Believe It's You 1976
Dock of the Bay 1977
Time Race 1977

Albums

PAG 1972
PAGLIARO I 1976
TIME RACE 1977

AVANT 1987
SOUS PEINE D'AMOUR 1988

The Parachute Club

KEITH BROWNSTONE (*guitar*)
BILLY BRYANS (*drums, percussion*)
LAURI CONGER (*keyboards, synthesizer, vocals*)
MARGO DAVIDSON (*saxophone, percussion, vocals*)

DAVE GRAY (*guitar*)
JULIE MASI (*percussion, vocals*)
LORRAINE SEGATO (*vocals, guitar, percussion*)
STEVE WEBSTER (*bass*)

The history of The Parachute Club goes back to 1977 when Lorraine Segato met Billy Bryans. Both were members of Mama Quilla II, a seven-piece rock 'n' roll band, and then V, which was comprised of prominent reggae, pop, and funk musicians who played in and around Toronto in 1981-82. When neither of these two groups were unable to perform at the opening night party of the 1982 Festival of Festivals, Lorraine and Billy organized The Parachute Club.

One member of the group, Margo Davidson, had played with Gary O and Craig Russell. Julie Masi joined The Parachute Club in December 1982. Raised in Winnipeg, Manitoba, she moved to Toronto, where she worked with Kerr Whitely and the Paradise Revue, then the Cuban Fence Climbers. On guitar was Dave Gray, recruited to play on The Parachute Club's debut album, RISE UP, in 1983. In 1984, Keith Brownstone became the eighth and newest member. He had played funk and reggae in the bands R.Z. Jackson and David Bendeth.

After a string of hit singles, the group broke up in 1989. Lorraine Segato went on to pursue a solo career. She recorded *Good Medicine*, her first single in 1989, and in 1990 released her debut album, PHOENIX. In 1990 she had hits with *Stealin' Fire* and *Givin' It All We Got*.

Singles		
Rise Up 1983	*Love Is Fire* 1986	
Alienation 1984	*Love and Compassion* 1987	
Boy's Club 1984	*Walk to the Rhythm* 1987	
At the Feet of the Moon 1985	*Big Big World* 1988	
Act of an Innocent 1985		

Albums/CDs		
THE PARACHUTE CLUB 1983	SMALL VICTORIES 1986	
AT THE FEET OF THE MOON 1984	WILD ZONE: THE ESSENTIAL	
MOVING THRU' THE MOONLIGHT 1985	PARACHUTE CLUB 1992	

Paradox

FRANCOIS COSSETTE (*vocals, guitar*)

SYLVAIN COSSETTE (*vocals, guitar*)

JEAN-FRANCOIS HOULE (*vocals, bass*)

DENIS LAVIGNE (*vocals, drums*)

Denis Lavigne, Jean-Francois Houle, and Sylvain Cossette formed Paradox in late 1984 in Grand-Mère, Quebec, as a cover band. They soon earned a reputation as one of Eastern Canada's premiere live acts. In June 1988 they received the Canadian Factor Award, which became a stepping-stone to recording their debut album with MCA Music America. About this time Francois Cossette, Sylvain's younger brother, joined the group as lead guitarist.

Their first hit single was *Waterline* in 1989 from their self-titled debut album. In the 1991 they had success with their second album, OBVIOUS PUZZLE, and its first single, *Kiss Me on the Lips*.

Singles	*Waterline* 1989	*Catch Me in the Act* 1990
	Another Day 1989	*Kiss Me on the Lips* 1991
Albums/CDs	PARADOX 1989	OBVIOUS PUZZLE 1991

Partland Brothers

CHRIS PARTLAND (*vocals, guitar*)
G.P. PARTLAND (*vocals, percussion*)

The Partland Brothers grew up in Colgan, a small rural community north of Toronto. G.P. and Chris were first members of the Toronto bar band Oliver Heavyside in 1979. In 1983 this band won the Homegrown Contest sponsored by Toronto radio station Q107.

When Oliver Heavyside split up in the late 1980s, impresario James Martin encouraged Chris and his brother to become a duo. In 1987 they signed a record contract with Capitol Records. Their first album, ELECTRIC HONEY, contained an upbeat collection of light pop tunes, and the first single, *Soul City*, was a Top 30 hit on Billboard's Hot 100 in June 1987. Their second album, BETWEEN WORLDS, came out in 1990. It produced the single *Honest Man*.

Three years later, the Partland Brothers were on a new label, Kinetic Records. Their debut, PART LAND, PART WATER, was released in 1993. Produced by Ken Greer at Metalworks Studio in Mississauga, the first single was *Lift Me Up*.

Singles	*Soul City* 1987	*Untouched* 1990
	One Chance 1990	*Christmas Day* 1991
	Honest Man 1990	*Lift Me Up* 1993
CDs	ELECTRIC HONEY 1986	PART LAND, PART WATER 1993
	BETWEEN WORLDS 1990	

The Paupers

CHUCK BEALE (*lead guitar*)
DANNY GERARD (*bass*):
    Replaced by BRAD CAMPBELL

BILL MISENER (*guitar*)
    Replaced by ADAM MITCHELL
RONN (SKIP) PROKOP (*vocals*)
PETER STERBACH (*organ*)

Formed in 1965 in Toronto, The Paupers were originally a quartet known as The Spats comprised of Chuck Beale, Danny Gerard, Bill Misener, and Skip Prokop. In the summer of 1966 Bill Misener left to pursue a career as a solo artist and producer. He was replaced by Brad Campbell. The addition of Peter Sterback on organ made the group a quintet.

Their first hit was *If I Call You by Some Name* in 1966, written by Prokop and Mitchell, the band's principle songwriters. Albert Grossman believed The Paupers were the next biggest thing after The Beatles and became their manager. He also managed Bob Dylan and Peter, Paul and Mary. The Paupers played in L.A.'s Whiskey a Go Go, the Fillmore Auditorium in San Francisco, and Boston's Tea Party. Their big break came in 1967 when they backed up Jefferson Airplane at New York's Cafe à Go Go. Their first album, MAGIC PEOPLE, was released in 1967; ELLIS ISLAND came out a year later.

Prokop left the band in 1968 and was in demand as a session drummer, working with Mama Cass Elliott, Richie Havens, Pozo Seco Singers, and Ian and Sylvia. Prokop had played with Peter, Paul and Mary on their 1967 hit, *I Dig Rock and Roll Music*, and later with Al Kooper and Mike Bloomfield on the second SUPER SESSION album project on Columbia Records. Prokop also helped Albert Grossman re-form Big Brother and the Holding Company after Janis Joplin left. In 1969 he met Paul Hoffert and together they formed Lighthouse.

Bill Misener joined Sun Bar Productions and produced the Quebec group, Morse Code Transmission. He had a major hit with the song *Little Ol' Rock 'N' Roll Band* in 1972. Adam Mitchell's turn as a solo artist came in the late 1970s and early 1980s. He had two hits, *Fool For Love* in 1979 and *Dancing Round and Round* in 1980.

Singles *If I Call You by Some Name/Copper Penny* 1966
Simple Deeds/Let Me Be 1967
One Rainy Day/Tudor Impressions 1967
Magic People/Black Thank You Package 1967
Think I Care/White Song 1967
Another Man's Hair on My Razor/Cairo Hotel 1968

Albums MAGIC PEOPLE 1967   ELLIS ISLAND 1968

The Payola$

PAUL HYDE (*vocals*)   CHRIS TAYLOR (*drums*)
BOB ROCK (*vocals*)   LARRY WILKINS (*bass*)

The Payola$ were founded in Victoria, British Columbia, by Paul Hyde and Bob Rock. They recorded the single *China Boys* on their own Slophouse label, which led to a contract with A&M Records.

In 1982 the release of *Soldier* established them on Canadian radio. Three years later, A&M dropped the group and they broke up. Rock and Hyde continued to record together as a duo until Paul Hyde left to go solo. Bob Rock later formed the heavy rock band Rockhead in Vancouver.

(As The Payola$)

Singles

China Boys 1979	*You're the Only Love* 1985
Eyes of a Stranger 1982	*Stuck in the Rain* 1985
Soldier 1982	*Here's the World* 1985
Where Is this Love 1983	*It Must Be Love* 1986
I'll Find another You	
(Who Can Do It Right) 1983	

Albums/CDs

NO STRANGER TO DANGER 1982	HERE'S THE WORLD FOR YA 1985
HAMMER ON A DRUM 1983	BETWEEN A ROCK AND A HYDE
IN A PLACE LIKE THIS 1984	PLACE: THE BEST OF THE
	PAYOLA$ 1993

(By Paul Hyde)

Singles *America Is Sexy* 1989   *What Am I Supposed To Do* 1989

(As Rock & Hyde)

Single *Dirty Water* 1987

Pear of Pied Pumkin

JOE MOCK (*guitar*)   SHARI ULRICH (*vocals*)
RICK SCOTT (*dulcimar*)

Formed in the late 1960s by Joe Mock and Rick Scott, Pear of Pied Pumkin was one of Vancouver's most popular folk acts. Scott, born in San Antonio, Texas, moved to Canada in the late 1960s to avoid the draft. After living in British Columbia, he toured Japan as a member of the Lotus Eaters. Monk was born in Regina but moved to Vancouver to go to university. He eventually formed his own band, Mock Duck, which had a local following. When it broke up he joined Scott to form Pied Pumkin. Their first two albums on their own Squash label, PIED PUMKIN STRING ENSEMBLE and PIED PUMKIN ALLAH MODE sold 3,000 copies each. Their third, THE PEAR OF PIED PUMKIN came out in 1971.

Shari Ulrich made it a trio in the mid-1970s, but she left in 1976 to join Valdy's backup group, Hometown Band. In 1978 she pursued a solo career.

Scott and Mock continued to perform as Pear of Pied Pumkin. Their next album on Squash Records was PIED PEAR in 1980, recorded at Vancouver's Pinewood Studios. Ulrich was featured on sax on *Caught in the Rain*. Backing up Scott and Mock were Claire Lawrence (sax), Robbie King (organ), Rene Worst (bass), and drummers Geoff Eyre and Duris Maxwell of The Powder Blues. In 1989, Mock and

Scott went on a cross-country tour to promote the independent release of THE LOST SQUASH TAPES.

Albums PIED PUMKIN STRING ENSEMBLE   THE PEAR OF PIED PUMKIN 1977
1975   PIED PEAR 1980
PIED PUMKIN ALLAH MODE 1976   THE LOST SQUASH TAPES 1989

Pepper Tree

CHRIS BROCKWAY   BOB QUINN
TIM GARAGON   JIM WHITE

Originally from the Maritimes, Pepper Tree signed with Capitol Records in 1970 after they were discovered by a talent scout. The group then moved to Alliston, Ontario, where they concentrated on their first album, YOU'RE MY PEOPLE, released by Capitol in 1971. The album yielded the Top 40 hit *Mr. Pride*.

Singles *Everywhere* 1970   *You're My People* 1971
Mr. Pride 1970   *Love Is a Railroad* 1972
Try 1971   *Midnight Lady* 1973

Album   YOU'RE MY PEOPLE 1971

Percy and the Teardrops

B.J. BOOMER   PERCY MORAN
SMITTY GILLES   IKE "FINGERS" TAYLOR
SIMON J. LEMOX

Like Sha Na Na, their American counterparts, this Kingston-based band, formed in 1971, specialized in performing classic rock 'n' roll hits from the 1950s and 1960s. By 1980 there were only two original members left, Percy Moran (Tom Revell) and Simon J. Lemox (Joe Brady). With the popularity of the ABC-TV show *Happy Days* and the Paramount film *Grease* (1978), Percy and The Teardrops were in demand. In 1980 they recorded their only album, ALMOST LIVE, on their own Drop label at Marc Sound in Ottawa. They broke up in 1986.

Album   ALMOST LIVE 1980

Perth County Conspiracy

MICHAEL BUTLER (*bass*)   CEDRIC SMITH (*guitar, vocals*)
RICHARD KEELAN (*guitar, vocals*)

This trio from Stratford, Ontario, in Perth County, was formed in 1969 by Cedric Smith and Richard Keelan.

Their songs blended the words of Dylan Thomas, William Shakespeare, and British poet Christopher Logue with gentle and satirical lyrics about love, freedom, and peace.

Perth County Conspiracy recorded two albums with Columbia Records called THE PERTH COUNTY CONSPIRACY DOES NOT EXIST and PERTH COUNTY LIVE. Their first single, *You've Got to Know*, was an edited version from the first album. Its flip side, also from the same album, was called *Keeper of the Key*. The band recorded a live album called BREAK OUT IN BERLIN in 1976.

Cedric Smith and Terry Jones collaborated in 1977 on one album, TEN LOST YEARS — AND THEN SOME. With the breakup of the group in the late 1970s, Cedric Smith turned to acting. His most notable role was Alec King in the CBC family series *Road to Avonlea*.

Singles	*You've Got to Know/Keeper of the Key* 1971	*Uncle Jed* 1971-72

Albums   PERTH COUNTY CONSPIRACY DOES NOT EXIST 1970
PERTH COUNTY CONSPIRACY LIVE 1971
BREAK OUT IN BERLIN 1976
TEN LOST YEARS — AND THEN SOME 1977

Colleen Peterson

Born in 1950, Colleen Peterson has been playing music since she bought her first guitar with Lucky Green stamps at age thirteen in Peterborough, Ontario. While still in her teens, she played a part in the Toronto production of *Hair*. She soon was playing the coffeehouse circuit which led her to Three's a Crowd, a folk trio based in Ottawa that also included Bruce Cockburn and David Wiffen.

In 1970 she moved to Kingston and with singer Mark Haines became half of the duo Spriggs and Bringle. They toured Canada and the United States for the next four years. BEGINNING TO FEEL LIKE HOME was the name of her first album in 1976. Released on Capitol Records, it contained *Souvenirs*, which became her signature song. The year 1977 saw went back in Toronto, where she co-hosted, with Rick Neufeld, the CBC-TV series *On the Road*.

When her days with Spriggs and Bringle were over, she headed to Nashville to tour with such country and western singers as Charlie Daniels, Roger Miller, and Waylon Jennings. By the end of the 1970s she had recorded two more albums, COLLEEN and TAKIN' MY BOOTS OFF.

The next decade she performed at the Mariposa Folk Festival and Expo 86 and released a series of hit singles, including *I Had It All* and *Weather the Storm*. She also recorded two duets with singer Gilles Godard, *I Still Think of You* and *Life Is Just a Holiday*.

Colleen moved back to Toronto in 1988 and now lives in Lakefield, just outside of her hometown.

Singles	*I Had It All* 1986
	What a Fool I'd Be 1987
	Basic Fact of Love 1987
	Gently Lay Me Down 1987
	Mr. Conductor 1988

I Still Think of You
   (with Gilles Godard) 1988
Weather the Storm 1989
If You Let Me Down Easy 1990
Life is Just a Holiday
   (with Gilles Godard) 1990

Albums/CDs BEGINNING TO FEEL LIKE HOME 1976
COLLEEN 1977

TAKIN' MY BOOTS OFF 1978
BASIC FACTS 1988
LET ME DOWN EASY 1991

Photograph ANDY FORGIE (*vocals*)
JOHN PAUL MURPHY (*drums, percussion*)

MARK RASHOTTE (*guitar*)
MARK WILKINS (*bass, vocals*)

From Belleville, Ontario, this band started out as Creed in 1969. Signed to Buddah Records, they failed to have a hit. A name change to The Elevators did not help the band achieve success. The turning point came in November 1979 when they signed to Capitol Records. Now known as Photograph, they scored three hits from their self-titled debut album, produced by Gene Matynec and Stacy Heydon. Although none of them was a huge hit, they did gain national exposure. The group broke up in 1984.

Singles *The Last Dance* 1981   *Blow Away* 1981
Sarah 1981

Album PHOTOGRAPH 1981

Pinky Victor "Pinky" Dauvin from Sackville, New Brunswick, played with Lighthouse and other groups before going solo in 1972. Signed to United Artists Records, his first hit was *Tell Me Who* in 1972.

Singles *Tell Me Who* 1972   *Cheatin' Mistreatin'* 1972
Don't Send Someone 1972

Platinum Blonde SERGIO GALLI (*guitar*)
MARK HOLMES (*vocals*)

KENNY MacLEAN (*bass*)
CHRIS STEFFER (*percussion*)

Platinum Blonde was one of Canada's major pop groups in the mid-1980s. Their second album, ALIEN SHORES went quintuple-platinum. In 1990 they made an album as The Blondes. Mark Holmes became a member of the group Breed in 1992.

Singles		
	Standing in the Dark 1984	*Somebody Somewhere* 1986
	Sad Sad Rain 1984	*Contact* 1987
	It Doesn't Really Matter 1984	*Connect Me* 1988
	Not in Love 1985	*Fire* 1988
	Crying over You 1985	*If You Go this Time* 1988
	Hungry Eyes 1986	*Yeah Yeah Yeah*
	Situation Critical 1986	(as The Blondes) 1990

Albums/CDs

STANDING IN THE DARK 1983   CONTACT 1987
ALIEN SHORES 1985   YEAH, YEAH, YEAH (as The Blondes)
  1990

The Pointed Sticks

TONY BARDACH (*sax*):   BILL NAPIER-HEMY (*guitar*)
  Replaced by JOHN FARANO   GORD NICOLL (*keyboards*)
NICK JONES (*vocals*)   SCOTT WATSON (*bass*)
KEN MONTGOMERY (*drums*)

Formed in 1978 in suburban Vancouver, The Pointed Sticks, whose name was inspired by a Monty Python skit, won a battle of the bands TV contest on the CBC show *Great Canadian Gold Rush*. Signed to Stiff Records in 1979, they became the first Canadian group to record with the English label and quickly established themselves in the U.S. at San Francisco's Deaf Club and Los Angeles's Starwood.

In 1980 they released three singles on the Vancouver-based Quintessence label: *What Do You Want Me to Do?*, *Lies*, and *The Real Thing*. Their debut album, PERFECT YOUTH, was released in 1981.

Singles

What Do You Want Me To Do?   *Lies* 1980
  1980   *The Real Thing* 1980

Album   PERFECT YOUTH 1981

The Poppy Family

SUSAN JACKS
TERRY JACKS

The husband and wife team of Susan and Terry Jacks started recording together as The Poppy Family in the fall of 1968 with the song *Beyond the Clouds*. With their third single, *Which Way You Goin' Billy?* they achieved national success in 1969. A year later, it became a big hit in the United States and sold two million copies.

Born in Winnipeg, Terry grew up in Vancouver. His first band made one record, *The Way You Feel*, which was a minor hit in Western Canada. He appeared regularly on CBC's *Music Hop* in Vancouver as leader, rhythm guitarist, and vocalist of The Chessmen.

Susan Pesklevits was eighteen when she met her future husband and singing partner. They first played together in a group called Powerline. With guitarist Craig McCaw, they formed a new group, Winkin' Blinkin' and Nod. They first played as The Poppy Family in a small coffeehouse in Blubber Bay, British Columbia in the winter of 1966. *That's Where I Went Wrong* went to the top of the French charts in Quebec as *Le Bateau du Bonheur* in the fall of 1970.

In 1973 Susan and Terry were divorced. The next year he fronted the band Hood who recorded on his own Goldfish label. Their first and only national hit was *Cause We're In Love*. He continued to write songs during the 1980s and produced such groups as Chilliwack. In 1983 he signed a contract with A&M Records. His first single release was *You Fooled Me*. He was the first Canadian artist to achieve platinum on a single (over 150,000 in sales) for *Seasons in the Sun*, which The Kingston Trio first recorded in 1964.

Susan Jacks recorded a solo album called MEMORIES ARE MADE OF YOU in 1976. Early in 1980 she returned to the recording studio and the result was the album GHOSTS and the single *All the Tea in China*.

(As The Poppy Family)

Singles

Beyond the Clouds 1968	*That's Where I Went Wrong* 1970
What Can the Matter Be 1969	*I Was Wondering* 1971
Which Way You Goin' Billy? 1969	*Where Evil Grows* 1971
	I'll See You There 1971
You Took My Moonlight Away 1970	*No Good to Cry* 1971
	Good Friends 1972

Albums/CDs

THAT'S WHERE I WENT WRONG 1970	POPPY SEEDS 1971
WHICH WAY YOU GOIN' BILLY? 1970	THE POPPY FAMILY'S GREATEST HITS 1989

(By Susan Jacks)

Singles

You Don't Know What Love Is 1973	*Anna Marie* 1975
I Thought of You Again 1973-74	*Memories Are Made of This* 1976
	All the Tea in China 1980
I Want You to Love Me 1974	*Evergreen* 1980-81
Build a Tower 1974	*Twice as Strong* 1980
You're a Part of Me 1975	*Fool Such as I* 1980
Love Has No Pride 1975	*Tell Me about It* 1988

Albums

DREAM 1976	FOREVER 1982
GHOSTS 1980	

(By Terry Jacks)

Singles

I'm Gonna Capture You 1970
Someone Must Have Jumped
    1972
Concrete Sea 1972
I'm Gonna Love You Too 1973
Seasons in the Sun 1973
If You Go Away 1974
Rock and Roll (I Gave You the
    Best Years of My Life) 1974

Christina 1975
Holly 1975
Y' Don't Fight the Sea 1976
In My Father's Footsteps 1976
Hey Country Girl 1977
In the Dark 1982
You Fooled Me 1983
Voice of America 1984
Tough Guys Don't Dance 1985

Albums/CD

SEASONS IN THE SUN 1974
Y'DON'T FIGHT THE SEA 1976

PULSE 1983
INTO THE PAST 1989

Powder Blues Band

GORDIE BERTRAM (*sax*)
MARK HASSELBACH (*trumpet*)
WAYNE KOZAK (*sax*)
JACK LAVIN (*bass*)

TOM LAVIN (*guitar*)
DURIS MAXWELL (*drums*)
WILLIE MCCALDER (*keyboards*)
DAVID WOODWARD (*sax*)

The Vancouver-based Powder Blues Band was founded in 1978 by Chicago-born guitarist Tom Lavin, his brother Jack, and Willie McCalder. All eight members came from other groups: Tom used to be with Prism; Jack with Teen Angel; McCalder with Willie and The Walkers; Duris Maxwell with Doucette and Skylark; David Woodward with Downchild; Wayne Kozak with Cobra, Prism and Denise McCann; Gordie Bertram with Foreman Byrnes; and Mark Hasselbach with the jazz group Airbrush.

Their first big break came at a music store called the A&B in Vancouver when the store manager sold all copies of the group's album UNCUT in two days. When a CFOX deejay started playing their music, demand for the group increased, and they eventually signed a contract with Capitol Records. Their first single was *Doin' It Right* in 1980.

Singles

Doin' It Right 1980
Boppin' with the Blues 1980
What've I Been Drinking 1980
Thirsty Ears 1981

Hear that Guitar Ring 1981
Lovin' Kissin' & Huggin' 1981
I'm on the Road Again 1985

Albums/CDs

UNCUT 1980
POWDER BLUES 1980
THIRSTY EARS 1981
PARTY LINE 1982

RED HOT/TRUE BLUE 1983
FIRST DECADE-GREATEST HITS 1990
LET'S GET LOOSE 1993

Peter Pringle Born in 1955, Peter Pringle first became involved with music while he was growing up in Toronto where he studied classical piano and sang with the Canadian Opera Company. His career in opera ended when he turned thirteen and his voice changed from soprano to baritone. He later studied Indian music with Ravi Shankar.

His first major Top 40 hit was *You Really Got Me Needing You Now* in 1977. In 1979 Pringle headlined his own CTV network special and in 1981 recorded *It Just Occurred to Me*, a song written by Skip Prokop (formerly with Lighthouse) and Bob Johnson. Pringle currently lives in Quebec, where he continues to write and record. In 1981 he recorded his first French album, MAGICIEN. In 1992 he toured in the title role of Noel Coward in the stage production of *Coward: A Portrait* and drew rave reviews.

Singles

Gonna Get a Lady 1976
You Really Got Me Needing You Now 1977
Let Me Love You 1977-78
Outside and Inside 1979

I Could Have Been a Sailor 1980
It Just Occurred to Me 1981
Stranger 1981
Hold on to the Night 1981
Why Did I Wait So Long 1982

Albums

PETER PRINGLE 1975
MAGICIEN 1981
RAIN UPON THE SEA 1981
FIFTH AVENUE BLUE 1982
POUR UNE FEMME 1982
SOURIS-MOI 1984

FANTASIES 1984
CHANSONS D'AMOUR 1985
PORTRAIT D'UN ADIEU 1985
PAUVRE CASANOVA 1986
NOEL COWARD: A PORTRAIT 1987
LE JEU D'AMOUR 1991

Prism JOHN HALL (*keyboards*)
ALLAN HARLOW (*bass*)
LINDSAY MITCHELL (*guitar*)

ROCKET NORTON (*drums*)
RON TABAK (*vocals*):
Replaced by HENRY SMALL

This Vancouver band emerged in 1976 as Stanley Screamer. The name was changed when graphics specialist James O'Mara came up with a visual concept for the group. Signed to the now defunct GRT label, Prism recorded several albums, including PRISM, SEE FOREVER EYES, and ARMEGGEDON, before switching to Capitol.

Prism went through some personnel changes between labels. Ron Tabak was replaced by Henry Small, who had previously played with Small Wonder, Scrubbaloe Caine, Gainsborough Gallery, and Burton Cummings. John Hall also left a few months later. After selling two million records, the group split up in 1982.

Six years later, original members Rocket Norton, Lindsay Mitchell, and Allan Harlow were joined by vocalists Darcy Deutsch and Andy Lorimer to record the album OVER 60 MINUTES WITH...PRISM.

Singles

Spaceship Superstar 1977	*You Walked Away Again* 1979-80
Take Me Away 1978	*American Music* 1980
Take Me to the Captain 1978	*Night to Remember* 1980
Flyin' 1978	*Young and Restless* 1980
Armageddon 1979	*American Music* 1980
You're Like the Wind 1979	*Cover Girl* 1980
Virginia 1979	*Don't Let Him Know* 1981

Albums

PRISM 1977	SMALL CHANGE 1981
SEE FOREVER EYES 1978	BEAT STREET 1983
ARMAGEDDON 1979	OVER 60 MINUTES WITH...PRISM
YOUNG AND RESTLESS 1980	1988

The Pukka Orchestra

NEIL CHAPMAN (*guitar*)   GRAEME WILLIAMSON (*vocals*)
TONY DUGGAN-SMITH (*guitar*)

Formed in 1979 in Toronto, The Pukka Orchestra (pronounced puck-a from a Hindu word meaning first rate, permanent, genuine) signed to Solid Gold Records and released their self-titled debut album in 1984. The group's first single, *Listen to the Music*, was a cover version of the Tom Robinson/Peter Gabriel song originally entitled *Atmospherics*.

Singles

Listen to the Radio 1984	*Might as Well be on Mars* 1984-85
Cherry Beach Express 1984	

Albums

THE PUKKA ORCHESTRA 1984	THE PALACE OF MEMORY 1987

Pure

JORDY BIRCH (*vocals*)   MARK HENNING (*keyboards*)
LEIGH GRANT (*drums*)   TODD SIMKO (*guitar*)
DAVE HADLEY (*bass*)

From Vancouver, this band was first called After All and then Grin Factory before they changed their name to Pure. They self-produced and recorded a few songs on tape which were enthusiastically received at a music conference in Vancouver in February 1991. This led to a contract with Reprise/Warner.

In May 1992 a seven-inch green vinyl single, *Greedy/Laughing Like a Fiend*, was released, followed a month later by a four song EP entitled GREED. The song *Greedy* was featured in the Paramount film *Cool World*, directed by Ralph Bakshi of Fritz the Cat fame.

PUREAFUNALIA, the group's debut album on Reprise, came out in September 1992. From it came the first single *Blast*, followed in early 1993 by *Spiritual Pollution*.

Singles *Blast* 1992   *Blissful Kiss* 1993
        Spiritual Pollution 1993   *Pure* 1993

CD   PUREAFUNALIA 1992

The Pursuit of Happiness

TAM AMABILE (*vocals*)	DAVE GILBEY (*drums*)
TASHA AMABILE (*vocals*)	RACHEL OLDFIELD (*vocals*)
MOE BERG (*guitar, vocals*)	JOHNNY SINCLAIR (*bass, vocals*):
SUSAN MURUMETS (*vocals*):	Replaced by BRAD BARKER
Replaced by KRIS ABBOTT	LESLIE STANWYCK (*vocals*)

The Pursuit of Happiness (TPOH) has gone through a number of personnel changes since its inception in 1985. By the time their third album came out in 1993, Moe Berg and Dave Gilbey were the only original members left. Moe Berg was a veteran of several Edmonton bands, such as Modern Minds, Troc '59, and Face Crime. Gilbey had occasionally played with Berg. Johnny Sinclair came from Saskatoon, as did the Amabile sisters who had fronted a Winnipeg band called Dash and the Dots.

In 1986 TPOH made a video of the song *I'm an Adult Now* which was filmed on Queen Street West in Toronto. Its exposure on Much-Music helped them achieve success throughout the rest of Canada. In 1992 they signed with Mercury/Polygram, and their first album on this label, THE DOWNWARD ROAD, was released in 1993, produced by Ed Stasium in Los Angeles. The first single was *Cigarette Dangles*.

Singles *I'm an Adult Now* 1986   *Two Girls in One* 1990
        Killed by Love 1987   *New Language* 1990
        Hard to Laugh 1988   *Cigarette Dangles* 1993
        Beautiful White 1989   *Ashamed of Myself* 1993
        She's So Young 1989   *Pressing Lips* 1993

Albums/CDs LOVE JUNK 1988   THE DOWNWARD ROAD 1993
          ONE SIDED STORY 1990

Queen City Kids

ALEX CHUAQUI (*guitar, keyboards*)
JOHN DONNELLY (*bass*)

KEVIN FYHN (*guitar*)
JEFF GERMAIN (*percussion*)

Originally known as Cambridge, this quartet started out in Regina, Saskatchewan, in 1970. Eleven years later, with a contract from Columbia Records, they released their self-titled debut album. They changed their name to Queen City Kids.

Album   QUEEN CITY KIDS   1981

CHERRILL RAE
ROBBIE RAE

The Raes

The husband and wife team of Cherrill and Robbie Rae started their careers as singers quite by accident. When they heard the song *Que Sera Sera* on the radio, they decided they wanted to record it. Their updated version of Doris Day's 1956 classic was more upbeat, with a disco feel to it.

Robbie's first taste of success came in Wales where he recorded solo a Welsh version of The Lord's Prayer which was banned in Britain because it was deemed blasphemous. In the 1970s The Raes were hosts of CTV's popular *Circus* show.

Singles | *Que Sera Sera* 1977 | *I Only Wanna Get Up and Dance* 1979
A Little Lovin' Keeps the Doctor Away 1979 | *Don't Turn Around* 1979
| *Two Hearts* 1980

Albums | WINNING COMBINATION 1978 | TWO HEARTS 1980
DANCIN' UP A STORM 1979 |

The Rankin Family

COOKIE RANKIN (*vocals*)
HEATHER RANKIN (*vocals*)
JIMMY RANKIN (*vocals*)

JOHN MORRIS RANKIN (*piano, fiddle*)
RAYLENE RANKIN (*vocals*)

From Mabou, Cape Breton, The Rankin Family musical career began in the family home where neighbors would gather every third weekend for a party or ceilidh, as it is known in Gaelic. With their father on violin and mother on piano, the eldest Rankin children would learn Celtic dance steps and songs. As the older siblings grew up and left the family fold, the younger ones would replace them. They played at local weddings and dances.

In 1989, Cookie, Heather, Raylene, Jimmy, and John Morris Rankin were encouraged to perform at various folk festivals. Raylene, who had graduated with a law degree from Dalhousie University, handled most of their bookings, while their mother looked after mail orders for their two independent cassettes, THE RANKIN FAMILY and FARE THEE WELL LOVE.

The Rankin Family was honored in 1991 with three East Coast Awards for Best Live Artists, Best Traditional Artists, and Best Recording Band of the Year. One year later, they won three East Coast Awards and three Juno Award nominations for Best Roots/Traditional Album, Best Country Duo or Group, and Most Promising Group. They made their national TV debut on CBC's *On the Road Again* with host Wayne Rostad, and have performed at the Glen Echo Folk Festival and Winnipeg Folk Festival. In September 1990 the CBC network televised their appearance at the Baddeck and Winnipeg festivals for a one hour special called *Here Come the Rankins*.

To help celebrate Canada's 125th birthday on July 1, 1992, they performed on Parliament Hill in front of Her Majesty the Queen Elizabeth II.

In 1992 they signed a contract with EMI, who re-released their two independent cassettes. In August 1993 the label released NORTH COUNTRY. Its first single was *Rise Again*.

Singles		
Mo Run Geal, Dileas 1989	*Gillis Mountain* 1993	
Orangedale Whistle 1992	*Rise Again* 1993	
Fare Thee Well Love 1992-93	*North Country* 1993	

CDs		
THE RANKIN FAMILY 1989	NORTH COUNTRY 1993	
FARE THEE WELL LOVE 1990		

Tom Cochrane & Red Rider

ROB BAKER (*drums*)
PETER BOYNTON (*vocals, keyboards*)
TOM COCHRANE (*vocals, guitar*)
JEFF JONES (*bass*)
KEN GREER (*vocals, guitar*)

Tom Cochrane & Red Rider were formed in Toronto in 1976. Originally a trio comprised of Rob Baker, Peter Boynton, and Ken Greer, they toured with Pure Prairie League and backed up Bo Diddley in 1977. In November, Tom Cochrane, from Lynn Lake, Manitoba, joined the group and became the main writer. Cochrane had enjoyed a solo hit in 1974 called *Hang on to Your Resistance* for Daffodil Records. He also wrote the music for Al Waxman's film, *My Pleasure Is My Business*. In 1978 bassist Jones made the band a quintet.

Two years later, Capitol Records released the group's debut album, DON'T FIGHT IT, and from it, their first single, *White Hot*. Other albums quickly followed: AS FAR AS SIAM, NERUDA, and BREAKING CURFEW. With the release of their next album in 1986, they became officially known as Tom Cochrane & Red Rider, thus confirming Cochrane's influence as lead songwriter.

Boy Inside the Man was their next single release, followed by the albums VICTORY DAY and SYMPHONY SESSIONS, a collaboration with the Edmonton Symphony Orchestra.

By 1990-91, the original members of the group disbanded. Cochrane dropped the name Red Rider with the release of MAD MAD WORLD. His backup group consisted of drummer Mickey Curry, bassist Spider Sinnaeve, and keyboardist John Webster. The first single from the album, *Life Is a Highway*, was a huge hit in Canada in 1991 and a Top Ten hit in the U.S. in the summer of 1992. It was featured in an episode of Fox TV's *Baywatch* in the 1992-93 season.

(As Tom Cochrane & Red Rider)

Singles *White Hot* 1980
Don't Fight It 1980
What Have You Got to Do 1981
Human Race 1983
Young Thing, Wild Dreams (Rock Me) 1984
Breaking Curfew 1984
Boy Inside the Man 1986
The Untouchable One 1986

One More Time 1987
Ocean Blues (Emotion Blue) 1987
Big League 1988
Different Drummer 1989
Victory Day 1989
Good Times 1989
White Hot (Live) 1990
Bird on a Wire 1990

Albums/CDs DON'T FIGHT IT 1980
AS FAR AS SIAM 1981
NERUDA 1983
BREAKING CURFEW 1984

TOM COCHRANE & RED RIDER 1986
VICTORY DAY 1987
THE SYMPHONY SESSIONS 1989

(By Tom Cochrane)

Singles *Hang on to Your Resistance* 1974
You're Driving Me Crazy 1974
Life Is a Highway 1991
No Regrets 1991-92

Sinking Like a Sunset 1992
Mad Mad World 1992
Washed Away 1992
Bigger Man 1992-93

CD MAD MAD WORLD 1991
ASHES TO DIAMONDS: A COLLECTION 1993

Annie Reisler Annie Reisler was inspired to write music after seeing an article in a Toronto newspaper about a song contest. Reisler first learned to play the piano in one of the foster homes she lived in as a child. When she turned nineteen she wrote a few songs for amusement, but dropped music when she married and had children.

On her fifty-ninth birthday she received a keyboard. Before she knew, it she was writing down melodies, about one a month. In one year she composed twelve children's songs.

In May 1990 she wrote *Solitude*, the story of her life from her days at the orphanage where her father left her at a young age. It was the first of many instrumentals included on an RDR Promopak CD released in November 1991. Another instrumental, *Reminiscing*, came out in March 1992, followed by an album called LOVE INSTRUMENTAL STYLE.

Singles   *Solitude* 1991   *After the Storm* 1993
              Reminiscing 1992

CD   LOVE INSTRUMENTAL STYLE 1992

Ginette Reno   Ginette Reno grew up in Montreal's East Side, where her father was a butcher at the St. Laurent Market. She called herself "the Piaf of Market Street" and sang to people who gathered around. Radio station CKVL let her sing on their Saturday morning amateur show.

Her vocal teacher was Professor Roger Lariviere. To help pay for her lessons, she delivered newspapers. When her voice broke, she could not sing for six months, but in 1961 she heard Connie Francis sing *Where the Boys Are* and her interest in singing came back again.

From 1969 to 1974 she had several chart hits on the Parrot label, distributed by London Records, notably *Beautiful Second Hand Man*. In 1992 she acted in the film *Léolo*.

Singles   *Don't Let Me Be Misunderstood/ Everything* 1969
That I Am 1970
Crowded by Emptiness 1970
Beautiful Second Hand Man
    1970
So Let Our Love Begin 1971
I've Got to Have You 1971
Fallin' in Love Again 1972
Can't Get Hurt Anymore 1972
Everyday Working Man 1973
Light of Love 1974
I'll Bring You Apples 1974
I Just Want to Love 1979-80
T'es Mon Amour
    (with J.P. Ferland) 1974
Des croissants de soleil 1974
J'ai besoin de parler 1984
C'est beaucoup mieux comme ca
    1985

Albums/CDs   GINETTE RENO 1968
LES GRAND SUCCES D'UN
    VEDETTE,GINETTE RENO
    1968
GINETTE RENO A LA COMEDIE-
    CANADIENNE 1969
GINETTE RENO (Parrot) 1970
AIMEZ-LE SI FORT 1970
GINETTE RENO COLLECTION
    NOS. 1 & 2 1970
BEAUTIFUL SECOND HAND MAN
    1971
GINETTE RENO A LA COMEDIE-
    CANADIENNE, A QUICHET
    FERME 1971
GINETTE RENO ALBUM SOUVENIR
    1971
GINETTE RENO EN SPECTACLE
    AU CASA LOMA 1971
QUELQU'UN A AIMER 1971
TOUCHING ME, TOUCHING YOU
    1972
THE BEST OF GINETTE RENO 1975
TOUTE MA CARRIERE/21 DISQUES
    D'OR 1977
CE QUE J'AI PLUS BEAU 1978
JE NE SUIS QU'UNE CHANSON
    1979
TRYING TO FIND A WAY 1979
QUAND ON SE DONNE 1981

PARIS-QUEBEC 1982
SOUVENIRS TENDRES 1983
EN CONCERT 1983
SI CA VOUS CHANTE/DE PLUS
EN PLUS FRAGILE 1986

NE M'EN VEUT PAS 1988
COMPILATION 1990
L'ESSENTIEL 1991

Riverson

RAYBURN BLAKE
BRIAN EDWARDS

FRANKI HART

From Montreal, Riverson was made up of two members of Mashmakhan, Rayburn Blake and Brian Edwards, along with former solo singer Franki Hart. Their first hit was *Clear Night* in 1973.

Singles
Clear Night 1973
Sittin' Waitin' 1973

Eleanor Rigby 1973

Robbie Robertson

Born in 1943 to a Jewish father and a Mohawk mother, Robbie Robertson has been singing professionally since 1958 when he became a member of Ronnie Hawkins's backup group, The Hawks. His first exposure to music was on the Six Nations reserve near Brantford, Ontario, where he spent his summers as a young boy. As a teenager he played in such Toronto bands as The Robots and The Consuls.

By 1960 The Hawks had become a well known rock band in their own right and changed their name to Levon and the Hawks. Five years later, Bob Dylan saw them perform at Friar's Tavern in Toronto and signed them up. They then became known as The Band.

The Band's farewell concert in 1976 was filmed as a movie directed by Martin Scorsese. Robertson decided to try acting himself in *Carny* (1980) with Gary Busey. He then worked as music director on Scorsese's *The King of Comedy* (1983). In 1987 he released his first self-titled solo album. A second album, STORYVILLE, followed in 1991.

Singles
Showdown at Big Sky 1987
Somewhere Down the Crazy River 1988

What About Now 1991
Go Back to Your Woods 1991-92

CDs
ROBBIE ROBERTSON 1987

STORYVILLE 1991

Rockhead   STEVE JACK (*vocals*)   BOB ROCK (*guitar*)
               JAMEY KOSH (*bass*)   CHRIS TAYLOR (*drums*)

The two founding members of this Vancouver-based rock band are Bob Rock and Chris Taylor who had worked together in Rock & Hyde (1986-89) when The Payola$ disbanded in 1985. In between Rock & Hyde and the formation of Rockhead, Rock established himself as a producer for such acts as Motley Crue, Cher, and Metallica.

When Rock & Hyde separated, Capitol Records expressed interest in keeping Rock signed to the label. He and Taylor decided to form their own band and recruited Jamey Kosh and Steve Jack from the Vancouver area. Jack had been a member of the metal cover band Lovehunter. By the end of 1992 Capitol had released the group's debut album.

Singles   *Heartland* 1992-93   *Chelsea Rose* 1993

CD   ROCKHEAD 1992

Garnet Rogers   Between 1973 and 1983, Garnet Rogers of Hamilton, Ontario, served as accompanist and arranger for his older brother Stan. After Stan's untimely death in an airplane crash, Garnet went on to have a successful solo career. His rich, baritone voice distinguished him as a more contemporary pop singer. He toured with noted Scottish singer Archie Fisher, with whom they recorded the album OFF THE MAP in 1986.

Garnet also formed his own record label, Snow Goose Songs. His self-titled debut album came out in 1984.

Albums/CDs   GARNET ROGERS 1984   SPEAKING SOFTLY IN THE DARK
              THE OUTSIDE TRACK 1985   1988
              OFF THE MAP 1986   SMALL VICTORIES 1990

Stan Rogers   Born in 1949 in Hamilton, Ontario, Stan Rogers died in 1983 at the height of his career as a folk singer/songwriter. With his brother Garnet on fiddle and Jim Morrison on bass, Stan Rogers played the coffeehouse circuit, graduating to larger forums as his reputation grew. His appearance at various folk festivals across Canada endeared him to hundreds of folkies who appreciated his storytelling style. Part of his inspiration was drawn from the stories of the Maritimes, such as the tales of the Nova Scotia privateers from the War of 1812 which led him to write *Make and Break Harbour*. One of his most famous songs was the sea ballad *The Mary Ellen Carter*.

He recorded two singles for RCA Records in the early 1970s:

Here's to You Santa Claus in December 1970 and *The Fat Girl Rag* in February 1971. Rogers's self-titled debut album on RCA was released in 1971. While under contract with RCA, he wrote some songs recorded by the Montreal rock group Le Maitre.

His first independent album, FOGARTY'S COVE, came out in 1976. It was followed by TURNAROUND, the live album BETWEEN THE BREAKS, NORTHWEST PASSAGE and FOR THE FAMILY.

On June 2, 1983 Stan was among twenty-three people who died when a Canadian Airlines DC9 caught fire in flight and made an emergency landing in Cincinnati, Ohio, while traveling from Dallas to Toronto. In 1989, the CBC aired the memorial documentary, *One Warm Line*.

Singles		
Here's to You Santa Claus 1970	*Night Guard* 1981
The Fat Girl Rag 1971	*Canal Road* 1982
Passed Fifty 1973-74	

Albums/CDs		
FOGARTY'S COVE 1977	NORTHWEST PASSAGE 1981
TURNAROUND 1978	FOR THE FAMILY 1983
BETWEEN THE BREAKS — LIVE 1979	FROM FRESH WATER 1984
	HOME FROM HALIFAX 1993

Roq

TOM HARPELL (*guitar*)   ROB WATKINS (*vocals, bass*)
DUNCAN HOLT (*drums*)

The three members of Roq hail from Amherstview, Ontario. They landed a recording contract with Access Record Productions in Toronto in 1985. With help from the disc jockeys at CHUM in Toronto, *Empty Hall* became a hit single. It was added to CHUM's playlist in April 1985, and turned out to be their only hit.

Single   *Empty Hall* 1985

Rough Trade

JOHN CESSINE (*percussion*)   HAPPY RODERMAN (*bass*)
MARV KANAREK (*percussion*)   SHARON SMITH (*piano*)
CAROLE POPE (*vocals*)   KEVAN STAPLES (*guitar*)

The origins of Rough Trade go back to 1968 when Carole Pope and Kevan Staples began singing as a folk duo in Yorkville. A year later they formed a band called O and appeared in the film, Osaka '70.

In 1971 they worked as The Bullwhip Brothers, and three years later they became Rough Trade.

Pope's leather outfit helped bring female sexuality to Canadian rock. Lorraine Segato of Parachute Club, another Canadian group, described

Pope's new look as breaking new ground for female singers in Canada. In 1984 Rough Trade made their last album together.

Singles		
Fashion Victim 1981		*Crimes of Passion* 1983
High School Confidential 1981		*Sexual Outlaw* 1984
All Touch 1982		*On the Line* 1985

Albums/CDs		
ROUGH TRADE LIVE! 1976		SHAKING THE FOUNDATIONS 1982
AVOID FREUD 1981		WEAPONS 1983
FOR THOSE WHO THINK YOUNG 1982		O TEMPORA!, O MORES! 1984
		BIRDS OF A FEATHER 1985

Craig Ruhnke

This Toronto-born singer/songwriter's musical career began in the late 1960s when he was a member of the Groovin' Company. He was supplementing his income as a guitar teacher and trying to make ends meet.

He soon realized that songwriting was his niche. John Pozer, then A&R director at WEA in Toronto, signed Craig to the company's publishing arm, Don Valley Music. One of his songs, *I'll Always Love You* was recorded by Pinky. In 1974 WEA urged Ruhnke to record his own material. His first single for the label was *My World* that same year.

By 1974 he had signed with United Artists who released his first Top 10 hit, *Summer Girl*. It was released in Canada, the United States, France, Japan, England and South Africa. Mike Graham, a country vocalist recording for United Artists, played most of the instruments on *Summer Girl*.

Rahnke had several hits during the late 1970s and early 1980s. In 1980 he switched to A&M Records. His biggest hit with the label was *You're a Heartbreaker*. Both it and the flip side, *You and I*, were penned by the artist. Throughout the 1980s he released new songs on A&M Records, and his own record label, Pinnacle Records.

Singles		
My World 1974		*The First Time* 1979
Summer Girl 1974		*It's Time to Fall in Love* 1979
Sweet Feelin' 1974		*Wear My Love* 1979
I Need My Woman 1975		*I Need You to be There* 1979-80
Summer Love 1975		*You're a Heartbreaker* 1980
Surfin' All Summer Song 1975		*Heartache* 1980-81
It's Good to Know 1976		*I Can't Live without Your Love* 1981
Why Don't You Come Up and See Me 1976		*Reach Out* 1981
Wear My Love 1978		*Baby Blue* 1982
It's Time to Fall in Love 1978		*Lovin' Eyes* 1985

Album	
JUST LIKE THE OLD TIMES 1982	

Saga

IAN CRICHTON (*guitar*)
JIM CRICHTON (*bass*)
STEVE NEGUS (*drums*)

PETER RACHON (*keyboards*):
Replaced by JIM GILMOUR
MICHAEL SADLER (*vocals*)

Originally known as Pockets, Saga, like Rush and Max Webster, were part of the Canadian progressive music scene. Formed from the nucleus of Fludd (Jim Crichton, Steve Negus, Peter Rachon), an ex-member of Truck (Michael Sadler) and Kickback (Ian Crichton), Saga's first single, *It's Time (Chapter Three)*, was a huge hit in Toronto due to its exposure on CHUM. Although they never had the same commercial success as Rush, they did have a loyal following. They broke up in 1985.

In 1992 they reunited to play a few dates in Europe. It encouraged them to stay together, and in 1993 Saga recorded a new album, SECURITY OF ILLUSION. It sold over 100,000 copies in Germany.

Singles	
It's Time (Chapter Three) 1980	*Wind Him Up* 1982
See Them Smile 1980	*Scratching the Surface* 1984
Don't Be Late 1981	*What Do I Know* 1985

Albums/CDs	
SAGA 1978	HEADS OR TAILS 1983
IMAGES AT TWILIGHT 1979	BEHAVIOUR 1985
SILENT KNIGHT 1980	ALL THE BEST 1993
WORLDS APART 1981	SECURITY OF ILLUSION 1993
IN TRANSIT 1982	

Buffy Sainte-Marie

Born to Cree Indian parents on the Piapot Reserve at Craven, Saskatchewan, in 1942, Buffy Sainte-Marie was orphaned when she was only a few months old. She was later adopted by Winifred Kendrick Saint-Marie. Her adoptive parents were also part Micmac.

They moved Buffy to Wakefield, Massachusetts where she became a U.S. citizen. Growing up she taught herself to play the piano and, later in her teens, the guitar. Buffy went to the University of Massachusetts and there she started her career as a folksinger. In 1963 she received her degree in philosophy. She then went to New York where she performed at the Gaslight Cafe in Greenwich Village. *The New York Times* hailed her as a promising new talent and she continued to play at other Village nightspots.

Herbert S. Gart, a New York talent agent helped her sign her first recording contract with the Vanguard Recording Society. In 1964 her debut album, IT'S MY WAY, was released. In 1965 she made her first appearance at New York's Carnegie Hall, the Newport Folk Festival, and Royal Albert Hall in London. Other artists, such as Neil Diamond (*Until It's Time*), and Glen Campbell (*Universal Soldier*) have recorded her material.

In 1982, Buffy won an Oscar as co-writer of *Up Where We Belong*, the theme for the film, *An Officer and a Gentleman*. She released her fourteenth album, COINCIDENCES AND LIKELY STORIES, in 1992. She has appeared as a regular on Sesame Street, and earned her doctorate in fine arts from the University of Massachusetts. She holds dual citizenship papers for both Canada and the United States.

Singles

Circle Game 1970
I'm Gonna Be a Country Girl Again 1972
Mister Can't You See 1972
He's an Indian Cowboy in the Rodeo 1972

Can't Believe the Feelin' 1974
I Can't Take It 1974
Fallen Angels 1992
The Big Ones Get Away 1992

Albums/CDs

IT'S MY WAY 1964
MANY A MILE 1965
LITTLE WHEEL SPIN AND SPIN 1966
FIRE AND FLEET AND CANDLELIGHT 1967
I'M GONNA BE A COUNTRY GIRL AGAIN 1968
ILLUMINATIONS 1969
THE BEST OF BUFFY SAINTE-MARIE, VOLUME I 1970

SHE USED TO WANNA BE A BALLERINA 1971
MOONSHOT 1972
QUIET PLACES 1973
BUFFY 1974
CHANGING WOMAN 1975
SWEET AMERICA 1976
COINCIDENCE AND LIKELY STORIES 1992

The Sands of Time

ERIC BARAGAR
TIM CAMPBELL

MICHAEL GOETTLER
STEVE SMITH

Formed in 1966, this Belleville, Ontario band had only one hit, *I've Got a Feeling* in 1970. They performed at Man and His World at Expo 67, and were the youngest band in Canada to tour the east coast. In 1969 they played at the Canadian National Exhibition in Toronto and toured the west coast.

By the early 1970s the Sands of Time had disbanded. Eric Baragar had a brief solo career in 1972. Six years later, the former members of Sands of Time and vocalist Don Thompson of Noah organized a new band, Bentwood Rocker.

Single *I've Got a Feeling* 1970

Eddie Schwartz

Born in 1949, Eddie Schwartz enjoyed his first big success as a songwriter in 1980 with the single, *Hit Me with Your Best Shot*, recorded by Pat Benatar. Others who have recorded his songs include The Doobie Brothers (*The Doctor*), Joe Cocker (*Two Wrongs*), Paul Carrack (*Don't Shed a Tear*), and Gowan (*All the Girls in the World*).

In 1976 Eddie was a guitarist in Charity Brown's backup band. Three years later he signed a contract with Infinity Records but the label folded before anything was released. Early in 1980 he released his debut single, *Two Hearts Full of Love*, on Atco Records. His songs have been recorded by more than 100 artists in sixty countries. In the 1990s, he continues to write and produce songs for such acts as Gowan and Alias.

Singles

Two Hearts Full of Love 1980	*All Our Tomorrows* 1982
Does a Fool Ever Learn 1981	*Over the Line* 1982
Heart on Fire 1981	*Strike* 1984

Albums

SCHWARTZ 1980	PUBLIC LIFE 1983
NO REFUGE 1981	

Jack Scott

Born in 1936 in Windsor, Jack Scott (a.k.a. Jack Scafone) moved to Detroit, Michigan in his teens with his New York-born mother and Italian father, who taught him how to play the guitar. He started singing in high school with his brother Jerry in the country and western band, The Southern Drifters. When a local deejay in Detroit heard Jack at a high school dance, he was invited to make some demos. Response to Jack's songs led to a recording contract at ABC-Paramount in 1957. His first two hits with the label were *Baby She's Gone* and *Two-Timin' Woman*. Backing him up were Stan Getz and The Tom Cats (David Rohiller on lead guitar and Dominic Scafone on drums).

A year later, he signed to Carlton Records. A new group from Windsor, The Chantones, became his backup band. Scott's biggest hit at Carlton was *My True Love* in 1958, the same year he was drafted into the army. Discharged in 1959, he began recording for a new label, Top Rank; *What in the World's Come over You* was a Top 5 hit.

In 1961, he signed to Capitol Records. Three years later, Capitol put out a greatest hits album called BURNING BRIDGES AND MORE OF THE ALL-TIME GREAT HITS OF JACK SCOTT. By the mid-1960s, Scott's appeal began to fade. He signed to three different labels (ABC-Paramount, GRT, and Jubilee) before switching from rock to country in 1974. In 1990 Capitol released a special CD on the artist in its Collectors Series.

Singles		
	Baby She's Gone 1957	*A Little Feeling (Called Love)* 1961
	Two-Timin' Woman 1957	*My Dream Come True* 1961
	Leroy/My True Love 1958	*Steps 1 and 2* 1961
	Geraldine 1958	*Sad Story* 1962
	Goodbye Baby/Save My Soul 1958-59	*Part Where I Cry* 1962
	I Never Felt like This 1959	*Cry Cry Cry* 1962
	The Way I Walk 1959	*If Only* 1962
	There Comes a Time 1959	*Strangers* 1963
	What Am I Living For 1960	*All I See Is Blue* 1963
	Go Wild Little Sadie 1960	*There's Trouble Brewin'* 1963
	What in the World's Come Over You 1960	*Jingle Bells Slide* 1963
	Burning Bridges 1960	*I Knew You First* 1964
	Oh, Little One 1960	*Thou Shalt Not Steal* 1964
	It Only Happened Yesterday/ Cool Water 1960	*What a Wonderful Night Out* 1964
	Patsy 1960	*I Don't Believe in Tea Leaves* 1965
	Is There Something on Your Mind 1961	*Don't Hush the Laughter* 1965
		Looking for Linda 1965
		Before the Bird Flies 1966
		My Special Angel 1967

Albums/CDs		
	JACK SCOTT 1958	BURNING BRIDGES... AND OTHER ALL-TIME HITS 1964
	WHAT AM I LIVING FOR 1960	HERE'S JACK SCOTT 1964
	I REMEMBER HANK WILLIAMS 1960	JACK SCOTT 1990
	WHAT IN THE WORLD'S COME OVER YOU 1961	

Scrubbaloe Caine

PAUL DEAN (*guitar*)
AL FOREMAN (*keyboards, harmonica, vocals*)
JIM HARMATA (*guitar*)

JIM KALE (*bass, vocals*)
BILL MCBETH (*drums, percussion, vocals*)
HENRY SMALL (*electric violin, vocals*)

From Winnipeg, Scrubbaloe Caine had three hits in the 1970s. Bassist Jim Kale was a former member of The Guess Who.

Singles		
	Feelin' Good on Sunday 1973	*Travelling* 1974
	I'm a Dreamer 1974	

Albums		
	ROUND ONE 1973	STREET LEVEL 1974

The Seguins   Born as twins in 1952 in Pointe-aux-Trembles in the east end of Montreal, Richard and Marie-Claire Seguin did not share a common interest until they were in their teens and Richard started playing the guitar. In 1966 they started their first group, Les Nochers, and became a duo a year later, billing themselves as Marie *et* Richard. Le Patriote, a nightclub in Montreal, honored them as the Most Promising Newcomers of 1968. With four other musicians, they founded the group La Nouvelle Frontiere in 1969 which recorded one album on the Gamma label in 1970.

In 1971, Marie and Richard became a duo again known as Seguin until they both went solo in December 1976. Between December 1973 and 1976 the twins made four albums: SEGUIN and EN ATTENDANT for Warner Brothers; RECOLTE DES RÊVES for United Artists; and FESTIN D'AMOUR for CBS.

After their breakup, Richard Seguin collaborated with Serge Fiori of Harmonium on the album DEUX CENTS NUITS A L'HEURE which was released in 1977. By 1979 he released his first solo album, LA PARCEE, and his second in 1981, TRACE ET CONTRASTE, which Quebec novelist Louky Bersianik co-wrote. After some voice training Richard returned to the studio in 1985 to record the album DOUBLE VIE. The turning point in his solo career came at the ADISQ Awards in 1986: he won three Felix Awards. The albums JOURNEE D'AMERIQUE and AUX PORTES DE MATIN followed in the wake of his success.

Marie-Claire has recorded MARIE-CLAIRE SEGUIN (1979), MINUIT UN QUART (1986) and UNE FEMME UNE PLANETE (1990).

Albums   SEGUIN 1973   RECOLTE DE RÊVES 1975
             EN ATTENDANT 1974   FESTIN D'AMOUR 1976

Graham Shaw   Born in Calgary, Graham Shaw lived in Montreal and Regina before moving with his parents to Winnipeg in the early 1960s, where he played with various rock bands such as The Devrons.

Shaw played briefly with The Serenaders in 1971. He reunited with the group in 1977 and quickly established himself as their singer on several singles in the early 1980s.

Singles   *Can I Come Near* 1980   *Can't Say No* 1981
              French Lady 1980   *Jolene* 1981-82
              Roll All Nite Long 1981

Albums   GRAHAM SHAW AND THE SINCERE SERENADERS 1980
             GOOD MANNERS IN THE 80S 1981

Sherriff Freddy Curci (*vocals*)   Wolf Hassel (*bass*)
Steve De Marchi (*guitar*)   Arnold Lanni (*keyboards*)
Rob Elliott (*drums*)

Sherriff formed in Toronto in 1979. In 1983 after four years of touring, the band signed with Capitol Records. Their biggest hit was *When I'm with You* in 1983, re-released in 1989 by Capitol. The second time around it reached number one on Billboard's Hot 100.

Shortly after the initial release of *When I'm with You*, Sheriff disbanded. Arnold Lanni and Wolf Hassel went on to form the group Frozen Ghost in 1985. Freddy Curci and Steve De Marchi started their own band, Alias.

Singles *You Remind Me* 1982
When I'm with You 1983 (re-released 1989)

Album SHERRIFF 1983

Shingoose An Obijwa Indian, Shingoose (Curtis Jonnie) was born in 1946 on the Roseau River Reserve. At the age of four he was adopted by a Mennonite missionary family from Steinbach, Manitoba, and soon began singing in church choirs and playing church music. In his teens he moved to the United States where he joined the Nebraska-based Boystown Concert Choir. By the mid-1960s, he had graduated to rock music and played in various pop/rock and rhythm & blues bands in Washington, D.C. and New York.

He returned to Winnipeg in 1973 and became an activist on behalf of Native peoples. At various folk festivals across Canada, Curtis chose to sing under the name "Shingoose," the name of his great-grandfather. His first recording was an EP called NATIVE COUNTRY, which came out in 1975. Four years later came the album, BATTLE OF NORVAL.

The year 1983 saw him tour Canada in the native musical *In Deo*, which featured some of his own songs. Two years later, he hosted his own Native current affairs TV show, *First Nations Magazine*. In 1988 he released his first cassette, NATURAL TAN on the new Headband Records label and starred along with other Native singer/songwriters in the CTV prime time special, *Indian Time*.

Albums BATTLE OF NORVAL 1979   NATURAL TAN 1988

Shooter (see The Greaseball Boogie Band)

Jane Siberry

Jane Siberry was born in 1955 and raised in Toronto. Before launching her solo career, she performed in the acoustic duo Java Jive. Her self-titled independent album in 1981 was mostly an acoustic collection of folk songs. NO BORDERS HERE, the follow-up album on Duke Street Records, produced the hit *Mimi on the Beach*, a seven-and-a-half minute song about a woman floating on a pink surfboard. Her next album, released in 1985, was THE SPECKLESS SKY, followed in 1987 by THE WALKING. She continued to impress both fans and critics with her 1989 album, BOUND BY THE BEAUTY.

Jane loves to act in her videos and in 1989 she directed a twelve-minute movie, *The Bird in the Gravel*.

Singles

You Don't Need 1984
Mimi on the Beach 1984
I Muse Aloud 1984
One More Colour 1985
Bound by the Beauty 1989

Everything Reminds Me of My Dog 1989
Calling All Angels (with k.d. lang) 1992
Sail across the Water 1993
Temple 1994

Albums/CDs

JANE SIBERRY 1981
NO BORDERS HERE 1984
THE SPECKLESS SKY 1985

THE WALKING 1987
BOUND BY THE BEAUTY 1989
WHEN I WAS A BOY 1993

Silverlode

GEOFF GIBBONS
KEN KIRSCHNER

Both members of this duo from Vancouver were twenty-one when they had a big hit with *Sky High* in 1980. Kirschner began performing at age thirteen and after some vocal training he was invited to be a tenor soloist with the British Columbia Boys Choir. Gibbons was also a member of the B.C. Boys Choir where he spent two of his four years as soprano soloist. His voice was featured on two records the choir put out. At sixteen, he became singer, guitarist, and songwriter for a local band called Cove Company. Gibbons and Kirschner were in Australia playing separately when they decided to get together as Silverlode. They won second prize in a battle of the bands contest and also wrote and recorded several jingles for a radio station in Melbourne. In February 1981 Silverlode released their self-titled debut album.

Single *Sky High* 1981

Album SILVERLODE 1981

Gordon Sinclair Veteran CBC broadcaster Gordon Sinclair made only one record for Avco Embassy Records in 1974, an editorial he called *The Americans* which was part of his *Let's Be Personal* program on radio station CFRB in Toronto. The piece told how the Americans were unappreciated and unjustly maligned. The song stirred up a lot of controversy and was later recorded as a hit by Detroit broadcaster Bryon MacGregor.

Single *The Americans* 1974

Les Sinners ARTHUR LOUIS PARIZEAU
FRANCOIS GUY DANIEL VALOIS
ALAIN JODOIN

Les Sinners go back to 1965 when Francois Guy, Louis Parizeau, and Charles Linton formed a rock 'n' roll group called The Silver Spiders. Two months after they began playing together, they changed their name to Les Sinners. In 1968 Guy left the group to start another trio, La Revolution français, with Richard Tate and Angelo Finaldi. They recorded one song, *Quebecois*, which sold over 130,000 copies. Six months later, the trio broke up.

Guy formed another trio with Jay Brown and Jean-Guy Durocher before he left to concentrate on a solo career. He signed a contract with the Montreal-based label Pumpkin Records, which released his first single, *Mary-Go-Round*, in 1974.

Les Sinners returned with a new lineup in 1970. For the most part they were a studio group. The first single for the reconstituted band was *Je Chante* in 1970, which featured singer Alain Jodoin. In 1972 they established their own studios in Montreal. Their 1975 album on the Celebration label featured songs in French and English.

Singles *Quebecois* 1968 *Douce Folie* 1974
Je Chante 1970

Album LES SINNERS? 1975

The Skydiggers PETER CASH (*vocals, guitar*) RONNIE VON JOHNNY (*bass*)
JOHN FINLAYSON (*guitar*) WAYNE STOKES (*drums*)
ANDY MAIZE (*vocals*)

Founded in 1987 by Andy Maize, Peter Cash, and Josh Finlayson, The Skydiggers (named by Peter Cash's older brother Andrew) released their critically acclaimed self-titled debut album in 1990. From it came the singles *Monday Morning* and *I Will Give You*

Everything, one of the top five songs to receive radio airplay in 1991.

In 1992, The Skydiggers and John Oliveira formed the fre label, distributed by Capitol. That same year the group's second album, REST-LESS, came out. It was recorded over a six week period at Hamilton's Grant Avenue studio and mixed at Mississauga's Metalworks. Shortly after finishing RESTLESS, Wayne Stokes left the group to spend more time with his family. JUST OVER THIS MOUNTAIN, the group's third album, was released in September 1993.

Singles	*Monday Morning* 1990	*A Penny More* 1992
	I Will Give You Everything 1991	*Feel You Closer* 1992-93
		I'm Wondering 1993

CDs	THE SKYDIGGERS 1989	JUST OVER THIS MOUNTAIN 1993
	RESTLESS 1992	

Skylark

BONIE COOK (*vocals*)	DURIS MAXWELL (*drums*):
DAVID FOSTER (*keyboards*)	Replaced by BRIAN HILTON
DONNY GERARD (*vocals*)	NORMAN McPHERSON (*guitar*):
CARL GRAVES (*percussion*)	Replaced by ALLAN MIX
	STEVEN PUGSLEY (*bass*)

From Vancouver, Skylark recorded for Capitol Records in the early 1970s. The biggest of their three hits was *Wildflower*, written by Vancouver studio musician Doug Edwards and Victoria policeman Dave Richardson. They disbanded shortly after the release of *I'll Have to Go Away* in 1973.

Donny Gerard went on to have minor success with *Words Are Impossible* in 1976. Carl Graves had two hits in 1975 with *Baby, Hang Up the Phone* and *Hey Radio*. The most famous member was David Foster. In 1985 he recorded the theme from *St. Elmo's Fire* and released his self-titled debut solo album on Atlantic Records in 1986. On it was included a duet called *The Best of Me* with Olivia Newton-John. Foster also became one of the top producers of the 1980s. In 1985 he co-wrote and produced *Tears Are Not Enough*, the Ethiopian famine relief hit recorded by a group of Canadian celebrities. He also had solo hits with *Who's Gonna Love You Tonight* in 1986 and *Winter Games* in 1988. In 1993 he produced Color Me Badd's version of *Wildflower*.

(as Skylark)

Singles	*What Would I Do without You* 1972	*Wildflower* 1973
		I'll Have to Go Away 1973

Album SKYLARK 1972

(by David Foster)
Singles *The Love Theme from St. Elmo's Fire (Man in Motion)* 1985
The Best of Me (with Olivia Newton-John) 1986
Who's Gonna Love You Tonight 1986
Winter Games 1988

Albums DAVID FOSTER 1986 THE DAVID FOSTER CHRISTMAS
THE SYMPHONY SESSIONS 1988 ALBUM 1993

Slik Toxik

ROB BRUCE (*guitar*) PAT HOWARTH (*bass*)
NEIL BUSBY (*drums*) DAVE MERCEL (*vocals*)
KEVIN GALE (*guitar*) NICK WALSH (*vocals*)

Formed in October 1988, Slik Toxik established themselves playing the club circuit in Toronto where they opened for such acts as Succesexx and Slick Kitty. When the group began to develop a following, their manager Bob Luhtala made the rounds of the record companies with a demo tape. Capitol-EMI signed them, and in 1991 a CD maxi-single, SMOOTH AND DEADLY, was released, featuring five songs, including *Riff Raff* and *Mass Confusion*. In December 1991 Slik Toxik was awarded the 1991 Toronto Music Award for Live Club Band of the Year.

Their first album, DOIN' THE NASTY, was simultaneously released in Canada and the U.S.A. From it came their first single, *Helluvatime*, in 1992. The band became the last act to play in Toronto's legendary Rock 'n' Roll Heaven nightclub before it closed in February of 1992.

Singles *Helluvatime* 1992 *By the Fireside* 1992
I Hear It Raining 1992 *Doin' the Nasty* 1992
White Lies Black Truth 1992 *Sweet Asylum* 1992

CD DOIN' THE NASTY 1992

Sloan

JAY FERGUSON PATRICK PENTLAND
CHRIS MURPHY ANDREW SCOTT

The story of Sloan begins in Halifax, Nova Scotia, where their brand of "indie" rock established them as one of the top grunge bands on the East Coast music scene in 1991.

Chris Murphy, a former member of Blackpool, is the principal song-writer of the group. He and guitarist Jay Ferguson previously played together in the band Kennedy Lake Rd. Managed by Pete Rowan, who had his own record company, DTK Records, Sloan recorded the independent EP HERE AND NOW, which included *Underwhelmed*, the first single from their debut album, SMEARED on DGC/Geffen in October 1992.

Singles	*Underwhelmed* 1992	*500 Up* 1993
	Sugartune 1993	
CD	SMEARED 1992	

Snow Born in the Toronto suburb of North York, this Irish-Canadian learned to rap Jamaican DJ style from going to parties of his black friends. Snow (a.k.a. Darrin O'Brien) loves reggae music and is a fan of Barrington Levy and Junior Reid.

His debut album, 12 INCHES OF SNOW, features songs about his life as a criminal, *Lonely Monday Morning* and *Informer*, the album's first single. *Informer* became a huge hit in Canada and the United States, where it reached number one on Billboard's Hot 100.

Snow's experiences in jail include a year in the Metro East Detention Centre for two attempted murder charges of which he was acquitted. He also served a year for assault causing bodily harm.

In May 1993 Warner released *Girl, I've Been Hurt* as the second single from 12 INCHES OF SNOW.

Singles	*Informer* 1992-93	*Runway* 1993
	Girl, I've Been Hurt 1993	
CD	12 INCHES OF SNOW 1992	

Gino Soccio Gino Soccio is a multi-instrumentalist session musician and producer known as Kebekelektrik. Under his own name, he recorded his first album, OUTLINE, in 1979 for Quality Records. From it came the international number one disco hit, *Dancer*. In 1980, his long-awaited second album, S-BEAT, which was recorded in Montreal at Studio St. Charles, was released.

Singles	*Dancer* 1979	*It's Alright* 1982
	Les Visiteurs 1979-80	*Turn It Around* 1984
Albums	OUTLINE 1979	FACE TO FACE 1982
	S-BEAT 1980	REMEMBER 1984
	CLOSER 1981	

Southcote BEAU DAVID (*vocals*)   CHARLIE WHITE (*guitar*)
BREEN LeBOEUF (*vocals,*   LANCE WRIGHT (*drums*)
keyboards, bass)

Based in Toronto, Southcote had a major hit in 1974 with *She*, a fast-paced number written by Beau David, the leader of the group. The band had been together a little over a year when their record company, Smile Records, called them "the next supergroup." Southcote's only big hit was *She*.

Singles   *She* 1973-74   *Who Knows His Name* 1974

The Sparrows   LARRY BYRON   JACK LONDON
DENNIS EDMONTON   GOLDIE McJOHN
JERRY EDMONTON   BRUCE PALMER: replaced by
JOHN KAY   NICK ST. NICHOLAS

The Sparrows formed in Yorkville in Toronto, where bands like The Hawks, The Paupers, and The Ugly Ducklings were also performing. One member of the group was John Kay, who came to Canada from West Germany as a young teenager in 1958, and soon became involved in the Yorkville scene, playing in various bands before taking part in an impromptu session with Jack London and the Sparrows. He joined the group in May of 1966.

The Sparrows quickly gained a loyal following and their success led to their debut album on Columbia Records. Known eventually as John Kay and The Sparrows, their popularity began to grow in the United States. In 1967 the group broke up, but Kay and several other members went on to form Steppenwolf, the quintessential late-1960s hard rock band whose song, *Born to Be Wild*, became an anthem for the 1960s generation.

(As Jack London and the Sparrows)
Singles   *If You Don't Want My Love*   *I'll Be the Boy* 1965
1965   *Our Love Has Passed* 1965

Album   PRESENTING JACK LONDON AND THE SPARROWS 1965

(As The Sparrows)
Singles   *Hard Times with the Law* 1965

(As John Kay and the Sparrows)
Singles   *Tomorrow's Ship* 1966   *Green Bottle Lover* 1967

Album   JOHN KAY AND THE SPARROWS 1966

Gered Mankowitz

Gary Fjellgaard
Kim Mitchell
Robbie Robertson
National Velvet
Alannah Myles

Robert John

John Phillips

Victor Dezio

Big House
Marc Jordan
Lee Aaron
James Keelaghan
The Skydiggers

Matthew Wiley

Deborah Samuel

Denise Grant

Frank Mills
Mae Moore
Rita McNeil
Shingoose
Moxy Früvous

Rush
David Wiffen
Platinum Blonde
Sue Medley
Rockhead

Gregory Heisler

**West End Girls
Loreena
    McKennitt
Anne Murray
Murray
    McLauchlan**

Elisabeth Feryn

Denise Grant

Alison Dyer

The James Leroy Group
Catherine McKinnon
Colleen Peterson
Sloan
Three's a Crowd

Joakim Blockstrom

Jay Blakesberg

Maestro Fresh Wes
Snow
Pure
Lisa Lougheed
The Spoons

Neil Young
Buffy Sainte-Marie
The Irish Rovers
The Nylons
Valdy

Spice LAURIE CURRIE (*drums, vocals*) SUZANNE MORIER (*vocals*)
CHUCK GORLING (*organ, piano*) PHIL O'CONNELL (*guitar*)
BRIAN MIESSNER (*bass, vocals*) BOB WALKER (*bass*)

From Winnipeg, this band was first known as Sugar and Spice. They had two hits in 1969 on Franklin Records: *Cruel War* and *Something to Believe*. In 1972, Suzanne Morier and Bob Walker left, and the group became known as Spice.

Singles *Sweet Talkin' Woman* 1972   *Just a Little Love* 1972
Strawberry Wine 1972

Spirit of the West VINCE DITRICH (*drums*) J. KENNETSON (*mandolin, bass*):
GEOFFREY KELLY (*flute, bodhran, guitar*) Replaced by HUGH McMILLAN
JOHN MANN (*vocals, guitar*) LINDA McRAE (*bass, accordion, vocals*)

Founded by John Mann and Geoffrey Kelly in 1983, Spirit of the West's first album, TRIPPING UP THE STAIRS was produced with the help of fellow Vancouverite Barney Bentall. From 1984 to 1986, the band toured Finland, Scotland, and Canada. In the summer of 1990 the group toured England with the UK pop group The Wonder Stuff. The response to Spirit of the West in England was good enough for them to be invited back in June 1991 to play before an enthusiastic crowd of 20,000 fans in a football stadium outside Birmingham, England. In 1993, Spirit of the West released a new album called FAITHLIFT. *And if Venice Is Sinking* was the first single.

Singles *The Crawl* 1987   *Political* 1991
Save this House 1990   *And if Venice Is Sinking* 1993
D for Democracy 1991   *Five Free Minutes* 1994

CDs TRIPPING UP THE STAIRS 1986   SAVE THIS HOUSE 1990
LABOUR DAY 1988   GO FIGURE 1991
OLD MATERIAL 1984-1986 1989   FAITHLIFT 1993

The Spoons COLIN CRIPPS (*guitar*) ROB PREUSS (*keyboards*): Replaced
GORDON DEPPE (*vocals, guitar*) by SCOTT MacDONALD
SANDY HORNE (*bass*) DERRICK ROSS (*drums*):
Replaced by IAN HENDRY

Sandy Horne and Gordon Deppe formed The Spoons while both were attending high school in Burlington, Ontario, in 1979. Their debut album, STICK FIGURE NEIGHBORHOOD, on the independent Ready Records label, was released late in 1981, while their first single, *Nova Heart*, was a hit in 1982.

Four years later, the band went through some personnel changes, adding three new members, keyboardist Scott MacDonald, drummer Ian Hendry, and guitarist Colin Cripps. They also switched to Anthem Records in the spring of 1986 to record the album BRIDGES OVER BORDERS.

Singles		
	Nova Heart 1982	*Tell No Lies* 1984
	Arias and Symphonies 1982	*Romantic Traffic* 1985
	Smiling in Winter 1983	*When Time Turns Around* 1988
	Old Emotions 1983	*Waterline* 1989

Albums/CDs		
	STICK FIGURE NEIGHBORHOOD 1981	TALKBACK 1983
		BRIDGES OVER BORDERS 1986
	ARIAS AND SYMPHONIES 1982	VERTIGO TANGO 1988

The Staccatos

MIKE BELL *(drums, vocals)* LES EMMERSON *(guitar, vocals)*
RICK BELL *(drums, vocals)* TED GEROW *(keyboards)*
VERN CRAIG *(guitar, vocals)* BRIAN RADING *(bass, vocals)*

The Staccatos began playing together in Ottawa in 1963. Dean Hagopian, a local radio personality, was the group's first singer in 1963-64, and they released their first single, *Small Town Girl*, on Capitol Records in 1965. In the mid-1960s, they appeared on network television and built up a loyal following on both the Ontario and Quebec club circuits. They also did a series of Coke jingles that led to the album WILD PAIR, a collaborative effort with The Guess Who.

In 1967 *Half Past Midnight* became one of the biggest Canadian rock singles of the year. Written by Les Emmerson and produced in a four-track studio in Montreal, it sold just under 20,000 copies. The City Stompers, an Australian group, recorded the song a year later. In March 1968 the Staccatos released an album called THE FIVE MAN ELECTRICAL BAND. They officially adopted the album's name for the group in 1969. Their first single under their new name was *It Never Rains on Maple Lane*.

Capitol Records continued to release other singles by the group but none was very successful, and by the end of the 1960s they had no record company, though their song *Moonshine (Friend of Mine)* was used in the MGM film, *Moonshine War* (1970) and released as a single. The song was a minor hit in Canada. The band then recorded *Signs* on Lionel Records in the United States; the song was an instant hit in

Augusta, Georgia, Baton Rouge, Louisiana, and at CKLW in Windsor, Ontario. The attention it received from radio made it a national hit. In Canada, *Signs* was on the Polydor label.

Les Emmerson enjoyed success as a solo artist beginning with *Control of Me* in 1973 while remaining as the group's singer. When the band broke up later in 1973 in Los Angeles, Emmerson returned to Ottawa and three years later started his own group, The Emmerson Electrical Band. In 1980 he had a new backup band called Blue Blood. They released one single, *One Way Life (U-Turn Sign)* in 1980. Today, he is a member of the trio Cooper, King and Emmerson.

The Five Man Electrical Band has reunited for the occasional tour since 1986.

(as The Staccatos)

Singles
Small Town Girl 1965
Move to California 1965
Do You Mind if I Dance with You, Girl 1965
It's a Long Way Home 1966
C'Mon Everybody 1966
Let's Run Away 1966
Half Past Midnight 1967
Catch the Love Parade 1967
Walker Street 1968
Didn't Know the Time 1968

Albums
INITIALLY THE STACCATOS 1965
THE FIVE MAN ELECTRICAL BAND 1968

(as The Five Man Electrical Band)

Singles
It Never Rains on Maple Lane 1969
Private Train 1969
Sunrise to Sunset 1969
Moonshine (Friend of Mine) 1970
Hello Melinda Goodbye 1970-71
Signs 1971
Absolutely Right 1971
Julianna 1972
Devil and Miss Lucy 1972
Money Back Guarantee 1972
I'm a Stranger Here 1973
Baby Wanna Boogie 1973
Werewolf 1974
Johnny Get a Gun 1975

Albums
GOODBYES AND BUTTERFLIES 1971
COMING OF AGE 1972
SWEET PARADISE 1973
THE POWER OF THE FIVE MAN ELECTRICAL BAND 1974

The Stampeders
KIM BERLY
RACE BERLY
RICH DODSON
RONNIE KING
VAN KING
BRENDAN LITTLE
LEN ROEMER

The Stampeders formed in Calgary, Alberta in 1963 when Rick Dodson, Brendan Lyttle, Len Roemer, and Kim Berly practiced together as The Rebounds. Lyttle knew Mel Shaw, co-producer and talent co-ordinator of Calgary TV's *Guys and Dolls*, who booked The Rebounds on the show and later became their manager. Shaw also changed the group's name to The Stampeders in December 1964. In 1965 Mel arranged for the group to play regularly at a local Calgary club called The Conquistador. He also decided to bring in two new members: Van King because he was showman and had a flamboyant personality, and Race Berly, Kim's Brother. Later that same year Roemer decided to leave and was replaced by Ronnie King, whose experience was with another Calgary band, The Paint Brushes.

The group began a cross-Canada tour. Arriving in Montreal in 1967 they recorded *Morning Magic* at RCA. Shaw released it on MWC, his own record label. It was a hit only in Canada.

By the end of 1968 the rigors of touring had taken their toll on band members, and The Stampeders became a trio — Kim Berly, Rich Dodson, and Ronnie King. In 1970 they made their first album, and the first single was the hit *Carry Me*.

The Stampeders finally received recognition in the United States in 1971 with *Sweet City Woman* which went to number one and sold over a million copies.

The CBC-TV network produced a documentary about the group called *A Short Visit to Planet Earth* which aired on November 15, 1973. Simulated space effects were used to celebrate the terrestrial landing of Ronnie, Rich, and Kim as they sang some of their old hits plus some new songs from their then soon-to-be released album, FROM THE FIRE. The show's finale featured the songs *Wild Eyes* and *Johnny Lightning*. In 1976 a second drummer and a three-man brass and reed section were added. Dodson left to go solo in 1977. He was replaced by Doug Macaskill, former guitarist with Deja Vu. In 1978 Berly left to go solo. King switched to the guitar and was joined by his brother Roy on bass. The group was now billed as The Stampeders featuring Ronnie King.

By the end of the decade, the group had split up. Rich Dodson continues to record for Marigold Records and also has written and published his own material under the name of Sleepy Cat Music. In 1988 he wrote Toronto singer Debbie Johnson's 1988 hit, *Just Like Magic*.

In 1992 The Stampeders were reunited on CTV's *The Dini Petty Show* and that same year they performed at the Calgary Stampede.

The summer of 1993 saw them reunite for another series of concerts; they also signed a new contract with Aquarius Records.

Singles

House of Shake 1965
You Never Know until You Cry
 1966
Morning Magic 1967
Be a Woman 1968
Crosswalk 1969
Carry Me 1970-71
Sweet City Woman 1971
Devil You 1971-72
Monday Morning Choo Choo
 1972
Then Came the White Man
 1972
Wild Eyes 1972
Julia Get Up (Rich Dodson)
 1972
Johnny Lightning 1972-73

Oh My Lady 1973
Minstrel Gypsy 1973
Running Wild 1973-74
Me and My Stone 1974
Ramona 1974
Hit the Road Jack 1975
New Orleans 1975
Playin' in the Band 1976
Blue-eyed Woman (Kim Berly)
 1976
Sweet Love Bandit 1976
San Diego 1976
Give You that Love (Rich Dodson)
 1979
Natalie (Rich Dodson) 1980
Looking Back (Rich Dodson) 1981
Holiday (Rich Dodson) 1988

Albums/CDs

AGAINST THE GRAIN 1971
CARRYIN' ON 1972
RUBES, DUDES AND ROWDIES
 1973
FROM THE FIRE 1973
NEW DAY 1974
BACKSTAGE PASS 1975

STEAMIN' 1975
HIT THE ROAD 1976
PLATINUM 1977
BALLSY 1979
OVER 60 MINUTES WITH THE
 STAMPEDERS 1989

Steamer

GORDON HENDERSON
 (*vocals, piano*)

MIKE HILLIARD (*guitar*)
ED HILLIARD (*drums*)

Steamer, from Kamloops, British Columbia, was formed in 1977. They took their name from a character in the movie, *Walking Tall: Part Two*. During their first two years, they toured with Steppenwolf and The Guess Who.

Their debut album was titled LOOK AT ME NOW on Pickwick's Intercan label. From it came the single release *Don't Say Goodbye*.

Single *Don't Say Goodbye* 1980

Album LOOK AT ME NOW 1980

Steel River

ROB COCKELL (*bass*)
JOHN DUDGEON (*vocals*)
TONY DUNNING (*guitar*)

BOB FORRESTER (*keyboards*)
DENNIS WATSON (*drums*)

Steel River started playing in 1965 when the four original members performed together in small clubs and high schools in Toronto. In 1969 they played professionally for the first time as Steel River, and the following year producer Greg Hambleton signed them to his Tuesday label. Their first hit was *Ten Pound Note* from their debut album, WEIGHIN' HEAVY. It was not until the song became a national hit that they learned there actually was a namesake river near Ottawa. After three more hits, the group disbanded in 1974 but six years later the original four were reunited and a drummer added to record the single *Armoured Car.*

Singles		
Ten Pound Note 1970		*Mexican Lady* 1971-72
Walk by the River 1971		*Just Remember* 1974
Southbound Train 1971		*Armoured Car* 1980

Albums		
WEIGHIN' HEAVY 1970		A BETTER ROAD 1971

Suzanne Stevens

Suzanne Stevens was a receptionist in Montreal when she entered a talent scout show and won a chance to sing with French singer Renee Claude in concert at the Salle Claude Champagne, which led to a recording contract with Capitol Records. Her first single was *Le soleil* in May 1973. Her biggest English hit was *Make Me Your Baby* in 1976. She made her American debut that same year with the album THE TOWER.

LOVE'S THE ONLY GAME IN TOWN, her 1976 English album, included songs written by four different Canadian composers: Sylvia Tyson, Gene MacLellan, Ives Lapierre, and Judi Richards. In 1985 she joined other Canadian artists for *Tears Are Not Enough.*

Singles		
Le soleil 1973		*L'as-tu vu le soleil* 1976
En Route 1974		*Knowing How Knowing When* 1976
Je ne vivais pas avant toi 1975		*Let It Burn* 1979
Make Me Your Baby 1976		
Doesn't It Seem Like a Miracle 1976		

Albums		
EN ROUTE 1974		LOVE'S THE ONLY GAME IN TOWN 1976
MOI DE LA TETE AUX PIEDS 1974		

Stitch in Tyme

PINKY DAUVIN	BOB MURPHY
GRANT FULLERTON	BRUCE WHEATON
DANNY MORRIS	

Stitch in Tyme was formed in northwest Nova Scotia in the mid-1960s when two bands, The Untouchables and The Continentals, amalgamated. They later moved to Toronto where they became part of the Yorkville music scene. Signed to Yorkville Records, they had two hit singles in 1967, *Got to Get You into My Life* and *New Dawn*.

When the band split up in 1969, Wheaton formed the group Everyday People while Fullerton and Davin joined Lighthouse. In the late 1980s the Stitch in Tyme reunited for annual concerts.

Singles	*Got to Get You into My Life* 1967	*New Dawn* 1967
		Stop Wastin' Time 1968

Stonebolt

DANNY ATCHISON (*bass*)   JON WEBSTER (*keyboards*)
BRIAN LOUSLEY (*drums*)   DAVID WILLS (*vocals*)
ROY ROPER (*guitar*)

Stonebolt's origins go back to the late 1960s when Roy Roper and Brian Lousley, two North Vancouver schoolmates, wanted to start their own band. They listened to records and studied the older bands that came to their school dances. Not long after, bassist Danny Atchison made it a trio. They first called themselves Perth Amboy before they settled on Stonebolt. The addition of Jon Webster and David Wills made the band complete.

Based in Vancouver, their critics called the band's music "formula rock" while others said they were Canada's answer to The Eagles. It was not until 1977 that their career took off. Walter Stewart, an associate of Johnny Rivers, heard them in Vancouver and was impressed by their demo of *Sail On*. Stewart added the group to his roster at Walter Stewart Productions and signed them to Parachute Records, an affiliate of Casablanca. From their debut album came the first single, *Queen of the Night*, which was a modest hit early in 1978. A second single, *I Will Still Love You*, released in June, became the group's biggest hit, the only one to reach Billboard's Hot 100.

In 1979 the group's future was in limbo when Parachute Records went bankrupt. A year later they signed with RCA Records and released the album KEEP IT ALIVE.

Singles	*Queen of the Night* 1978	*Don't Ya Hide It* 1980
	I Will Still Love You 1978	*Crying Again Tonite* 1980
	Love Struck 1980	

Albums	STONEBOLT 1978	KEEP IT ALIVE 1980

Strange Advance

DREW ARNOTT   DARRYL KROMM
PAUL IVERSON

Strange Advance began as a concept band created by producer Bruce Fairbairn of Loverboy and Prism. In 1983 their debut album, WORLDS AWAY, went gold shortly after its release. The first single, *She Controls Me*, and the title track were instant hits with radio programmers across Canada.

Singles

She Controls Me 1983   *We Run* 1985
Kiss in the Dark 1983   *Love Becomes Electric* 1985
Worlds Away 1983

Albums/CDs

WORLDS AWAY 1983   OVER 60 MINUTES WITH STRANGE
2WO 1985   ADVANCE 1989
THE DISTANCE BETWEEN 1988

Streetheart

PAUL DEAN (*guitar*)   JOHN HANNAH (*guitar*)
MATT FRENETTE (*drums*)   KEN SHIELDS (*vocals*)
DARYL GUTHEIL (*keyboards*)   KIM SINNAEVE (*bass*)

The origins of Winnipeg's Streetheart go back to 1975 when Ken Shields formed the Saskatoon group Wascana with Daryl Gutheil and Kim Sinnaeve. The band was renamed Witness a year later, and when guitarist Paul Dean and drummer Matt Frenette joined the group, the band changed its name to Streetheart. Two years later they recorded their first album, MEANWHILE BACK IN PARIS.

By 1979 Dean and Frenette left to form Loverboy in Vancouver. The rest of the band continued to play hard rock and became a popular bar act. They disbanded in 1984.

Singles

Here Comes the Night 1979   *Joke's on You* 1980
Under My Thumb 1979   *Tin Soldier* 1980-81
Draggin' You Down 1980   *What Kind of Love Is This* 1982

Albums/CDs

MEANWHILE BACK IN PARIS 1978   DRUGSTORE DANCER 1981
UNDER HEAVEN OVER HELL 1979   ACTION: BEST OF STREETHEART 1981
QUICKSAND SHOES 1980   DANCING WITH DANGER 1983

Stringband

BOB BOSSIN (*banjo*)   MARIE-LYNN HAMMOND (*vocals*)
TERRY KING (*fiddle*)

Formed in 1971 in Toronto, Stringband began playing campus pubs for little remuneration. On stage this trio played an eclectic mix of

Acadian nonsense songs, thirties jazz, bilingual satire, and vintage folk.

The members of the band personally financed their first album of fifteen songs called CANADIAN SUNSET in 1974. It exceeded all expectations, and by 1977 they had two more equally successful albums out: NATIONAL MELODIES and THANKS TO THE FOLLOWING. The group's only commercial success came in 1975 when radio stations played *Dief Will Be Chief Again*, from NATIONAL MELODIES. They held their final concert on New Year's Eve in 1977, which was billed as "Stringband's Annual Farewell Concert" and was held at Bathurst Street United Church in Toronto.

Co-leader Marie-Lynn Hammond left to form her own band. In 1979 she released her self-titled debut album on Black Tie Records.

Single   *Dief Will Be Chief Again*   1975

Albums   CANADIAN SUNSET   1974   THE MAPLE LEAF DOG   1979
             NATIONAL MELODIES   1975   STRINGBAND — LIVE!   1980
             THANKS TO THE FOLLOWING   1977

The Sugar Shoppe   VICTOR GARBER (*vocals*)   LAURIE HOOD (*piano*)
                       LEE HARRIS (*vocals*)   PETER MANN (*vocals*)

The four members of the Toronto group The Sugar Shoppe came from diverse backgrounds. Peter Mann went to school in Miami and worked as an arranger/writer in New York. He had just joined The Sugar Shoppe when he wrote his own arrangement of Bobby Gimby's *Canada*. Lee Harris had three years of vocal training and had never been in front of a microphone. Laurie Hood had earned a scholarship to the University of Toronto Faculty of Music in her last year of high school. It was there that she joined the group. Victor Garber was a veteran of the stage. Born in London, Ontario, he was, at age fifteen, the youngest member of the University of Toronto's Hart House acting group. He performed in various Toronto workshop productions and also made TV appearances. In the evenings he played the city's coffeehouse circuit.

The Sugar Shoppe was popular from 1967 to 1969. Their hit *The Attitude* was a Canadian psychedelic rock song. The Sugar Shoppe recorded one album for Capitol Records in 1968.

Singles   *Canada*   1967   *Skip-A-Long Sam*   1968
              The Attitude   1967   *Privilege*   1968

Album   THE SUGAR SHOPPE   1968

Sven Gali DEE CERNILES (*guitar*)   SHAWN 'TT' MAHAR (*bass*)
ANDY FRANK (*guitar*)   DAVE WANLESS (*vocals*)
GREGG GERSON (*drums*)

Sven Gali, from Hamilton, Ontario, formed in 1987. They started out as a cover band until they began writing and singing their own material. Signed to BMG Records, they released their self-titled debut album in 1992, featuring a cover version of Teenage Head's *Disgusteen*. The video of the group's first single, *Under the Influence*, was shot in Toronto.

Singles *Under the Influence* 1992   *Love Don't Live Here Anymore*
Tie Dyed Skies 1993   1993
In My Garden 1993   *Sweet Little Gypsy* 1993

CD SVEN GALI 1992

Sweet BRUCE BARROW (*bass*)   DON MEEKER (*vocals*)
Blindness BOBBY DUPONT (*vocals*)   BILL MURRAY (*guitar*)
RONNIE GANT (*bass*)   SONNY MILNE (*drums*)
CURTIS LEE (*guitar, vocals*)   GABOR SZEPESI (*keyboards*):
AL MARINE (*bass*)   Replaced by PHIL SMITH

First known as The Statlers when the band was formed in 1967, they changed their name to Sweet Blindness in the mid-1970s, and became popular in bars and nightclubs in Southern Ontario. The group's lineup changed throughout the 1970s. American guitarist Curtis Lee joined in 1974. Gabor Szepesi on keyboards and Al Marnie on bass were also added the same year. Szepesi left in September 1975 and was replaced by former Statler Phil Smith. In 1976 Barrow joined the group when it toured Ontario.

On stage Sweet Blindness played soul and progressive jazz. Their biggest hit was *Cowboys to Girls*.

Singles *Cowboys to Girls* 1975-76   *National Poddy* 1976
Sweet Blindness (Music You   *Quebec* 1976
Can Ride On) 1976

Albums SWEET BLINDNESS 1976   ENERGIZE 1977

Syrinx JOHN MILLS-COCKELL (*piano,*   MALCOLM TOMLINSON (*drums,*
organ)   *voice*)
DOUG PRINGLE (*saxophone*)   ALLAN WELLS (*percussion*)

In the late 1960s John Mills-Cockell began experimenting with the Moog and Arp synthesizers in the studio and during live performances. Syrinx evolved in 1970 when Mills-Cockell joined forces with Doug Pringle, Allan Wells, and Malcolm Tomlinson.

The music of Syrinx combines Chinese, Balinese, African, North American Indian, Eskimo and ethnic folk in abstract forms.

John Mills-Cockell grew up in Toronto, where he attended Malvern Collegiate and spent two years studying at the Faculty of Music at the University of Toronto. He studied composition under Dr. Samuel Dolin at the Royal Conservatory of Music. In 1966 Mills-Cockell studied electronic music with Gustav Ciamaga at the then new electronic music studio at the Conservatory. He was awarded a Canada Council grant to perform in Vancouver, and in June 1967 received a BMI Student Composer's Award.

In 1968 he performed with a group called Intersystems, and, a year later, with Toronto's Kensington Market and Vancouver's Hydro-Electric Streetcar.

Syrinx created the music for the Paul Zindel play *Effect of Gamma Rays on Man-In-The Moon Marigolds*, which was directed by Henry Tarvainen and performed at the St. Lawrence Centre in Toronto. The group split up in 1972, but Mills-Cockell continued to record on his own. In 1973 he recorded under the name of JFC Heartbeat on the single *Instant Replay*.

Singles *Tillicum* 1971
Instant Replay (as JFC Heartbeat) 1973

Albums SYRINX 1970
LONG LOST RELATIVES 1971
NEON ACCLERANDO 1976

GATEWAY: A NEW MUSIC ADVENTURE 1977

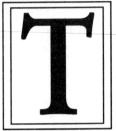

Tapestry

JUDY HARMON
JACK WINTERS

HEATHER WOODBURN

Tapestry had five hits in the early 1970s on Polydor Records. Their first, *Love Me Brother*, was produced by Cliff Edwards of The Bells. In 1973, Judy Harmon left the group. Jack Winters and Heather Woodburn became a duo, and were complemented by a backup group. *Everything Is Bringin' Me Down* was the first release by the new version of Montreal-based Tapestry.

Singles *Love Me Brother* 1971-72
*Music Doesn't Seem to Be
   Going Anywhere* 1972
Down by the Maple River 1973

California 1973
Everything Is Bringin' Me Down
   1973

Album DOWN BY THE MAPLE RIVER 1973

Michael Tarry

In the mid-1960s Michael Tarry MacDermott came to Canada from Manchester, England and changed his name to Michael Tarry. He signed a contract with Columbia and recorded a single which did not achieve chart success. In 1973 WEA's John Pozer signed him and the result was his only major Canadian hit, *Rosalie*, produced at Eastern Sound in Toronto.

Singles *All that I Love* 1969

Rosalie 1973

Album MICHAEL TARRY 1973

Bobby Taylor & the Vancouvers

THOMAS CHONG (*guitar*)
WES HENDERSON (*bass*)
ROBBIE KING (*keyboards*)

TED LEWIS (*drums*)
EDWARD PATTERSON (*guitar*)
ROBERT "BOBBY" TAYLOR (*vocals*)

This Vancouver-based band established itself on the city's club circuit in the mid-1960s. Their future changed when Diana Ross was in Vancouver with the rest of the Supremes and saw the Canadian group perform. She was so impressed that she set them up with a record deal with Motown's subsidiary label, Gordy Records. Their first single was *Does Your Mama Know about Me* in August 1968. After two more hits they broke up.

Chong became half of the comedy duo Cheech and Chong. Bobby Taylor is credited for discovering Michael Jackson and the Jackson Five.

Singles *Does Your Mama Know
   about Me* 1968

I Am Your Man 1968
Melinda 1968-69

Singles	*Somethin' on My Mind* 1980	*Tornado* 1983
	Let's Shake 1980	*Frantic Romantic* 1986
	Some Kinda Fun 1982	

Albums/CDs	TEENAGE HEAD 1979	SOME KINDA FUN 1982
	FRANTIC CITY 1980	ELECTRIC GUITAR 1988
	BACKWARDS IN BED WITH	
	TEENAGE HEAD 1981	

Diane Tell

Growing up in her native Quebec City, Diane Tell (a.k.a. Diane Fortin) studied music and learned to play the guitar. When her parents separated, she and her two older brothers moved to Montreal.

By the time she was in her teens, the Quebec music scene was flourishing with such groups as Offenbach, Beau Dommage, and Harmonium. She became Quebec's brightest young star in the early 1980s, singing in Old Montreal bars for two years until her big break came with the song *L'Eveche*.

Her album EN FLECHE sold more than 150,000 copies and in 1981 she won four Felix Awards. That same year she was a guest on Elton John's TV special and Perry Como's annual Christmas show from Quebec City. The following year she played at the now defunct new wave club, The Edge, in Toronto and appeared at the Juno Awards. She won the Pop Song of the Year Award for *Si j'etais un homme*. She returned to the recording studio in 1987 to record the album, PARIS COLLECTION.

Albums/CD	LES CINEMAS-BAS 1977	FAIRE A NOUVEAU CONNAISSANCE
	ENTRE NOUS 1979	1986
	EN FLECHE 1980	PARIS COLLECTION 1987
	CHIMERES 1982	PARIS*MONTREAL 1987
	ON A BESOIN D'AMOUR 1984	DEGRIFFE-MOI 1988

The Tenants

GARY BROWN (*vocals*)   ANDY MCLEAN (*vocals*)
DEREK GASSYT (*drums*)   LEWIS MELE (*bass*)
FRASER MACDOUGALL
    (*keyboards*)

The Tenants, from Scarborough, Ontario, began as an exchange of ideas and interests at a party where Andy McLean and Gary Brown first met. They soon became songwriting partners and decided to form a group with Fraser MacDougall, Derek Gassyt, and Lewis Mele. Signed to CBS Records who released their self-titled album and the single *Sheriff* in

1983, The Tenants began a cross-Canada tour in April of the same year, opening for Streetheart and Rough Trade. They broke up in 1984.

Singles *Sheriff* 1983

Album THE TENANTS 1983 VISIONS OF OUR FUTURE 1984

13 Engines

JOHN CRITCHLEY (*vocals, guitar*) JIM HUGHES (*vocals*)
GRANT ETHIER (*drums*) MIKE ROBBINS (*guitar*)

13 Engines evolved in 1985 from The Ikons, a group from York University in Toronto. They signed a record deal with EMI/Capitol, and in 1987 recorded their first album, BEFORE OUR TIME, at the Old Schoolhouse studio near Detroit, the home of the Motor City Five and Ig and The Stooges. In 1989 came their second album, BYRAIN LAKE BLUES and, a third, A BLUR TO ME NOW, in 1991. Early in 1993 they released their fourth which was recorded at Le Studio in Morin Heights, Quebec.

Singles *Beached* 1989 *More* 1993
Big Surprise 1991 *Smoke and Ashes* 1993
King of Saturday Night 1991 *Bred in the Bone* 1993

CDs BEFORE OUR TIME 1987 A BLUR TO ME NOW 1991
BYRAM LAKE BLUES 1989 PERPETUAL MOTION MACHINE 1993

Ian Thomas

Before his hit *Painted Ladies* became an international success in 1973, Burlington native Ian Thomas had been lead singer/songwriter for Tranquility Base. He wrote the group's two single releases, *If You're Lookin'* and *In the Rain*. Tranquility Base evolved from the Dundas, Ontario folk group, Ian, Oliver and Nora.

In 1971 Thomas left the group to work as a producer at the CBC where his credits include *The National Fireworks Company* on radio and *The Barbara McNair Show*, *Ian Tyson* and *Music Machine* on TV. The 1980s saw Thomas gain international success as a songwriter. On his 1985 album, ADD WATER, there were two songs that became big hits in Australia for Daryl Braithwaite, formerly lead singer of the 1970s band The Sherbs: *As the Days Go By* and *All I Do*. Gina recorded *As the Days Go By* in French, a Top Ten hit in Quebec in 1989.

By the 1990s, Thomas had formed a new group called The Boomers, comprised of veteran Canadian musicians Bill Dillon, who has worked with Robbie Robertson; bassist Peter Cardinali, a former sideman to Rick James and B.B. King; and drummer Rick Gratton, who has toured with Long John Baldry and Rough Trade. They became a sensation in Germany but are virtually unknown in Canada. Their self-titled debut album, WHAT WE DO, was released in 1991. THE ART OF LIVING was The Boomers second album. Released in 1993, it contained the singles, *You've Got to Know* and the title track.

(By Ian Thomas)

Singles

Painted Ladies 1973	*Coming Home* 1978
Come the Son 1974	*Time Is the Keeper* 1979
Long Long Way 1974	*Pilot* 1979
Mother Earth 1975	*Hold On* 1981
Julie 1975	*Chains* 1981
The Good Life 1975	*I'll Do It Right* 1984
Liars 1976	*Levity* 1988
Right Before Your Eyes 1977	*Back to Square One* 1989

Albums

IAN THOMAS 1973	GLIDER 1983
DELIGHTS 1975	RIDERS ON DARK HORSES 1984
CALABASH 1976	ADD WATER 1985
STILL HERE 1978	LEVITY 1988
THE RUNNER 1981	

(As the Boomers)

Singles

You've Got to Know 1993	*Good Again* 1994
Art of Living 1993	

CDs

WHAT WE DO 1991	ART OF LIVING 1993

Three's a Crowd

BRUCE COCKBURN	COMERIE SMITH
SANDY CRAWLEY	BRENT TITCOMB
KEN KOBLUN	TREVOR VEITCH
RICHARD PATTERSON	DONNA WARNER
DENNIS PENDRITH	DAVID WIFFEN
COLLEEN PETERSON	

Founded in 1964 in Vancouver by Donna Warner, Trevor Veitch, and Brent Titcomb, this folk/rock band was first known as The Bill Schwartz Quartet, with apologies to Schwartz's absence since he did not exist. They performed in coffeehouses in Western Canada for a year then moved to Toronto in 1965. The following year they released their first hit single, *Bound to Fly*, on Columbia Records. In 1966 singer-songwriter David Wiffen and bass guitarist Comerie Smith were added when the trio played at Ottawa's Le Hibou Coffee House. Richard Patterson, who was a member of The Children at the time, also joined on drums. The new group moved to Toronto and played at many venues throughout Canada and the northeastern United States. They also performed at the Ontario Pavilion at Expo 67. When Mama Cass Elliott and Papa Denny Doherty saw them play, the former arranged for Three's a Crowd to record a demo tape in New York. Signed to Dunhill they made two hit singles, *Bird without Wings*, which was written by Bruce Cockburn, and *Let's Get Together*, as well as the album CHRISTOPHER'S MOVIE MATINEE.

After a tour of the United States, the band drifted apart, but in 1969, independent TV producer Sid Banks contacted them about appearing on a weekly TV variety series on the CBC called *One More Time*, hosted by Broadway star Gilbert Price. Three's a Crowd now was comprised of Richard Patterson (drums), David Wiffen (vocals, guitar), Bruce Cockburn (guitar, vocals), Colleen Peterson (vocals), Sandy Crawley (guitar, vocals), and Dennis Pendrith (bass). When Bruce Cockburn left to pursue a solo career, Three's a Crowd broke up. Although this version of the group never made a record, they did make a video of Cockburn's song, *Electrocution of the Word*, which was showcased at the Youth Pavilion of Ottawa's Central Canadian Exhibition.

Wiffen had a brief solo career in the early 1970s, and Patterson went to work with the CBC in Ottawa and became a member of the country/swing band The Radio Kings. Cockburn and Peterson went on to have successful solo careers.

Singles	*Bound to Fly* 1966	*Bird without Wings* 1968
	Coat of Colours 1968	*Let's Get Together* 1968
Album	CHRISTOPHER'S MOVIE MATINEE 1968	

Thundermug JAMES CORBETT (*bass*)   BILL DURST (*keyboards*)
JOE DE ANGELIS (*guitar*)   ED PRANSKUS (*drums*)

Thundermug, from London, Ontario, was the first Canadian group to have two singles on RPM's Top 100 at the same time, a cover hit of the Kinks' 1964 smash *You Really Got Me* and *Africa*. They recorded three albums in the 1970s, THUNDERMUG STRIKES, ORBIT, and TA-DAA.

Singles	*You Really Got Me* 1972	*I Wanna Be with You* 1974
	Africa 1972	*Let's Live Together* 1975
	Orbit 1973	*Clap Your Hands and Stamp*
	Breaking up Is Hard to Do 1974	*Your Feet* 1976
Albums	THUNDERMUG STRIKES 1972	TA-DAA 1975
	ORBIT 1973	

Ken Tobias   From Saint John, New Brunswick, Ken Tobias began his career in the music business as a songwriter. Between 1970-71 he wrote *Stay Awhile* for The Bells, *Some Birds* for Anne Murray, *My Songs Are Sleeping* and *Get Yourself Some Sunshine* for Cliff Edwards, and *Keep on Changing* for the British group The King Sisters.

Although he was born in the Maritimes, he made Toronto his home and appeared on CBC's *Singalong Jubilee* with Anne Murray, her future husband Bill Langstroth, and the late Fred McKenna. In 1977 his albums, EVERY BIT OF LOVE and SIREN SPELL were released internationally in West Germany, Italy, Australia and South Africa.

Singles		
You're Not Even Going to the Fair 1969		*Lover Come Quickly* 1974
Now I'm in Love 1971		*Lady Luck* 1975
I'd Like to Know 1971		*Run Away with Me* 1975
Dream No. 2 1972		*Every Bit of Love* 1976
I Just Want to Make Music 1973		*Give a Little Love* 1976
Fly Me High 1973		*Dancer/Lovelight* 1977
On the Other Side 1974		*I Don't Want to Be Alone* 1978
		New York City 1978

Albums		
DREAM #2 1972		STREET BALLET 1977
MAGIC'S IN THE MUSIC 1973		GALLERY 1984
EVERY BIT OF LOVE 1975		

Top Sonart   SERGE BOUDREAULT   CLAUDE FREGEAU
GAETAN BOUDREAULT   MARIE-JOSEE MORIN
ERIC COITEAUX

Top Sonart was discovered by Marc Racine and the Gendron Brothers in 1981 at the *Festival international des radios francophones*. By 1984 the band was a duo comprised of Marie-Josee Morin and Eric Coiteux, but in 1985, the other members joined to record an album. Top Sonart also made several TV and radio appearances and went on tour to promote their image as Quebec's most promising young rock group. By the end of the year they became famous for playing dance-rock in french. A mini-album of electro-pop dance music, recorded in french, was released in October 1985. They had four hit singles in 1985-86 before their debut album, PAN DE PANIQUE, was released in March 1987.

Singles		
Une soiree 1985		*Donne-moi une chance* 1986
C'est pas necessaire 1985		*Fauve* 1986

Albums		
TOP SONART 1985		PAS DE PANIQUE 1987

Toronto BRIAN ALLEN (*guitar*)   JIM FOX (*drums*)
SHARON ALTON (*guitar*)   HOLLY WOODS (*vocals*)
NICK COSTLELLO (*bass*)

Toronto was fronted by Holly Woods (a.k.a. Annie Woods) and Brian Allen. Handled by the same agency as Chilliwack and The Raes, Toronto adopted a street-wise image. Their debut single, *Even the Score*, was released in the spring of 1980. They broke up in 1984.

Singles *Even the Score* 1980   *Start Tellin' the Truth* 1982
Lookin' for Trouble 1980   *All I Need* 1983
5035 1980   *Ready to Make Up* 1984
Your Daddy Don't Know 1982 *New Romance* 1984
Enough Is Enough 1982

Albums LOOKIN' FOR TROUBLE 1980   GIRLS NIGHT OUT 1983
HEAD ON 1981   GREATEST HITS 1984
GET IT ON 1982

Toulouse HEATHER GAUTHIER   LORRI ZIMMERMAN
JUDI RICHARDS

The members of this female trio from Montreal were all active as backup singers when they decided to get together in 1975. They were all bilingual and felt comfortable singing in both languages. Their second album, EXPORT, was an English translation of their first album.

Singles *It always Happens this Way*   *Don't Play with My Heart* 1978
1977   *Rock My Love* 1980
A.P.B. 1977   *11 AM 'n' Rainin'* 1980
What Would My Mama Say
1977-78

Albums TOULOUSE 1976   EXPORT 1977

The Townsmen PAUL HUOT (*drums, vocals*)   DAVID MILLIKEN (*guitar*)
ANDRE LEGAULT (*guitar, vocals*) FRANK MORRISON (*vocals*)
WAYNE LESLIE (*bass, vocals*)

This Ottawa band began as The Darnells in the early 1960s with Frank Morrison, Dave Milliken, and Wayne Leslie. In 1965, they changed their name to The Townsmen when they added two new members, Andre Legault and Paul Huot, formerly with The Esquires. Signed to the Regency label, The Townsmen's first hit was *I'm a Dreamer* in 1965.

They toured Canada, opening for The Rascals, The McCoys, The Turtles, and Gary Lewis and the Playboys.

In 1966 Andre Legault left, and two new members were added, Buddy Stanton on piano and vocals, and John Bocho on guitar and vocals.

The Townsmen initially broke up in 1967.

Singles

I'm Such a Dreamer 1966
Funny How Love Can Be 1966
The Lion Sleeps Tonight 1966
He's in Town 1967
We're Doin' Fine 1967

Heaven in the Middle of Town 1968
Rockin' Chair 1968
Winds Blowin' Diamonds Tonite 1968
I Can't Find My Way Home 1969

The Tragically Hip

BOBBY BAKER (*guitar*)
GORDON DOWNIE (*vocals*)
JOHNNY FAY (*drums*)
PAUL LANGLOIS (*guitar*)
GORD SINCLAIR (*bass*)

Formed in 1983, this Kingston-based band took its name from ex-Monkee Michael Nesmith's *Elephant Parts* video. Gordon Downie, Rob Baker, and Gord Sinclair were students at Queen's University, while Johnny Fay was in high school. Together they played the local clubs and toured across Canada catching the attention of MCA Records President Bruce Dickinson after seeing their performance at Toronto's Horseshoe Tavern. Their first of hit was *Blow at High Dough* in 1989 taken from the album UP TO HERE. *New Orleans Is Sinking* became their signature song. Internationally, The Tragically Hip have large followings in Holland, Belgium, Australia, and the United States.

Their 1992 release, FULLY COMPLETELY, was one of the year's top selling albums. From it came the smash Top Ten hit *Locked in a Trunk of a Car*. The video for *At the Hundredth Meridian* was shot in Australia, south of Melbourne.

Singles

Smalltown Bringdown 1987
Blow at High Dough 1989
New Orleans Is Sinking 1989
Boots or Hearts 1990
38 Years Old 1990
Little Bones 1991
Three Pistols 1991
Twist My Arm 1991
Long Time Running 1991

On the Verge 1991
Locked in a Trunk of a Car 1992-93
Courage 1993
At the Hundredth Meridian 1993
Looking for a Place to Happen 1993

CDs

THE TRAGICALLY HIP 1987
UP TO HERE 1989

ROAD APPLES 1991
FULLY COMPLETELY 1992

The Travellers

1952 Lineup:
SID DOLGAY (*mando-cello*)   JERRY GOODIS (*vocals*)
JERRY GRAY (*banjo, singer*)   OSCAR ROSS (*vocals*)
HELEN GRAY (*vocals*)

1980 Lineup:
JERRY GRAY (*banjo, singer*)   TED ROBERTS (*guitar*)
AILEEN LAWRENCE (*vocals*)   DON VICKERY (*drums*)
JOE LAWRENCE (*bass*)

Formed in 1952 at the suggestion of Pete Seeger, The Travellers became one of Canada's best known folk-singing groups. The founding members were part of the choir of United Jewish Peoples Order. They got their start in folk clubs like The Chelsea Club in Toronto and made their TV debut in 1954 on CBC's *Pick the Stars*.

The Travellers made *This Land Is Your Land* the nation's second national anthem when they Canadianized the lyrics of the late Woody Guthrie's classic song. All the proceeds from the sale of sheet music went to Guthrie's family. They made their first album, ACROSS CANADA WITH THE TRAVELLERS in 1957.

The Travellers headlined the first Mariposa Folk Festival in 1961. That same year they went on a six-city tour of Russia as part of a cultural exchange. During Canada's Centennial Year the Travellers played 135 concerts across the country, toured several army bases, and performed at Expo 67. They also were asked to play at the opening ceremonies of the Yonge Street subway in Toronto, and appeared before Queen Elizabeth and Prince Philip at the 1964 opening of the Charlottetown Confederation Arts Centre.

The 1970s saw the group entertain at Expo 70 in Osaka, Japan, and at Canadian Armed Forces in Cyprus with Harry Belafonte, Oscar Brand, Anne Murray, Gordon Lightfoot, Oscar Peterson, Judy Collins, and Catherine McKinnon. In 1980 The Travellers released their fifteenth album, MERRY GO ROUND and continued to play on a part-time basis, Jerry Gray being the only original member. The Travellers celebrated their fortieth anniversary on October 3, 1993 with a concert at the Minkler Auditorium at Seneca College in Toronto.

Singles   *This Land Is Your Land*   1955

Albums   ACROSS CANADA WITH THE TRAVELLERS   1957
THE TRAVELLERS SING SONGS OF NORTH AMERICA   1959
QUILTING BEE   1960
INTRODUCING THE TRAVELLERS   1961
THE TRAVELLERS ON TOUR   1962

SOMETHING TO SING ABOUT 1963
WE'RE ON OUR WAY AGAIN 1964
THE TRAVELLERS STILL TRAVELLING 1966
A CENTURY OF SONG 1967
THIS LAND, THE TRAVELLERS CENTENNIAL ALBUM 1967
THE TRAVELLERS APPLAUD CANADA 1968
THE TRAVELLERS SING FOR KIDS 1970
THE TRAVELLERS 1970
MERRY-GO-AROUND 1980

Triumph

RIK EMMETT (*guitar*)   PHIL X (*guitar*)
MIKE LEVINE (*bass*)   RICK SANTERS (*guitar*)
GIL MOORE (*vocals, drums*)

Formed in mid-1975 in Toronto, this trio of heavy metal rockers first established themselves on the city's club circuit, and also developed a following south of the border, in Texas. It was not until they recorded a remake of Joe Walsh's *Rocky Mountain Way* that Triumph became well known back home. In 1978 the group headlined their own show at Toronto's Massey Hall.

Triumph continued to have commercial success on the charts into the late 1980s. Rik Emmett left the group in 1987 to pursue a solo career and the group broke up. In 1992, Mike Levine and Gil Moore reunited and added Phil X and Rick Santers. That same year Triumph released the album EDGE OF EXCESS and had their first Top 40 hit, *Trouble Maker*, which was featured on the soundtrack of the 1992 film *Hellraiser III: Hell on Earth*.

Singles

Rocky Mountain Way 1978   *Somebody's Out There* 1986
Hold On 1979   *Just One Night* 1987
Lay It on the Line 1979-80   *Let the Light (Shine on Me)* 1987
I Can Survive 1980   *Trouble Maker* 1992
Magic Power 1981   *Child of the City* 1992-93
Say Goodbye 1982   *Somewhere Tonight* 1993

Albums/CDs

TRIUMPH 1976   NEVER SURRENDER 1983
ROCK AND ROLL MACHINE 1977   THUNDER AS SEVEN 1984
JUST A GAME 1979   STAGES 1985
PROGRESSIONS OF POWER 1980   THE SPORT OF KINGS 1986
ALLIED FORCES 1981   EDGE OF EXCESS 1992

Trooper RAMON MCGUIRE (*vocals*)   FRANK LUDWIG (*piano, keyboards*):
BRIAN SMITH (*guitar*)   Replaced by ROB DEANS
HARRY KALINSKY (*bass*):   TOMMY STEWART (*drums*)
   Replaced by DONI UNDERHILL

This Vancouver-based group began as a duo, Ramon McGuire and Brian Smith, eventually named Applejack in 1972. They later called themselves Winters Green. In September of 1972 Bruce Allen and Sam Feldman of the Bruce Allen Talent Promotion agency heard the group and began to book dates for them. Later that year, drummer Tommy Stewart made it a trio, and in 1974 bassist Harry Kalinsky was added.

In September 1974 Randy Bachman asked the band to play at a dance at the Mormon Church where he was a youth co-ordinator. He was impressed by their sound and signed them to his Legend label, distributed by MCA. By the time the label released their first hit single, *Baby Woncha Please Come Home* in 1975, they had changed their name to Trooper.

Doni Underhill replaced Kalinsky in 1976 and Frank Ludwig was added on piano. In 1979, Ludwig was replaced by Rob Deans.

Throughout the 1970s and 1980s, Trooper had many hits, but their biggest was the ballad *Oh, Pretty Lady* in 1978. In 1991, Warner Music released TEN, their last album for the label. Today, Trooper is still touring.

Singles *Baby Woncha Please Come*   *The Boys in the White Sports*
       Home 1975   *Car* 1979
General Hand Grenade 1976   *Janine* 1980
Two for the Show 1976   *Good Clean Fun* 1980
Santa Maria 1977   *Real Canadians* 1980
Here for a Good Time 1977   *Are You Still My Baby* 1980
Oh Pretty Lady 1978   *Just One Kiss* 1981
Raise a Little Hell 1978   *Only a Fool* 1982
Round Round We Go 1978   *Boy in the Beat* 1986
Three Dressed Up as Nine 1979 *The Best Way (To Hold a Man)*
The Moment that It Takes   1989
   1979   *American Dream* 1991

Albums/CDs TROOPER 1975   FLYING COLORS 1979
TWO FOR THE SHOW 1976   HOT SHOTS 1979
KNOCK 'EM DEAD KID 1977   THE LAST OF THE GYPSIES 1989
THICK AS THIEVES 1978   TEN 1991

True Myth   Tony Cook (*guitar*)   Steve McKenna (*bass*)
Kirk Devereux (*drums*)   Bob Stirajs (*guitar*)
Malcolm McGuigan (*vocals*)   Tom Treumuth (*keyboards*)

The rock group True Myth was formed in September 1977 at Fanshawe College in London, Ontario by Tom Treumuth. When Warner Bros. released their self-titled debut album in 1979, it was Canada's first digital recording and the second album of its kind to be released in the world. In 1981 came their second album, TELEGRAM, and the single *Give It Up*.

Single   *Give It Up* 1981

Albums   TRUE MYTH 1979   TELEGRAM 1981

Tundra   Formed in 1970 this Toronto bar band began as a quartet called Manning and played covers of Tom Jones and Engelbert Humperdinck songs. After the addition of a fifth member and a name change to Tundra, they signed a contract with A&M Records. Their single *Band Bandit*, released in 1970, was not a huge hit.

Single   *Band Bandit* 1970-71

DAVE BINGHAM (*vocals*)   ROGER PAYNE (*guitar*)
GLYNN BELL (*guitar*)   JOHN READ (*bass*)
ROBIN BOERS (*drums*)

Formed in 1965, The Ugly Ducklings quickly established themselves as one of the top bands in Yorkville and released their first hit single, *Nothin'*, a year later. Their biggest hit on the Yorkville Record label was *Gaslight* in the fall of 1967. At the end of the year they disbanded.

The Ugly Ducklings

Singles	*Nothin'* 1966	*Just in Case You Wonder* 1967
	10:30 Train/She Ain't No Use to Me 1966	*Gaslight* 1967

Shari Ulrich

Originally from the San Francisco Bay area, Shari immigrated to Vancouver in 1972. She played with various folk and rock groups before joining Rick Scott and Joe Mock in The Pear of Pied Pumkin in 1973. Their strong harmonies and distinctive sound made them popular on the folk music circuit.

In 1976 she quit Pied Pumkin to join Valdy's backup group, The Hometown Band. After two years she left to concentrate on a solo career. She performed at folk festivals until 1980 when she recorded her first solo album, LONG NIGHTS. Two more albums followed, ONE STEP AHEAD in 1981 and TALK AROUND TOWN in 1982. Seven years later, she met Bill Henderson of Chilliwack and Roy Forbes (Bim) for a special one night concert at Vancouver's Winter Roots Festival. They realized their voices complemented each other well and formed a trio called UHF (Ulrich, Henderson, and Forbes). In 1991 they recorded their self-titled debut album on Tangible Records.

In between performances with Henderson and Forbes, Ulrich recorded another solo album, EVERY ROAD, in 1990, and a year later came her BEST OF SHERI ULRICH collection.

Singles	*Bad Bad Girl* 1980	*Save It* 1982
	Long Nights 1981	

Albums/CDs	LONG NIGHTS 1980	EVERY ROAD 1990
	ONE STEP AHEAD 1981	BEST OF SHARI ULRICH 1991
	TALK AROUND TOWN 1982	

Union RANDY BACHMAN *(guitar)* Frank Ludwig *(keyboards)*
CHRIS LEIGHTON *(drums)* Fred Turner *(vocals)*

With the demise of Ironhorse, Randy Bachman, Frank Ludwig, and Chris Leighton became three quarters of Union on Bachman's U.S.-based Portrait label. Fred Turner, formerly with Brave Belt and BTO, rejoined his old friend Randy to make Union a quartet.

Singles *Mainstream USA* 1981 *Next Stop London* 1981
Album ON STRIKE 1981

Uranus DEXTER BEAUREGARDE *(drums)* FRANK RIDSDALE *(vocals, guitar)*
JERRY FLETCHER *(bass)* JACK WHITESIDE *(vocals, guitar)*

Uranus formed in London, Ontario, in 1976 and played mainly 1950s and 1960s remakes along with some original rockabilly material. When producer Ross Munro heard about the group through a radio programmer in London, he encouraged the band to record at Phase One Studios in Scarborough. The result was their only hit, *You're So Square*, on Trilogy Records, released in the spring of 1980.

Single *You're So Square* 1980
Album YOU'RE SO SQUARE 1980

Valdy

Born of Danish parents in 1946 in Ottawa, Valdy (Valdemar Horsdal) began playing the guitar as a teenager, took piano lessons for five years, and learned orchestration from Professor Robin Wood, the dean of a music school in Victoria.

In the mid-1960s, Valdy was a member of the London Town Criers. He went on to play with The Prodigal Sons in Montreal and later worked as a bassist for country singer Blake Emmons and for various groups in Victoria. In 1972 he signed with Haida Records, distributed by A&M. His first single was *Rock and Roll Song* that summer.

By 1976 Valdy had recorded five albums and was second to Gordon Lightfoot in record sales for a Canadian folk singer. In August, he represented Canada at the International Song Festival in Sopot, Poland. One of the highlights of his career was his association with The Hometown Band, with whom he recorded VALDY AND THE HOME-TOWN BAND in 1977. In 1978 he recorded a more upbeat environmental album called HOT ROCKS. The title song refers to spent nuclear fuel.

In 1982 he left A&M. Three years later he recorded one album for Duke Street Records.

Over the years, Valdy has collaborated with other singer/songwriters, such as Max Bennett on *Simple Life* and Bob Ruzicka on *Leaving Ain't the Only Way to Go* and *Easy Money*. In 1992 he signed an eight year contract with the adult arm of the children's label Oak Street Music. His first album, HEART AT WORK, was released in April 1993. *Double Solitaire* was the first single.

Singles

Rock and Roll Song 1972	*Leavin' Ain't the Only Way to Go* 1982
A Good Song 1973	*Daddy's Okay* 1983
Landscapes 1973	*It's that Melody* 1985
Simple Life 1973	*Sonny's Dream* 1986
Renaissance 1974/75	*Roll Man Roll* 1987
Yes I Can 1976	*Living Next to a Candy Store* 1988
Peter And Lou 1977	*Hey Mr. Michael Wilson* 1990
Dirty Old Man 1977	*Double Solitaire* 1993
Hot Rocks 1978	*Link in a Chain* 1993
Sister I Love You 1979	
Easy Money 1980	
Movie Scene 1981	

Albums/CDs

COUNTRY MAN 1972	VALDY & THE HOMETOWN BAND 1976
LANDSCAPES 1973	HOT ROCKS 1978
FAMILY GATHERING 1974	PASSPORT: BEST OF VALDY 1979
SEE HOW THE YEARS HAVE GONE BY 1975	1001 1980

VALDY'S KIDS RECORD 1982   VALDY: A CLASSIC COLLECTION 1988
NOTES FROM PLACES 1985   HEART AT WORK 1993

Gino Vannelli

Gino Vannelli's father Russ played in the bands of Bix Belair and Maynard Ferguson. While growing up in Montreal, he learned to play the drums and studied music theory at McGill University, where he formed a rhythm and blues band with his older brother Joe. Another brother, Ross, joined them later.

In 1970 Gino recorded under the name of Vann Elli for RCA, but success did not come until four years later when he signed with A&M Records and recorded *People Gotta Move*, which was a big hit in both Canada and the United States. One of his most successful albums was BROTHER TO BROTHER in 1979, which featured a symphonic suite performed by the Royal Philharmonic Orchestra under his direction. Vannelli was one of the few singers to perform on the syndicated TV show *Soul Train*, hosted by Don Cornelius. He released many hit singles during the 1980s and in 1993 he recorded a duet with Quebec singer Martine Saint-Clair.

Singles

Gina Bold 1970
People Gotta Move 1974
Powerful People 1975
Love Me Now 1975
Keep on Walking 1976
Love of My Life 1976
I Just Wanna Stop 1978
Wheels of Life 1979
The River Must Flow 1979
Living Inside Myself 1981
Nightwalker 1981

Black Cars 1985
Hurts to Be in Love 1985
Just a Motion Away 1985
Wild Horses 1987
In the Name of Money 1987
Cry of Love 1991
The Time of Day 1991
If I Should Lose this Love 1991
L'Amour est loi (Duet with
   Martine Saint-Clair) 1993

Albums/CDs

CRAZY LIFE 1973
POWERFUL PEOPLE (RE-TITLED
   PEOPLE GOTTA MOVE) 1974
STORM AT SUNUP 1975
GIST OF GEMINI 1976
A PAUPER IN PARADISE 1977

BROTHER TO BROTHER 1978
NIGHTWALKER 1981
BLACK CARS 1985
BIG DREAMERS NEVER SLEEP 1987
INCONSOLABLE MAN 1990
LIVE IN MONTREAL 1992

Roch Voisine

From St. Basile, New Brunswick, Roch Voisine was born in 1963. He was a gifted athlete who wanted to be a professional hockey player but was sidelined by a serious knee injury when he was eighteen. It was during this time that he began writing songs. Roch continued to write while attending the University of Ottawa, where he studied for a degree in physiotherapy.

In 1989 he teamed up with his friend Stephane Lessard to write the romantic ballad *Helene*, a song inspired by Stephane's breakup with a girlfriend. The song was a success in Quebec and in France where it sold over a million copies.

Known by his fans as "Le Beau Roch," Voisine and writer/producer David Foster performed together in Ottawa on July 1, 1992 to celebrate Canada's 125th birthday. In 1993 Voisine's first all-english album, I WILL ALWAYS BE THERE was released.

Singles		
Las bas dans l'ombre 1989		*La legende de oochigeas* 1992
Helene 1989/90		*L'idole* 1993
La bercuse du petit diable 1990		*Oochigeas (Indian Song)* 1993
Pretty Face 1990		*I Will Always Be There* 1993
A Fishing Day 1991		*Lost without You* 1994
On the Outside 1991		*There's No Easy Way* 1994
Waiting 1991		

CDs		
ROCH VOISINE 1988		DOUBLE 1990
HELENE 1989		I'LL ALWAYS BE THERE 1993

The Waltons

JASON WALTON PLUMB *(vocals, guitar)*
DAVID COONEY *(drums)*
KEITH NAKONECHY *(vocals, bass)*

This acoustic pop trio from Regina first came together in 1987. After playing various clubs in Western Canada, they decided it was time to break into the Toronto music scene. They began playing regularly and toured across Canada with The Pursuit of Happiness, The Barenaked Ladies, The Northern Pikes, and The Tragically Hip. The Waltons released two independent cassettes, 89 DEMONSTRATIONS and DEMO SANDWICH, as well as two MuchMusic/Videofact-funded videos of *Old* and *Alone Again*.

In 1992 the trio released their debut album, LIK MY TRAKTOR, which was recorded at Orchard Studios and produced by John Switzer. The first single was *Colder than You* in late 1992.

Singles		
Colder Than You 1992-93		*The Naked Rain* 1993
In The Meantime 1993		*Colder Than You* 1994

CD LIK MY TRAKTOR 1992

Christopher Ward

Born in 1950, Christopher Ward began singing and playing guitar while attending Trent University in Peterborough, Ontario. He almost graduated but left to travel around the world with his friend and co-writer, Stephen Stohn. While at Trent Ward founded the campus radio station (with Stohn). He later hosted his own all-night radio station on Peterborough's CKPT.

In 1975 he signed a recording contract with Warner Music and enjoyed a brief solo career with such songs as *Lost in a Love Song* in 1976 and *Once in a Long Time* in 1977. By the early 1980s he gave up recording to become a veejay at MuchMusic, the nation's first all-video station.

He continued to write songs and in the late 1980s helped launch the career of Alannah Myles. Some of Ward's songs were on her debut album on Atlantic Records, namely *Love Is* and *Black Velvet*, which went to number one on Billboard's Hot 100 in 1990.

Singles		
Lost in a Love Song 1976		*Imagine a Song* 1978
Once in a Long Time 1977		*No Time to Cry* 1979
Maybe Your Heart 1978		*So Long Baby Jane* 1981

Albums: SPARK OF DESIRE 1978   CHRISTOPHER WARD 1987

The Watchmen DANNY GREAVES *(vocals)* PETER LOEWEN *(bass)*
SAMMY KOHN *(drums)* JOEY SERLIN *(guitar)*

Formed in Winnipeg in 1988, The Watchmen released their debut album, MACLAREN FURNACE ROOM in 1992. The group's first single, *Run and Hide*, stirred up controversy because it dealt with violence towards women.

Singles *Run and Hide* 1992 *Must To Be Free* 1993
Cracked 1992

CD MACLAREN FURNACE ROOM 1992

Weather Permitting GARY MCGIRR *(drums)* ANDREW STEINMETZ *(guitar, vocals)*
BRUNO STEINER *(bass, vocals)* PETER STEINMETZ *(guitar, vocals)*

The four members of Weather Permitting have been performing together since 1985. Peter Steinmetz started playing the guitar at seventeen. He earned a Bachelor's degree in science before joining Weather Permitting, his first group. Peter's brother Andrew began playing the guitar in 1983 and the band's first folk songs were written by him. His musical education included one year of classical training. Bruno Steiner is a classically trained pianist who was introduced to dance music when he was eighteen. He also learned how to play the bass guitar and was an original member of The Ethnic Drivers. Other groups Bruno has played with include What Th—? and The Reptiles. Born in North Bay, Ontario, Gary McGirr was a figure skater for eighteen years who played drums in his high school band. In 1988 he moved to Montreal and began practicing at night with the other members of Weather Permitting.

The group's first song, *I Needed You*, was included on the VOT Records compilation album LISTEN in the fall of 1985. Another song, *Almost Happy*, was their contribution to LISTEN 2 the following year. In June 1987, their debut album, INTO THE GROUND, was released by VOT Records. Two years later came their second album, CODE OF LIFE.

Singles *I Needed You* 1985 *Almost Happy* 1986
Albums INTO THE GROUND 1987 CODE OF LIFE 1989

Wednesday

RANDY BEGG *(drums, guitar, vocals)*
JOHN (JOSE) DUFEK *(bass, harp, vocals)*
MIKE O'NEIL *(guitar, harp, vocals)*
PAUL ANDREW SMITH *(guitar, keyboards, vocals)*

From Oshawa, Wednesday gained instant fame in the fall of 1973 with a version of *Last Kiss*, which was originally released in 1964 by J. Frank Wilson and the Cavaliers. After Wednesday had made the record, John Driscoll, the band's producer, took it to 680 CFTR in Toronto. Its immediate response on Canadian radio made the group an overnight success. Late in 1973 it was added to Billboard's Hot 100 in the U.S. Two months after its release in the United States, sales of the record were in excess of 200,000. Some of Wednesday's other hits have been versions of other rock 'n' roll classics, such as Mark Dinning's *Teen Angel*, Bobby Vinton's *Roses Are Red*, and Dion's *Ruby Baby*.

Singles

Last Kiss 1973
Teen Angel 1974
Roses Are Red 1974
Fly Away 1975
Here Today, Gone Tomorrow 1975

Loving You Baby 1976
Doing the Best that I Can 1976
Ruby Baby 1976
Ride Me 1977
Elenore 1981

Albums

LAST KISS 1974

LOVING YOU BABY 1976

Maestro Fresh Wes

Born of Guyanese parents in 1968 in Toronto, Wes Williams grew up in the suburb of North York. His first experience with rap music was in elementary school in Scarborough. At age seven he was writing poetry and at eleven he was writing his own rap music. Under the tutelage of New York hip-hop pioneers Grandmaster Flash and the Furious Five, Sponnie G., Jimmy Spicer, and Kurtis Blow, the eleven-year-old began performing.

In 1983 under the stage name of Melody MC, he took part in a rap fest on college station CKLN. He later joined a fellow rapper, Ebony MC (a.k.a. Marlon Bruce) to form the Vision Crew, which lasted until 1987. Although they developed a local following, they never recorded any material.

By 1988 Williams had changed his name to Maestro Fresh Wes and recorded his first demo, *You Can't Stop Us Now*. Another demo, *I'm Showin' You*, with partner DJ LTD (a.k.a. Alva Swaby) was also made. Accompanied by Farley Flex and DJ LTD, Wes recorded *Let Your Backbone Slide* in 1989. A visit to New York resulted in a contract with the independent LMR Records, and Al Mair of Attic Records agreed to distribute the U.S. label in Canada.

Maestro Fresh Wes's commercial success paved the way for other aspiring Canadian rap artists. He was the first rap artist ever to perform at the Juno Awards.

Singles *Drop the Needle* 1990   *Conductin' Thangs* 1991
Private Symphony 1990   *Nothing at All* 1991
Let Your Backbone Slide 1990   *It's on the Mike Mechanism* 1993
Don't Play SHARE-AIDS   *Fine Tune Da Mic* 1993
    (with D-SHAN) 1990   *Search without the Retsin* 1994

CDs SYMPHONY IN EFFECT 1990   NAAAH, DIS KID CAN'T BE
BLACK TIE AFFAIR 1991   FROM CANADA?!! 1994

West End Girls

CAMILLE HENDERSON: Replaced by CELIA-LOUISE MARTIN
AIMEE MACKENZIE
SILVANA PETROZZI: Replaced by JANELE WOODLEY

West End Girls came together in 1991 in Vancouver. Camille Henderson, the daughter of Bill Henderson of Chilliwack recorded her first single at eleven. Silvana Petrozzi formed her first band at fourteen. Aimee MacKenzie had won a number of dance contests before joining the band. The three first met at Johnny Jet Records, where producer John Dexter helped them record their first album for A&M Records in April 1991. *I Want You Back*, a cover of the old Jackson Five hit, was their first release.

In 1992 Silvana left the group to join Big Bottom Swing. She was replaced by Janele Woodley. Early in 1993 Camille also left to pursue other musical interests. Celia-Louise Martin replaced her. During the summer of 1993 the group released their second album, WE BELONG TOGETHER. *R U Sexin' Me* was the first single.

Singles *I Want You Back* 1991   *R U Sexin' Me* 1993
Not like Kissin' You 1991   *State Of The Heart* 1993
Say You'll Be Mine 1991/92   *Pure (You're Touching Me)* 1994
Show Me the Way 1992

CDs WEST END GIRLS 1991   WE BELONG TOGETHER 1993

David Wiffen

Born in England in 1942, English-born singer/songwriter David Wiffen came to Canada in 1958 when he was a teenager. He began his singing career at the folk club The Village Corner on Pears Avenue in Toronto.

He later hitch-hiked across Canada and ended up in Calgary, where he briefly managed The Depression coffeehouse.

In 1965 he was invited to play with other artists at the Bunkhouse folk club in Vancouver, a session which was also going to be recorded for an album. David was the only one who showed up. The recording session ended up being a solo album called DAVID WIFFEN LIVE AT THE BUNKHOUSE. He then played with The Pacers from Northern British Columbia, and when they were offered a record deal in Montreal, Wiffen followed them east. The deal, however, fell through, and he went to Ottawa, where he joined one of its first folk/rock bands, The Children, comprised of Bill Hawkins, Bruce Cockburn, Sneezy Waters (a.k.a. Peter Hodgkinson), Neville Wells, Sandy Crawley, and Richard Patterson, formerly of The Esquires.

Late in 1966 the Vancouver folk trio Three's a Crowd played in Ottawa at the Le Hibou Coffee House. During their visit they met Wiffen, who knew them from his days as manager of The Depression in Calgary. They asked Wiffen to join as lead male vocalist and rhythm guitarist. In addition to him, they added Comerie Smith of Toronto on bass, and Richard Patterson on drums. When Three's a Crowd played at the Bitter End, a folk club in New York, Wiffen was spotted by a talent scout and signed to a solo contract with Fantasy Records. His self-titled debut album came out in 1971 and produced two hit singles, *One Step* and *More Often than Not*, which has been recorded by many artists, including Ian and Sylvia, Jerry Jeff Walker, Eric Anderson, and Bill Hughes. In 1973 United Artists released Wiffen's album COAST TO COAST FEVER, which was nominated for a Juno Award but was not a commercial success.

While recovering from a back injury, he found an artistic outlet in painting, sculpture, and poetry. Two volumes of his poetry and other writings have been published. In 1991 he created a series of paintings and sculptures called Vernissage.

Singles	*One Step* 1971	*More Often than Not* 1971
Albums	DAVID WIFFEN LIVE AT THE BUNKHOUSE 1965 DAVID WIFFEN 1971	COAST TO COAST FEVER 1973 (re-released in 1994)

Wild 'T' and The Spirit

DANNY BILAN (*drums*)
BRIAN DICKIE (*bass*)
WILD 'T' (*vocals*)

Wild 'T' (a.k.a. Tony Springer) took his name from his Trinidadian home town of Tunapuna. In his teens he moved to Toronto and eventually established himself on the local club circuit with his Tunapuna Jam Sessions. In 1982, he received the award for Best Guitarist by the Canadian Black Musicians's Association. He was also nominated for a Toronto Music Award as Best Blues Guitarist and a finalist in Toronto radio station Q-107's annual Homegrown competition. Wild 'T' has toured with Carole Pope and Rough Trade and was a session musician on the latter's last album. Arnold Lanni of Frozen Ghost co-wrote and produced Wild 'T''s debut album, LOVE CRAZY for Warner Music in 1991.

The members of Spirit included Brian Dickie, a well known R&B bassist who has played in Toronto since the early 1980s, and Danny Bilan, who has played drums with Moxy, among others.

Released in 1993, GIVIN' BLOOD was the second Wild 'T' and the Spirit album. *Freedom Train* was the first single.

Singles	*Love Crazy* 1991	*Yvonne* 1991
	Midnight Blue 1991	*Freedom Train* 1993
CDs	LOVE CRAZY 1991	GIVIN' BLOOD 1993

Willie and the Walkers

BILL HARDIE *(guitar)*
ROLAND HARDIE *(drums)*

WILLIE MACCALDER *(vocals, keyboards)*
DENNIS PETRUK *(guitar)*

Formed in 1963, Willie and the Walkers were a quartet with matching guitars bought at Harmony Kids, a music store in their home town of Edmonton, Alberta. In the mid-1960s, they opened for many acts, including The Guess Who, Dino, Desi & Billy, Paul Revere and the Raiders, and Cream. They also recorded in Clovis, New Mexico with Norman Petty, Buddy Holly's former manager and producer.

By 1967 they had signed with Capitol Records. Their first single was *Diamonds and Gold*, followed by *Alone in My Room*.

The original group split up in the early 1970s, with Willie MacCalder going on to join The Powder Blues Band.

Twenty-five years after they first played together, the original members reunited for Edmonton's First Annual Rock and Roll Reunion in 1988. They were suddenly in demand again. However, the pressure and demands of touring took their toll on the band, and there were some personnel changes. Dennis Petruk's brother Nick replaced Roland Hardie on drums. There were three new additions: Rick Francis on vocals, R. J. Smarton on keyboards, and guitarist Sam Paladino. They are now known as The Walkers.

Singles	*Diamonds and Gold* 1967	*Alone in My Room* 1967/68

Jesse Winchester Born in Shreveport, Louisiana, in 1944, Jesse Winchester moved to Canada in 1967 to avoid being drafted into the armed forces. He settled in Montreal and became a Canadian citizen in 1973.

Winchester has recorded five albums and his songs have been recorded by such artists as Jimmy Buffett, The Weather Girls, New Grass Revival, Joan Baez, The Everly Brothers, and Jonathan Edwards.

Singles

Yankee Lady 1970
Isn't that So 1973
Snow 1973/74
Third Rate Romance 1974
Let the Rough Side Drag 1976

Nothing But a Breeze 1977
Say What 1981
Baby Blue 1981
Want to Mean Something 1989

Albums/CDs

JESSE WINCHESTER 1970
THIRD DOWN, 110 TO GO 1972
LET THE ROUGH SIDE DRAG 1976

TALK MEMPHIS 1981
THE BEST OF JESSE WINCHESTER 1989

Witness Inc. ALLAN AYERS *(bass guitar)*
LES BATEMAN *(organ, electric piano)*

ED CLYNTON *(guitar)*
CRAIG KALEAL *(drums)*
KENNY SHIELDS *(vocals)*

The motivating force behind Witness Inc. from Saskatoon, Saskatchewan is vocalist Kenny Shields. With an exciting stage show and a contract with Apex Records, they built up a following wherever they played. Their first hit on the label was *I'll Forget Her Tomorrow*. They also were a smash stage act who had conquered Western Canada by the summer of 1967. *Jezebel*, their follow-up single, failed to have any impact in Toronto, but sold well in the West. Three successive singles — *Harlem Lady, Visions of Vanessa*, and *So Come with Me* — were hits in Ontario and the Maritimes in 1968-69.

Singles

I'll Forget Her Tomorrow 1967
Jezebel 1967
Harlem Lady 1968

Visions of Vanessa 1968
So Come with Me 1969

Wizard GEORGE BOWSER *(guitar)*
MIKE DRISCOLL *(drums)*

HARRY MARKS *(bass)*

Wizard, from Montreal, was organized in 1970 by Harry Marks while working as musical director of the comedy series *Crackers* on CBC television. Marks studied classical bass at the Conservatoire de Quebec in Montreal. While he studied there he formed a jazz trio which performed regularly at The Playboy Club. It was there that Dale Barnes, one of the top producers at the CBC, approached him for *Crackers*.

When the season of *Crackers* finished, Marks wanted to continue playing, and along with fellow musicians Mike Driscoll and George Bowser, he formed Wizard. They went through a number of personnel changes during the next two years. In 1972 Wizard split up.

Marks had minor success as a solo performer. His biggest hit was *Sad and Simple Man*.

(As Wizard)
Singles   *Come Away*   1970   *A Familiar Story*   1970

(By Harry Marks)
Singles   *Sad and Simple Man*   1972   *Sou'western Morning*   1974
           Every Reason to Be Proud   1973

Michelle Wright   Chatham, Ontario native Michelle Wright left home in 1980 at the age of nineteen to pursue a singing career. After years of touring and performing, her first album, DO RIGHT BY ME was released by Savannah Records. Her second, MICHELLE WRIGHT, was released by Arista Records' Nashville label.

Singles   *New Kind of Love*   1990   *He Would Be Sixteen*   1992
           Woman's Intuition   1990   *The Change*   1993
           All You Really Wanna Do   1990   *If I'm Ever Over You*   1993
           A Heartbeat Away   1991   *Guitar Talk*   1993
           Take It Like a Man   1992   *Now and Then*   1994
           One Time Around   1992

CDs   DO RIGHT BY ME   1988   TAKE IT LIKE A MAN   1992
       MICHELLE WRIGHT   1990

Priscilla Wright   In 1955 Priscilla Wright was the youngest Canadian performer to have a hit in both the United States and Canada with *Man in the Raincoat* on Unique Records. Written by Warwick Webster, it went on to sell half a million copies. At the time she was only fourteen and still living with her parents. The popularity of her only hit brought her appearances on *The Ed Sullivan Show*, CBC, and with Elvis Presley in a U.S. musical movie short.

After her initial success she became a vocalist with Ottawa bandleader Moxie Whitney for fourteen years. She also sang with the National Press and Allied Jazz Band. In 1991 she was contacted by Al Mair, President and co-founder of Attic Records, who offered Wright a chance to record again. By Valentine's Day 1992 her new album, WHEN YOU LOVE SOMEBODY was released.

Singles	*Man in the Raincoat* 1955 (reissued in 1988)	*Say You'll Stay Forever* 1985
	Me and My Bestest Feller 1957	*Midnight Man* 1993
		Woman's Intuition 1993

CD	WHEN YOU LOVE SOMEBODY 1992

Neil Young

Born in Toronto in 1945, Neil Young first became interested in music in 1958 when his father bought him an ukulele for Christmas. Later when his parents separated, Neil moved with his mother to Winnipeg, where he learned to play the banjo and guitar. At Kelvin High in the early 1960s he played in a group called The Squires. In the fall of 1962 Young dropped out of school to write songs and play music full-time.

In 1964 he moved back to Toronto, where he joined Ricky James and the Mynah Birds, who broke up after a making a record in Detroit. He later joined another group, Danny and the Memories,which had brief success with the hit *Can't Help Lovin' That Girl of Mine* in 1964 on Valiant Records. With bassist Bruce Palmer, Young headed for Los Angeles in 1966, where he met Stephen Stills and Richie Furay and formed Buffalo Springfield.

For the next two years Young was a member of Buffalo Springfield, but when they broke up in 1968, he decided to go solo and formed his own backup group first called The Rockets, then Crazy Horse, comprised of Danny Whitten on lead guitar, Billy Talbot on bass, and Ralph Molina on drums. Nils Lofgren and Frank Sampredo joined later on organ and rhythm guitar, respectively. Their producer and arranger, Jack Nitzsche, would often join the group on stage on piano.

In August 1969 Young joined Crosby, Stills, and Nash at Woodstock. His association with them lasted two years before he returned to Crazy Horse. Crosby, Stills, Nash and Young reunited in the summer of 1974.

From 1970 on he established himself as one of North America's top performers. He wrote the soundtracks for such movies as *The Landlord* (1970) and *The Strawberry Statement* (1970). In 1972 he had his first number one hit with *Heart of Gold*, from the album HARVEST, recorded in Nashville with The Stray Gators.

Today, Neil Young continues to be successful as a mainstream pop troubadour. His album HARVEST MOON and the single of the same title released in 1992 again topped the charts.

(As Danny and the Memories)
Single   *Can't Help Lovin' That Girl of Mine*   1964

(By Neil Young)
Singles

Sugar Mountain 1968	*Heart of Gold* 1972
Cinnamon Girl 1970	*Old Man* 1972
Only Love Can Break Your Heart 1970	*War Song* 1972
Oh Lonesome Me 1971	*Time Fades Away* 1973
When You Dance I Can Really Love 1971	*Walk On* 1974
	Lookin' for a Love 1976
	Drive Back 1976

Homegrown 1977
Hey Babe 1977
Like a Hurricane 1977
Rust Never Sleeps 1979
Southern Pacific 1981
Little Thing Called Love 1983
Computer Age 1983
Wonderin' (with The Shocking
   Pinks) 1983
*Are There Anymore Real
   Cowboys?*
   (with Willie Nelson) 1985
Get Back to the Country 1985
Touch the Night 1986
People on the Streets 1986
Weight of the World 1986

Ten Men Workin' 1988
This Note's for You 1988
Needle and the Damage Done
   1989
*Rockin' in the Free World/
   No More* 1989/90
*Crime in the City
   (Sixty to Zero) Part One* 1990
Mansion on the Hill 1990
Over and Over 1990-91
Cinnamon Girl 1991
War of Man 1992-93
Harvest Moon 1992-93
Unknown Legend 1993
From Hank to Hendrix 1993
Long May You Run 1993

Albums/CDs

NEIL YOUNG 1969
EVERYBODY KNOWS THIS IS
   NOWHERE 1969
AFTER THE GOLDRUSH 1970
HARVEST 1972
JOURNEY THROUGH THE PAST
   1972
TIME FADES AWAY 1973
ON THE BEACH 1974
TONIGHT'S THE NIGHT 1975
ZUMA 1975
DECADE 1977
AMERICAN STARS AND BARS
   1977
COMES A TIME 1978
HAWKS AND DOVES 1979

RUST NEVER SLEEPS 1979
LIVE RUST 1979
RE-ACT-OR 1981
EVERYBODY'S ROCKIN' 1983
TRANS 1983
OLD WAYS 1985
LANDING ON WATER 1986
LIFE 1987
THIS NOTE'S FOR YOU 1988
FREEDOM 1989
RUGGED GLORY 1990
WELD 1991
HARVEST MOON 1992
LUCKY THIRTEEN 1993
UNPLUGGED 1993

Young Saints

DARREN CHURCHILL *(bass)*
ROBIN COOK *(vocals, guitar)*

ALEX MACFARLANE *(drums)*
IAN ROE *(guitar)*

All four members of the Young Saints grew up in Newfoundland. Robin Cook and Darren "Dirt" Churchill lived only a few houses apart and were boyhood pals.

In the late 1980s, Young Saints played almost every club within a 200 mile radius of St. John's and made enough money to convince themselves to go professional. They first moved to Toronto, where success eluded them, so they went to Vancouver. While playing at one of the clubs there, Cliff Jones, who had managed The Payola$, Blvd, and Idle Eyes, among others, helped Young Saints gain exposure. They opened for Sue Medley, and she liked them enough to mention them in the *Vancouver Sun* as one of her favorite bands. Polygram was impressed enough to sign them to a record contract, and their self-titled debut album was released in 1991.

Singles	*Live for Today* 1991	*New Solution* 1991
	Weight of the World 1991	
CDs	YOUNG SAINTS 1991	NEW SOLUTION 1991

Zappacosta

Singer/songwriter Alfie Zappacosta decided he wanted a music career in his teens when he first learned to play the guitar. His first foray into recording occurred in 1979 when he fronted the five piece band Surrender, which he left in 1983. Zappacosta recorded his self-titled debut album in 1984, and from it came his first single, *Passion*. A second single from the album, *We Should Be Lovers* was a Top 30 hit in 1985.

That same year Zappacosta turned his attention to the stage and portrayed Ché Guevara in Richard Ouzounian's production of the hit musical *Evita*, at the Neptune Theatre in Halifax, Nova Scotia. Also in 1985, he joined other Canadian artists to record *Tears Are Not Enough* to aid in the African famine relief effort.

His second solo album, A-Z, was released in 1986. In 1988 one of his songs *Overload* was included on the soundtrack of the movie *Dirty Dancing*. In 1990 his third album, QUICK!... DON'T ASK ANY QUESTIONS, came out on the artist's own label, A-Zee Records, distributed by Capitol.

Singles	*Passion* 1984	*Nothing Could Stand in Your Way* 1987
	We Should Be Lovers 1985	*Overload* 1988
	Start Again 1985	*Letter Back* 1990
	When I Fall (In Love Again) 1986	*I'll Be the One* 1991
		Simple Words to Say 1991

Albums/CDs	ZAPPACOSTA 1984	QUICK... DON'T ASK ANY QUESTIONS 1990
	A-Z 1986	

Zon

HOWARD HELM *(keyboards)*	JIM SAMPSON *(bass)*
KIM HUNT *(drums)*	YOUNG *(vocals)*
BRIAN MILLER *(guitar)*	

Toronto-based Zon began recording together in 1977 when they signed to a major multi-national label, recording two albums, ASTRAL PROJECTOR in 1977 and WORRIED ABOUT THE BOYS in 1980. The label dropped the group after their second album. Zon then caught the attention of Falcon Records, a Canadian Independent label distributed by A&M Records, who released their first single, *For You* in 1981.

Single	*For You* 1981

Albums	ASTRAL PROJECTOR 1978	I'M WORRIED ABOUT THE BOYS 1980

Zylan   STEVE ANNAN   DONALD HANN
        HELENE BOLDUC   REAL PELLETIER
        PETER FRAZER   DAVE SKINNER

This band from Halifax, Nova Scotia had one national hit, *Darlin'*, in the summer of 1973.

Single   *Darlin'* 1973

Album   RAINBOWS, DREAMS AND FANTASIES 1973

Appendix A: The following recording artists and bands released songs in the 1960s
Noteworthy and 1970s that reached the charts. Information on these acts is scant
Artists or sketchy. The author would be delighted to receive letters or news
clippings telling their story for possible inclusion in another edition
of this Encyclopedia.

Aaron Space
Keep on Movin' 1971-72
Abbey Tavern Singers
Off to Dublin in the Green 1966
Airlift
You Got Me Dancin' 1975-76
Tell Me 1976
James Robert Ambrose
Brand New Sunny Day 1972
Antique Fair
Fuddle Duddle 1971
Your Eyes 1971
Anne Attenborrow
We Will Find Love 1970
I Shall Be Released 1972
Claudja Barry
Boogie Tonight 1979
Everybody Needs Love 1979-80
(You Make Me) Feel the Fire 1980
Radio Action 1981
Blakewood Castle
Lynnie Lynnie 1970
Gimmie Little Lovin' 1971
Bronze
Lady Lover 1976
Easy Come, Easy Go 1976
Buckstone Hardware
Pack It In 1969
Buxton Kastle (a.k.a. Buxton Castle)
Kagie 1971
Red Red the Rocking Horse 1972
Lovin' Games 1972
Shorty McKenna 1972
Checkerlads
Baby Send for Me 1966
Behind Ev'ry Man 1967-68
Jack Cornell
Happy Dreamer 1973
Good to Be by You 1973-74
In the Park 1974
On My Way Out West 1975

Counts (a.k.a. Fabulous Counts)
He Will Break Your Heart 1966
Patricia Dahlquist
Keep Our Love Alive 1975
Bang a Boomerang 1975
Waiting for the Rain 1976
Wes Dakus
(a.k.a. Wes Dakus & the Club 93 Rebels)
Hobo 1965
The Hoochi Coochi Coo 1965-66
We've Got a Groovy Thing Goin' 1966
Shotgun 1967
Dee & the Yeomen
Take the First Train Home 1965
A Love like Mine 1966
Baby It's All Worthwhile 1966
In a Minute or Two 1966
Dublin Corporation
Come and Join Us 1972
Jimmie Dybold
(a.k.a. Jimmy Dybold & the Proverbial Nee Hi)
You're Breaking My Heart 1966
A Bit of Love 1966
Do You Remember 1966
Fergus
Same Old Feelin' 1972
Ice on the Road 1973
Down on My Knees 1973
Five Canadians
Writing on the Wall 1966
Lois Fletcher
I Am What I Am 1974
Man Smart, Woman Smarter 1974
Freedom
Doctor Tom 1970
Don Goodwin
This Is Your Song 1973-74
Time to Cry 1974
Diana 1974
The Gospelaires
Preachin' Man 1969
Only Believe 1971

Anthony Green & Barry Stagg
  To Love Means to Be Free 1970
  Face of the Sun 1970
  It's Been a Long Time 1971
  Hail to the World 1972
  Window of Your Life 1973
Greenfield (a.k.a. **Barry Greenfield**)
  New York Is Closed Tonight 1972
  Sweet America 1973
  Canada Sky 1975
Happy Feeling
  Happy Feeling 1968
  Hey Little Man 1969
  Still Hill 1970
  Sacroiliac Boop 1970
Jayson Hoover (a.k.a. **Trials of Jayson Hoover**)
  King Size 1969
  Freedom Train 1971
  Love Will Get You 1974
  She's My Lady 1975
House of Commons
  Do the Fuddle Duddle 1971
  C'Mon Baby 1972
Incredible Bongo Band
  Bongo Rock 1973
  Let There Be Drums 1973-74
James, John & Francois
  Run Run 1971
  Six O'Clock in the Morning 1971
Kurt & Noah
  There Are Things 1971
  When I Was Young 1971
Pierre Lalonde
  Ticket to Ride 1968-69
  I'll Catch the Sun 1969
C'est Toujours Comme Ca
  La Premiere Fois 1971
Last Words
  I Symbolize You 1966
  Give Me Time 1967
Larry Lee (a.k.a. **Larry Lee & the Leesures**)
  Stood Up 1963
  Toodle Oo Kangeroo 1966
  Barefootin' 1967
Les Sultans
  Le poupee qui fait non 1966
Life
  Hands of the Clock 1969
  Strawberry Fields 1970

Lisle
  Goin' Away 1973
  Shelley Made Me Smile 1973-74
  Stormy Eyes 1974-75
Terry McManus
  Sunshower in the Spring 1971
  Carolyn 1972
  Love Is Wine 1972
Tom Middleton
  It Wouldn't Have Made Any Difference 1973
  One More Chance 1974
  One Night Lovers 1976
  I Need a Harbour for My Soul 1976
  Marie 1976
A Mythical Meadow (a.k.a. **Meadow**)
(formerly **The Elastic Band**)
  You've Got That Lovin' Look 1969
  Oh Darling 1970
  Fight Today 1971
Naked Lunch
  Mad Man 1970
New City Jam Band
  Lazy Love 1976
  Our Love Is Getting Better 1977
Noblemen (featuring Harry Youngs)
  Child of My Sleeping Mind 1969
Nocturnals
  Because You're Game 1965
  This Ain't Love 1966
Nomads (a.k.a. **Lennie Richards & the Nomads**)
  Cry Baby 1967
  Walkin' Mary Home 1967
  Bittersweet 1967
A Passing Fancy
  I'm Losing Tonight 1967
  I Believe in Sunshine 1967
  People in Me 1967-68
  Island 1968
Poor Souls
  Lookin' Round 1970
  Comin' Round 1970
  In the Land of the Few 1971
Rain
  Out of My Mind 1971
  Stop Me from Believing in You 1972
  I Don't Want to Leave You 1972
  Find Our Love 1972
Regents
  Me and You 1965

Bob Ruzicka
- *Storm Warning* 1972
- *Down and Losing* 1972
- *Lately Love (Laughter Don't Come Easy)* 1973
- *Thank God He's a Stranger* 1973-74
- *Outrageous* 1976

Allen J. Ryan
- *PM Pierre* 1968
- *True Fine Virginia* 1971

St. Thomas Four
- *Cherry Brook/Why the Rain* 1968
- *Bobby/You Got the Light* 1968

Scepters
- *I Never Had a Love like That* 1967
- *Juicy Morning* 1968

Sea Dog
- *It's a Hot Night* 1971
- *I Don't Wanna Hear* 1972
- *Holding Your Hands* 1973

Seeds of Time
- *My Home Town* 1970-71
- *Cryin' the Blues* 1971
- *Long Time Ago* 1971

Showdown
- *Rodeo Song* 1981

Smyle
- *Glory Glory* 1971

Sound Box
- *Warm Your Mind and Soul* 1968

Sound 80
- *The Theme* 1972

Spring
- *As Feelings Go* 1970
- *A Country Boy Named Willy* 1971
- *I Turn to You* 1971-72

Barry Stagg
- *Blue* 1977
- *Like You and Me (My Love)* 1978
- *Children of the Dream* 1978
- *The Warm Maritimes* 1980

J.C. Stone
- *Carrie's Gone* 1974
- *Rocky Mountain Boy* 1975
- *Laura's Song* 1976

THP Orchestra
- *Theme from SWAT* 1976
- *Early Riser* 1976
- *Fightin' on the Side of Love*   1977
- *Too Hot for Love* 1978
- *Good To Me* 1979-80

Russell Thornbury
- *Rosaline* 1971
- *Miss January* 1971
- *Michelle's Song* 1977
- *She's an Outlaw* 1978

Michael Vincent
- *That Girl Becomes a Woman* 1971
- *We Are All of Us* 1973

The Wackers
- *Day and Night* 1972-73
- *Hey Lawdy Lawdy* 1973

Wishbone
- *You're Gonna Miss Me* 1971
- *First Sign of Love* 1971

Young
- *Going to the Country* 1971
- *Happy Song* 1972

Yukon
- *Understanding Is Sorrow* 1971
- *Fallen Angel* 1973

Appendix B:
Beyond the Border

Certain Canadian artists have found success in groups based outside of Canada. Among them are:

Richard Bell   Toronto, Ontario
Pianist for the Full Tilt Boogie Band (one of Janis Joplin's backup bands).

Kerry Chater   Vancouver, British Columbia
Bassist for Gary Puckett and the Union Gap.

Gene Cornish   Ottawa, Ontario
Part of the Young Rascals and The Rascals from 1965-71.

August Darnell   Montreal, Quebec
Bassist for Dr. Buzzard's Savannah Band from 1976-80. Formed Kid Creole and the Coconuts in 1980.

Denny Doherty   Halifax, Nova Scotia
One of the Mamas and the Papas from 1965-68 and The New Mamas and the Papas from 1982-present.

Jerry Edmonton   Oshawa, Ontario
Drummer for Steppenwolf.

Roy Kenner   Toronto, Ontario
Vocalist for The James Gang.

Corky Laing   Montreal, Quebec
Drummer for Mountain.

Dewey Martin   Chesterville, Ontario
Drummer for Buffalo Springfield.

Ken Pearson   Woodstock, Ontario
Keyboardist for the Full Tilt Boogie Band.

Floyd Chester Sneed
Calgary, Alberta
Drummer for Three Dog Night.

Domenic Troiano
Toronto, Ontario
Guitarist for The James Gang.

Zalman Yanovsky
Toronto, Ontario
Part of the Mugwumps in 1964. Lead Guitarist for The Lovin' Spoonful.

Appendix C: Juno Award Winners, 1964-1994

The Juno Awards have been awarded, in one form or another since 1964. In December of that year, *RPM Weekly*, a new music trade magazine, published a readers poll that would metamorphose, by February 1970, into an awards presentation at St. Lawrence Hall. In July 1970 the awards were nicknamed the Juno Awards after CRTC Chairman Pierre Juneau, and in October 1977, the present organizers, the Canadian Academy of Recording Arts and Sciences (CARAS), took control of the awards.

1964

Male Vocalist of the Year ...... Terry Black
Female Vocalist of the Year..... Shirley Matthews
Most Promising Male Vocalist .. Jack London
Most Promising Female Vocalist Lynda Layne
Female Vocal Group .... The Girlfriends
Vocal Instrumental Group ..... The Esquires
Folk Group of the Year........ Courriers

1965

Male Vocalist of the Year ...... Bobby Curtola
Female Vocalist of the Year..... Catherine McKinnon
Most Promising Male Vocalist .. Barry Allen
Most Promising Female Vocalist Debbie Lori Kaye
Vocal Instrumental Group ..... Guess Who
Female Vocal Group .... The Girlfriends
Folk Group of the Year........ Malka & Joso
Folk Singer of the Year .... Gordon Lightfoot

1966

Male Vocalist of the Year ...... Barry Allen
Female Vocalist of the Year..... Catherine McKinnon
Most Promising Male Vocalist .. Jimmy Dybold
Most Promising Female Vocalist Lynda Layne
Vocal Instrumental Group ..... The Staccatos
Female Vocal Group .... Allan Sisters
Folk Group of the Year........ Three's a Crowd
Folk Singer of the Year .... Gordon Lightfoot

1967

Male Vocalist of the Year ...... Gordon Lightfoot
Female Vocalist of the Year..... Debbie Lori Kaye
Most Promising Male Vocalist .. Tom Northcott
Most Promising Female Vocalist Colleen Peterson
Vocal Instrumental Group ..... The Guess Who
Folk Group of the Year........ Three's a Crowd
Folk Singer of the Year .... Leonard Cohen

1968

Top Male Vocalist .... Andy Kim
Top Female Vocalist .... Debbie Lori Kaye
Top Vocal Instrumental Group . Guess Who
Top Folk Group.............. Irish Rovers
Top Folk Singer .... Gordon Lightfoot

1969

Top Male Vocalist .... Andy Kim
Top Female Vocalist .... Ginette Reno
Top Vocal Instrumental Group . Guess Who
Top Folk Singer (or Group) .... Gordon Lightfoot

1970

Top Male Vocalist .... Gordon Lightfoot
Top Female Vocalist .... Anne Murray
Top Vocal Instrumental Group . Guess Who
Top Folk Singer (or Group) .... Bruce Cockburn

1971

Male Vocalist of the Year ...... Gordon Lightfoot
Female Vocalist of the Year..... Anne Murray
Vocal Instrumental Group ..... The Stampeders
Folk Singer of the Year .... Bruce Cockburn
Outstanding Performance (Male) .... Joey Gregorash
Outstanding Performance (Female)..................... Ginette Reno
Outstanding Performance (Group)..................... Lighthouse

1972

Male Vocalist of the Year ...... Gordon Lightfoot
Female Vocalist of the Year..... Anne Murray
Vocal Instrumental Group ..... Lighthouse
Folk Singer of the Year .... Bruce Cockburn
Outstanding Performance (Folk) Valdy
Outstanding Performance (Female)..................... Ginette Reno

Outstanding Performance
(Group) . . . . Edward Bear

1973

Male Vocalist of the Year . . . . . . Terry Jacks
Female Vocalist of the Year. . . . . Anne Murray
Folk Singer of the Year . . . . Valdy
Group of the Year . . . . Lighthouse
Most Promising Male Vocalist . . Ian Thomas
Most Promising Female Vocalist Cathy Young
Most Promising Group . . . . Bachman-Turner
 Overdrive
Most Promising Folk Singer . . . Dave Nicol

1974

Male Artist of the Year . . . . Gordon Lightfoot
Female Artist of the Year . . . . . . Anne Murray
Folk Singer of the Year . . . . Murray
 McLauchlan
Group of the Year . . . . Bachman-Turner
 Overdrive
Most Promising Male Artist . . . . Gino Vannelli
Most Promising Female Artist . . Suzanne Stevens
Most Promising New Group . . . Rush

1975

Male Artist of the Year . . . . Gino Vannelli
Female Artist of the Year . . . . . . Joni Mitchell
Folk Singer of the Year . . . . Gordon Lightfoot
Group of the Year . . . . Bachman-Turner
 Overdrive

Best New Male Artist . . . . Dan Hill
Best New Female Artist. . . . . Patricia Dahlquist
Best New Group . . . . Myles & Lenny

1976

Male Vocalist of the Year . . . . . . Burton Cummings
Female Vocalist of the Year. . . . . Patsy Gallant
Folk Singer of the Year . . . . Gordon Lightfoot
Group of the Year . . . . Heart
Best New Male Vocalist. . . . . Burton Cummings
Best New Female Vocalist. . . . . . Colleen Peterson
Best New Group . . . . T.H.P. Orchestra
Best Selling Single. . . . . *Roxy Roller*
 — Sweeney Todd
Best Selling Album . . . . NEIGES
 — Andre Gagnon

1977

Male Vocalist of the Year . . . . . . Dan Hill
Female Vocalist of the Year. . . . . Patsy Gallant
Group of the Year . . . . Rush
Folk Singer of the Year . . . . Gordon Lightfoot
Best New Male Vocalist. . . . . David Bradstreet
Best New Female Vocalist. . . . . . Lisa Dal Bello
Best New Group . . . . Hometown Band
Best Selling Single . . . . *— Sugar Daddy*
 Patsy Gallant
Best Selling Album. . . . . LONGER FUSE
 — Dan Hill

1978

Male Vocalist of the Year . . . . . . Gino Vannelli
Female Vocalist of the Year. . . . . Anne Murray
Group of the Year . . . . Rush
Folk Artist of the Year. . . . . Murray
 McLauchlan
Most Promising Male Vocalist . . Nick Gilder
Most Promising Female Vocalist Claudja Barry
Most Promising Group
of the Year. . . . . Doucette
Best Selling Single. . . . . *Hot Child in the
City*
 — Nick Gilder
Best Selling Album. . . . . DREAM OF A CHILD
 — Burton
 Cummings

1979

Male Vocalist of the Year . . . . . . Burton Cummings
Female Vocalist of the Year. . . . . Anne Murray
Group of the Year . . . . Trooper
Folk Artist of the Year. . . . . Bruce Cockburn
Most Promising Male Vocalist . . Walter Rossi
Most Promising Female Vocalist France Joli
Most Promising Group . . . . Streetheart
Single of the Year . . . . *I Just Fall in Love
Again*
 — Anne Murray
Album of the Year . . . . NEW KIND OF
 FEELING
 — Anne Murray

1980

Male Vocalist of the Year . . . . . . Bruce Cockburn
Female Vocalist of the Year. . . . . Anne Murray
Group of the Year . . . . Prism
Folk Singer of the Year . . . . Bruce Cockburn
Most Promising Male Vocalist . . Graham Shaw
Most Promising Female Vocalist Carole Pope
Most Promising Group . . . . Powder Blues Band
Single of the Year . . . . *Could I Have this Dance* — Anne Murray
Album of the Year . . . . GREATEST HITS — Anne Murray

1981

Male Vocalist of the Year . . . . . . Bruce Cockburn
Female Vocalist of the Year. . . . . Anne Murray
Group of the Year . . . . Loverboy
Folksinger of the Year . . . . Bruce Cockburn
Most Promising Male Vocalist . . Eddie Schwartz
Most Promising Female Vocalist Shari Ulrich
Most Promising Group . . . . Saga
Single of the Year . . . . *Turn Me Loose* — Loverboy
Album of the Year . . . . LOVERBOY — Loverboy

1982

Male Vocalist of the Year . . . . . . Bryan Adams
Female Vocalist of the Year. . . . . Carole Pope
Group of the Year . . . . Loverboy
Most Promising Male Vocalist . . Kim Mitchell
Most Promising Female Vocalist Lydia Taylor
Most Promising Group . . . . Payola$
Single of the Year . . . . *Eyes of a Stranger* — Payola$
Album of the Year . . . . GET LUCKY — Loverboy

1983-84

Male Vocalist of the Year . . . . . . Bryan Adams
Female Vocalist of the Year. . . . . Carole Pope
Group of the Year . . . . Loverboy
Most Promising Male Vocalist . . Zappacosta
Most Promising Female Vocalist Sherry Kean
Most Promising Group . . . . The Parachute Club

Single of the Year . . . . *Rise Up* — The Parachute Club
Album of the Year . . . . CUTS LIKE A KNIFE — Bryan Adams

1985

Male Vocalist of the Year . . . . . . Bryan Adams
Female Vocalist of the Year. . . . . Luba
Group of the Year . . . . The Parachute Club
Most Promising Male Vocalist . . Paul Janz
Most Promising Female Vocalist k.d. lang
Most Promising Group . . . . Idles Eyes
Single of the Year . . . . *Never Surrender* — Corey Hart
Album of the Year . . . . RECKLESS — Bryan Adams

1986

Male Vocalist of the Year . . . . . . Bryan Adams
Female Vocalist of the Year. . . . . Luba
Group of the Year . . . . Honeymoon Suite
Most Promising Male Vocalist Billy Newton-Davis
Most Promising Female Vocalist Kim Richardson
Most Promising Group . . . . Glass Tiger
Single of the Year . . . . *Don't Forget Me (When I'm Gone)* — Glass Tiger
Album of the Year . . . . THIN RED LINE — Glass Tiger

1987

Male Vocalist of the Year . . . . . . Bryan Adams
Female Vocalist of the Year. . . . . Luba
Group of the Year . . . . Red Rider
Most Promising Male Vocalist . . Tim Feehan
Most Promising Female Vocalist Rita MacNeil
Most Promising Group . . . . Frozen Ghost
Single of the Year . . . . *Someday* — Glass Tiger
Album of the Year . . . . SHAKIN' LIKE A HUMAN BEING — Kim Mitchell

1989

Male Vocalist of the Year . . . . . . Robbie Robertson
Female Vocalist of the Year. . . . . k.d. lang
Group of the Year . . . . Blue Rodeo

Most Promising Male Vocalist .. Colin James
Most Promising Female Vocalist Sass Jordan
Most Promising Group .... Barney Bentall &
the Legendary
Hearts
Single of the Year .... *Try* — Blue Rodeo
Album of the Year .... ROBBIE ROBERTSON
— Robbie
Robertson

1990

Male Vocalist of the Year ...... Kim Mitchell
Female Vocalist of the Year..... Rita MacNeil
Group of the Year .... Blue Rodeo
Most Promising Male Vocalist .. Daniel Lanois
Most Promising Female Vocalist Alannah Myles
Most Promising Group .... The Tragically Hip
Single of the Year .... *Black Velvet*
— Alannah Myles
Album of the Year .... ALANNAH MYLES
— Alannah Myles

1991

Male Vocalist of the Year ...... Colin James
Female Vocalist of the Year..... Céline Dion
Group of the Year .... Blue Rodeo
Most Promising Male Vocalist .. Andy Curran
Most Promising Female Vocalist Sue Medley
Single of the Year .... *Just Came Back*
— Colin James
Album of the Year .... UNISON
— Céline Dion

1992

Male Vocalist of the Year ...... Tom Cochrane
Female Vocalist of the Year .... Céline Dion

Group of the Year .... Crash Test
Dummies
Most Promising Male Vocalist .. Keven Jordan
Most Promising Female Vocalist Cassandra Vasik
Most Promising Group .... Infidels
Single of the Year .... *Life Is a Highway*
— Tom Cochrane
Album of the Year .... MAD MAD WORLD
— Tom Cochrane

1993

Male Vocalist of the Year ...... Leonard Cohen
Female Vocalist of the Year..... Céline Dion
Group of the Year .... Barenaked Ladies
Most Promising Male Vocalist .. John Bottomley
Most Promising Female Vocalist Julie Masse
Most Promising Group .... The Skydiggers
Single of the Year .... *Beauty and the Beast*
— Céline Dion &
Peabo Bryson
Album of the Year .... INGENUE
— k.d. lang

1994

Male Vocalist of the Year ...... Roch Voisine
Female Vocalist of the Year..... Céline Dion
Group of the Year .... The Rankin Family
Best New Solo Artist.......... Jann Arden
Best New Group .... The Waltons
Single of the Year .... *Fare Thee Well Love* — The
Rankin Family
Album of the Year .... HARVEST MOON
— Neil Young

Bibliography

"Abraham's Children — A New Chapter." *RPM Weekly*, Vol. 18, No. 9 (October 14, 1972), 2.

"Abraham's Children Finally Gets A Name And A Hit Record As Well." *Canadian Composer*, No. 74 (November 1972), 40.

"All About The Stampeders." *Music Canada Quarterly (Special Edition)*, Vol. 2, No. 3 (1973).

Allan, Chad. "The Pop Scene In Winnipeg." *Music Scene*, No. 242 (July/August 1968), 6-7.

"Amherstview Band to Release Record." *The Heritage*, 13 March 1985.

Andrews, Marke. "'Disco Queen' the Title but Not the Style of Denise McCann." *Music Scene*, No. 301 (May/June 1978), 5.

Andrews, Marke. "Seven Years Later Stonebolt Is Making It." *Music Scene*, No. 304 (November/December 1978), 6.

"Art Snider, 60 Helped to Launch Lightfoot's Career." *The Toronto Star*, 30 May 1987.

"The Band that Links the Worlds of Jazz and Pop [Downchild]." *Canadian Composer*, No. 67 (February 1972), 30-32.

Bateman, Jeff. "The Art of Not Falling Apart." *Music Scene*, No. 348 (March/April 1986), 4-6.

Bateman, Jeff. "Rock and Hyde." *Music Scene*, No. 353 (January/February 1987), 4-7.

Batten, Jack. "Christopher Kearney's Album: Different Moods." *Canadian Composer*, No. 71 (June 1972), 24-26.

"Beginnings — Ginette Reno." *Today Magazine*, (July 18, 1981), 18.

Bell, Karen and Kevin Pope. "A Visit with Loreena McKennitt." *Performing Arts*, Vol. 27, No. 3 (Summer 1992), 12-14.

"Bim." *Prime Cut* (Summer 1976).

Bist, Dave. "Mashmakhan's Success Based On People Contact." *Music Scene*, No. 258 (March/April 1971), 8-9.

Blanks, Tim. "Honeymoon Suite — Champagne and Caviar Nuptials for Niagara Rockers." *Music Scene*, No. 342 (March/April 1985), 6-7.

Bliss, Karen. "New Blood." *Network*, Vol. 6, No. 2 (April/May 1992), 23.

Bliss, Karen. "The Road to Success: Two Very Different Bands Win Record Deals [National Velvet and Cowboy Junkies]." *Canadian Composer*, No. 235 (November 1988), 12-15.

"Bobby Gimby's 'Canada' a Phenomenal Success Story." *Canadian Composer*, No. 20 (July/August 1967), 4-7.

"Bobby G. Griffith Ready for the Big Time." *RPM Weekly*, Vol. 18, No. 13 (November 11, 1972), 7.

Bomph. "Sudbury's Cano Bridges Language Barrier." *Music Express*, (March 1978), 21-22.

"Brighton Rock Calling It Quits." *The Toronto Star*, 17 June 1992.

Burman, Terry. "Steamer Debuts on Pickwick's Intercan Label." *RPM Weekly*, Vol. 33, No. 11 (June 7, 1980), 12-13.

Burman, Terry. "Sheriff — A Three Year Plan Worked!" *Music Scene*, No. 330 (March/April 1983), 8-9.

Burman, Terry. "The Success Story Continues for the Powder Blues." *RPM Weekly*, Vol. 33, No. 16 (July 12, 1980), 12-13.

"Butler and Bilyk: Montreal's Answer to Bacharach and David." *Canadian Composer*, No. 60 (May 1971), 22, 24.

Callwood, June. "Sh-Boom! The Crazy Career of the Crew-Cuts." *Maclean's*, Vol. 67, No. 23 (December 1, 1954), 26-27, 97-99.

"Canadian Teen Who Sang with Elvis Starts Her Comeback with New Disc." *The Toronto Star*, 17 May 1992.

"CANO." *Prime Cut*, Vol. 2 No. 2 (Xmas 1976).

"Capitol's Pepper Tree Growing 45 And Lp Action." *RPM Weekly*, Vol. 16, No. 2 (August 28, 1971), 4, 11.

"Celtic Roots and Rock." *The Globe and Mail*, 22 February 1978.

Champagne, Jane. "Ryan's Fancy: Modern Troubadours Sing Out." *Canadian Composer*, No. 81 (June 1973), 14-21, 46 .

"Chandells Reunite and Issue Single After Ten Years." *RPM Weekly*, Vol. 32, No. 26 (March 22, 1980), 17.

"Charity Brown." *Prime Cut*, (Summer 1976).

"Charlebois in English Canada." *Canadian Composer*, No. 52 (September, 1970), 20-23.

"Charlebois in Overtime." *The Toronto Star*, 20 June 1993.

"Chilliwack Hopes This Is It." *The Toronto Star*, 2 September 1981.

Chown, Susan. "Sylvia Tyson Off On a Solo Career." *RPM Weekly*, Vol. 23, No. 16 (June 14, 1975), 4, 11.

Chycki, Richard. "Ipso Facto." *Canadian Musician*, Vol. 14, No. 3 (June 1992), 32-34.

Clinton, Barry J. "Agent—Jingles and Record Deals." *Music Scene*, No. 343 (May/June, 1985), 18.

Collie, Ashley. "Déjà-Vu." *Cheap Thrills*, (July 1976).

"CRTC Eases Rule After Adams Uproar." *The Toronto Star*, 30 January 1993.

Current Biography. New York: The H.W. Wilson Company, 1969, 1970.

Current Biography. New York: The H.W. Wilson Company, 1992.

Dafoe, Chris. "A Story of Evolution [Lisa Dal Bello]." *Canadian Composer*, No. 239 (March 1989), 6-10.

"Debut For Toronto on Solid Gold Records." *RPM Weekly*, Vol. 32, No. 26 (March 22, 1980), 12.

"Debut Single for Uranus on Trilogy Records." *RPM Weekly*, Vol. 32, No. 24 (March 8, 1980), 22.

DeVoss, David. "Rock 'n' Roll's Leading Lady [Joni Mitchell]." *Time*, Vol. 104, No. 25 (December 16, 1974), 59-62.

Dolgy, Michael. "A Direct Hit for this Trooper." *RPM Weekly*, Vol. 24, No. 3 (September 13, 1975), 8.

Dolgy, Michael. "A Funny Sight for Soaring Eyes [Sweet Blindness]." *RPM Weekly*, Vol. 25, No. 3 (April 17, 1976).

"Don Walsh Forms Mister Downchild." *Canadian Composer*, No. 136 (December 1978), 38.

Doole, Kerry. "Sheree Jeacocke: Twisting And Turning." *SoundCan*, Vol. 1, No. 6 (July, 1993), 8.

Dostie, Bruce. "Pop Music from a Quebec Perspective." *Canadian Composer*, No. 124 (October, 1977), 26-32.

Dostie, Bruce. "Quebec's Rock and Roll Bad Guys Make the Push into English Canada [Offenbach]." *Canadian Composer*, No. 118 (February, 1977), 4-9.

"Downchild." *RPM Weekly*, Vol. 24, No. 4 (September 20, 1975), 4, 12.

Druckman, Howard. "The Box — A Gust of Fresh Air with Closer Together." *Music Scene*, No. 356 (July/August 1987), 4-5.

Druckman, Howard. "Living in a Chalk Circle." *Canadian Composer*, No. 222 (July 1987), 12-15.

Dunne, Bob. "Peter Foldy's Past May Be His Recording Future." *Music Scene*, No. 277 (May/June 1974), 15.

"The Education of Robert Goulet." *The Toronto Star*, 22 May 1993.

"Edward Bear — A Product of Capitolism." *RPM Weekly*, Vol. 18, No. 26 (February 10, 1973).

"Eight Seconds Beats Clock to Top." *The Toronto Star*, 2 January 1987.

Elliott, Kate. "Suzanne Stevens — Quebec's Cinderella." *RPM Weekly*, Vol. 23, No. 12 (May 12, 1975), 12.

Encyclopaedia of Music in Canada. Toronto: University of Toronto Press, 1992 (Second Edition).

"Farewell to the Greasiest Group." *Time*, Vol. 104, No. 9 (August 26, 1974), 10.

"The Father of Paunch Rock Is No Slug at Selling Records." *The Toronto Star*, 2 January 1981.

"Ferron Takes the Big Step with Testimony." *RPM Weekly*, Vol. 33, No. 16 (July 12, 1980), 5.

Ferguson, Jeremy. "Musical Raes of Sunshine." *Starweek*, (Nov. 5, 1977), 4.

Ferguson, Jeremy. "Shooting for Stardom." *Starweek* (July 24, 1976), 5.

Filion, Sylvain. "Renowned Quebec Songwriter and Copyright Advocate Diane Juster Returns to the Spotlight after Years Behind the Scenes." *Canadian Composer*, Vol. 4, No. 3 (Summer 1993), 16-17.

Flohil, Richard. "Fludd: Canada's Incredible Exploding Rock Band." *Canadian Composer*, No. 84 (October 1973), 10-15.

Flohil, Richard. "For Colleen Peterson: No More Compromises." *Canadian Composer*, No. 113 (September 1976), 4-9 .

Flohil, Richard. "Getting Luke Gibson off from the Farm Isn't Easy." *Canadian Composer*, No. 66 (January 1972), 4-9.

Flohil, Richard. "Greg Adams: Making a Career as a Songwriter." *Canadian Composer*, No. 127 (January 1978), 4-7, 46.

Flohil, Richard. "Harry Marks: A Composer Taking Care of Business." *Canadian Composer*, No. 76 (January 1973), 28-31.

Flohil, Richard. "Mae Moore Gets Rid of the Day Job and Gets into Recording." *Canadian Composer*, No. 243 (September, 1989), 30-33.

Flohil, Richard. "A Magical Mystery Band from Canada, Klaatu." *Canadian Composer*, No. 121 (May 1977), 12-15.

Flohil, Richard. "Noah." *Canadian Composer*, No. 70 (May 1972), 4-7, 46.

Flohil, Richard. "Portrait of an Artist in an Alien Surrounding." *Canadian Composer*, No. 74 (November 1972), 4-6, 46.

Flohil, Richard. "Rough Notes on a Gentle Conspiracy." *Canadian Composer*, No. 58 (March 1971), 28-31, 46.

Flohil, Richard. "Teenage Head Rides to the Top of the Heap." *Canadian Composer*, No. 163 (September, 1981), 20-23.

Flohil, Richard. "The White Hair Has Gone but Les Classels Are Certainly Not Forgotten." *Canadian Composer*, No. 59 (April 1971), 19-23, 37.

"Flying Circus Now a Part of Beaver Patrol." *RPM Weekly*, Vol. 18, No. 11 (October 28, 1972), 15.

"40 Years On: Travellers Return." *The Toronto Star*, 2 October 1993.

Fulton, E. Kaye. "Queen Céline." *Maclean's*, Vol. 105, No. 22 (June 1, 1992), 40-42.

Gabiou, Alfrieda. *Gordon Lightfoot*. Toronto: Gage Publishing Limited., 1979.

Gallo, Nancy. "Zon Resurfaces with Falcon Power." *RPM Weekly*, Vol. 34, No. 5 (October 25, 1980), 16-17.

Gelmon, Larry. "The Dumptrucks: Bluegrass Country-Opera In Saskatoon." *Canadian Composer*, No. 102 (June 1975), 16-19.

Goddard, Peter. "The Blues Boy." *Saturday Night*, Vol. 107, No. 8 (October 1992), 26, 28, 32, 116.

Goddard, Peter. "Leroy: Rural Values Keep His Music Warm and Open." *Canadian Composer*, No. 90 (April 1974), 24-27.

Goddard, Peter and Philip Kamin. *Shakin' All Over: The Rock 'n' Roll Years in Canada*. Toronto: McGraw-Hill Ryerson Limited, 1989.

Godfrey, Larry. "Harlequin's Success Begins with Switch to Original Tunes." *Music Scene*, No. 319 (May/June, 1981), 5, 18.

Gungras, Peter. "Mahogany Rush Launched from Quebec." *Music Scene*, No. 274 (November/December, 1973), 7.

Graves, Leif. "Getting to Know Ms. Shirley Eikhard." *Canadian Composer*, No. 93 (September 1974), 14-19.

Grealis, Walt. "How Elaine Wilson Found the Walkers." *RPM Weekly*, Vol. 56, No. 17 (October 24, 1992), 10.

Gregory, Hugh. *Bryan Adams: The Inside Story*. London, England: Box Tree Limited, 1992.

Gudgeon, Chris. "Monkeywalk's Home-Made Soul." *Canadian Musician*, Vol. 14, No. 7 (August 1992),42-44.

Guettel, Alan. "Bill Amesbury's Career Spans North America and Europe." *Music Scene*, No. 295 (May/June 1977), 10.

Guettel, Alan. "Suzanne Stevens Is Well on Her Way." *RPM Weekly*, Vol. 25, No. 7 (May 15, 1976), 7.

Guinness Encyclopaedia Of Popular Music, Volume I. Guinness Publishing Ltd., England, 1992.

Hall, Ron. *The CHUM Chart Book*. Etobicoke: Stardust Productions, 1990.

"Hampshire — Exciting New Presence." *RPM Weekly*, Vol. 19, No. 12 (May 5, 1973), 1, 5.

Hansen, Kim. "Headpins — Invasion from the West." *Music Scene*, No. 329 (January/February 1983), 8.

Hansen, Kim. "Payola$ Won't Compromise Despite Industry Criticism." *Music Scene*, No. 326 (July/August 1982), 12.

"Happiness Is . . . Chester." *RPM Weekly*, Vol. 19, No. 25 (August 4, 1973), 1, 5.

Harrison, Tom. "54-40's Record Deal: Breaking the Barriers." *Canadian Composer*, No. 212 (June/July 1986), 26-31.

Harry, Isobel. "Keeping Traditional Music Alive." *Canadian Composer*, No. 185 (November 1983), 4-9.

Harry, Isobel. "Profile: Messenjah." *Canadian Composer*, No. 190 (April 1984), 14, 16.

Harry, Isobel. "This Child Star Grew up Fast [France Joli]." *Canadian Composer*, No. 188 (February 1984), 16-18, 44-45.

"Helix Lead Guitarist Killed as Van Overturns." *The Toronto Star*, 7 July 1992

Hensel, Karen. "Mighty Pope Finds Heaven on the Seventh Floor." *Music Express*, (March 1978),18.

"He Relives Days of Crew-Cut Fame." *The Toronto Star*, 30 January 1979.

Holt, James. "Tenants Look for Song Contest." *Music Scene*, No. 332 (July/August 1983), 12-13.

Howell, Bill. "The End of a Maverick [Stan Rogers]." *Canadian Forum*, Vol. 63, No. 734 (December 1983), 7-11, 21.

"Ian and Sylvia Encore." *The Globe and Mail*, 2 August 1986.

"It's Official. Anka's American." *The Globe And Mail*, 8 September 1990.

"Jackie Allan, 50, Renowned Country Singer." *The Toronto Star*, 28 December 1985.

Jackson, Marni. "High-Flying Gino Vannelli: More than Meets the Eye." *Maclean's*, Vol. 92, No. 22 (May 28, 1979), 4-6.

"James Leroy Is Denim." *RPM Weekly*, Vol. 19, No. 19 (June 23, 1973), 1, 5.

Jasmin, Helene. "Beau Dommage: Canada's Most Successful New Pop Group Proves that True to Yourself Pays Off." *Canadian Composer*, No. 106 (December 1975), 4-6, 33.

Jennings, Nicholas. "Plucking for Glory — The Rankin Family Fiddles with Tradition." *Maclean's*, Vol. 105, No. 32 (August 10, 1992), 46.

Jennings, Nicholas. "Songs for a Native Son [Robbie Robertson]." *Maclean's*, Vol. 100, No. 47 (November 23, 1987), 52, 54.

Kelley, Linda. "Jane Siberry's Musical Dance In and Out of Time." *Canadian Composer*, No. 204 (October 1985), 4-11.

"Kelly Jay and Crowbar Back on the Road Again." *Canadian Composer*, No. 129 (March 1978), 44.

"Kings' 'Blue Skies' Breaking Nationally." *RPM Weekly*, Vol. 22, No. 4 (September 14, 1974), 8.

Krewen, Nick. "Gowan: Making a Strange Animal." *Canadian Composer*, No. 201 (May/June 1985), 8-11, 40-41.

Kroll, Stephen. "Twin Talent [Richard and Marie Seguin]." *Canadian Composer*, No. 80 (May 1973), 4-9.

Land, Court. "Brussel Sprout." *Cheap Thrills*, (July 1976).

Laurier, Andree. "Smarts, Sass and Songwriting." *Canadian Composer*, No. 242 (June 1989), 6-9.

Laurier, Andree. "Top Sonart Is Making Waves in Quebec." *Canadian Composer*, No. 206 (December 1985), 30-33.

"Lawrence Novels Inspire Diviners' Songwriting Duo." *The Toronto Star*, 7 January 1993.

Lazier, Kate. "Happily Blue [Annette Ducharme]." *Canadian Composer*, No. 242 (June 1989), 20-23.

Lazier, Kate. "In a Room of Her Own [Mary-Margaret O'Hara]." *Canadian Composer*, No. 238 (February 1989), 4-8.

Leblanc, Larry. "Carl Dixon and Coney Hatch." *Music Scene*, No. 336 (March/April 1984), 8.

Leblanc, Larry. "Five Man Electrical Band." *Music Scene*, No. 265 (May/June 1972), 14-15.

Leblanc, Larry. "Terry Jacks' One Commitment Is His Music." *Music Scene*, No. 264 (March/April 1972), 6-7.

Lepka, Stan. "Motherlode Recorded Before Performing." *Music Scene*, No. 251 (January/February 1970), 11-12.

Lepka, Stan. "Witness." *Canadian Composer*, No. 41 (June 1969), 32-35.

Linden, J.J. "Anne Murray — Hanging on to Superstardom." *RPM Weekly*, Vol. 33, No. 23 (August 30, 1980), 4-5.

Linden, J.J. "B.B. Gabor — An Unusual Artist, An Unusual Career." *RPM Weekly*, Vol. 32, No. 26 (March 22, 1980), 26-27.

Linden, J.J. "Gino Soccio — Another Big Step Forward with S-Bcat." *RPM Weekly*, Vol. 33, No. 12 (June 14, 1980), 13, 17.

Linden, J.J. "Ken Tobias — A New Album for a Seasoned Pro." *RPM Weekly*, Vol. 28, No. 11 (December 10, 1977), 19-21.

Linden, J.J. "The Kings' Beat Rock Offers Unfamiliar Familiarities." *Music Scene*, No. 316 (November/December 1980), 14.

Linden, J.J. "Loverboy — New Band Ready to Break Internationally." *RPM Weekly*, Vol. 33, No. 18 (July 26, 1980), 12-14.

Linden, J.J. "Max Webster — The Band to Break in 1977." *RPM Weekly*, Vol. 27, No. 20 (August 13, 1977).

Linden, J.J. "Streetheart — Alive and Kicking with Quicksand Shoes." *RPM Weekly*, Vol. 33, No. 14 (June 28, 1980), 13-14.

Linden, J.J. "Trooper." *RPM Weekly*, Vol. 27, No. 15 (July 9, 1977), 6-8.

Linden, J.J. "Vancouver's Ironhorse Part with Scotti Bros." *RPM Weekly*, Vol. 33, No. 18 (July 26, 1980), 18-19.

Littlejohn, Maureen. "Blvd. Makes the Grade." *Canadian Musician*, Vol. 10, No. 4 (August 1988), 78.

Littlejohn, Maureen. "Lee Aaron — Canadian Sweetheart in Wolf's Clothing." *Music Scene*, No. 346 (November/December, 1985), 14-15.

Littlejohn, Maureen. "The Spoons: Fighting Old Scars." *Canadian Musician*, Vol. 9, No. 1 (February 1987), 10.

"Local Rock Band Max Webster Breaks Up." *The Toronto Star*, 23 April 1981.

"A Long Time for . . . Copperpenny." *RPM Weekly*, Vol. 19, No. 23 (July 21, 1973), 1, 5.

"Lost Dakotas." *The Toronto Star*, 11 March 1993.

"Lorence Hud — Guilty of Rock 'N Roll." *RPM Weekly*, Vol. 20, No. 17 (December 8, 1973), 1, 15.

Lyttle, Brendan J. *A Chartology of Canadian Popular Music*.

MacIntosh, Dave. "Sarah McLachlan: The Positive Touch." *Music Scene*, No. 367 (May/June 1989), 16-17.

MacIntyre, John. "John Allan Cameron: Cape Breton's Musical Ambassador." *The Atlantic Advocate*, Vol. 81, No. 2 (August 1991), 11-13.

MacLauren, Doug. "Mills-Cockell's Music Expressed Electronically." *Music Scene*, No. 258 (March/April 1971), 10.

"Madrigal Again." *Canadian Composer*, No. 102 (June 1975), 36.

Marsh, Rodney. "Take a Ride with Myles Cohen." *Music Express*, (March 1978), 19.

Martin, Peter. "Leskiw's Songs Come to Forefront through Kilowatt." *Music Scene*, No. 330 (March/April 1983), 8-9.

Martin, Peter. "Prism Tours in Support of New and Decisive Album." *RPM Weekly*, Vol. 35, No. 17 (November 21, 1981), 4.

Martin, Peter. "Teddy Boys Debut Album Tells about Experiences." *RPM Weekly*, Vol. 34, No. 9 (November 22, 1980), 12.

McMullen, Richard. "The Odds — Rockin' Heteros." *National Chart*, Vol. 4, No. 2 (August 1993), 15.

Melhuish, Martin. "Craig Ruhnke's 'Summer Girl' Released in Six Countries." *Music Scene*, No. 279 (September/October 1974), 6.

"Melody's Rough 'n' Sweet When Gravelberrys Jam." *The Toronto Star*, 20 February 1993.

"Memories Are Made of This." *The Sunday Sun*, 5 September 1976.

"Mike Mainlines the Blues." *The Toronto Star*, 25 July 1986.

Morris, John. "Life on the Rockpile: Four Toronto Bands out there Looking for Fortune." *Canadian Composer*, No. 102 (June 1975), 4-9.

"Moxy Hopes To Jumps from Stars to Bars." *The Sunday Sun*, 26 September 1976.

"Mr. CA-NA-DA Leads the Band at Retirement Leisure World." *The Toronto Star*, 4 May 1993.

"New Faces: The Pukka Orchestra." *Canadian Composer*, No. 337 (May/June 1984), 15.

"Northcott Marks LP Release at Riverboat." *RPM Weekly*, Vol. 16, No. 7 (October 2, 1971), 2.

"Ocean Creating Waves in Business." *RPM Weekly*, Vol. 16, No. 4 (September 11, 1971), 2.

O'Connor, Tim. "Pulling Gold from the Well." *Canadian Musician*, Vol. 9, No. 6 (December 1987), 45, 48.

O'Day, Ellie. "Headpins — The Year of Living Patiently." *The Music Scene*, No. 347 (January/February 1986), 12-13.

O'Day, Ellie. "The Power of Persistence." *Canadian Musician*, Vol. 11, No. 6 (August 1989), 54-55, 57.

O'Hara, Phil. "Skip Prokop's Energies Directed Toward Solo Career." *Music Scene*, No. 296 (July/August, 1977), 5.

Osborne, Jerry and Bruce Hamilton. *Popular Rock Records 1948-1978*. Phoenix: O'Sullivan Woodside Co., 1978.

"Patsy Gallant Breaks into English Canada." *RPM Weekly*, Vol. 18, No. 12 (November 4, 1972), 10.

Pedneault, Helene. "Morse Code Provides Inspiration for Composer Christian Simard." *Music Scene*, No. 288 (March/April, 1976), 10.

"Percy and the Teardrops Release Almost Live." *RPM Weekly*, Vol. 33, No. 18 (July 26, 1980), 20.

"Peter Pringle's Pick Pricks Placidity." *RPM Weekly*, Vol. 39, No. 18 (April 11, 1981), 2.

Petrowski, Nathalie. "Diane Tell — This Quebec Star Is Now Moving Up." *Canadian Composer*, No. 135 (November 1978), 18-23.

Petrowski, Nathalie. "Edith Butler: The Voice from Acadia." *Canadian Composer*, No. 148 (February 1980), 4-9.

Petrowski, Nathalie. "Leyden Zar: 'American Rock' from Quebec." *Canadian Composer*, No. 162 (June 1981), 10-15.

Petrowksi, Nathalie. "Maneige: An Eight-Year Formula." *Canadian Composer*, No. 150 (April 1980), 26-31.

Petrowski, Nathalie. "Interview: Monique Leyrac." *Canadian Composer*, No. 140 (April 1979), 10-17.

"Photograph — Twelve Years in the Making." *RPM Weekly*, Vol. 34, No. 20 (April 25, 1981), 2.

"Pianist Jane Vascy Dies at 32." *Canadian Composer*, No. 173 (September 1982), 38.

Porteous, John A. "The Paupers — Music Made in Canada." *Music Scene*, No. 239 (January/February 1968), 7.

"The Queen City Kids — Eleven Years in the Making." *RPM Weekly*, Vol. 35, No. 2 (June 20, 1981), 4.

Ray, Randy and Mark Kearney. *Canadian Music Fast Facts*. London, Ontario: Sparky Jefferson Productions, 1992.

"Recording Star Now Sings Ads." *The Whig-Standard*, 14 April 1978.

"Rapper Snow Drifts out of Jail and into Hip-Hop Big Time." *The Toronto Star*, 30 January 1993.

Rocco, Rino. "The Carlton Showband — 13 Years and 20 Albums Later." *RPM Weekly*, Vol. 34, No. 3 (October 11, 1980), 24-26.

Rocco, Rino. "Hagood Hardy — The Master Returns." *RPM Weekly*, Vol. 34, No. 7 (November 8, 1980), 13.

"Rock Band Has the Goods, Talent and Uncle Miltie." *The Financial Post*, 24 March 1973.

"Rock Veteran Dies in Smash." *Canadian Composer*, No. 183 (September, 1983), 40.

Roxon, Lillian. *Rock Encyclopaedia*. New York: Grosset & Dunlap, 1971.

"Services Set for Sax Player Keith Jollimore." *The Toronto Star*, 14 January 1976.

Sharp, Keith. "Triumph — Toronto's Rock 'n Roll Machine." *Music Express*, (March 1978), 12.

"Snowbird Anne Still All Business after 25 Years." *The Toronto Star*, 20 March 1993.

"The Song Is Ended — The Memory Lingers On." *The Whig-Standard*, 25 August 1976.

"The 'Spirit and Energy' Still Exists as Parachute Club Falls to Earth." *Canadian Composer*, No. 240 (April 1989), 34.

"Stampeders Classic and Proud of It." *Canadian Composer*, Vol. 3, No. 2 (Fall 1992), 9.

"Stampeders Reformed by Ronnie King." *Canadian Composer*, No. 144 (October 1979), 34.

Stewart, Scott. "Dan Hill — Almost There." *RPM Weekly*, Vol. 23, No. 25 (August 16, 1975), 8-9.

Stewart, Scott. "MCA's Octavian Spotlights Capital." *RPM Weekly*, Vol. 23, No. 23 (August 2, 1975), 6.

"Tarry Makes It All Worthwhile." *RPM Weekly*, Vol. 19 No. 14 (May 19, 1973), 1, 14.

Tattrie, Boyd. "Speeding Ahead — Rush" *RPM Weekly*, Vol. 25, No. 4 (April 24, 1976), 7.

Taylor, Alex and Marc Coulevain. "1-2-5: The Haunted's Early Days." *Canadian Wax Hound*, Vol. 1, No. 2 (December 1992), 1-2.

"Then and Now — Patsy Gallant." *Canadian Composer*, No. 243 (September 1989), 14.

"Then And Now — The Stampeders." *Canadian Composer*, No. 244 (October 1989), 10.

"Ian Thomas — Feeling Fine Mama." *RPM Weekly*, Vol. 20, No. 15 (November 24, 1973), 1, 12.

"Thunder Who? . . . Establishes Name." *RPM Weekly*, Vol. 17, No. 26 (August 12, 1972), 22.

"Tommy Graham, World Tour Over, Returns to the Recording Studio." *Canadian Composer*, No. 56 (January 1971), 28-30.

Topalovich, Maria. "Versatility of New Album Indicative of Myles and Lenny." *Music Scene*, No. 287 (January/February 1976), 12.

"Toronto's Martha and the Muffins Break across Canada." *RPM Weekly*, (May 17, 1980), 3.

"Toulouse." *The Toronto Star*, 6 August 1977.

"Touring Lyell Gasses Up at Reopening of Gasworks." *The Toronto Star*, 8 April 1993.

"Travellers Still Manage to Roll Along." *The Toronto Star*, 26 May 1980.

Tremblay, Denis. "Les Sinners: Quebec's Tough Rock Group Is Now Ready for Another Hit." *Canadian Composer*, No. 72 (September 1972), 4-7.

"True Myth Concentrating on European Market." *RPM Weekly*, Vol. 34, No. 25 (May 30, 1981), 2

"Van's Pointed Sticks Catching Nationally." *RPM Weekly*, Vol. 34, No. 13 (December 20, 1980), 8.

Vautour, Chris. "Sloan Crunchy Grungsters." *Canadian Composer*, Vol. 3, No. 2 (Fall 1992), 20-21.

Vincent, Pierre. "Michel Pagliaro." *Music Scene*, No. 253 (May/June 1970), 12.

Waxman, Ken. "Crack Of Dawn: In Demand on the Disco Club Circuit." *Canadian Composer*, No. 112 (June 1976), 20-25.

Waxman, Ken. "The Dream Never Dies for Ottawa's Pop-Rock Writer Richard Cooper." *Canadian Composer*, No. 150 (April 1980), 4-9.

Waxman, Ken. "Alberta's Gift to Canadian Rock 'n Roll [Fosterchild]." *Canadian Composer*, No. 136 (December 1978), 10-15.

Waxman, Ken and Richard Flohil. "Battered Wives: How Publicity Pays Off." *Canadian Composer*, No. 140 (April 1979), 4-8.

Waxman, Ken. "Folk Duo Maintains Control over All Aspects of Business." *Music Scene*, No. 296 (July/August 1977), 8.

Waxman, Ken. "New Ronney Abramson Album Reaches Far beyond Folk." *Music Scene*, No. 296 (July/August 1977), 4.

Waxman, Ken. "Paul Hoffert's Versatility Keeps Boredom Away." *Music Scene*, No. 300 (March/April 1978).

Waxman, Ken. "Vancouver's Jerry Doucette Turns into a Rock 'n' Success." *Canadian Composer*, No. 138 (February 1979), 18-22.

Waxman, Ken. "Writing Songs and Jingles Sure Keeps Tommy Ambrose Busy." *Canadian Composer*, No. 153 (September 1980), 26-30.

"Wednesday — Last Kiss — First Hit." *RPM Weekly*, Vol. 20, No. 16 (December 1, 1973), 1, 19.

"Whiskey Howl Gets Its Chance to Again." *The Globe And Mail*, 23 July 1980.

Whitburn, Joel. *Top Pop Singles 1940-1955*. Wisconsin: Record Research, Inc., 1973.

Whitburn, Joel. *Top Pop Singles 1955-1986*. Wisconsin: Record Research, Inc., 1987.

Wilson, Elaine. "Willie and the Walkers: 25 Years Later." *RPM Weekly*, Vol. 56, No. 16 (October 17, 1992), 15.

Wilson-Smith, Anthony. "A Bashful Candidate for Pop Stardom [Luba]." *Maclean's*, Vol. 99, No. 31 (August 4, 1986), 46.

Yorke, Ritchie. *Axes, Chops & Hot Licks*. Edmonton: M.G. Hurtig Ltd., 1971.

Yorke, Ritchie. "Materick — Into the International Marketplace." *RPM Weekly*, Vol. 26, No. 8 (November 20, 1976), 7.

Yorke, Ritchie. "Terry Jacks — Nine Million 'Seasons' Later" *RPM Weekly*, Vol. 22, No. 13 (November 16, 1974), 1, 13.

Photograph Credits

We would like to thank the following organizations and individuals for supplying the photographs reproduced in this book:

A&M Records: Jann Arden, Bryan Adams, The Doughboys, Figgy Duff, Paul Janz, West End Girls

Attic Records: Haywire, Lee Aaron, Maestro Fresh Wes, The Nylons, The Irish Rovers

Backstage Productions: Ronnie Hawkins

BMG Music Canada Inc.: Big House, 13 Engines, Jeff Healy Band, Crash Test Dummies, Cowboy Junkies

Bernie Dobbin: The Bells, Bentwood Rocker

Canadian Press File: Robbie Robertson

Canadian Broadcasting Corporation: Leonard Cohen

EMI Music Canada: The Grapes of Wrath, Glass Tiger, National Velvet, Rockhead, Anne Murray, Buffy Sainte-Marie, Sass Jordan, Kim Mitchell, The Skydiggers, Tom Cochrane, The Band, The Rankin Family, 13 Engines

Flood Ross Entertainment: April Wine

MCA Records Canada: Alanis, Andrew Cash (Sumo), Rik Emmett (Duke Street Records), Sloan (Geffen Records), Joni Mitchell (Geffen Records), The Tragically Hip

Richard Patterson: Shingoose, The James Leroy Group, Colleen Peterson, Ronnie Hawkins, Platinum Blonde, Three's a Crowd, David Wiffen, Bruce Cockburn, Shirley Eikhard

Paul Simmons Management: Catherine MacKinnon

Jean-Marc Pisapia: The Box

PolyGram: Bootsauce, Sue Medley

Rolling Stone Records: Neil Young (black and white)

Savannah Music: Gary Fjellgaard, One Horse Blue

Shantero Productions: John Allan Cameron, Frank Mills, Rita MacNeil, Valdy, James Keelaghan

The Showtime Music Archive (Toronto): Paul Anka, The Guess Who, Bobby Curtola

Sony Music: Céline Dion, Barney Bentall and the Legendary Hearts, Mitsou, 54-40, Mae Moore, Gowan, Gordon Lightfoot

Warner Music Canada: Meryn Cadell, Jane Child, The Boomers, Corey Hart, Spirit of the West, k.d. lang, Loreena McKennitt, Jane Sibbery, Lisa Lougheed, Alannah Myles, Moxy Fruvous, Snow, Marc Jordan, Neil Young (Color), The Waltons, Daniel Lanois, Wild 'T' and the Spirit, Blue Rodeo, The Barenaked Ladies

PAUL
ANKA

MAESTRO
FRESH WES

LEONARD
COHEN

CÉLINE
DION

MITSOU

Finally, someone has incorporated the whole history of Canadian rock, pop, and folk music into one book. I found that while reading the pages memories came back to me . . . As you read this encyclopedia you'll find yourself remembering events, people, love, break-ups, school, weddings, grads . . .

Bands at the front edge can and will succeed. However, after that initial success they must forever answer the question, "What have you done for us lately?" Well, this book answers that question and any others that might be asked. It will help preserve this country's musical legacy.

— Terry David Mulligan

RONNIE
HAWKINS

BRUCE
COCKBURN

RUSH

KIM
MITCHELL

APRIL
WINE